THE YEAR'S WORK
IN CRITICAL AND CULTURAL THEORY 1992

The Year's Work in Critical and Cultural Theory

Volume 2 • 1992

Edited by
STEPHEN REGAN

Advisory Editors
STEVEN CONNOR (Birkbeck College, London)
TERRY EAGLETON (St Catherine's College, Oxford)
LINDA HUTCHEON (University of Toronto)
FREDRIC JAMESON (Duke University)
CHRISTOPHER NORRIS (University of Wales)
ELAINE SHOWALTER (Princeton University)
ALAN SINFIELD (University of Sussex)
STAN SMITH (University of Dundee)
PATRICIA WAUGH (University of Durham)

Published for
THE ENGLISH ASSOCIATION

by
BLACKWELL PUBLISHERS, OXFORD

Copyright © The English Association 1996

First published 1996
2 4 6 8 10 9 7 5 3 1

Blackwell Publishers Ltd
108 Cowley Road
Oxford OX4 1JF
UK

Blackwell Publishers Inc.
238 Main Street
Cambridge, Massachusetts 02142
USA

British Library Cataloguing in Publication Data

A CIP catalogue record for this book is available from the British Library.

Library of Congress Cataloging-in-Publication Data has been applied for.

ISBN 0–631–18859–2

Typeset in 10 on 12pt Times by Acorn Bookwork, Salisbury, Wilts
Printed and bound in Great Britain by T.J. Press (Padstow) Ltd, Padstow, Cornwall

Printed on acid-free paper

The English Association

The object of the English Association is to promote the knowledge and appreciation of English language and literature. The Association pursues these aims by creating opportunities of co-operation among all those interested in English; by furthering the recognition of English as essential in education; by discussing methods of English teaching; by holding lectures, conferences, and other meetings; by publishing a journal, books, and leaflets; and by forming local branches overseas and at home.

Publications

The Year's Work in English Studies. An annual bibliography. Published by Blackwell Publishers, Oxford and Cambridge, MA.

The Year's Work in Critical and Cultural Theory. An annual bibliography and collection of theoretical essays. Published by Blackwell Publishers, Oxford and Cambridge, MA.

Essays and Studies. An annual volume of essays by various scholars assembled by the collector covering usually a wide range of subjects and authors from the medieval to the modern. Published by Boydell and Brewer, Woodbridge, Suffolk.

English. The journal of the Association, *English*, is published three times a year by the English Association.

Use of English. This journal is published three times a year by the English Association.

Benefits of Membership

Institutional Membership

Full members receive copies of *The Year's Work in English Studies, Essays and Studies, English* (three issues), and three *News-Letters*.

Ordinary Membership covers *English* (three issues) and three *News-Letters*.

Schools Membership covers two copies of each issue of *English*, one copy of *Essays and Studies* (optional), three *News-Letters*, and preferential booking for Sixth Form Conference places.

Individual Membership

Individuals take out basic membership, which entitles them to buy all regular publications of the English Association at a discounted price.

For further details write to The Secretary, The English Association, The University of Leicester, University Road, Leicester LE1 7RH.

Contents

CONTENTS

Part II Critical Theory: An International Perspective

Preface

The Year's Work in Critical and Cultural Theory is a companion volume to *The Year's Work in English Studies*, also published for the English Association by Blackwell Publishers. Part I of each volume is a narrative bibliography that records and evaluates books and articles on specific areas of research in the humanities. This second volume covers books and articles published in 1992. As well as recording significant developments in literary theory, the volume offers a comprehensive survey of new publications and critical essays on art history, popular music and media studies.

Part II of each *Year's Work in Critical and Cultural Theory* will contain a collection of specially commissioned essays on current theoretical issues and debates. Volume 2 includes a selection of essays which look at critical theory from a broad international perspective. Readers in Britain and the United States will have an opportunity to learn about recent developments in critical theory in Germany, France and Italy, and will also acquire some understanding of new theoretical approaches to literary and cultural studies that have begun to emerge in Russia, Bulgaria and Poland in the 1990s.

No bibliography of this kind can claim to be complete in its review of new publications. Authors, publishers and editors are therefore invited to submit review copies of journals, books and articles for inclusion in future volumes. Items for review should be addressed to The Secretary, The English Association, The University of Leicester, University Road, Leicester LE1 7RH.

Stephen Regan
The Open University

Part I

The Year's Work in Critical and Cultural Theory

1

Critical Theory: General

STUART SIM

This chapter has eight sections: 1. Postmodernism; 2. Narrativity; 3. The Politics and Ideology of Theory and Criticism; 4. Textuality; 5. Theory of Humour; 6. Online Literacy; 7. Education; 8. Reference Works.

1. Postmodernism

The phenomenon of postmodernism continues to fascinate critical and cultural theorists. In *Modern Conditions, Postmodern Controversies* Barry Smart offers a useful, if not perhaps particularly original or contentious, sociologically-based survey of the major theorists of postmodernism and post-industrialism (Lyotard, Baudrillard, Bell, Toffler, Gorz, etc.) and the implications of their ideas for movements such as Marxism. Smart's is an even-handed account which can find something of value in almost everyone it considers, and is concerned to combat the more hostile responses to thinkers such as Baudrillard and Lyotard. Thus Baudrillard is to be rescued from the charge of celebrating the 'new techno-cultural configurations and their effects', and Lyotard from being an *advocate* of the postmodern condition rather than, as Smart regards him, an *analyst* of it. Such a line tends to neutralize the force (not to mention the shock-value) of these two theorists, and it also involves a highly selective reading of texts like *America* or *The Postmodern Condition*: what else, one wonders, is the rejection of 'grand narrative' and the enthusiastic espousal of 'little narrative' but an advocacy of the postmodern condition? Smart is also skating on thin ice when he tries to play down Lyotard's rejection of Marxism; even a cursory glance at *Libidinal Economy* (particularly the chapter entitled 'The Desire Called Marx') should be enough to indicate just how estranged Lyotard becomes from the Marxist project in his later career. Writing from a broadly post-Marxist perspective, Smart seems anxious overall to lower the temperature of the postmodernism debate, reassuring us that 'the belated discovery that the social world is more complex than we might have been led to believe should not increase despair'.

Gianni Vattimo's premise in *The Transparent Society* is that the postmodern condition is closely linked to the explosive growth of the mass media: 'the society in which we live is a society of generalized communication'. Far from creating a 'transparent' society, the rapid expansion of the information market – 'telematics' so called – has brought about the dissolution of 'centralized perspectives' (or 'grand narratives'), making us increasingly aware of the bewildering diversity of our world. The postmodern condition for Vattimo is one of cultural complexity and chaos, and therein lies its liberatory potential: confronted by a plurality of languages, dialects and differences, 'we are made to realize the contingency and relativity of the "real" world in which we live'. The mass media, he feels, can help us to achieve the desired state of 'heterotopia', where democratic pluralism can reign. Aesthetics, with its ability to dislocate our cultural perceptions and lead us into other possible worlds (Benjamin and Heidegger being the major points of reference), is assigned a key role in this process. Despite powerful plugs from those postmodern heavyweights Richard Rorty and Jean-François Lyotard, this is an uneven book which promises more than it delivers. Heterotopia is no doubt a desirable ideal but how achievable is it in socio-political reality? Recent historical developments such as Bosnia in the 1990s and the Lebanon in the 1980s make one highly sceptical of the positive effect of the recognition of cultural diversity on either group or individual consciousness. Vattimo has some thought-provoking things to say about Nietzsche (an advocate of moderation in this reading), Schopenhauer (an undervalued precursor of the postmodern), and Habermasian hermeneutics (dismissed as 'the thought of the epoch of the end of metaphysics . . . of modernity and its consummation, and nothing more'), but the whole remains less than the sum of its parts.

Arthur Kroker's *The Possessed Individual: Technology and Postmodernity* is a revisionist account of French theory from existentialism through poststructuralism and postmodernism, which takes this body of thought to present a description of technology as cynical power. Kroker's thesis is that recent French theory (Sartre onwards) provides the key to how power functions in America, the 'global hologram' of today's world. Several old postmodern favourites put in an appearance here – Baudrillard, Lyotard, Deleuze and Guattari – although Paul Virilio, whom Kroker deals with at some length, will be less familiar to most Anglo-Saxon readers. In Kroker's opinion we have moved past postmodernism into what he calls 'bimodernism', the bimodern condition being life at 'the violent edge of primitivism and simulation', where 'possessed individualism' (defined as 'subjectivity to a point of aesthetic excess that the self no longer has any real existence') is the norm. French theory, Kroker contends, is our way into the mechanisms lying behind this condition. There are various drawbacks to Kroker's presentation of his thesis. In the first place he is rather prone to talk of 'the French mind' ('the French mind has always exhibited a fascination for the study of subjectivity as the ruins within' . . . 'In the French mind, there is no agency, no subject capable of appropriation, no acquisitive self'), which sounds an unhealthily essentialist concept for a postmodernist to be espousing. Neither should we feel under any obligation to accept the blithe assumption of cultural homogeneity concealed in such a concept: French thought of the last few decades cannot simply be *reduced* to that of the poststructuralist/postmodernist mafia. Kroker's style is also an acquired taste and all too often sounds like someone trying too hard for effect in a creative writing class: exhortations to 'read Baudrillard with the violence of a particle accelerator' will leave most readers none the wiser, and precisely what does it mean to 'inscribe alterity into the disappearing centre of things'? For all these drawbacks the book has its moments. Kroker's forays into postmodern art can yield some thought-provoking analogies with theory; the reading of Lyotard as a latter-day sophist is worth further exploration, and he also features in what is surely one of the most arresting chapter openings in recent theoretical literature: 'When I think of Jean-François Lyotard what first comes to mind is Moose Jaw, Saskatchewan . . .' It would seem unkind to spoil potential readers' pleasure by revealing any more of this fascinating connection here.

Christopher Norris continues his recent opposition to the postmodernist movement in *Uncritical Theory: Postmodernism, Intellectuals, and the Gulf War*. For Norris postmodernism (and its fellow-traveller neopragmatism) is an orthodoxy that urgently needs to be challenged and the Gulf War provides a focus for such a project, 'by showing what follows when scepticism is pushed to the point where it becomes just a pretext for strategies of moral and political evasion'.

Chief amongst the villains is Jean Baudrillard with his now infamous pronouncements that the Gulf War would not happen, and then, after the event, that it had not happened. Norris is incensed by Baudrillard and takes him as a starting-point for a wide-ranging attack on postmodernist-neopragmatist thought. Lyotard, Foucault, and Rorty are among those censured, although Norris is careful to exempt Derrida from what he clearly feels is a very misguided and intellectually sloppy form of philosophical discourse. For Norris 'there are factual truths . . . which don't come down to a mere disagreement between rival viewpoints', and philosophers who deny this (Baudrillard, Lyotard, Foucault, Rorty, et al.) are sophists at best, indirect apologists for a repressive political system at worst. The effect of both philosophical ultra-relativism and media-managed Western ideology (especially in its American-led Gulf War manifestation) is, Norris notes, to render dissent from consensus almost unthinkable. Norris is always good value and he succeeds in making a mockery of the Baudrillardean line on the Gulf War, without perhaps entirely demolishing postmodernism as an intellectual position in the process. In particular Lyotard seems a much more complex thinker than Norris pictures him, as well as a much more politically-oriented one (although to be fair Norris is not claiming to offer any more than the briefest summary of anyone's work in this study). Then, too, Norris seems over-inclined to find fault with Foucault's notion of the 'specific intellectual', treating it as part of the moral and political evasion he abhors, rather than a possible gesture of political good faith. It is also a bit worrying for postmodernism to be written off, as it so often is by Norris, as mere fashion, as if its iconoclasm were a mere whim rather than a response to deep-seated cultural problems. Neither should it simply be dismissed as the product of a series of misreadings of Kant and Saussure. First and foremost, however, *Uncritical Theory* should be judged on its success as polemic – and as polemic it is first-rate. David H. Hirsch would most likely dissent from such a judgement, however, and in 'A Postmodernist and Post-Marxist World' (*The Sewanee Review* 100.343–6) he dismisses Norris's 1990 study *What's Wrong with Postmodernism?* (Harvester) as 'superficial' and 'tedious'. In Hirsch's eyes Norris is guilty of a simplistic application of Marxist doctrine to the British political scene.

Norris's doubts about Lyotard are echoed to some extent in Robert Weimann's '(Post)Modernity and Representation: Issues of Authority, Power, Performativity' (*New Literary History* 23.955–81), where the French theorist's concept of power as a 'closed system' is criticized on the grounds that it conceals areas of conflict within systems, as well as the factor of mediation. Weimann's two case-studies look at problems of representation in German theatre and architecture under circumstances of 'a deep crisis in authority'. Lyotard receives a better press in Mark Poster's 'Postmodernity and the Politics of Multiculturalism: The Lyotard–Habermas Debate over Social Theory' (*Modern Fiction Studies* 38.567–80), and in Alex Segal's 'Language Games and Justice' (*Textual Practice* 6.210–24). Poster generally takes Lyotard's part over Habermas, even though he considers postmodern thought ultimately to be no more than 'a fledgling position' on the way to something more culturally liberating. Segal identifies two distinct conceptions of justice in Lyotard's *Just Gaming*, and proceeds to defend them against what he takes to be Eagleton's misreading.

Whereas Norris sees postmodernism as all too often politically suspect, Richard Kearney, in 'Postmodernism and Nationalism: A European Perspective' (*Modern Fiction Studies* 38.581–93), is altogether more positive about its political potential. For Kearney postmodernism helps to undermine the concept of the nation-state, and he makes a case for its application to the Irish political agenda where traditional notions of sovereignty are proving such a stumbling-block.

Brian McHale's *Constructing Postmodernism* is in some sense a response to his own earlier *Postmodernist Fiction* (Methuen, 1987). He now considers the latter study to present too neat a picture of literary history – 'first modernist poetics, then, *because* of a change of dominant, postmodernism' – and proposes instead 'a plurality of constructions' of literary postmodernism. The philosophical basis for his new 'story' of postmodernism is Nelson Goodman's 'constructivism', whose basic epistemological principle is that all our cognitive operations are theory-dependent. The emphasis is very much on construction; postmodernism is simply the latest in a line of literary constructions, rather than something given or found, and McHale's interest lies in how it works as a discourse. Critics of *Postmodernist Fiction* remarked on its lack of sustained textual analysis, so McHale offers us a series of readings of postmodernist (and in some cases part-postmodernist) texts in *Constructing Postmodernism*. Joyce, Pynchon, Eco, Joseph McElroy, and Christine Brooke-Rose all come in for extended treatment, as does the phenomenon of cyberpunk. Although at one point McHale states that the question of whether a given text is postmodernist or not is a 'vacuous' one, he does seem to spend rather a lot of time and effort on the categorization problem. *Ulysses*, he argues, is 'a literary-historical scandal' since it is part-high modernist and part-postmodernist (whether that would constitute a scandal to anyone not embroiled in the categorization problem is a moot point); *The Name of the Rose* is described as being 'poised on a cusp between modernist and postmodernist poetics', *Foucault's Pendulum* as more straightforwardly postmodernist (and possibly in consequence less interesting). Such category-chopping soon loses its appeal, and McHale is far more stimulating when showing how difficult texts like *Gravity's Rainbow* and *Vineland* can open up under a postmodernist construction. McHale has more to say about cyberpunk in 'Elements of a Poetics of Cyberpunk' (*Critique* 33.149–75), where he undertakes to demonstrate an overlap between postmodernist and cyberpunk poetics.

Anthony J. Cascardi's *The Subject of Modernity* seeks to challenge some of the assumptions of the postmodern project, such as 'the widespread belief that whatever follows the culture of enlightened modernity must in some way be a rejection of it', through a wide-ranging exploration of the genealogy of subjectivity (including, crucially, subjective desire) from the seventeenth century to the present, postmodern, world. Subjectivity is taken to be central to our understanding of the world picture of modernity, with Cascardi claiming that existing analyses of subjectivity and modernity simply accept the Cartesian model of self-consciousness as dominant, even when, as is the case with poststructuralists and postmodernists for example, they are arguing against it. For Cascardi the self-consciousness of the modern subject is a contradictory one, and that subject is in fact situated 'within a field of conflicting discourses', where individual desires cannot be linked to society as a whole and desire is generally conceived of as an iconoclastic force – whether of a threatening kind (as in Hobbes) or an emancipatory one (Deleuze and Guattari). If desire is read as constitutive of subjectivity rather than as an external threat to it, then, Cascardi contends, its transformative and emancipatory power might be recovered for the general good of the community. Cascardi draws on Kant for his theory of 'aesthetic liberalism', whose goal is to reconcile individual desire and the community by allowing for the coexistence of each in the manner of Kantian antinomies – although exactly how one achieves this objective in hard political terms of reference is not entirely clear. In effect Cascardi is trying to retain what he sees as best from both the modern and postmodern projects, and even if most postmodernists are likely to regard this as too much of a concession to outmoded 'grand narratives', the alternative account he offers of the genealogy of the subject is worth consideration. Cascardi further explores the problem of divided subjectivity in terms of the project of enlightened modernity in 'Totality and the Novel' (*New Literary History* 23.607–27).

Another commentator anxious to salvage something from modernism is Marianne DeKoven, who in 'The Politics of Modernist Form' (*New Literary History* 23.675–90) argues that modernist form gives us a means of both maintaining difference and denying hierarchy, and suggests that we should use 'this aesthetic of *sous-rature*' as a model 'for our efforts at overcoming the seemingly hopeless polarizations that characterize contemporary cultural-political life'. In a thoughtful piece entitled 'Postmodernism and Enlightenment, or, Why Not a Fascist Aesthetics?' (*SubStance* 67.24–43), Larry L. Langford tries to reconcile the conflict between modernism and postmodernism by arguing that they are in reality part of the same dialectical process within the Enlightenment project. Langford is keen to emphasize the positive side of postmodernism, claiming that, no less than is the case with modernism, it 'entails a project to reconceptualize enlightened thought'.

A less problematical conception of subjectivity than Cascardi's emerges from Richard Levin's 'Son of Bashing the Bourgeois Subject' (*Textual Practice* 6.264–70), an entertaining sequel to the same author's 'Defence of the Bourgeois or Humanist Subject' (or BHS) against its many detractors, or 'bashers', in a 1989 *Textual Practice* article. Such celebrated bashers as Catherine Belsey, Alan Sinfield and Francis Barker are roundly criticized for beliefs about the BHS (that it is self-created, for example) and capitalism ('natural', 'universal', 'unchanging') that Levin declares 'were never held by anyone outside a mental institution'. In fact, Levin contends, the bashers have produced the BHS to give themselves an easy target for their political theorizing – 'an empty and infinitely expansible discursive space into which they can dump everything that they disapprove of'. This is knockabout stuff which will no doubt cause hackles to rise across the far left. More reflections on the relationship between modernity and postmodernity can be found in Vassiliki Kolocotroni and Margerie Metzstein's 'Modernity–Postmodernity: A Dialogue' (*Textual Practice* 6.478–90), where a *Symposium*-style dialogue makes use of Wildean personae 'to mimic and parody discourses of modernity and postmodernity' from a feminist perspective.

Postmodernism's popularity has acted as a spur to the production of anthologies, such as Peter Brooker's *Modernism/Postmodernism* and Patricia Waugh's *Postmodernism: A Reader*. In the main the readings in the Brooker volume are fairly predictable (Lukács, Benjamin, Adorno, and Williams on modernism, Habermas, Lyotard, Baudrillard and Eco on postmodernism, for example), although they come with useful headnotes putting the authors into socio-historical context. There is a succinct introductory essay, of leftish slant, by the editor on the cultural history of the terms 'modernism' and 'postmodernism'. The Waugh collection contains many of the same authors, but ranges somewhat more widely than Brooker (back to Kant, for example), reflecting the editor's belief that the roots of postmodernism (in her reading 'a theoretical and representational "mood"') can be traced back at least as far as the phenomenon of European Romanticism. Again, the introduction is a useful one, with its emphasis on the aesthetic dimension of post-modern theory. Many of the same theorists turn up in Antony Easthope and Kate McGowan's *A Critical and Cultural Theory Reader*, whose remit is to provide an introduction to the study of the texts of high and popular culture together.

Finally in this section, two works on Foucault, a seminal figure of the postmodern movement whose genealogical and archaeological studies continue to cast a long shadow over the field of critical and cultural studies: Simon During's *Foucault and Literature: Towards a Genealogy of Writing*, and *Michel Foucault Philosopher*, a collection of essays by an international cast of philosophers and critics, with French and German translation provided by Timothy J. Armstrong. During sets out to explore the implications for literary studies of Foucault's 'transgressive thought'. While conceding that Foucault himself rarely dealt with literature as a category or institution, During nevertheless claims a pivotal role for literature in Foucault's career, drawing attention to his subject's deep interest in, and in some cases overt championship of, such writers as Blanchot, Bataille, Klossowski, Roussel, and Robbe-Grillet in the 1960s and 1970s. What we learn from transgressive thought, During maintains, is that 'the big, big terms – "being," "reason," "history," "humanism," and so on – can no longer thread our thoughts together'. Given the problematization and loss of integrity of such terms, literature must subsequently appear in a different light than traditional literary studies would have us believe; it can no longer be considered to form sensibility, nor provide role models for the young reader, nor communicate a set of stable cultural values over time. During offers sound readings of Foucault's major works (*Madness and Civilization*, *Birth of the Clinic*, *History of Sexuality*, etc.), with excursions into the work of such Foucault-influenced critics as Ian Hunter (*Culture and Government*) and Stephen Greenblatt (*Shakespearean Negotiations*). Despite the fact that he has misgivings about some aspects of the latter two texts (a certain arbitrary quality to Greenblatt's choice of case-studies, for example), During still sees much to commend the Foucauldian approach to literary analysis, with its encouragement to us to 'work at the level of local relations between events' rather than in the more rarefied reaches of 'grand narratives'. Literature students new to Foucault should find this a useful introduction.

Michel Foucault Philosopher consists of a series of papers read and discussed at an international colloquium organized by the Michel Foucault Centre in Paris in 1988, featuring such luminaries as Étienne Balibar, Georges Canguilhem, Gilles Deleuze, Manfred Frank, Pierre Macherey and Richard Rorty. The volume's five sections consider Foucault's work in terms of the history of philosophy, style and discourse, power and government, ethics and the subject, and rationalities and histories. Volumes II–III of *The History of Sexuality* loom large in the proceedings, and there is an overall concern to apply the genealogical method back on to Foucault's own work. The emphasis throughout is on the provisional and tactical nature of Foucauldian thought and methodology, and the contributors are at pains to resist any unproblematic incorporation into the philosophical mainstream of a thinker who, as Georges Canguilhem reminds us, began his work iconoclastically enough with a history of madness. Foucault himself continues to defy easy categorization as a writer: 'How many Michel Foucaults would it be necessary to construct in order that they should figure in at least one of his complete works?' . . . 'What could be said of the authorial function of a writer who, as he put together histories in philosophy, was actually constructing fictions?', wonder Denis Hollier and Raymond Bellour respectively. This is a wide-ranging, and by no means hagiographically-inclined collection – the shortcomings of 'genealogy' and 'archaeology' are frequently alluded to – which contributes significantly to the Foucault debate.

2. Narrativity

Postmodernism and poststructuralism have had a lot to say about narrative and, as is only too well known, have tended to question many of the assumptions made by traditional narrative and its defenders. Two articles to address this issue are Martin Kreiswirth's

'Trusting the Tale: The Narrativist Turn in the Human Sciences' (*New Literary History* 23.629–57), and Alex Agyros's 'Narrative and Chaos' (*New Literary History* 23.659–73). Kreiswirth posits a 'narrativist turn' to discourse in recent years (with Lyotard being seen to play a crucial role in the process), and notes that narrative has increasingly come to displace argument and explanation in a wide range of disciplinary contexts. The cultural importance of narrative is emphasized, as well as the need to keep it a subject of theoretical investigation. Lyotard comes off far less lightly in Agyros's thought-provoking piece, which sets out to present an 'affirmative theory of narrative' and to argue, contra-Lyotard, that 'oppression does not result from grand narratives, it results from evil grand narratives'. The 'affirmative theory' proves to be a heady mixture of biogenetic anthropology, information theory and the science of chaos, and is designed to rehabilitate narrative as an agent of cultural change. All the sources of the affirmative theory listed above suggest to Agyros that human beings are creatures predisposed to 'organize material in a narratival manner'. Neither is traditional narrative as simplistically linear as poststructuralists and postmodernists would have us believe; in the light of chaos theory, Agyros claims, traditional narrative can be understood 'as an evolutionary adaptation which is able to tap the remarkable ability of chaotic systems to be simultaneously conservative and innovative'. This is a densely-structured argument which could well merit more elaborate treatment in book form.

The theory of narratology outlined by Barthes in such studies as *S/Z* comes under scrutiny from Frank Whitehead in 'Roland Barthes's Narratology' (*The Cambridge Quarterly* 21.41–64). Whitehead has little time for Barthes, whom he regards as the source of 'some highly unrealistic prescriptions for both the writing and the reading' of literature, but it would have to be said that *S/Z* hardly seems a burning issue in current theoretical circles.

3. The Politics and Ideology of Theory and Criticism

Next come several studies dealing with the politics and ideology of theory and criticism. The current 'theory paradigm' (or 'constructivist anti-humanism' as the authors term it) comes under severe attack in Richard Freadman and Seumas Miller's *Re-Thinking Theory: A Critique of Contemporary Literary Theory and an Alternative Account*, an unashamedly humanist-oriented broadside against the practices and underlying assumptions of Althusserian Marxism and the various streams of post-Saussurean language theory. There are three main aspects of the paradigm to which Freadman and Miller take particular exception: (1) the commitment to a non-referential view of language; (2) the rejection of substantive accounts of the individual; (3) the repudiation of moral and aesthetic evaluation. By espousing such notions, Freadman and Miller contend, constructivist anti-humanists are led progressively more deeply into contradiction in their theorizing. Thus Catherine Belsey's enthusiastic championship, in *Critical Practice* (Routledge, 1980), of the reader as the active originator of textual meaning simply cannot be squared with her 'official denial of the substantial self' in the same work. Similar contradictions are located in the work of Eagleton, Derrida, Spivak, Foucault, and Greenblatt, as Freadman and Miller work their way through a series of case-studies designed to demonstrate the general incoherence of constructivist anti-humanist thought. Freadman and Miller have a point when they identify 'at the very least, subliminally totalitarian' tendencies in the paradigm, with its assumption that only those who accept the constructivist anti-humanist line can be permitted to lay claim to an emancipationist politics, as well as the effective demonization of 'the complex and varied phenomenon' of humanism. As a piece of negative polemic revealing some serious inconsistencies in constructive anti-humanist writing, *Re-Thinking Theory* can be considered relatively successful. Where the study falls down is in its alternative account, which in effect amounts to the statement of a set of ethical principles (such as a firm belief in moral agency) rather than any kind of alternative methodology for dealing with texts – which, one suspects, is what most non-constructive anti-humanists are likely to be looking for. Disappointing though the final stages of the book may be, it is nevertheless fascinating to observe humanism slowly but surely re-establishing a niche for itself within theoretical discourse.

Yet more evidence for such a trend can be found in Jean-Jacques Thomas's 'Poststructuralism and the New Humanism' (*SubStance* 67.61–76). Thomas approvingly notes a general movement towards the 'salvaging of Modernism' which involves a 'return of the subject' and a recognition of 'the accomplishments of humanism'. The villain of the piece in this reading is poststructuralist thought and its 'aggrandized disorder'.

Denis Donoghue's scepticism about the modern (and postmodern) theoretical enterprise is well documented, and *The Pure Good of Theory*, the sixth volume in the 'Bucknell Lectures in Literary Theory' series, provides him with yet another platform to continue his attack on the perceived excesses of deconstruction, Marxism, etc. The volume consists of two lectures by Donoghue, plus an interview with him, two introductory essays on his work by Pauline Fletcher and Harold Schweizer, and a complete bibliography of Donoghue's writings up to 1991. Donoghue's line is that most recent literary theory is really a form of ideology: 'what we encounter is not theory at all,' he claims, 'it is merely a number of ideologies going about their business'. In the main he finds theory/ideology coercive and intolerant, and is puzzled as to where its air of conviction comes from, 'in the absence of any ground of ultimacy'. Drawing on a phrase from R. P. Blackmur he accuses the likes of Derrida, Jameson, Rorty and de Man of turning theory into a 'technique of trouble'. While conceding that some forms of trouble are worth making and can lead ultimately to the common good, he remains highly sceptical that current theory will yield much of benefit. Most theorists, he argues, have no real feeling for literature, and theory is only really justifiable to Donoghue if it helps us to understand literature better. There is no denying the force of many of Donoghue's objections, but one cannot help wondering if the theoretical imperative is so easily explained away as he pretends. The roots of 'trouble-making' call for far more exploration than he is willing to give them (surely it is more than just trouble for trouble's sake?), and even if theory were just a 'concatenation of largely independent ideologies', as he claims, one would want to ask what set of cultural circumstances generated such a response. For all his declared intention to 'make peace' with the proponents of theory, there is not a great deal of bridge-building going on in Donoghue's lectures.

Paul Bove's *In the Wake of Theory*, a 'critique of the politics and practice of intellectuals and disciplines in postmodern society' as it styles itself, is a fairly bitter attack on the current American academic scene. For Bove the 'moment of theory' has passed, the victim of a combination of Reaganite politics and the various malign cultural and intellectual forces that its success unleashed: 'In my work', he notes in a despair-tinged introduction, 'I generally tell a sad story of the defeat of criticism by institutions, of knowledge and seriousness by posture and fashion, of memory by amnesia.' This proves to be the signal for some very biting criticism indeed of the work of, amongst others, Sacvan Bercovitch, Stephen Greenblatt, Alan Bloom, and the 'anti-theory' duo of Steven Knapp and Walter Benn Michaels. Bove sees ideological surrender all around him, a prevalent feature in American intellectual life from the days of I. A. Richards and the New Critics right through to the present and New Historicism, a critical movement which 'merely functions to contain resistance within a state institution, within the academy'. Bove identifies a loss of nerve amongst the vast majority of American academics, whom he collectively accuses of failing to live up to their duty – as he sees it – of providing the basis for an oppositional critique of American culture. Drawing extensively on the work of Gramsci and Foucault (whose notion of the 'specific intellectual' is found highly attractive) Bove argues that what critical training ought to inspire is a desire to engage in an ongoing critique of a society's institutions, rather than, as he feels is more usually the case in late twentieth-century America, merely an exercise in the development of marketable skills. Bove's impassioned plea for intellectual regeneration will strike a chord in non-American no less than American academics, but his critique founders to some extent on the twin rocks of conspiracy theory and false consciousness. Neither is a very satisfactory explanation for the current state of the American intellectual establishment, and there is a suspect air of nostalgia hanging around that notion of a lost 'moment of theory'. One can also query whether intellectuals are quite as important in the overall cultural scheme of things as Bove clearly seems to believe they are.

The 'anti-theory' debate, one of the key debates about the politics and practice of theory in the 1980s, surfaces again in the pages of *Critical Inquiry*. In 'Again, Theory: On Speaker's Meaning, Linguistic Meaning, and the Meaning of a Text' (*Critical Inquiry* 19.164–85) George Wilson attacks Knapp and Benn Michaels (whose *Critical Inquiry* article sparked off the original debate) for failing to take enough account of developments within the philosophy of language. In 'Reply to George Wilson' (*Critical Inquiry* 19.186–93) Knapp and Benn Michaels respond that their concern rests not with philosophy of language but with interpretation. Given that the original exchanges also generated a book (W. J. T. Mitchell, ed., *Against Theory*, University of Chicago Press, 1985), most readers are likely to conclude that this is a debate that has probably run its course.

The value of a theory-led approach to literary studies is questioned by David Gervais in 'Literary Criticism and the Literary Student' (*English* 41.149–61), an article communicating a definite air of nostalgia for pre-theoretical times. In 'Towards a Critical Renewal: At the Corner of Camus and Bloom Streets' (*College English* 54.46–63) Quentin G. Kraft calls for a new balance to be struck between theory and critical practice, arguing that 'we need to find some way to reassert the value of individual texts'. K. M. Newton, on the other hand, is entirely positive about the cultural and political value of literary theory, and in 'Literary Theory and the Rushdie Affair' (*English* 41.235–47) argues that the application of theory could help to resolve the affair in question. Newton's claim is that literary theory – in particular de Manian deconstruction and New Historicism – could be used to support Muslim opposition to *The Satanic Verses*. The admission by literary critics and theorists that Muslim readers are justified in finding Rushdie's narrative 'offensive' would, Newton believes, help to promote a spirit of dialogue and compromise 'rather than intolerance and conflict'. It is a bold claim, although one suspects it is also a highly idealistic one, given how high passions have run in this affair. Value itself comes under analysis in Lindon Barrett's 'Exemplary Values: Value, Violence, and Others of Value' (*SubStance* 67.77–94), the contention being that 'value originates in excess and violence'. While this might suggest a commendable concern to sketch out a politics of value, Barrett's argument is highly abstract and not always easy to decipher.

The politics of textual analysis are scrutinized in Bob Hodge and Alex McHoul's 'The Politics of Text and Commentary' (*Textual Practice* 6.189–209), where the various kinds of relationship (authoritarian and otherwise) involved in textual commentary are explored. Joseph Cleary's concern in 'Theory in an Age of Mechanical Reproduction' (*Textual Practice* 6.452–77) is with the impact of militarism on socio-politically radical theories such as classical Marxism, neo-Marxism, and poststructuralism. In Cleary's view the 'invocations of catastrophe' so prominent in these theories harbour 'an explicit or implicit military referent'.

Studies such as Norris and Freadman/Miller suggest that we are witnessing a return to humanism, value and the subject in theoretical discourse, and the various contributors to Stephen Regan's collection of essays *The Politics of Pleasure: Aesthetics and Cultural Theory* provide further evidence that this is indeed the case. The editor announces a 'return to the aesthetic', whose goal is to overcome the negative associations that have grown up around the term over the course of the twentieth century, such that it can begin to function as 'a politics of culture'. Terry Eagleton's 'The Ideology of the Aesthetic', a 1988 essay which rehearses many of the themes of the 1990 book of the same name, sets the tone for the collection in its recognition of the simultaneously repressive and liberating connotations of the term 'the aesthetic' – a view that finds echoes throughout the collection. Michèle Barrett counsels against the assumption, so often made in Marxist circles, that all questions about aesthetic pleasure and value are irretrievably contaminated by bourgeois humanism. Steven Connor hopes that the aesthetic can be turned into a realm in which the political value of pleasure can be 'pleasurably' renegotiated; Adrian Page that a concept of value based on social function can be reinstated in literary–critical discourse. Patricia Waugh's contribution 'Stalemates?: Feminists, Postmodernists and Unfinished Issues in Modern Aesthetics' might be more at home in a collection addressing postmodernism, but it is in many ways the most stimulating essay in the volume: a commendably closely-argued piece that draws our attention to the many 'patriarchal metanarratives' lurking behind the scene of postmodernist theory. Waugh is not afraid, even in these generally metanarrative-hostile times, to counter with some 'grand and totalizing narratives' in the name of feminism. One criticism of the volume would have to be the treatment of Lukács in Geoff Wade's 'Marxism and Modernist Aesthetics: Reading Kafka and Beckett'. Wade argues that Lukács demanded 'a clear socialist drive' in modern narrative if it was to meet with his approval, and queries, somewhat maliciously, where this drive might be found in Thomas Mann, 'whom Lukács reveres'. In point of fact Lukács's doctrine of 'critical realism' makes no such demand of the bourgeois author, asking only that such an author not be actively hostile to socialism. Neither was Lukács likely to insist on 'born-again proletarian heroes' in the pages of the bourgeois novel, far less to 'rhapsodise' over them in the manner of a 'Soviet Minister of Culture' as is suggested. There are many things questionable about Lukácsian aesthetics, but not what he is being accused of by Wade.

The aestheticization of politics is usually taken to be a postmodern phenomenon, but an earlier example of the tendency can be found in fascism, as David Carroll argues in 'Literary Fascism, or the Aestheticizing of Politics: The Case of Robert Brasillach' (*New Literary History* 23.691–726). Brasillach, a French fascist writer executed for collaborationist activities in 1945, becomes for Carroll a case-study of the complex relationship between fascist politics and literary aesthetics. Carroll's claim is that fascism should be regarded as a product of modernity, 'an extreme manifestation' of modernist aesthetics and political theory.

4. Textuality

John Mowitt's *Text: The Genealogy of an Antidisciplinary Object* offers a history of the 'theory of the text', identifying the phenomenon as a response to a crisis of disciplinarity in modern (particularly French) culture noticeable from the work of Barthes and the *Tel Quel* group of theorists onwards. In Mowitt's reading 'text' is an antidisciplinary object in that it makes us aware of the limits of disciplinary knowledge, and, ultimately, calls into question the cultural logic of the entire project of disciplinarity. Whereas the theory of the text has generally been taken to sanction a move into interdisciplinarity (encouraging the growth of film and media studies in the process), Mowitt sees this as something of an evasion of textuality's revolutionary potential, suggesting that we should always query what tactical point lies behind the desire 'to subsume ever more social experience under an academically inflected variant of disciplinary power'. The ultimate goal is to encourage 'the emergence of a more productive notion of textuality' that will enable us to confront cultural paradigms. Mowitt argues that the notion of textuality is essentially derived from literature and that this has proved restrictive to film studies and musicology, whose practitioners find themselves forcing their analyses to fit what are inappropriate literary models. As a result they are prevented from engaging in what Mowitt regards as the proper task of criticism: 'seeking to transform the institutional conditions of their own authority'. No doubt Mowitt has done a service by demonstrating how deeply the literary paradigm infiltrates interdisciplinarity, but antidisciplinarity remains a vague concept at best, whose revolutionary potential is never very convincingly demonstrated. While the study makes some moves towards addressing the politics of textuality, it promises more than it delivers, and all too often the argument breaks down into banal, and fairly empty, exhortations to 'oppose disciplinary power' or 'transform institutional conditions of authority'.

5. Theory of Humour

The Language of Jokes, by Delia Chiaro, is a volume in the 'Interface' series whose declared aim is to examine topics at the interface of language and literary studies and to find common ground between the two areas. Chiaro ranges over issues such as the narrative organization of jokes, the role of established conventions in joke-telling and joke-reception, discourse strategies in making jokes, and the creative uses of puns, word play and ambiguities, all from a broadly sociocultural perspective. This is a disappointing book, however, which rarely lives up to the 'two major points of principle' outlined by the series editor: namely, 'that the term "literature" cannot be defined in isolation from an expression of ideology', and that contributors are expected, as far as they can, 'to explore the role of ideology at the interface of language and literature'. In fact, ideology receives little detailed attention in this work, whose special concern with the role of humour in British life and literature yields mainly descriptive statements of the kind that 'word play may well be more pervasive in Britain than elsewhere', and 'its expressions of humour remain mysterious to all but its most proficient speakers', with little in the way of analytical back-up (such as an exploration of the role of class in British life, for instance). Chiaro works her way through a series of jokes, considering how and why they work (diagrams copiously provided), and offering some practical hints as to how to effect translation from one language-context to another, but overall I fear there is not a great deal to engage the literature student in this volume.

Ideology is given more attention in Debbora Battaglia's 'Displacing Culture: A Joke of Significance in Urban Papua New Guinea' (*New Literary History* 23.103–17), an analysis of a collection of jokes from the Trobriand Islands which treats the jokes as 'historically specific ideological formations'. Esoteric though the article undoubtedly is, it does succeed in making a general point about the roles of jokes within a culture.

6. Online Literacy

The exact nature of the impact of the new computing technologies on thought and literacy is still a matter of considerable debate amongst scholars, and Myron C. Tuman's *Word Perfect: Literacy in the Computer Age* constitutes a welcome addition to that debate in the balanced assessment it presents of the competing claims of print and online literacy. While enthusiastic about the potential of online literacy Tuman is no mere zealot – one of the constant refrains of his study is that there are losses as well as gains involved in the shift from a print to an online culture. 'There is much of value to salvage from that older tradition,' he cautions, 'the sanctity it places on individual experience, its respect for privacy, its respect for innovation.' Tuman is sceptical of some of the wilder claims made for online literacy, hypertext, and the 'networked classroom', and brings a keen historical consciousness to bear on the evaluation of the two literacies. Print literacy is viewed as that necessary to enable an individual 'to prosper in a given historical moment', and Tuman's ultimate concern is to work out the relationship of online literacy to the current, postmodern, historical moment. One of the likely consequences of online literacy is the fostering of a collaborative, as opposed to competitive, attitude in the individual. While appreciating the undoubted benefits this brings (the strengthening of the community ethic and the breakdown of hierarchy, for example), Tuman also sounds a warning note about the threat it poses to the dissenting individual – the group ethic can only too easily become a conformist ethic serving the needs of the multinational corporations. Neither does Tuman's enthusiasm for online literacy extend to an uncritical acceptance of hypertext, a genre he feels has been wildly oversold by its champions: poorly-implemented hypertext, he points out, can, as one leading computer scientist has put it, 'also lead to hyperchaos'. This is a stimulating book which may well convince the still considerable ranks of the print-literate to revise their position regarding the virtues, and possibilities, of online literacy. It might (and it certainly *should*) even persuade some of the online-literate to pay more attention to the ideological implications of their new technology.

Tuman is also the editor of *Literacy Online: The Promise (and Peril) of Reading and Writing with Computers*, a collection of conference-derived essays confronting key issues in the online literacy debate. The contributors are in the main partisan, although by no means all of them unquestioningly so, and dissenting views do put in an appearance. No one is more zealous, however, than Theodor Nelson, the coiner of the term 'hypertext', for whom 'the purpose of computers is human freedom' and 'the universal electronic docuverse' the goal to which we should all be aspiring. What hypertext represents to Nelson is little less than the liberation of mankind, and there is an unmistakably messianic note to his pronouncements on the subject that will grate on defenders of print literacy. Nelson and the concept of hypertext form something of a central focus for the collection's contributors, some of whom, like Eugene F. Provenzo Jr, are sceptical of Nelson's view that machines are essentially neutral. Provenzo's Foucault-inspired analysis of the computer's role in modern culture is based on the premise that computer technology just *cannot* be neutral. Computers, he reminds us, empower 'both good and evil people'. There is considerable disagreement overall as to whether this particular medium should be blamed for the message when the technology is turned to evil ends, and some contributors (Victor Raskin being a case in point) also express fears that the use of computers in schools might be having the effect of dehumanizing education. Possibly the most serious doubt of all is raised by the editor in his 'final thoughts': is the very notion of critical thought tied to print technology?

7. Education

Edwin Webb's *Literature in Education: Encounter and Experience* comes from an entirely different world from that of postmodernism, hypertext or online literacy. What we have here instead is a determinedly rearguard action on behalf of literature as a humanizing phenomenon, something that 'vivifies our sense of being, and through that enrichment of our sensibilities, enables us to begin to make sense of the world of our realities'. Webb sees himself in an English cultural tradition stretching from Arnold through Eliot and Leavis and their disciples to the present, and argues that theories such as structuralism and poststructuralism trivialize the literary experience, and, eventually, act to stultify our imagination. He has little time in general for the treatment accorded literature in current higher education, which in his opinion fails to pay enough attention to the subject's aesthetic field; anecdotal evidence is duly produced of narrow-minded graduates and insensitive lecturers, although that hardly clinches Webb's general point. The goal is to find in literature what John Stuart Mill found in the poetry of Wordsworth: access to a world of the imagination that can transcend the utilitarian world most of us inhabit in our daily lives. Webb writes as if we can simply ignore the poststructuralist problematization of notions like personal identity – 'self-expression' lives on as a relatively unproblematical ideal in his world – or of 'literature' as a special category. One does not have to be a card-carrying poststructuralist to find this questionable practice. Perhaps this is to be unfair to Webb, however, since his real target is not so much the theoretical establishment as a utilitarian-minded British school system where literary study is being superseded by language study in the curriculum, on the grounds that subjects such as literature are 'of little consequence to the "real world" of affairs'. It is possible to sympathize with Webb's concern on this score, and indeed Arts academics will be only too familiar with the spectre of cultural philistinism raised in these pages. Whether an increased dose of self-expression or Arnoldian tradition is the remedy for such philistinism is much more arguable.

Peter Erickson's concern lies with the literary syllabus in American higher education, and in 'The Question of the Canon: The

Examples of Searle, Kimball and Kernan' (*Textual Practice* 6.439–51) he mounts an attack on three defenders of the traditional canon. The traditionalist cultural line pursued by such defenders is traced back to a political source in the Reagan presidency and the forces it released in American society. In Erickson's view the effect of thinkers like Searle, Kimball and Kernan has been entirely negative, acting to inhibit engagement with the new literature of multiculturalism. Kimball's views are defended in Joseph Epstein's 'The Academic Zoo: Theory – In Practice' (*Hudson Review* 44.9–30), which, like the Gervais article above (see p. 15), evinces an air of nostalgia for the days before the modern theory revolution. Sander L. Gilman adopts a positive attitude to recent changes in higher education, and in 'Whose Classroom Is It Anyway?: Teaching and Researching in the Humanities from a Transdisciplinary Perspective' (*University of Toronto Quarterly* 61.443–9) argues that the ability continually to problematize disciplinary boundaries is one of the humanities' great strengths.

8. Reference Works

The explosive growth of the discourse of literary theory over the last couple of decades has created a large demand for reference works, and Jeremy Hawthorn's *A Glossary of Contemporary Literary Theory* is one of the more notable contributions to the field. It is designed to provide a guide to the rapidly-expanding specialized vocabulary of recent (roughly from 1970 onwards) literary theory and critical discourse, although it also includes glosses on certain older terms such as 'New Criticism'. The latter are excluded from the volume's edited version, *A Concise Glossary of Contemporary Literary Theory*.

Books Reviewed

Armstrong, Timothy J., trans. *Michel Foucault Philosopher*. Harvester Wheatsheaf. pp. 351. £12.99. ISBN 0 7450 0885 2.

Bove, Paul. *In the Wake of Theory*. Wesleyan University Press. pp. 181. hb £27.25, pb £11.50. ISBN 0 8195 5244 5, 0 8195 6254 8.

Brooker, Peter, ed. *Modernism/Postmodernism*. Longman. pp. 268. hb £25.00, pb £9.99. ISBN 0 582 06358 2, 0 582 06357 4.

Cascardi, Anthony J. *The Subject of Modernity*. Cambridge University Press. pp. 316. hb £35.00/$49.95, pb £11.95/$16.95. ISBN 0 521 41287 0, 0 521 42378 3.

Chiaro, Delia. *The Language of Jokes: Analysing Verbal Play*. Routledge. pp. 129. £9.99. ISBN 0 415 03090 0.

Donoghue, Denis. *The Pure Good of Theory*. Blackwell. pp. 146. hb £30.00, pb £9.95. ISBN 0 631 18474 0, 0 631 18475 9.

During, Simon. *Foucault and Literature: Towards a Genealogy of Writing*. Routledge. pp. 259. £10.99. ISBN 0 415 01242 2.

Easthope, Antony, and Kate McGowan, eds. *A Critical and Cultural Theory Reader*. Open University Press. pp. 270. hb £37.50, pb £10.99. ISBN 0 335 09944 0.

Freadman, Richard, and Seumas Miller. *Re-Thinking Theory: A Critique of Contemporary Literary Theory and an Alternative Account*. Cambridge University Press. pp. 296. £35.00. ISBN 0 521 38035 9.

Hawthorn, Jeremy. *A Glossary of Contemporary Literary Theory*. Edward Arnold. pp. 282. £35.00. ISBN 0 340 53912 7.

——. *A Concise Glossary of Contemporary Literary Theory*. Edward Arnold. pp. 210. £9.99. ISBN 0 340 53911 9.

Kroker, Arthur. *The Possessed Individual: Technology and Postmodernity*. Macmillan. pp. 176. £12.99. ISBN 0 333 57550 4.

McHale, Brian. *Constructing Postmodernism*. Routledge. pp. 342. hb £35.00, pb £11.99. ISBN 0 415 06013 3, 0 415 06014 1.

Mowitt, John. *Text: The Genealogy of an Antidisciplinary Object*. Duke University Press. pp. 245. hb £37.95, pb £13.50. ISBN 0 8223 1251 4, 0 8223 1273 5.

Norris, Christopher. *Uncritical Theory: Postmodernism, Intellectuals, and the Gulf War*. Lawrence and Wishart. pp. 218. £9.99. ISBN 0 85315 752 9.

Regan, Stephen, ed. *The Politics of Pleasure: Aesthetics and Cultural Theory*. Open University Press. pp. 225. £12.99. ISBN 0 335 09759 6.

Smart, Barry. *Modern Conditions, Postmodern Controversies*. Routledge. pp. 241. £10.99. ISBN 0 415 06952 1.

Tuman, Myron C., ed. *Literacy Online: The Promise (and Peril) of Reading and Writing with Computers*. University of Pittsburgh Press. pp. 284. £11.95. ISBN 0 8229 5465 6.

——. *Word Perfect: Literacy in the Computer Age*. University of Pittsburgh Press. pp. 150. hb $49.95, pb $19.95. ISBN 0 8229 3735 2, 0 8229 5489 3.

Vattimo, Gianni. *The Transparent Society*. Polity Press. pp. 129. hb £29.50, pb £9.95. ISBN 0 7456 0926 0, 0 7456 1047 1.

Waugh, Patricia. *Postmodernism: A Reader*. Edward Arnold. pp. 226. £10.99. ISBN 0 340 55050 9.

Webb, Edwin. *Literature in Education: Encounter and Experience*. Falmer Press. pp. 159. hb £32.00, pb £11.95. ISBN 1 85000 767 5, 1 85000 768 3.

2

Rhetoric and Deconstruction

ROBIN JARVIS

This year's harvest of books and articles is distinguished by a number of studies taking serious philosophical stock of Derrida (with a corresponding diminution of interest in 'literary' deconstruction), and a flurry of projects exploring the relations of deconstruction with other intellectual traditions and with less familiar thinkers (among which the Derrida–Levinas connection comes into some prominence).

Let's take some of Derrida's own main publications first. *The Other Heading* brings together in book form two long newspaper articles, one on Europe, one on 'public opinion', with – something of a convention of Derrida's translated works – an introduction that is over half the length of the text it accompanies. In the light of growing anti-Eurocentrism, of the collapse of the Soviet empire and the fragmentation of Eastern Europe, and of developments such as the dominion of the tele-image, Derrida attempts to rethink the problem of European cultural identity in a way that is wary equally of the opposing models of monopoly and dispersion. Avoiding the abyss of 'a multiplicity of self-enclosed idioms or petty nationalisms, each one jealous and untranslatable', this identity must never come under the 'heading' of 'a centralizing authority that, by means of trans-European cultural mechanisms . . . would control and standardize, subjecting artistic discourses and practices to a grid of intelligibility, to philosophical or aesthetic norms, to channels of immediate and efficient communication, to the pursuit of ratings and commercial profitability'. The deconstructive logic is familiar, and it is pursued with a flickering brilliance, but as the case for an 'impossible' cultural identity built on such an aporia gathers steam one's empiricist reflexes begin to twitch. One of Derrida's main contentions (one is strongly aware of the similarity of his speculations to Lyotard's in this connection) is that ethics and politics cannot be reduced to prescription and 'scientific' judgement without becoming *ir*responsible: one must respect the singularity of each decision, each experience of responsibility, whilst simultaneously heeding the 'universal' values which Europe has always seen it as its destiny to uphold and propagate. So it is urged that power be exercised, and the idea of Europe determined, in response to 'two contradictory injunctions': one stemming, it would seem, from the tired value-base of Western bourgeois democracy, the other stemming from . . . well, the Other. Europe as the experience and experiment of the impossible: one wonders what message of hope or consolation this might carry to the people of Bosnia-Herzegovina.

Under the heading of *The Other Heading*, one might also consider Derrida's 'Onto-Theology of National-Humanism (Prolegomena to a Hypothesis)' (*Oxford Literary Review* 14.3–23), which reports on the accompaniment of the 'intensification of so-called international exchanges' by an 'exasperation of national identities and identifications'. The problem of nationality, Derrida suggests, does not impinge on philosophy from outside, because it is a characteristic of nations to see themselves as the unique bearers of a potentially universal discourse.

Cinders is one of Derrida's more experimental 'literary' works. First published in 1982, then revised in 1987 and issued with an accompanying cassette, Nebraska have now published it in a bilingual edition with an English translation by Ned Lukacher (but minus the cassette). It exploits Derrida's favourite devices of parallel texts, a polylogic conversation, citation and allusion, and so on, counterfacing excerpts from Derrida's work from 1968 onwards on the theme of ashes and cinders (a now seemingly privileged metaphor for the linguistic trace) with a prose poem centred on the gnomic phrase, '*il y a là cendre*' (wherein the homophonic *la cendre* marks the gap between speech and writing). Bizarrely described by the publisher's blurb as 'uniquely accessible to readers who have only recently begun to read Derrida', I found it one of the least rewarding of the latter's texts that I have read. One reason it irritates is its sumptuous coffee-table format and matching price-tag. Some of the same themes are traversed more economically in 'Given Time: The Time of the King' (*Critical Inquiry* 18.161–87), which uses the paradoxical structure of the gift (mere recognition of the gift by donor or donee completes a symbolic exchange, thereby annulling the gift) to reflect on the forgetting that is constitutive of

Being and Time: 'the structure of this impossible of the *gift* is also that of Being . . . and of time'.

Hot on the heels of Peggy Kamuf's *A Derrida Reader*, which I reviewed last year (*YWCCT* 1.21), Derek Attridge has produced another Derrida anthology, *Acts of Literature* – which, as its title indicates, has a distinctive focus on Derrida's writings on literary texts and the institution of literature, and can therefore justly be regarded as a complementary rather than a rival volume. Particularly useful to have are the texts appearing for the first time in English, at least in the particular version translated: 'Mallarmé' (1974), 'Before the Law' (1982, on Kafka), 'Aphorism Countertime' (1986, on *Romeo and Juliet*), and an extract from *Shibboleth*, on Paul Celan (1984). Also included are 'The First Session', 'The Law of Genre', 'Ulysses Gramophone', a section from *Of Grammatology* on Rousseau, and excerpts from 'Psyche: Invention of the Other' and *Signsponge*. There is also a lengthy interview with Derrida in which he speaks of the origins of his writing in an 'autobiographical dream' that is still his 'most naïve desire'. He talks of the varying appeals of literature, an institution which allows one to say anything, and philosophy, which poses the kinds of questions about the essence of literature which 'literary' writers seem unable to ask. Derrida refuses Attridge's invitation to generalize either about literature's complicity with metaphysical assumptions or about literary criticism's enslavement to logocentrism – in either case, 'the possibilities of rupture are always waiting to be effected'. Challenged on whether he objects to the kind of naïve enjoyment that most readers find in literature, he rather cheekily counters that 'there is no efficient deconstruction without the greatest possible pleasure'. An insistent theme in the interview is the use of the opposition – unstable, of course – of singularity and iterability to characterize the constitution, production and reception of literary texts. It is a theme picked up in Attridge's lucid introduction, which tactfully steers the reader between two influential misreadings of Derrida: that which privileges 'philosophical deconstruction' as a model for an undeluded critical methodology, while ignoring Derrida's own discussions of literature; and that which draws on Derrida's 'style' to cultivate a 'playfully literary' reading of literary texts. Both misreadings reaffirm the classical separation of philosophy and literature which, as these essays plainly illustrate, Derrida persistently calls into question. This anthology will undoubtedly be valued by scholars, and may also be found serviceable in postgraduate teaching.

In *The Ethics of Deconstruction* Simon Critchley reflects on, and develops, the dialogue that has taken place between Derrida and Emmanuel Levinas, in order to validate the claim that deconstruction obeys a categorical imperative construed as a 'yes-saying to the unnameable'. Critchley begins by theorizing what he terms *clôtural* reading, which seems indistinguishable from common notions of deconstructive practice: a first stage of doubling commentary 'faithful' to a scholarly consensus about the meaning of a text, followed by a second stage wherein a position of alterity is sought from which the intended meaning is brought into contradiction with an unassimilable other. Critchley then reads Derrida reading Levinas, and Levinas reading Derrida. He argues that Derrida avoids the trap of reading Levinas unethically ('gratefully', fulfilling the economy of the Same) by reading him *as a woman*: Levinas, according to Derrida, maintains that ethical difference is sexually *in*different, but marks the wholly other with male pronouns; the second moment of a *clôtural* reading therefore consists in establishing the feminine as the 'other to the wholly other', thus receiving Levinas's work 'ungratefully' and maintaining ethical alterity. Reversing the roles, Critchley looks at Levinas's analysis of Derrida's reading of Husserl. Levinas shows how Derrida captures the originary contamination of expression by indication, but fails to register the ethical nature of the indicative relation, where 'that which is indicated cannot be reduced to being an object for self-consciousness' but confronts one as the 'absolutely other', with roots ultimately in non-verbal, bodily discourse. In his final chapter, Critchley suggests that Levinas offers a way through the deconstructive log-jam that has prevented a passage from ethics (where deconstruction has arguably had something to say) to politics (where it has been accused of evasion, or impotence, or worse). Levinas, he claims, shows how one's infinite responsibility for the Other within ethical discourse is always already implicated in the order of political justice, where abstract rights supersede personal duties; Levinas demonstrates that in a just *polis* 'the equality and symmetry of the relations between citizens must be interrupted by the inequality and asymmetry of the ethical relation'. An interestingly knotty, genuinely ground-breaking book.

Having had his relationship with Levinas sorted out, in Andrew J. McKenna's *Violence and Difference* Derrida finds himself confronted with Girardian anthropology – a move self-consciously designed to rescue deconstruction from the formalism to which it is deemed to be fatally attracted. McKenna's comparison of Girard's hypothesis of arbitrary sacrifice as the foundation of culture, with Derrida's theory of the originary repression of writing, looks tenuous on first acquaintance, but grows on one as he proceeds to elaborate it across a range of interesting topics. Among his more arresting analyses is his application of Girard's ideas of mimetic desire and scapegoating to humanity's collective survival after Auschwitz – to, as Derrida puts it, the 'living on' that characterizes postmodernity, in which our 'moral and cognitive imperative' is to forgo the sacrificial mechanism by which human cultures have historically re-established their identity in difference. In an intriguing chapter on the French government's sinking of the *Rainbow Warrior* in a New Zealand harbour in 1985, McKenna finds the same anthropological law at work in such covert actions of the modern state as in primitive sacrificial rites: the Greenpeace affair, which 'reveals the state as heir to sacrifice', demonstrates that 'national security' is the mystified object in the name of which modern communities misrecognize their own desire for violence. This book provides plenty of food for thought, chewy though the prose is at times, and despite some lingering doubt as to whether Derrida, whom McKenna openly acknowledges is being used to re-upholster Girardian themes, is strictly necessary to its project.

Derrida and Negative Theology, edited by Harold Coward and Toby Foshay, is a contribution to the field explored so incisively by Kevin Hart in his *The Trespass of the Sign* (see *The Year's Work in English Studies* 71.50). It reprints two of Derrida's major essays on apophatic thought, 'Of an Apocalyptic Tone Newly Adopted in Philosophy' and 'How to Avoid Speaking: Denials', and then presents responses to them from both Western and Eastern perspectives in essays by Michel Despand, Mark C. Taylor, Harold Coward, David Loy and Morny Joy. Derrida re-enters the debate in a concluding 'Post-Scriptum'. This is a well-conceived volume, but definitely one for hard-nosed specialists only; literary scholars without the requisite philosophical background are unlikely to get much purchase on it.

Nevertheless, they might care to move on to it after reading Coward's own *Derrida and Indian Philosophy*, which provides a more accessible introduction to the apophatic strain in Derrida's thought, along with much else besides. The major aim of the book is to build a bridge between Western and Eastern philosophies of language by exploring parallels between Derridean deconstruction and the writings of important figures from the Hindu and Buddhist traditions. Hinduism is represented by Bhartrhari (fifth century), Śankara (seventh century), and the contemporary Aurobindo Ghose, Buddhism by Nāgārjuna (second century). For the uninitiated, at

least, the parallels are certainly beguiling: for both Derrida and
Bhartrhari 'language is a dynamic becoming that is the very stuff of
our experience of reality', with Bhartrhari's construal of Brahman as
Word-Principle anticipating Derrida's *différance* in its stress on the
sequencing power of time; Śankara shares with Derrida an emphasis
on language as a means to 'spiritual self-realisation', though for him
ultimate reality entails the loss of all distinctions, whereas for
Derrida difference is the real; Aurobindo and Derrida both value
poetry highly for its role in restoring a lost freedom of language,
insisting that this can only happen when normal language use and
the demands of the speaker's ego are suspended; whilst Derrida is in
broad agreement with the Buddhist Nāgārjuna on the 'illusions of
permanence, stasis, or presence' that beset experience, for him
language vitally participates in the reality that such illusions
obscure, whereas for Buddhism language is purely conventional and
must be negated before reality can be apprehended. As this bald
summary might suggest, for many Coward's portrayal of deconstruction as a form of spiritual discipline and self-realization will
seem misguided and question-begging, and they will bristle at the
tendency to see Derrida as a religious thinker, albeit as a negative
theologian: *différance* is all but equated with the final reality or God,
which in 'questioning [us] from the midst of silence' infuses us with
a 'divine demand for moral action'. Still, it would be unwise to
dismiss such claims out of hand, with the jury seemingly still out on
the Jewish–Kabbalistic influence on Derrida's philosophy and the
debate over deconstruction and negative theology with some way
still to run. Before leaving this whole area, I should note Kerry
McKeever's 'How to Avoid Speaking About God: Poststructuralist
Philosophers and Biblical Hermeneutics' (*Literature and Theology*
6.228–38), which takes its cue from Derrida's insistence that he has
not written on the Bible. In fact, McKeever suggests, his writing on
all texts constitutes a 'negative attendance to the divine', given the
relation of all books to the One Book and the notion of God as the
'deferred reciprocity of interpretation'.

In *Derrida, Heidegger, Blanchot*, Timothy Clark examines dialogic
texts by these three thinkers to see how a certain practice of literature opens the question of the other beyond language. The focal
issue, which is keyed in throughout with the philosophy of Levinas,
is how one can practise a 'heteronomy', whereby thought maintains
'a continual suspicion of itself and an openness to alterity'. Clark
begins polemically by briskly dismissing representative pieces of
literary theory by Hillis Miller and Jonathan Culler as forms of dis-

placed positivism that fail to move beyond the horizons of Wellek and Warren's *Theory of Literature*; after this, however, his argument gets a good deal thornier. He glosses Heidegger's thinking of the different senses of mimesis and representation, drawing attention not to the standard semiotic understanding of language but to Heidegger's sense of poetic language as 'a force that brings the apparent into its own to stand unconcealed before us' – an unconcealment that must precede mimesis in the accepted sense. Blanchot's development of the form of the *récit* is said to purge Heideggerian dialogue of the last phenomenological residues in performing a genuine heteronomy, 'a becoming intransitive of language such that a sentence remains solely as a trace of its own movement towards the other'. Derrida's writings on Blanchot are then used to deepen this exploration of the 'call of the other' that takes place through language, without, perhaps, satisfactorily answering Clark's own question of whether this amounts to much more than the 'well-known paradoxes of self-reference'. A separate chapter gamely tries to throw light on *Signsponge* as a 'science of the contingent' in which notions of singularity and generality enter into an abyssal interinvolvement. Charles Tomlinson's 'Poem' provides a testing-ground of disputable benefit for many of the ideas Clark explores. A postscript raises the question of how heteronomic thought as advocated here can be distinguished from the 'paralysed pietism of the later Heidegger', and indeed one's evaluation of the book's thesis will hinge on how far one is prepared to accredit Clark's high claims for the responsibility of deconstruction as a disciplined attentiveness that makes possible an 'affirmation of the other'.

Another branch of Clark's research is brought to notice in 'Modern Transformations of German Romanticism: Blanchot and Derrida on the Fragment, the Aphorism and the Architectural' (*Paragraph* 15.232–47), a dense exploration of common ground between Blanchot's reassessment of the fragment in Schlegel, and Derrida's speculations on the complicity between architecture and metaphysics. Clark's interest in heteronomy is shared by Bill Readings, whose 'Sublime Politics: The End of the Party Line' (*Modern Language Quarterly* 53.409–25) makes an interesting case for distinguishing between the politics of the sublime, which seeks to remake society in the conventionalized terms of the sublime (energy, terror), and sublime politics, which retains the indeterminacy of the Kantian sublime in heralding a 'heteronomous community in which there can be no absolutely authoritative instance and no consensus that might legitimate such an authority'. One is left with the difficulty of implementing such a programme, which resembles an ethics more than a politics.

The reader should by now have some sense of the remarkable overlapping of interests in what at first sight is a very disparate crop of books. To move into more arcane territory, those interested in what deconstruction might mean in architectural terms could take a peek at Papadakis and Toy's *Deconstruction: A Pocket Guide*. Measuring less than five inches by four inches, it certainly lives up to its name, but the combination of drawings and evanescent prose jottings is unlikely to help the uninitiated form an impression of whether architectural theorists have been more than superficially opportunistic in their appropriation of a philosophical term.

Those whose curiosity is more excited by the fate of deconstruction in Finland will rush out to buy Nicholas Royle's essay collection, *Afterwords*, the outgrowth of a convention at the University of Tampere in 1989. In so far as the collection addresses the national context, the picture it paints is ambiguous. Outi Pasanen, the first person to translate Derrida into Finnish, speaks of the difficulties of finding an audience for deconstruction owing to the 'cultural isolation' of Finnish readers. However, if the violently ill-tempered exchange between Matti Savolainen and Markku Eskelinen is anything to go by, deconstruction is already healthily at work setting the Finns at each other's throats. For the rest, *Afterwords* is another general collection of essays on deconstruction, loosely linked by themes of history and temporality. It includes Hillis Miller's 'Deconstruction Now: The States of Deconstruction or Thinking without Synecdoche', Royle's own 'Expositioning', Thomas Kent's 'The Institutionalization of Deconstruction: An American Perspective', Taina Rajanti's 'The Law of Babel', and, perhaps the most trenchant, Robert Young's 'White Mythologies'. The last-named studies the relations between the 'ontological imperialism' of a Western philosophical tradition dedicated to the appropriation of the other by the same, and the political and economic oppression practised by the developed world that sees its destiny writ large in a world History, and finds in this enduring complicity an opening for deconstruction to help to 'decolonise the forms of European thought'. Royle has invited Derrida to comment on the title of the volume, and Derrida accordingly expands on how an afterword cannot and should not be the *last* word, even in a country which might be translated as 'land of the end'.

What perhaps is missing in the various efforts I have described to find new contexts and collaborators for deconstruction, is any serious effort to link Derrida to the wider debate on postmodernity. It is doubly disappointing in this light that Gianni Vattimo's *The Transparent Society*, a book that explores postmodernity as the epoch of the 'end of metaphysics', makes no reference at all to Derrida's work, which surely has a considerable stake in the debate. Nevertheless, Vattimo's short book is a rich and suggestive discussion of the topic, engaging with thinkers like Heidegger, Benjamin, Gadamer and Habermas in a forceful and enthralling way. His title is fundamentally ironic, his major premise being that the 'giddy proliferation' of the mass media and new communications technologies has produced not a self-transparency at the level of the collective in fulfilment of Hegel's Absolute Spirit, but a dissolution of the entire 'programme of Enlightenment emancipation' through the multiplication of unsynthesizable histories, subcultures and world views. In pursuing the implications of this development, at one with the 'end of modernity', he analyses the place of myth in contemporary culture, the emergence of aesthetic 'heterotopia' in place of the false universality of traditional models of the beautiful, and the difficulties of constructing a positive morality on the basis of a hermeneutical understanding of the world as consisting not of facts but interpretations. This is one of those books that one wants to reread as soon as one has finished it.

Opposition to deconstruction (and poststructuralism more widely) has come too often in the shape of ill-informed blustering (often directed at secondary accounts rather than the key thinkers), and too rarely in the manner of the reasoned, knowledgeable critique which Seán Burke provides in *The Death and Return of the Author*. Neatly launching his argument with some remarks on the de Man affair, which is justly claimed to have galvanized the corpse of biographical criticism, Burke sets out to show, through close readings of Barthes, Foucault and Derrida, that the concept of the author is 'never more alive than when pronounced dead'. That this is so is demonstrated, in the case of Barthes, by the fact that the antitheological cast of his views on the death of the author are nowhere justified by the ways in which authorship is actually conceptualized in twentieth-century criticism; in the case of Foucault, it is illustrated by, among other things, the contradiction between his privileging of Nietzsche as the source of the 'death of man' and the transindividual nature of epistemic determination posited in *The Order of Things*. Burke begins his discussion of Derrida by asking why Rousseau is treated at such length in *Of Grammatology* when it is asserted that his *oeuvre* is merely symptomatic of the history of metaphysics. Derrida, according to Burke, fails to show the features Rousseau has in common with his age, and elaborates instead a 'highly idiosyncratic network of circumstances' converging on the exaltation of presence and the denunciation of supplementarity. Derrida, in his readings of Rousseau and Plato, forces the question of writing into a position of centrality in order to permit and justify the labour of deconstruction. Without Rousseau, Burke opines wryly, 'there would be neither a single example of logocentrism between Plato and Hegel, nor a single logocentric text of any length in the history of logocentrism'. In his conclusion; he makes the interesting point that whereas deconstruction made a kind of sense against the background of the pre-eminence of phenomenology in France, it made little in an Anglo-American context where subjectivity and intentionality had long been evacuated at the level of textual theory. This is an important and stimulating book which deserves to be widely read.

An example of the kind of bone-headed antagonism to deconstruction which Burke avoids is David Farley-Hills's 'Deconstruction: A Deconstruction' (*Essays in Criticism* 42.173–95), which attempts to destroy the 'whole edifice of Deconstruction theory [*sic*]' – which amounts to chapter 2 of *Of Grammatology*, 'Signature Event Context', Belsey's *Critical Practice* and Easthope's *Poetry and Discourse* – in twenty pages on the basis of a distinction between linguistic and non-linguistic concepts. More in the spirit of Burke's critique is John Elliott's 'The Ethics of Repression: Deconstruction's Historical Transumption of History' (*New Literary History* 23.727–45). Working with a broad, flexible notion of history as misprision, Elliott argues that deconstruction is 'a metalepsis of the historical process [the reign of the Book] it attempts to contain' by virtue of its concentration on one local *type* of misreading: 'intentionally naive' reading invariably accompanied by a thematics of repression and guilt. 'By understanding how [deconstruction's] best readings work', Elliott claims, 'we also understand where its critical movements are untimely and inaccurate.'

Perhaps the weightiest challenge to Derrida this year comes from J. Claude Evans's *Strategies of Deconstruction*. It is often pointed out that Derrida's writings have been most enthusiastically embraced not by fellow philosophers but by literary critics, and Evans, a philosopher, does nothing to redress the balance. He takes Derrida to task over two of the texts which have been imagined to be safest from the guard-dogs of the philosophical establishment: the early *Speech and Phenomena* and *Of Grammatology*. Although Evans

makes a persistent show of giving Derrida his due, according him
the respect of serious attention which he plainly feels is undeserved,
his final judgement on Derrida's project is that, 'instead of reading
the texts ostensibly under discussion, [he] enframes them as raw
material for a writing that, for whatever reasons, ultimately exhibits
no interest in those texts themselves'. His analysis of *Of Grammatology* takes the line that what Derrida sees as fatal contradictions in
Saussure's theory disappear when one attends to the 'shifting
contexts' of the *Course in General Linguistics*, in particular to the
methodological requirements of Saussure's elaboration and exposition of the new science of signs. Since these contexts are themselves
largely imputed, it is arguable that Evans's claim that Derrida's
deconstruction of Saussure 'has been performed with mirrors' can be
retorted upon his own reading. However, his response to *Speech and
Phenomena* – a painfully close, almost paragraph-by-paragraph dissection of Derrida's critique of Husserl – is a different proposition.
It would be impossible in a few words to give any sense of the
pattern of aberrations and distortions which Evans finds in Derrida's argument, even had I sufficient expertise to represent and
evaluate the former's account adequately, but this book undoubtedly
calls for consideration by all those interested in the purely 'philosophical' side of deconstruction.

I shall now deal with a few miscellaneous articles. The best one
published this year is Joseph N. Cleary's 'Theory in the Age of
Mechanical Annihilation' (*Textual Practice* 6.452–77), a superbly
incisive and thought-provoking piece which gives a new breath of
life to nuclear criticism. Taking inspiration from the spectre of
nuclearism which stalked Gulf War propaganda, Cleary analyses the
difficulties posed by the 'transition from conventional to nuclear
militarism' for the theoretical paradigms of classical 'revolutionary'
Marxism (Engels), Gramscian 'hegemonistic' Marxism (E. P.
Thompson), and poststructuralism (Derrida). He demonstrates the
crisis presented to classical Marxist eschatology by the prospect of a
catastrophe that would abolish rather than repossess the means of
production in their entirety. The New Left, the argument continues,
attempts to redeem society from its 'catastrophic tendencies' by a
programme of coalition-building, and in so doing loses sight of the
enduring 'institutional materiality of force'; Derrida, for his part,
subsumes this problematic of force under the 'generalised problematic of epistemic violence', and can only offer a Scheherazade-like
commitment to keep talking to defer apocalypse in place of a
concrete political agenda. Cleary concludes by advocating a form of

critique that resists the dichotomy of coercion and consent in its theorization of nuclear society.

In a lean year for studies focusing closely on deconstruction and literature in a practical way, Charles Eric Reeves, in 'Vice-Versa: Rhetorical Reflections in an Ideological Mirror' (*New Literary History* 23.159–71), negotiates between the 'absolutizing tendencies of both Marxism and deconstruction' in the service of the defence of realism undertaken by people like Raymond Tallis. He points away from the unhelpful 'mirroring' analogy to a Wittgensteinian conception of the 'weaving' of experience into literary form within the arena of motivations constituted by reading conventions. In 'Derrida, Heidegger, and Van Gogh's "Old Shoes"' (*Textual Practice* 6.87–100), Michael Payne explores a similar metaphor of 'interlacing', as found in the final section of Derrida's *Truth in Painting*. He also finds occasion to defend Derrida against the charge that he ignored Heidegger's Nazi sympathies until the publication of Farias's *Heidegger and Nazism*. Robert Stecker's 'Incompatible Interpretations' (*Journal of Aesthetics and Art Criticism* 50.291–8) distinguishes between interpretations that make statements about the work, which must be subject to the law of non-contradiction, and interpretations which are a possible 'making sense of' the work. Although Stecker aims to chastise the excesses of poststructuralism, much of his argument would be perfectly acceptable to poststructuralist literary critics, and his anxiety seems largely self-generated.

In a corner all its own, Dennis L. Stamps's 'Rhetorical Criticism and the Rhetoric of New Testament Criticism' (*Literature and Theology* 6.268–79) shows how a 'polarization over defining the nature and role of rhetorical criticism' is 'an illustration of the war being waged in New Testament studies over the nature of the text and the scope of the interpretive task'. This is a useful survey, for an outsider, of the impact of the new rhetoric on New Testament studies and of the associated factionalism and infighting, with a partisan but sweetly reasonable conclusion.

Those who have not tired completely of the de Man affair might find distraction in Gilbert Adair's sardonic and amusing novella, *The Death of the Author*, whose first-person narrator, Léopold Sfax, is a thinly disguised (in places, not disguised at all) Paul de Man. The story takes the hybrid form of a confession-cum-murder-mystery, beginning with de Man/Sfax's anguished but self-exculpatory account of his collaborationist past ('I was a gifted young man of twenty-two who had a desperate longing to write . . .'), then taking a generic swerve as violence breaks out in what the tabloids call the 'Graves of Academe' at 'New Harbor'. Adair's fictional sport fails to reconstruct de Man's mental and emotional life plausibly – Sfax is, at once, too vain and boastfully calculating on the one hand, and too bluntly importunate on the other, in his self-exposure; and it does not, as its jacket promises it will, offer anything approaching a 'serious critique' of de Man's theoretical enterprise. Nevertheless, there are some good moments: after two murders have been committed, Sfax, confronted by a reporter with his famous critical utterance that death is a displaced name for a linguistic predicament, is asked whether he has any idea 'who might have been responsible for these two regrettable linguistic predicaments that had just arisen in New Harbor'. There is a neat, if somewhat smugly adroit, ending. The book is short enough to be read on the train to a conference.

'Not even our own selves, as thought *of*, can be identified with any further actuality. No vision is that *of* which it is. No meanings are that which they would represent.' Who wrote this? Paul de Man? Hillis Miller? No: in fact, it was written by the septuagenarian I. A. Richards, in a 1968 essay included in Ann Berthoff's heavily but beneficially edited anthology, *Richards on Rhetoric*. Berthoff complains that Richards is 'virtually unread today', which is almost certainly true: one is hard pushed to find much reference to him in standard works on literary theory beyond formulaic mockery of a few ideas from *Science and Poetry* and *Principles of Literary Criticism*, and he seems to be ignored by linguisticians. On the evidence of this collection, which excerpts generously from Richards's later work, there is certainly much of interest in his writings on language (his idea of the meaning of a word as 'the missing parts of its contexts', for example), and much that could be brought into dialogue with wider developments in semiotics and with other pragmatist thinkers. However, perhaps one reason Richards is unread is because he shows so little interest in entering into such dialogue himself. Lamentably, the book lacks an index.

It is perhaps as well to be reminded that the revival of rhetoric has encompassed more than poststructuralist tropology. At the extreme pragmatic end of the market, *Persuading People*, by Robert and Susan Cockcroft, is a back-to-basics survey of 'persuasive techniques' (with chapters on *ethos*, *pathos* and *logos*, and an inventory of tropes and schemes illustrated by 'functional' and 'literary' uses) closely modelled on classical rhetoric. In an afterword, the Cockcrofts try to demonstrate the relevance of their practical rhetoric to current critical theory by looking briefly at the place of rhetoric in the criticism of Terry Eagleton and Harold Bloom. However, they fail to take on board the challenge posed by rhetoricians like Stanley Fish to their working opposition between pragmatic and literary language, or to their attempt to isolate what they call a 'Generic Persuasive Potential' as an objective property of different types of text. The book does what it sets out to do lucidly and engagingly, though a doubt lingers as to what kind of student, either at degree or sub-degree level, it is pitched at: are there really courses running in which students are encouraged to improve their persuasive skills by trying out a little *traductio* or *anadiplosis*? Perhaps there ought to be!

Georgio Agamben's *Language and Death: The Place of Negativity* (University of Minnesota Press), Andrew Benjamin's *Judging Lyotard* (Routledge), Robert C. Holub's *Crossing Borders: Reception Theory, Poststructuralism, Deconstruction* (University of Wisconsin Press), and David Jasper's *Rhetoric, Power and Community* (Macmillan) were all, sadly, unavailable for review.

Books Reviewed

Adair, Gilbert. *The Death of the Author*. hb Heinemann (1992), pb Minerva (1993). pp. 135. hb £13.99, pb £4.99. ISBN 0 434 00623 8, 0 7493 9806 X.

Burke, Seán. *The Death and Return of the Author: Criticism and Subjectivity in Barthes, Foucault and Derrida*. Edinburgh University Press. pp. 216. hb £35, pb £12.95. ISBN 0 7486 0355 7, 0 7486 0361 1.

Clark, Timothy. *Derrida, Heidegger, Blanchot: Sources of Derrida's Notion and Practice of Literature*. Cambridge University Press. pp. 219. £30. ISBN 0 521 40539 4.

Cockcroft, Robert, and Susan M. Cockcroft. *Persuading People: An Introduction to Rhetoric*. Macmillan. pp. 181. hb £35, pb £9.99. ISBN 0 333 47162 8, 0 333 47163 6.

Coward, Harold. *Derrida and Indian Philosophy*. Sri Satgaru. pp. 200. £13.95. ISBN 0 7914 0499 4.

Coward, Harold, and Toby Foshay, eds. *Derrida and Negative Theology*. State University of New York Press. pp. 337. hb $49.50, pb $16.95. ISBN 0 7914 0963 5, 0 7914 0964 3.

Critchley, Simon. *The Ethics of Deconstruction: Derrida and Levinas*. Blackwell. pp. 253. pb £13.99. ISBN 0 631 17786 8.

Derrida, Jacques. *Acts of Literature*, ed. Derek Attridge. Routledge. pp. 456. pb £12.99. ISBN 0 415 90057 3.

——. *Cinders*. University of Nebraska Press. pp. 80. £18.95. ISBN 0 8032 1689 0.

——. *The Other Heading: Reflections on Today's Europe*. Indiana University Press. pp. 129. £13.50. ISBN 0 253 31693 6.

Evans, J. Claude. *Strategies of Deconstruction: Derrida and the Myth of the Voice*. University of Minnesota Press (1991). pp. 207. hb $39.95, pb $14.95. ISBN 0 8166 1925 5, 0 8166 1926 3.

McKenna, Andrew J. *Violence and Difference: Girard, Derrida, and Deconstruction*. University of Illinois Press. pp. 239. hb $39.95, pb $15.95. ISBN 0 252 01837 0, 0 252 06202 7.

Papadakis, Andreas, and Maggie Toy. *Deconstruction: A Pocket Guide*. Academy Editions (1990). pp. 32. £2.50. ISBN 1 85490 033 1.

Richards, I. A. *Richards on Rhetoric: I. A. Richards, Selected Essays, 1929–1974*, ed. Ann E. Berthoff. Oxford University Press. pp. 287. pb £13.50. ISBN 0 19 506426 7.

Royle, Nicholas, ed. *Afterwords*. Outside Books. pp. 217. No price obtainable. ISBN 951 44 2997 4.

Vattimo, Gianni. *The Transparent Society*. Polity Press. pp. 129. hb £29.50, pb £9.95. ISBN 0 7456 0926 0, 0 7456 1047 1.

3

Semiotics

ADRIAN PAGE

It appears that the tide is turning against poststructuralism in semiotics as there are increasing attempts to stabilize meaning whilst not impinging on the creative potential of signifying systems. In *Critical Survey* (4:iii.1241–50) A. W. Lyle argues that semiotics as described by Michael Riffaterre validates the 'close reading' of practical criticism by offering a procedure which specifies clearly how the legitimate meaning of the text can be derived. The semiotic interpretation *à la* Riffaterre is based upon the belief that the text itself is the 'transformation of a structural matrix' which is never directly articulated. Thus a set of fundamental binary oppositions may be used to generate a poem whilst themselves remaining unspoken. The whole text acts as a signifier because it refers to this fundamental matrix through hypograms, or clichés which are intertextually related to the matrix. Riffaterre maintains that, as Lyle puts it, the hypogram is part of the reader's literary competence. It is necessary to be able to recall the hypogram in order to approach the matrix to which it is intertextually linked. Hypograms may be potential, i.e. they can be constructed from the text, or actual, i.e. they are actually to be found in another text.

Lyle demonstrates his approach in relation to the first three Shakespeare sonnets. The process of textual *production* as outlined by Lyle takes us from matrix to hypogram, to text. In criticism, it would seem that the semiotic process must be reversed. The first stage is to read the text as if it were a standard piece of information, the heuristic reading. On discovery of the 'ungrammaticalities' of the text we find that the heuristic reading has to be abandoned and the text must be regarded as referring to another sign-system which is best summarized through a hypogram. The hypogram is in turn intertextually related to the elements of the matrix.

Lyle's reading of Sonnet 1, however, immediately undermines this semiotic approach. He writes, 'we notice first of all that the text is based on a series of manifest oppositions – increase/decrease, we/ thou, famine/abundance, die/bear, tender heir/tender churl, waste/ niggarding, and so on. These all seem to be hypogrammatic variants of the cliché, 'preserve beauty before it is too late'. Here the binary oppositions are spotted before the hypogram is detected. According to Riffaterre's theory, this should not be possible. The poem should not be understandable before the hypogram has been found. In this case the matrix is used to discover the hypogram. It is true that Lyle goes on to identify the matrix as one particular opposition between 'bud' and 'buries', but there is no explanation as to why this should be the fundamental origin of the poem's complexity. Strictly speaking this is not even an opposition, as the terms are contraries not diametrical opposites. This deviation from Riffaterre's approach reflects the problem detected by Robert Young in his commentary on Riffaterre: 'The matrix or kernel word which is chosen will still depend on what the reader wishes to find, and will, in effect, depend upon his interpretation of the poem as a whole' (Robert Young, ed. *Untying the Text.* Routledge and Kegan Paul, 1981, p. 104). Riffaterre's theory can be offered retrospectively as a justification of the conclusions which the practical critic has derived intuitively in advance of any theoretical investigation.

It must be added that Lyle does not accept Riffaterre uncritically, and has some astute criticisms of his methodology. One in particular, however, might need further consideration, and that is the accusation that it is *reductive*. If the fundamental binary oppositions are the ultimate secret of interpretation, then once we reach them, criticism has come to a dead end. If language is 'a system of differences' which can never be fully explored, then the system can generate endlessly proliferating meanings, yet the semiotic reading *à la* Riffaterre stops short at the discovery of differences.

Umberto Eco leads the attempt to establish a firmer ground for critical readings on the principles of semiotics whilst not reducing the text to an elemental structure. In *Interpretation and Over-interpretation,* edited by Stefan Collini, Eco's Cambridge Tanner lectures are reproduced together with a series of essays by other leading academic figures, responding to Eco's remarks. Eco begins by informing his audience that he has repeatedly stressed the fact that unlimited semiosis, as advocated by Peirce, does not mean that there are no criteria for interpretation. The first lecture begins with the example of Jack the Ripper: if he told us that he did what he did as a result of an interpretation of the Gospel according to St Luke, argues Eco, we would be prepared to say he needed medical treatment. Some interpretations are clearly wrong. Eco's most controversial pronouncement is that '*there is an intention of the text*', or *intentio operis*, a meaning which is authorized by the text itself, although not dictated by the author. It may be the case that only a certain *range* of meanings may be legitimate on the basis of textual evidence, yet Eco seems to proceed at this point on the basis that the text has a specific semiotic value of its own.

With characteristic virtuosity, Eco connects contemporary critical thought with a vast range of classical theories. In particular, he establishes a connection between contemporary poststructuralist thought and the Hermetic tradition. The more that meaning is described in terms of symbols and metaphors, the more it becomes possible for likenesses to continue to be compared with likenesses endlessly. What Eco calls 'contemporary textual gnosticism' is parallel in many ways with its intellectual predecessors. The critic must continually suspect that a further secret is contained within each interpretation, in order to perpetuate the process of reading. Ultimately, 'The Real Reader is one who understands that the secret of a text is its emptiness.' In conclusion, Eco considers the view that a text divorced from its context and history becomes potentially subject to innumerable interpretations. He points out that some meanings would persist, no matter how far removed the text is from its origins. A text which alluded to a basket of figs would imply that there was at one time such a basket. The stance Eco adopts is that of the person who appreciates the power of language to communicate and marvels like the illiterate subject of his example, at the fact that language can convey meaning at all.

In his second lecture, Eco discusses the fact that anything may be said to resemble anything else. He argues that it is important to distinguish between paranoiac interpretations of similarity and those which are rationally grounded. 'Evidence', he writes, 'is considered as a sign of something else only on three conditions: that it cannot be explained more economically; that it points to a single cause . . . and that it fits in with the other evidence.' Such is the rhetorical power of Eco's prose that his examples are extremely convincing, as he adduces further proof that semiosis is bounded by logical rules of inference. Popper is invoked here to answer the objection that to limit the range of possible intepretations is not automatically to validate only one of them. Eco believes that he can confidently defend the negative hypothesis that some readings can be shown to be examples of overinterpretation, even if none can be conclusively proved to be valid. An example of overinterpretation from Rossetti is explored in detail.

In his treatment of Geoffrey Hartman's criticism of Wordsworth's poem, 'A Slumber Did My Spirit Seal', however, Eco illustrates how this reading can neither be disqualified on semiotic grounds nor proven. This might appear to vindicate the poststructuralist view that the text's meaning is in the hands of the reader, but Eco continues to demonstrate how even reader-oriented interpretation has its rules. Eco convincingly illustrates that if the isotopy of the text is heroism, then to compare Achilles with a duck is not legitimate, whereas to compare him with a lion is. The theme of the text, once assumed, is a governing principle which limits interpretation. If, however, it is true to say that, 'a text is a device conceived in order to produce its model reader', then Eco seems to stumble when it comes to the distinction between the intention of the text and the intention of the reader. He asserts that the text's intention can only be perceived as a result of a decision on the part of the reader to 'see' it. This sounds very much as if the reader produces the text rather than the text producing the reader. Of course it is true that the reader can only 'see' within certain logical limits, yet Eco has conceded that these limits, however narrow, may contain an infinite number of interpretations. The problem of textual semiosis revolves around the problem of combining freedom and necessity, yet in so doing the notions of the *intentio operis* and the *intentio lectoris* seem to become indistinguishable or, perhaps, inseparable. The only solution offered by Eco to the problem of how to check on an *intentio operis* is to refer to 'the text as a coherent whole', yet this manoeuvre reveals that the basis of the interpretation is merely internal coherence rather than semiotic principles.

In all this the author is not to be forgotten. The third lecture, 'Between Author and Text', seeks to reinstate the author, yet not permit the author to dictate meaning. The text's intention intervenes to coerce the model reader into a particular form of interpretation. Eco reminds us that the word 'gay' in Wordsworth cannot be taken to mean 'homosexual' as it might in *Playboy*: there are limits to interpretation. Eco draws a distinction between *using* a text (which may involve deliberately violating its historical intention) and *interpreting* it, which means appealing to some notion of legitimate conventions of meaning.

On the other hand, some associations which may not be fully apparent to an author can be significant. The Italian poem 'A Silvia' is used to demonstrate what Eco labels the 'liminal author', the writer who is not consciously intending certain meanings, yet is not reducible to the linguistic conventions of the text. The name of Silvia is echoed several times in the text, yet it can also be heard in many other Italian texts, according to Eco. The principle of economy can be invoked to render this apparent discovery rather facile.

With the aid of many examples, some of which are drawn from his own novels, Eco shows how the liminal author may be invoked to explain the surfacing of certain ideas which seem to invite critical interpretation. Sometimes, as with his own work, the explanation is simply that an idea has been forgotten and has made a reappearance. Some writers hover on the margins between the author and the text, occasionally coinciding with the text: 'Between the unattainable intention of the author and the arguable intention of the reader there is the transparent intention of the text which disproves an untenable interpretation.'

In his response to Eco's lectures (in the same volume), Richard Rorty asserts that he believed Eco to have abandoned 'code-cracking' in favour of an uninhibited pragmatism which sees using the text as the only option. Rorty describes some of the textual knowledge he has about Eco and his interests to show that *intentio operis* and *intentio lectoris* may be dangerously close in practice. In addition, Rorty maintains that internal coherence is not something which a text has before it is described. Interpretation may be necessary in order to arrive at *intentio operis*, in other words: the intention cannot lead to the interpretation. Rorty is staunchly opposed to the essentialist notion that the text has an implicit meaning, and this notion is inherent in the distinction between using and interpreting texts. Rorty, in fact, begins to formulate his own criterion of value in semiotics when he talks of using a text in order to 'help change your purposes' and so your life. Interpretation, he maintains, changes very little.

Jonathan Culler is convinced that Eco harbours a sneaking regard for what he calls 'overinterpretation'. Culler's contribution entitled 'In Defence of Overinterpretation', asks whether overinterpretation is not like what Wayne Booth calls 'overstanding': the process of asking questions of the text which are not strictly necessary for communication, yet which yield the best results. 'Overstanding consists of pursuing questions which the text does not pose to its model reader.' Culler attacks Rorty's view that it is superfluous to interpret the text, just as it is superfluous to attempt to discover how a computer works if one wishes to word process. Culler believes that the understanding of literature can be enhanced by such knowledge. 'Learning something about literature' is as important to him as learning what can be accomplished with it.

Culler's most important criticism of Eco, however, is expressed in his succinct account of the deconstructionist approach Eco is attacking. Culler maintains that 'Deconstruction stresses that meaning is context bound . . . but that context is boundless.' Thus Culler can assert that even Wittgenstein's famous nonsense word 'bububu' can have a meaning given that it now occurs in a philosophical context where we as readers of theory have encountered it. Culler claims that such an example shows that there is 'a lack of limits to semiosis'. This, however, misses the point which Eco has been trying to make. The fact that context can lead on to context in an infinite recursive chain, does not necessarily mean that we cannot specify the meaning which can be derived from a particular statement in one particular context. It is true that the word 'bububu' now has a semiotic value to readers of Wittgenstein, but only because we are familiar with a specific context. It is clear that this is an issue which will be revisited, perhaps in Eco's forthcoming work, *The Limits of Interpretation*.

Christine Brooke-Rose argues in her essay 'Palimpsest History' that whether an author was influenced by another book or not, the novel is still 'palimpsest history', or history conceived as a narrative which is endlessly re-inscribed in various forms. In his final reply, Eco reiterates his belief that '*It is not true that everything goes*'. Rorty's example of the screwdriver which pragmatically may be used for a number of purposes other than driving in screws, is adopted by Eco to argue that these purposes are also limited by cultural consensus. He appeals to the notion of communities which maintain traditions of interpretation and pass on such strategies. 'The communitarian control of our sane partners is enough to decide whether at a given moment it is raining or not', as Eco puts it. In his final rhetorical flourish, Eco reminds the reader that the colloquium has taken place and he is disputing other interpretations precisely because there are significant disagreements over interpretations and not because all readings are equally valid.

Patrice Pavis, in *Theatre at the Crossroads of Culture*, argues for a semiotic theory which would not aim at an exhaustive analysis of the 'object' of study, since as Keir Elam comments, the more precise such analyses, the less the theatrical community displays any interest in them. Pavis is therefore a little closer to Rorty than Eco in this regard. An empirical semiotics might be possible in which the study examined the actual cultural consequences of theatre. For this reason, Pavis refrains from linking the semiotics of the dramatic text and the performance text, as they belong to entirely different signifying systems.

Pavis represents the *mise-en-scène* of a dramatic text as a new 'situation of enunciation' in which the text acquires an innovatory meaning from its new 'social context of reception'. *Mise-en-scène* is thus rather like the process of inventing a context for a sentence which we do not immediately understand. The new context is not forced upon us by the sentence, but opens up the sentence to new possibilities of interpretation. As Pavis puts it, '*Mise-en-scène* is reading actualized'. Pavis makes a distinction between the auto-textual *mise-en-scène*, which is determined by the internal logic of the text, and ideotextual *mise-en-scène* which stages the 'political, social and psychological subtext'. Such a staging fulfils the 'communicative function' as specified by Mukarovsky. Pavis advocates the kind of semiotics which does not simply appeal to existing codes, but which generates new meanings. He draws on Barba and Lyotard to outline a new, non-Western semiotics which would enable the semiotician to become an 'ideal' spectator who can not only comprehend the object's significance but also follow the process of thought in motion and transition. The 'energetic semiotics' which Pavis seeks allows the swiftly-changing context of performance and movement to be apprehended. The ultimate goal is a semiotic approach which is sensitive to cultural traditions of meaning and artistic creativity.

Pavis may seem to be at odds with Eco, but between Eco's resilient insistence on some grounds for interpretation and the more imaginative semiotics of Pavis, there does appear to be some basis for the development of a semiotics which is neither purely creative nor slavishly dependent on existing conventions.

Books Reviewed

Eco, Umberto, with Richard Rorty, Jonathan Culler and Christine Brooke-Rose. *Interpretation and Overinterpretation,* ed. Stefan Collini. Cambridge University Press. pp. 151. £9.99. ISBN 0 521 42554 9.
Pavis, Patrice. *Theatre at the Crossroads of Culture,* trans. Loren Kruger. Routledge. pp. 219. £10.99. ISBN 0 415 06038 9.

4

Hermeneutics

KARIN LITTAU

Hans-Georg Gadamer's work figures prominently in the hermeneutics output for 1992. Whilst his brand of hermeneutics informs Shaun Gallagher's major study *Hermeneutics and Education*, many shorter pieces also share a Gadamerian slant, nicely rounded off by the publication of Gadamer's own essays, addresses and interviews, made available in English for the first time by Dieter Misgeld and Graeme Nicholson in *Hans-Georg Gadamer on Education, Poetry, and History: Applied Hermeneutics*. In Part I, Gadamer establishes his views on what university education was, is, and could be. Briefly, he situates a hermeneutically informed educational philosophy as a critique of mass education's incapacity, as he sees it, to promote the acculturation (*Bildung*) and development of the self, historically associated with the humanities. Part II picks up on these themes, but also affords a central role to the vitalizing cultural force of the poetry of Hölderlin, George, Benn and Celan (i.e. the Heideggerian canon), which 'educates toward poetizing', in order 'that the human essence and knowledge come to be realized . . . through always new creation'. Part III takes the broad view, where Gadamer sets out the strengths of and potential future for European culture(s) in the face of two major challenges: firstly the averaging attendant upon mass society and the culture of expertise; and secondly, as the editors put it, 'the drama of a worldwide conversation of cultures'. Problematically, Gadamer claims that Europe is in a 'privileged position' in this conversation because it has already had 'to learn to live with others, even when the others were different'. The much criticized fact that for Gadamer the other is only ever potentially an-other self, is exposed by his concluding sentence in this book: 'we may perhaps survive as humanity if we would be able to learn that we may not simply exploit our means of power . . . and if we would be able to experience the other and the others, as the other of our self, in order to participate with one another'.

Whilst Shaun Gallagher's *Hermeneutics and Education* adopts a Gadamerian 'moderate hermeneutics' to outline an educational theory, the author seizes on this inherent underestimation of hegemonic relations in Gadamer's work to argue that a moderate theory of education 'learns in its debates with critical and radical hermeneutics [about] the principle of power'. Gallagher's approach here, as elsewhere, in this fascinating book, illustrates how the four hermeneutic principles, which he identifies as conservative, critical, moderate and radical, can participate in a 'conversation' through which they can learn from each other's discourses. Conversation here becomes a 'vehicle of collaborative learning', which – unlike the textual hermeneutic model which Gallagher criticizes for its 'Romantic emphasis on the interior subject' – is adequate to describe 'explication, pedagogical presentation and educational experience'. This demonstrates that hermeneutics has something to say to educational theory, and conversely, that educational theory has something to say to hermeneutics. What Gallagher presents to us then is 'a plurality of paralogical conversations at a multiplicity of interpretive sites', and what he demonstrates to us is that 'many of the conversations cut across others, sometimes at cross-purposes and sometimes in a complementary way'. In short, Gallagher communicates the (in)commensurability between Gadamer and Lyotard, holds on to Gadamer's conversation whilst offering to accommodate Lyotard's paralogism. The question remains open whether this offer of *good will* by a hermeneut is acceptable to a postmodernist. I, for one, shall look out for the responses that Gallagher's momentous study will undoubtedly elicit.

The critical encounter between hermeneutics and postmodernism forms the basis of another SUNY publication, and another project by Shaun Gallagher, here as an editor with Thomas W. Busch of *Merleau-Ponty, Hermeneutics, and Postmodernism*. The contributors to this collection are 'deeply sensitive' to Merleau-Ponty's thinking, and in response to the general poststructuralist move away from phenomenology, these essays, eighteen in all, either engage with the importance of his work within a hermeneutic project, whether Ricoeurian, Gadamerian or Habermasian; or negotiate his work in relation to current postmodern thinkers such as Derrida, Lyotard, Foucault, and Deleuze. Part I therefore explicates and fleshes out specific aspects of his thinking, for instance on perspective, tempor-

ality, language and perception. Part II situates his work as part of a
postmodern discussion, suggesting on the one hand, as Gary
Madison does, that Merleau-Ponty was a 'poststructuralist avant la
lettre' who avoided its more garish current manifestations, or on the
other, stressing a radical potential in Merleau-Ponty's work, as
Hugh Silverman does, that made him as much of a 'polylogos as
Deleuze, Derrida, and Kristeva'. The agenda of this stimulating
collection, however, seems a little strained. Thus when, in the
introduction, Gallagher claims that Merleau-Ponty 'would remind
us that postmodernism can not afford to leave hermeneutics behind
– even if that were possible', the question remains whether the
editors, in having subsumed both phenomenology and postmodernism within the horizon of a hermeneutics, stretched it to breaking
point.

Robert Holub's *Crossing Borders: Reception Theory, Poststructuralism, Deconstruction* is also concerned with the encounter
between advocates of a German hermeneutic tradition and the
recent disciples of French postmodern thought, focusing in particular on the receptions, subsumptions and appropriations of theory
across cultural borders. Part I therefore deals with the
(non)reception of German reception theory in the United States.
Here, Holub illustrates how and why American critics have ignored
the bulk of German reception theorists, but more readily assimilated Wolfgang Iser's work, which (unlike Jauss's work, with its
broader socio-historical concerns) slotted more easily into a tradition of textual criticism or close reading, practised in the United
States since the New Criticism. In Part II Holub proceeds to
examine the rejection of poststructuralism in a German academic
frame which has largely been influenced by the traditions of hermeneutics and Marxism; but also examines poststructuralism's partial
absorption through critics such as Peter Szondi and Friedrich
Kittler. Manfred Frank is particularly appreciated by Holub, for
although critical of poststructuralism, he nevertheless integrates it
very successfully into a German hermeneutic tradition. Part III
focuses on the misappropriations of French deconstruction by
American criticism, which forfeits much of its 'inherent native' –
although, Holub insinuates, dubious – political value. Whilst outlining many important debates, the book nevertheless reads like a
record of grievances – especially as regards the hegemony of deconstruction in the United States – without really offering its own
direction, other than the call for a political criticism and the embracing of a rather sketchy, quasi-Habermasian 'communicative ethics',

in order to 'eliminate' the political errors – from fascism to political correctness – both of which Holub curiously associates with American deconstruction.

If Holub's book concentrates on the pitfalls of crossing borders in the context of conflictual cultural traditions, Zhang Longxi's *The Tao and the Logos: Literary Hermeneutics East and West*, constitutes an attempt to provide a final hermeneutic solution to the problems of cultural difference. Rather than 'applying a Western hermeneutic theory to the reading of Chinese literature', Zhang proceeds from the premise that the hermeneutic phenomenon is 'truly universal' and can as such reveal what is 'common to both Chinese and Western traditions'. By way of this 'search for the same' rather than falling for the faddish discourse of 'pure difference' (perhaps a rereading of *Différance* might avoid further confusions), Zhang hopes to avoid – following Steven Connor's polemic – the 'totalizing discourse of consensus' which characterizes the postmodern thematic of difference. Zhang goes on to 'identify common themes . . . that have emerged at various times in the East and West' as regards the nature of literary language, and literary interpretation. In this exercise in comparative literature as well as in comparative criticism, Zhang not only brings together Tao Qian and Rilke, or Qiu Zhao-ao and E. D. Hirsch, but also Wimsatt, Hirsch and Fish, amongst others, in order to advocate that all these 'opposing views' need only be fused into one friendly methodology (which he calls 'interpretive pluralism'), so that a 'deeper understanding of literature' may be gained. This naïve eclectic 'good will' for a better understanding aside, the 'ultimate goal of such thematic comparisons' then is, according to Zhang, to further the 'process of learning . . . in which the unfamiliar becomes familiar, adding to the repertoire of our knowledge, and the alien is absorbed till it becomes part of our-selves'. Zhang would do well to learn from Shaun Gallagher's critique of the Gadamerian underestimation of hegemonic relations, or from Nietzsche's good *will to power*. Before looking at this year's – rather scant, I'm afraid – journals, mention must be made of Georgia Warnke's *Justice and Interpretation*. This work 'borrows' a hermeneutic model 'from the humanities' in order to address the consequences of anti-foundationalism in contemporary political theory (Rawls, Rorty, Habermas, MacIntyre). To counter Haber-mas's avowed idealism as regards the virtues of 'unconstrained con-versation', Warnke suggests that hermeneutics, in particular, offers ways in which to redirect 'our political energies' towards instances of overt incommensurability in political discourse (as, for example, between Black Power and the Ku Klux Klan). Steering a similar middle way between the advocates of agonism and consensual idealism, Fred Dallmayr offers a historical account of the role of hermeneutics within contemporary legal theory in his 'Hermeneutics and the Rule of Law' in D. Cornell, M. Rosenfeld and D. G. Carlson's *Deconstruction and the Possibility of Justice*. In its rejection of foundationalism and abstraction, and its embracing of the hermeneutic grounding necessary, in his view, to a fully democratic political life, Dallmayr's essay could be read as a historical companion-piece to Warnke's contemporary addresses, in providing a brief but involved discussion of the role of hermeneutics in the social sciences. The theme of foundationalism crops up again, this time in a philosophical context, in Felix O. Murchadha's 'Truth as a Problem for Hermeneutics, Towards a Hermeneutical Theory of Truth', in *Philosophy Today* (36.122–30). This essay takes up the Heideggerian roots of Gadamerian hermeneutics to pose questions concerning the ontology, rather than the epistemology, of truth. In sketching a 'framework of a hermeneutical theory of truth', the author seeks to avoid the twin pitfalls of absolute historical relativism and absolute essentialism, to establish truth as a question. Thus, rather than closing the question in either essentialist or relativist terms, a hermeneutics of truth continually re-opens the larger historical, cultural and linguistic horizons within which this *guiding question* can be posed.

Finally, hermeneutics makes another appearance, this time on the theatrical stage. Thomas Postlewait's 'History, Hermeneutics, and Narrativity' reconsiders how narrative contributes to the interpretive process, although how it found its way into a collection of essays on *Critical Theory and Performance*, edited by Janelle G. Reinelt and Joseph R. Roach, without making any real mention of the theatre remains rather mysterious. The other contribution to the Hermeneutics and Phenomenology section of this volume is Bert O. States's 'The Phenomenological Attitude'. In working together the discourses of phenomenology and semiotics, States neatly outlines how the stage makes a twofold gesture at once corporeal and significative. Benjamin Bennett's rather dense essay 'Performance and the Exposure of Hermeneutics' in *Theatre Journal* (44.431–47) debates the ways in which a hermeneutics 'textualizes' the materiality of the body on stage, by turning it into a textual organ, so to speak, of its own interpretation system, thus simultaneously mummifying performance in a text and rescuing performance by repeatedly reinscribing this very process.

Books Reviewed

Busch, Thomas W., and Shaun Gallagher, eds. *Merleau-Ponty, Hermeneutics, and Postmodernism*. State University of New York Press. pp. 263. pb $16.95. ISBN 0 7914 1140 0.

Cornell, Drucilla, Michael Rosenfeld and David Gray Carlson, eds. *Deconstruction and the Possibility of Justice*. Routledge. pp. 304. pb £12.99. ISBN 0 415 90304 1.

Gadamer, Hans-Georg. *Hans-Georg Gadamer on Education, Poetry, and History: Applied Hermeneutics*, trans. Lawrence Schmidt and Monica Reuss. Ed. Dieter Misgeld and Graeme Nicholson (SUNY Series in Contemporary Continental Philosophy). State University of New York Press. pp. 238. pb $19.95. ISBN 0 7914 0920 1.

Gallagher, Shaun. *Hermeneutics and Education* (SUNY Series in Contemporary Continental Philosophy). State University of New York Press. pp. 402. pb $21.95. ISBN 0 7914 1176 1.

Holub, Robert C. *Crossing Borders: Reception Theory, Poststructuralism, Deconstruction*. University of Wisconsin Press. pp. 244. pb £14.95. ISBN 0 299 13274 9.

Reinelt, Janelle G., and Joseph R. Roach, eds. *Critical Theory and Performance*. University of Michigan Press. pp. 379. pb £16.95. ISBN 0 472 06458 4.

Warnke, Georgia. *Justice and Interpretation*. Polity Press. pp. 178. £35. ISBN 0 7456 0686 5.

Zhang Longxi. *The Tao and the Logos: Literary Hermeneutics East and West* (Series in Post-Contemporary Interventions). Duke University Press. pp. 238. pb £15.95. ISBN 0 8223 1218 2.

5

Intertextuality

GRAHAM ALLEN

This year's contributions attest to the range and diversity of subjects and approaches generated by intertextual theory and practice. I have decided upon various principles of selection which require explanation. Since the relationship between theory and practice is so fluid in this area, I have selected for review only those studies which attempt to make some kind of theoretical intervention. I have, however, looked at works which use those terms *intertextuality* was once thought to have replaced: principally *influence* and *allusion*. These 'traditional' terms continue to be revised in the light of intertextual theory and a number of studies this year have contributed to this process.

T. Jefferson Kline's *Screening the Text: Intertextuality in the New Wave French Cinema* presents one of this year's most original and important contributions to the field. As a medium, cinema has always identified itself against literature. Kline argues that New Wave French cinema is special in what it attempts to do with its ineradicable 'Other', literature. The French New Wave is centred not on a straightforward repression of all reference to literature (all representations of 'the text') but to a 'screening [of] the text'. The numerous allusions to literary texts in this cinema allow the films to contain and thus cancel their reliance on literary narratives. Kline writes of 'the conscious and unconscious relationships that French New Wave film-makers developed to a constituted-and-then-repressed authority: the literature(s) that subtend their films'. This process involves intertextual techniques such as 'figuring, ambivalence, misprision [and] misrepresentation'. One of the most satisfying features of Kline's study is the manner in which he employs the nowadays-obligatory Lacanian discourse of film theory. The analogy between the psychoanalytical notion of 'screen memory' and the New Wave's screening of (off) the text is obviously central to this approach. If film in general is symptomatic (if it generates meaning out of strategies of repression, defence and 'screened' identifications), then, as Kline demonstrates, the importance of film-makers such as Malle, Truffaut, Godard, Bresson, Rohmer, Chabrol and Resnais lies in how self-conscious they are about this fact. Time and again Kline's astute eye picks up a literary intertext and builds a convincing interpretation upon it. The study is a quite brilliant example of how intertextual analysis can proceed from specific intertextual relations to a recognition of the 'text's' cultural situatedness. It is a study which critics attempting to employ intertextual analysis as a technique for uncovering the cultural and ideological features of literary texts would do well to ponder and elaborate upon.

Intertextuality, after all, was a term meant to open the text to the cultural codes and discursive networks out of which and within which it has its meaning. From the strength of this year's work, however, it is still far from clear how the concept can actually perform such a function. Jonathan Culler's well-known examination of this problem in his 'Presupposition and Intertextuality' seems to have established a universal paradigm for discussing it. A good many of the works under review begin with or contain a survey of intertextual theory structured around the two nodal points in Culler's essay: the anonymous, infinite, spatialized realm of textuality first articulated by Kristeva and Barthes, as opposed to the specificities of, amongst others, Riffaterre's text–intertext model, with its pursuit of hermeneutical closure.

B. J. Leggett, in his *Early Stevens: The Nietzschean Intertext*, having rehearsed the above paradigm, argues for a combination of the Riffaterrean model and Pierre Macherey's account of the ideology of the text. Both models share an interpretive focus on the indeterminacies, ungrammaticalities and undecidabilities of the text. Leggett, in other words, argues for an intertextual practice in which analysis of the text's 'gaps, lapses, or contradictions' leads us not only to the intertextual relations 'behind' them but to their ideological significances as well. This approach is clearly a useful one and it allows Leggett to demonstrate an intense and complex interrelationship between Stevens's early work and the philosophical texts of Nietzsche. Leggett is also extremely useful on the role of Nietzsche in modern theory and Stevens criticism. Despite the book's merits, and it is surely one of the most sophisticated examinations of its subject that we have, it is difficult to concur fully with Leggett on how we locate the ideology of the text. Focusing on sites of semantic and formal indeterminacy and fragmentation is clearly a useful strategy. The question, however, is how we move from a formal analysis of the text itself through an analysis of the ideological implications of intertextual relations to the specific historical moment of writing and of reading. Despite the discussions of the place, within Stevens' early work, of a 'Nietzschean ideology' involving religion, epistemology, sexual politics and, for most of the second half of the book, perspectivism, there remains little sense of the social and cultural contexts within which this work was produced. As a consequence we are often presented with that strange phenomenon, a discussion of the 'ideology' of literary texts which avoids a historical placement of those texts.

Critics wishing to relate intertextuality to ideological trends are often more successful when dealing with more limited areas. Shu-mei Shih, in 'Exile and Intertextuality in Maxine Hong Kingston's *China Men*', an article collected in James Whitlark and Wendell Aycock's *The Literature of Emigration and Exile*, discusses the manner in which Kingston employs intertextual techniques to represent the 'doubleness' of the experience of exile. Special attention is paid here to the way in which Kingston's employment of Chinese fables helps the author foreground her own 'exilic imagination'. The material experience of exile, on various levels, helps to explain and *place* Kingston's employment of intertextual techniques.

Jill F. Durey's 'Tolstoj Speaks for Bachtin' (*Russian Literature* 32.357–92) argues that Bakhtin does not consider all 'realist' fiction (and Tolstoy in particular) monologic. Durey develops a complex reading of Tolstoy to extend this point, elaborating on seven kinds of intertextual (*qua* dialogic) elements within Tolstoy's work. Erika Greber, in 'The Metafictional Turn in "Russian Hoffmannism": Veniamin Kaverin and E. T. A. Hoffmann' (*Essays in Poetics* 17. 1–34), looks at how the Serapion Brothers, particularly Kaverin, engaged in a rigorous critique of the concepts of imitation, influence and plagiarism in their use of Hoffmann. Kaverin's key trope of the palimpsest, in particular, helps Greber to extend our understanding of pre-Bakhtinian notions of 'intertextuality' in Russian literature.

Brad Epps, in 'The Politics of Ventriloquism: Cava, Revolution and Sexual Discourse in *Conde Julián*' (*Modern Language Notes* 107.274–97), demonstrates how, on the basis of intertextuality's reversibility, Juan Goytisolo develops a modern version of the Spanish legend of King Rodrigo's rape of Cava. The textual violence presented via these intertextual techniques mimics the violence of modern Spanish history and, Epps argues, implicates the reader within that history. Even more impressive is Steve Boldy's 'Intertextuality in Carlos Fuentes's *Gringo viejo*' (*Romance Quarterly* 39.489–500). Boldy begins by analysing the accusations of plagiarism levelled at Fuentes's novel and asserts: 'Intertextuality and the notion of intellectual property form one of the most explicit motifs of the novel and are inseparable from major historical and symbolic clusters: land tenure, and questions of paternity and legitimacy within a revolutionary context.' With this kind of material and historical perspective, Boldy is able to demonstrate precisely why intertextuality stands 'at the core of Latin-American literature'.

Two books which also manage to negotiate the gulf between intertextual analysis and historical specificity are dedicated to the intertextual nature of the Chinese poetic tradition. Joseph R. Allen's *In the Voice of Others: Chinese Music Bureau Poetry* is a surprisingly easy-to-follow yet definitive account of *yuefu* or *yuefushi* poetry (Chinese Music Bureau poetry), a genre that sometimes seems rather like the Western 'After –' poem. Allen's instincts concerning the appropriate theoretical approach are patently good and I was pleased to be reminded of Vincent B. Leitch's description of the Barthesian/Kristevan brand of total textuality: 'a Salvation Army Outlet with unaccountable collections of incompatible ideas, beliefs and sources. . . . Manifested, tradition is a mess.' Allen spends considerable time developing a mid-way term between that kind of intertextuality and the textual relationship most of us would try to capture by reference to the term 'source study'. *Yuefu* poetry, he argues, exhibits an *intratextuality* in which the poet, free to speak 'in the voice of others', can transcend the limitations of the 'biographical self'. This poetry, therefore, requires an approach which can trace the intertextual chains 'behind' specific texts. And yet, because of the material history of this genre's production, the creation of specific anthologies at specific historical moments, *yuefu* poetry also relies on a certain active reader response. Such an approach seems particularly effective because it develops an inter-intratextual approach directly tied to the requirements of the specific genre being studied.

Jing Wang's *The Story of Stone* is not always as comfortable with its theoretical freight as Allen's study. However, if readers are willing to struggle through the more unwieldy parts of this monumental book they will discover one of this year's most sophisticated and ambitious contributions to the theory of intertextuality. As Allen states: 'The continuous depth and breadth of the Chinese literary tradition assures a nearly chronic intertextuality to all its poetry.' Wang takes great pains to explain the cultural formations behind this tradition. The notion of *wen* (script/sign/pattern/configuration/text/culture/literature), for example, suggests how deeply embedded within the Chinese tradition is a notion of interrelatedness close to, if not identical with, the Western notion of intertextuality. Wang's efforts to combine without confusing Chinese literary and cultural practices with modern, Western theory are impressive. The most important chapter for those concerned with the theory of intertextuality is the first, 'Intertextuality and Interpretation'. Like Allen, Wang is keen to establish the reader's 'freedom' to contain intertextual networks. His use of Greimas is helpful in this respect, as is his engagement with the hermeneutical notion of 'pre-understanding'.

Intertextuality continues to be an important term in Renaissance studies. Richard Hillman, in his *Intertextuality and Romance in Renaissance Drama*, also employs an approach which takes off from Riffaterre's notion of ungrammaticality, but argues that, when dealing with earlier literatures, allusion and citation must form a part of such an interpretive strategy. Taking up Kristeva's term 'idéologème' (that 'which gives a text . . . its historical and social coordinates'), Hillman argues that the only way to reduce the 'gap' between text and reader is to construct the necessary fiction of a 'reader' constructed from our own understanding of the ideological co-ordinates of Renaissance culture. Hillman's 'reader' is not the 'total' or 'perfect' reader of Barthes's 'The Death of the Author' and of countless other essays on intertextuality and interpretation. Rather, it is a flexible and self-conscious figure which emerges from an attempt to posit 'a subject position for the "modality of perception" which enable[d] the intertextual "act" of "decoding" texts in the light of other texts'. Hillman's is a refreshingly cautious yet capable theoretical mind, and he is particularly salutary on the illusions which can emerge from the apparently 'neat fit' between 'Renaissance habits of mind' and 'poststructuralist attitudes'. Intertextuality, as a term, he argues, is in some ways analogous to Renaissance typological theory. However, Hillman uses such analogies as suggestive 'openings' rather than as confirmations of theoretical assumptions. The other 'key coordinates' in the study are the Renaissance trope of 'theatre' (particularly in terms of the concept of imaginative space) and romance. These three co-ordinates, carefully arranged and developed, help Hillman to represent the period as a moment of cultural crisis in which social and material change generated a turn to the historical nostalgia, and to the positing and yet deferral of utopian goals, involved in the genre of romance. Staying with the use of intertextuality in Renaissance studies, D. N. C. Wood's 'Intertextuality, Indirection, and Indeterminacy in Milton's *Samson Agonistes*' (*English Studies in Canada* 18.261–72) is an attempt to use intertextual theory to argue for a reading of Milton's drama as a text in which a 'sustained multivalency [is] held poised, as it were, in delicate suspension'. Mention should perhaps also be made of Neil Thomas's *The Defence of Camelot*. This is a study of the influence of the mediaeval German Arthuriad on German romance works up to the mid-fourteenth century. Unlike Hillman's impressive study, however, intertextuality functions here as an undeveloped term which could as easily be substituted by any of its cognates (*sic*). Joseph C. Sitterson Jr's 'Allusive and Elusive Meanings: Reading Ariosto's Vergilian Ending' (*Renaissance Quarterly* 45.1–19) is more significant for our purposes, addressing, as it does, in complex ways, the 'analogy' we have already seen Hillman tackling between Renaissance and contemporary culture. Sitterson's theoretical points revolve around a fundamental distinction between two approaches to intertextuality: for Renaissance authors, it is a legitimating technique centred on the positing of origins; for contemporary authors (read 'theorists') it manifests a 'desire' (*sic*) for what one might be tempted to style the legitimating recognition of indeterminacy. Whether or not this particular distinction is completely water-tight, it seems necessary for those concerned with the historical implications of intertextual practice to develop similar period-specific frameworks.

Michael Vincent's *Figures of the Text*, another application of intertextual theory to seventeenth-century literature, is one of the most impressive theoretical contributions this year. Vincent's aims, stated programmatically at the beginning, are no less than daunting: 'to conjugate a theory of reading, of reception and perception, and a theory of textual production by drawing attention particularly to those aspects of the text that figure writing and reading'. These aspects include: 'scenes of reading; other modes of writing (emblematics, hieroglyphics, and their *mise-en-scène*); proper names; forms of intertextuality and citationality (proverbs, maxims, allusions); the relation of represented orality to textuality, of textuality to corporeality, of textuality to the visual arts; inscriptions and epitaphs; and the archaeology of textual figures (labyrinths, hieroglyphics, textiles, veils)'. That the book is only 150 pages long might in itself suggest that these 'aspects' are sometimes referred to rather than bound within one overarching 'theory of reading . . . reception and perception'. Despite its rhetorical posturing, however, the book is highly suggestive. Vincent, like other theorists this year, interrogates the intertextuality of the signature, producing an important examination of its relation to the ideology of authority and the dis-authorizing nature of writing. The non-signatory nature of fable, for example, does seem, on the strength of Vincent's argument, to disrupt the binarism of *doxa* and *para*(doxa) central to seventeenth-century French culture. What Vincent excels in is a highly condensed yet complex and suggestive intertextual approach in which the possibilities of meaning within an individual fable do begin to be understood in relation to aspects of their historical context. Vincent is theoretically astute with regard to textual mediation, the contemporary reading of La Fontaine, with its critical and cultural mediation, in many ways complementing as well as distancing and distorting La Fontaine's own highly mediated use of 'sources'. The strength of Vincent's book is that it convincingly shows ways in which the fables of La Fontaine 'figure' this fundamental aspect of writing and reading.

This last consideration, a fundamentally hermeneutic if 'playful' (ludic) issue, might serve to direct our attention to the year's contributions to biblical intertextuality. This is an area, after all, in which the question of historical interpretation predominates. There are two collections this year worthy of note. Virgil Nemonianu and Robert Royal's *Play, Literature, Religion* contains eleven essays structured around the concept of play. The essays themselves are wide-ranging and diverse, and Nemonianu attempts to give the collection some overall coherence by discussing, in his introduction, the 'play' (influence, conflictual relationship) between theology (or, rather, 'religion') and literary criticism. What has been missing in the recent critical tradition, Nemonianu argues, is a sustained analysis of the 'inter'-play between religious thought, religious experience and literature. Nemonianu argues that such a field of study would require a criticism open to modern, 'secular' theory and to religious experience and thought. This is the intertextuality of which the essays in the book are examples. However, such an approach means that the intertextuality in most of the essays is contained in a form of exemplary practice. There is little theoretical discussion of the term. One exception to this is Stanford Budick's 'Milton "Ridens": Reinventing the Temporality of Tradition and Faith' which, taking as its subject Milton's approach to the temporal nature of writing, produces an important

corrective to Bloom's de-historicized account of Milton's trans-
umptive style.

Danna Nolan Fewell's *Reading Between Texts: Intertextuality and
the Hebrew Bible* collects papers given to the Hebrew Bible Section
of the Society of Biblical Literature. The collection contains an
informative introduction by Fewell, a glossary of terms, three theoretical chapters – Tim Beal on the background and methodology of
intertextual theory, Peter Miscall on the potentially subversive
aspects of revisionism (*à la* Bloom), and Ilona Rashkow on the
reader-oriented nature of intertextual analysis – and then divides
into two further sections of close readings: the first dealing with
texts from the *Genesis* to *Kings* corpus; the second taking texts from
Kings and beyond. The quality of the essays is, not surprisingly,
varied. Beal is excellent on the necessity for 'strategies of containment' when performing intertextual analysis. Rashkow's essay complements Beal's well by adding, by way of an analogy between
intertextuality and the psychoanalytic concept of transference, a
more sophisticated analysis of the complex positionality of the text
with regard to the reader and of the reader with regard to the text.
From a theoretical point of view, the most significant of the close
readings are David Penchansky's analysis of *Genesis* 19 and 24 and
Judges 19 which ends with a candid statement of its ideological preoccupations, Stuart Lasine's attempt to recover the 'authorial
audience' for and thus the cultural and ideological significance of
1 *Kings* 12, and Francisco O. Gracía-Treto's interesting analysis of
the motif of 'the fall of the house' in 2 *Kings* 9 and 10 and a number
of other intertexts. The book as a whole presents an array of
readings in which a fluid, unstable, but usually constructive concept,
intertextuality, is employed in order to open up that (supposedly)
'closed' book known as the Bible. Though many of the readings
tend toward 'source study' rather than intertextual analysis, they all
have a sense of the cultural and ideological possibilities contained
within what we might call 'relational' reading.

One major figure still seen by many as offering ways of combining
some of the specificities of 'source study' with the theoretical
concerns attached to the concept of intertextuality is Harold Bloom.
John Welle, in his 'Dante and Poetic *Communio* in Zanzotto's
Pseudo-Trilogy' (*Lectura Dantis* 10.34–58), argues that Dante
situates the issue of poetic influence in the dialogic arena of
'communio' rather than in Bloom's 'Oedipal theory' of 'weak' and
'strong' poets. Ernest Fontana in his 'Rossetti's "On the Field of
Waterloo": An Intertextual Reading' (*Victorian Poetry* 30.179–82)

develops the work of Antony H. Harrison by looking at how Rossetti 'misreads' Wordsworth's 'After Visiting the Field of Waterloo' in his 'On the Field of Waterloo'. Harrison's *Victorian Poets and Romantic Poems* (University Press of Virginia, 1990), an important 'post-Bloomian' study of influence, in that it attempts to use influence-study to explore the ideological significance of Victorian poetic texts, is issued in paperback this year and is reviewed favourably by Lawrence Potson (*Studies in Romanticism* 31.117–21).

The most significant 'post-Bloomian' study this year is Leslie Brisman's '*Maud*: The Feminine as the Crux of Influence' (*Studies in Romanticism* 31.21–43). Brisman begins with Michael Cooke's 'The Feminine as the Crux of Value' and uses its thinking-through of what we might call the thematics of gender as a starting-point for a consideration of the gendered nature of poetic influence in Tennyson and, beyond that, the Romantic and post-Romantic poetic tradition. Brisman's focus is on the question 'whether it makes any sense to regard a certain kind of poetic influence as a masculine and acquisitive "institution"?' This question leads on to another: whether we can go any further in distinguishing 'masculine' and 'feminine' modes of influence in Romantic and post-Romantic literature. Cooke's taxonomies of the 'masculine' and the 'feminine' – '*force, aggression, explosiveness, acquisitiveness* and *institution*' as against '*balance, responsiveness, perseverance,* the *accumulative,* and *community*' – are applied to two chief precursors of Tennyson's poem: Byron and Keats respectively. Brisman's dense and rewarding essay leads to a possible reversal of Cooke's model, whereby the Tennyson/Byron relationship takes on 'the feminine "accumulative" mode', whilst the Tennyson/Keats relationship begins to seem of the 'masculine "acquisitive" sort'. Whilst Brisman's essay is pre-eminently a superb intervention at the level of close, intertextual analysis, her argument may help to discourage a too rigid 'gender-typing' in considerations of poetic influence and intertextuality. The point is that there may well be a gender of poetic influence in Romantic and post-Romantic poetry, but it is not open to a rigid, binary description. On the other hand, as James S. William's 'A Beast of the Closet: The Sexual Differences of Literary Collaboration in the Work of Marguerite Duras and Yani Andréa' (*Modern Language Review* 87.576–84) would seem to suggest, the modes of 'feminine' influence which have arisen to counter Bloom's patriarchal poetics of influence are still essential in our uncovering of the interrelations between female authors. Another important 'post-Bloomian' work, Christopher Beech's *ABC of Influence: Ezra Pound*

and the Remaking of American Poetic Tradition (University of California Press) has not been received for review.

Two essays this year deal directly with an issue close to the
Bloomian project, the issue of literary allusion. Adam Piette's '*Ill
Seen Ill Said*: Allusion and Cultural Memory', collected in Balz
Engler's *Writing and Culture*, looks, in interesting ways, at how
Beckett employs 'self allusions' to question 'the distinction between
personal creation remembered (personal past) and traditional
allusion (cultural memory)'. David Cohen's somewhat less sophisti-
cated essay, '"For This Relief Much Thanks"': Leopold Bloom and
Beckett's Use of Allusion' in Phyllis Carey's and Ed Jewinski's
Re:Joyce'n Beckett, makes distinctions between Beckett's and Joyce's
use of literary and cultural allusions.

The most important intervention in this area this year, however, is
Goran Hermerén's 'Allusions and Intentions' in Gary Iseminger's
Intention and Interpretation. As Hermerén suggests: 'We cannot take
for granted that "allude" and "allusion" are always by all critics
and scholars in all contexts used consistently in the same way or in
one sense only.' Given the preoccupations of this collection, it is
appropriate that Hermerén should begin with a distinction between
adaptation, which can be unintentional, and allusion, which, he
argues, cannot. This is an analytic study, in the philosophical sense
of the word, which should go some way to clarify this important
issue.

The essay just mentioned, for example, might have allowed Zoran
Konstantinovic to develop more thoroughly his distinction between
intertext and alteration as a paradigm for comparative literature
studies. His 'Intertext and Alteration: On the Modern Paradigm in
Comparative Literature' in the second volume of Vita Fortunati's
collection *Bologna, la cultura italiana e le letterature straniere
moderne*, moves us away from the analytic precision of Hermerén
and back to the nightmare scenario of the total, cultural text. Konstantinovic's declaration of intent is exemplary in its theoretical and
critical naïveté and deserves citing: 'Thus, not only every work of
art, but every human endeavour, generally – not only a picture or a
particular stage adaptation but, indeed, a city's entire life from the
moment it first awakens in the early morning to when the last lights
go out – can be understood as a woven text; it is up to us to
decipher and read this kind of text which, indeed, is to be found at
every step'. The answer to this might be given in two stages: firstly,
'understood' by whom? and, secondly, from what position are we
(*sic*) supposed to be able to survey all this? As an antidote to that

kind of theoretical hubris, the reader might like to turn to André Lefevre's review of Worton and Still's recent *Intertextuality* (Manchester University Press) (*Comparative Literature Studies* 29.218–22). Here Lefevre, whilst locating 'the (neo)positivistic search for "influences"' as the 'greatest danger' intertextual studies still has to confront, also points 'to the existence of the necessary complement to intertext in any discourse on literature: context'.

Studies of single authors also throw up some interesting points this year. Annette Shandler Levitt, in 'Joyce Cary's Blake: The Intertextuality of *The Horse's Mouth*' (*Mosaic* 25:iii.47–63), is rather shaky on the theory, although she does have interesting things to say about the intertextual relationship signalled by her title. Sharon Wood's 'Seductions and Brazen Duplications: Two Recent Novels from Italy' (*Forum for Modern Language Studies* 28.349–62) introduces two contemporary Italian novelists, Francesca Duranti and Sandra Petrigani, and traces their intertextual strategies in the context of Italian feminism. John R. Williams, in 'Emma Bovary and the Bride of Lammermoor' (*Nineteenth-Century French Studies* 20.352–60), discusses how Flaubert uses the story of Lucia, particularly Scott's version, to set up an intertextual relation between 'life' and 'fiction' which subjects romantic love to a deconstructive *mise en abîme*. Rudolf Bader's '*The Satanic Verses*: An Intertextual Experiment by Salman Rushdie' (*International Fiction Review* 19.ii.65–75) presents Rushdie's novel as a conscious attempt to generate dialogic patterns of meaning. What is interesting about this last essay is less Bader's own, rather limited, hold on intertextual theory than his use and extension of Manfred Pfister's 'model . . . for [the] scaling of intertextual references'. This 'model' can be found in Pfister's 'Konzepte der *Intertextualität*', collected in a volume entitled *Intertextualität* (Niemeyer, 1985).

Of more theoretical interest are Elizabeth Brunazzi's '"The Voice of an Unseen Reader" in *Giacomo Joyce*' and Kathryne V. Lindberg's 'Re-Signings, Re:Signatures: Joyce and Pound Reading Shakespeare's *Will*', both collected in *The Languages of Joyce: Selected Papers from the 11th International James Joyce Symposium, Venice, 12–18 June 1988*, edited by Bosinelli et al. Brunazzi discusses how references to sight and speech generate an allusive internal dialogue which prepares the way for Joyce's intertextual breakthrough in *Ulysses*. Lindberg's analysis of the intertextuality of the signature (proper name, unique mark), as a means of disclosing strategies of authorization and identification in Pound and Joyce, complements elements of Michael Vincent's work already discussed.

Eyal Amiran, in 'Proofs of Origin: Stephen's Intertextual Art in *Ulysses*' (*James Joyce Quarterly* 29.775–89) is an extremely interesting study which proves that the gradations between anonymous citationality and the specifics of intentional allusion provide not merely a critical problem but, often, a framework within which authors can work productively. Stephen's attitude towards interpretation changes during the day, Amiran argues; a movement which takes him from 'a poetics of mastery to the knowledge of unknowability'.

Charles D. Minahen's 'Correspondence Theory and the Case of Baudelaire's Sphinx Intertext' (*Romance Quarterly* 39.145–58) is a major contribution to studies of intertextuality in Baudelaire. Minahen's main point is that Baudelaire's theory of correspondences is predicated not simply on an effort to discover 'underlying simple structures' of analogy but, more significantly, to 'generate[s] their proliferation *tautologically* in intertextual enumerations'. Grant Crichfield's 'Gautier's Orient: Mask, Mirage, and "Decor D'Opera" in *Constantinople*' (*Romance Notes* 32.263–70) discusses the manner in which Gautier's intertextual focus posits an 'other' (the Orient) at the same time as avoiding the full recognition of Otherness.

Two other essays this year usefully incorporate elements from particular theoretical discourses into the examination of intertextual relations. Myriam Yvonne Jehenson, in 'The Dorotea–Fernando/ Lusinda–Cardenio Episode in *Don Quijote*: A Postmodernist Play' (*Modern Language Notes* 107.205–19), characterizes Cervantes's novel as a postmodernist text. Jehenson demonstrates how intertextual elements in the novel take on that postmodernist characteristic described by Baudrillard as 'the culture of the simulacrum' (the copy not being subservient to the original), and goes on to show how these elements are used by Cervantes to deconstruct a range of binary oppositions. Finally, David Lorenzo Boyd, in 'Compilation as Commentary: Controlling Chaucer's *Parliament of Fowls*' (*South Atlantic Quarterly* 91.945–64), uses Lee Paterson's notion of 'disambiguation' in order to discuss the material reproduction, transmission and distribution of mediaeval texts. Disambiguation, as the controlling of a text's meaning by placing it in a specific interpretive context or textual space, highlights here the strategies of control exercised over textual interpretation by mediaeval traditions of compilation and brings us back to a point similar to the one developed by Joseph R. Allen in his analysis of the Chinese poetic tradition. Boyd ends by encouraging others to develop this kind of intertextual approach, one which does indeed have fascinating implications for many different areas of the discipline.

Atle Kittang's *Intertextuality and Irony in 'Dag Solstad'* (University of Minnesota Press) has not been made available for review.

Books Reviewed

Allen, Joseph R. *In the Voice of Others: Chinese Music Bureau Poetry* (Michigan Monographs in Chinese Studies, vol. 63). University of Michigan Press. pp. 293. hb $20.00, pb $12.00. ISBN 0 892 64 096 0, 0 892 64 097 9.

Bosinelli, R., M. Bellettieri, C. Marengo Vaglio and Christine van Boheemen, eds. *The Languages of Joyce: Selected Papers from the 11th International James Joyce Symposium, Venice, 12–18 June 1988.* Benjamins North America. pp. 299. hb £42.00, pb £17.00. ISBN 90 272 2124 3, 90 272 2125 1.

Carey, Phyllis, and Ed Jewinski, eds. *Re:Joyce'n Beckett.* Ford University Press. pp. 199. hb $25.00, pb $19.95. ISBN 0 8232 1340 4, 0 8232 1341 2.

Engler, Balz, ed. *Writing and Culture* (Swiss Papers in English Language and Literature, vol. 6). Narr. pp. 253. DM48.00. ISBN 3 8233 4681 4.

Fewell, Danna Nolan, ed. *Reading Between Texts: Intertextuality and the Hebrew Bible* (Literary Currents in Biblical Interpretation). John Knox. pp. 285. pb $21.99. ISBN 0 664 25393 8.

Fortunati, Vita, ed. *Bologna, la cultura italiana e le letterature straniere moderne,* vol. 2. Longo. pp. 431. pb ISBN 1 19 447 303 0.

Hillman, Richard. *Intertextuality and Romance in Renaissance Drama: The Staging of Nostalgia.* Macmillan. pp. 214. £45.00. ISBN 0 333 56703 X.

Iseminger, Gary, ed. *Intention and Interpretation.* Temple University Press. pp. 275. $44.95. ISBN 0 87722 971 6.

Kline, T. Jefferson. *Screening the Text: Intertextuality in the New Wave French Cinema.* Johns Hopkins University Press. pp. 308. $34.95, £29.00. ISBN 0 8018 4267 0.

Leggett, B. J. *Early Stevens: The Nietzschean Intertext.* Duke University Press. pp. 285. $36.95. ISBN 0 8223 1201 8.

Nemonianu, Virgil, and Robert Royal, eds. *Play, Literature, Religion: Essays in Cultural Intertextuality.* State University of New York Press (SUNY series, The Margins of Literature). pp. 221. hb $44.50, pb $16.95. ISBN 0 7914 0935 X, 0 7914 0936 8.

Thomas, Neil. *The Defence of Camelot: Ideology and Intertextuality in the 'Post-Classical' German Romances of the 'Matter of Britain Cycle'.* Lang. pp. 255. £26.10. ISBN 3 261 04590 6.

Vincent, Michael. *Figures of the Text: Reading and Writing (in) La Fontaine* (Purdue University Monographs in Romance Languages, vol. 39). Benjamins North America. pp. 154. $49.00, £31.00. ISBN 1 55619 306 8.

Wang, Jing. *The Story of Stone: Intertextuality, Ancient Stone Lore, and the Stone Symbolism of 'Dream of the Red Chamber', 'Water Margin', and 'The Journey to the West'* (Post-Contemporary Interventions Series). Duke University Press. pp. 359. $37.50. ISBN 0 8223 1178 X.

Whitlark, James, and Wendell Aycock, eds. *The Literature of Emigration and Exile*. Texas Tech University Press. pp. 192. $24.95. ISBN 0 89672 263 5.

6

Psychoanalysis

VICKY LEBEAU

One of the most important publications this year is Dennis Porter's translation of Jacques Lacan's *The Ethics of Psychoanalysis*. Edited by Jacques-Alain Miller, this is the seventh of Lacan's seminars, delivered between 1959 and 1960. Divided into five sections – 'Introduction to the Thing [*Das Ding*]', 'The Problem of Sublimation', 'The Paradox of *Jouissance*', 'The Essence of Tragedy' and 'The Tragic Dimension of Analytical Experience' – the interdisciplinary scope of this rereading of Freud will be familiar from Lacan's previously-published seminars. The tone, too, is distinctively 'Lacan': 'Before coming here today I read in Jones a kind of celebration of the sublime virtues of social pressure, without which our contemporaries, our fellow humans, would be vain, egotistical, sordid, sterile, etc. One is tempted to comment in the margin, "What are they but that?".' This seminar is, at once, a sarcastic and angry denunciation of a 'general tendency' towards an 'all-embracing moralism' within a psychoanalysis which 'seems to have as its sole goal the calming of guilt' and an exploration of the 'revolution' in ethical thought required by, precisely, Freud's discovery of an 'exorbitant' and omnipresent sense of guilt 'which is exercised without the subject's knowledge'. Guilt, like ethics, goes beyond what can be described as moral command or obligation, touching instead on the sense of the good, the ideal, which Lacan relates to what is perhaps still the least familiar element of his explanatory triad, enigmatically defined here: 'The real, I have told you, is that which is always in the same place.'

With the symbolic and the imaginary, the concept of the real has become increasingly important in recent critical appropriations of

Lacan – for example, in Slavoj Žižek's *The Sublime Object of Ideology* (Verso, 1989) and his *Enjoy Your Symptom!* (reviewed below). In this sense, the translation of *The Ethics of Psychoanalysis* is timely. It also offers a series of stunning readings – of, for example, Freud's *Project for a Scientific Psychology* (1895) as a transposition of Aristotelian ethics on to a 'mechanistic' psychology, as an 'ethical' text for and within psychoanalysis, and as one of Freud's first attempts to articulate the relation between pleasure and reality, between the primary and secondary processes which not only lock the subject into conflict with itself and the other but also make access to 'reality' such a difficult and precarious process. That difficulty has immediate bearing on the structure of the superego and the pressure of what could be called social morality or conscience: 'Reality is precarious. And it is precisely to the extent that access to it is so precarious that the commandments which trace its path are so tyrannical.' Similarly, *Civilization and its Discontents* sustains Lacan's interrogation of what lies beyond the pleasure principle – and all the implications of that beyond for a type of ethical thinking that, at least since Aristotle, has so often tried to identify pleasure and the good, terms that are, for Lacan, 'fundamentally antithetical'.

But perhaps the most fascinating section of the seminar is Lacan's commentary on Sophocles' *Antigone*. For Lacan, *Antigone* represents a 'turning point' in the field of ethics: 'Is there anyone who doesn't evoke *Antigone* whenever there is a question of a law that causes conflict in us even though it is acknowledged by the community to be a just law?' It would be impossible to do justice to Lacan's treatment of Sophocles' play which, as he suggests, amounts to nothing less than 'the reinterpretation of the Sophoclean message'. For Mikkel Borch-Jacobsen (*Lacan: The Absolute Master*, Stanford University Press, 1991) such a claim may simply be read as evidence of Lacan's hyperbolic claims to originality. More generously, Lacan is engaged in a fundamental requestioning of the relation between law and desire, between affect and spectatorship, between the being of family and of community, which may be crucial to the debates taking place within critical theory about ethics, politics and the imperative, legislative aspects of our appeals to 'justice'. John Brenkman, in 'Family, Community, Polis: The Freudian Structure of Feeling' (*New Literary History* 23.923–54), for example, takes up some of the issues raised by the always-specific historical conditions in which the socialization of the psyche takes place. In the case of Antigone, there is conflict both within and outside of the psyche, within the individual and the community, in so far as there seems to be too much 'truth', too much 'judgement', which can be applied equally, though not perhaps equitably, to both parties.

It is in this context that Slavoj Žižek picks up on Lacan's reading of *Antigone* for its analysis of an authoritarian tautology which, for Žižek, has to be linked to the concept of the real: 'What one should bear in mind here is that, according to Lacan, Antigone's defense against Creon's accusations ultimately consists in precisely such an "authoritarian" tautology.' Antigone does not counter Creon's law of the polis with the 'subterranean divine law protecting the right of the deceased, as Hegel wrongly assumed'; on the contrary, she interrupts Creon's arguments 'by insisting that "It is so because it is so!"', that '"My brother is my brother!"' This can be described as Antigone's claim to know the 'real kernel of the designated object, what, in it, "always returns to its place" (Lacan's definition of the real) – in the case of Polynices [Antigone's dead brother, whose burial Creon has forbidden], it designates his absolute individuality that remains the same beyond the changing properties that characterize his person (his good or evil deeds)'. Žižek's comments on Antigone suggest the remarkable and innovative clarity which characterizes his critical appropriation of Lacan in *Enjoy Your Symptom! – Jacques Lacan in Hollywood and Out*. Žižek's strategy is to take Lacan's sometimes over-familiar maxims, chapter by chapter, in the form of a question – so that the Contents page of the book reads like a glossary which promises to explicate even the most baffling of Lacan's terms: '1. Why Does a *Letter* Always Arrive at Its Destination?' – which promises to explain that infinitesimal difference between Lacan and Derrida on Poe's 'The Purloined Letter' with reference to Charlie Chaplin's *City Lights*; '2. Why Is *Woman* a Symptom of Man?' – which takes on not only what has always been, for feminism at least, one of Lacan's more notorious statements but also, almost in passing, 'the fascination of the sacrifice' through one of the most uncomfortable pleasures of cinema: the fascination with the serial killer and the stalking of the woman 'alone in the house' in Fred Walton's *When a Stranger Calls*. Chapters 3 ('Why is Every Act a *Repetition*?'), 4 ('Why Does the *Phallus* Appear?') and 5 ('Why Are There Always Two *Fathers*?') repeat this strategy, locating Lacan's terms in a complex philosophical and psychoanalytic context and illustrating them through key elements of classic popular, usually cinematic, culture.

In one sense, Žižek's work is building on the privileged link between psychoanalysis and film theory supported by journals like

Screen through the 1970s and 1980s. Some of this earlier work on sexuality, psychoanalysis and cinema is republished this year in *The Sexual Subject: A Screen Reader in Sexuality*, edited by John Caughie, Annette Kuhn and Mandy Merck, with Introduction by Barbara Creed. The first section, 'Psychoanalysis and Subjectivity', includes what have become two 'set' texts for psychoanalytic film studies: Laura Mulvey's 'Visual Pleasure and Narrative Cinema' (22–34) and Stephen Heath's 'Difference' (47–106). Also included is the perhaps less well known article put together by Edward Buscombe, Christine Gledhill, Alan Lovell and Christopher Williams, 'Psychoanalysis and Film' (35–46), which expresses a number of reservations about the 'unproblematic acceptance of psychoanalysis' implicit in *Screen*'s presentations of its material in the late 1970s. The article makes interesting reading for any history of the reception of psychoanalysis within film, literary and cultural theory in the 1970s and, in particular, for the methodological problems raised by the attempts to 'apply' psychoanalysis outside its own sphere of practice. The third section of the book, 'The Female Spectator', includes Mary Ann Doane's (again classic) 'Film and the Masquerade: Theorizing the Female Spectator' (227–44) and Jackie Stacey's account of the three masculinized, marginalized or masochistic forms of looking available to the woman in the theories of the female spectator in 'Desperately Seeking Difference' (244–260). Doane's famous essay appropriates Joan Rivière's theory of femininity as a form of masquerade as a way of approaching the problem of the female spectator (see p. 73 for more on Rivière). 'Masculinity as Spectacle' (277–90), Steve Neale's response to Laura Mulvey's drastic sexing of the look as masculine in 'Visual Pleasure', explores the homoerotic dimensions of looking in the fourth section, 'Images of Men'. Without invoking Mulvey directly, Homi K. Bhabha's essay, 'The Other Question: The Stereotype and Colonial Discourse' (312–31) – in Section V, 'The Social Subject' – offers a way of resisting the residual functionalism which emerges at times in her profile of a spectator 'slotted' into place by the social formations that have moulded him in 'Visual Pleasure'. Bhabha's careful path through the work of, amongst others, Freud, Lacan, Edward Said and Frantz Fanon disturbs one of the most frequent accusations against psychoanalysis – that it has nothing to say about the 'social' and, in particular, about either race or class. In fact, a rereading of the papers included in *The Sexual Subject* shows up the engagement with the problem of social identity – of social identification as always sexed and sexual identification as always social – that runs through what is sometimes presented as the 'high' point of an exclusive focus on the sexual in psychoanalysis.

'Through an alternation of a literary and a clinical perspective, the present study strives to grasp and to articulate the obscure relation between witnessing, events and evidence, as what defines at once the common ground between literature and ethics, and the meeting point between violence and culture. . . .' Thus Shoshana Felman and Dori Laub introduce their collaborative work, *Testimony: Crises of Witnessing in Literature, Psychoanalysis, and History*, reinflecting, once again, the relation between ethics, psychoanalysis and the 'reality' of history: '[W]e propose to introduce the dimension of the real – the events and implications of contemporary history.' The key event of that history for this book is the Holocaust, the trauma of contemporary history which, by annihilating the position of the 'witness', ushers in what Felman calls the 'age of testimony': 'As a relation to events, testimony seems to be composed of bits and pieces of a memory that has been overwhelmed by occurrences that have not settled into understanding or remembrance.' The Holocaust represents the event that is always in excess of our frames of reference, the event which requires both literature and psychoanalysis to rethink, or, more strongly, to rearticulate, the relation between representation and history, representation and event. For psychoanalysis, the overwhelming reality of the Holocaust can be said to have forced a rethinking of the classical oppositions between, or implication of the one in the other of, fantasy, reality and memory. In his two chapters of the book, Dori Laub, a psychoanalyst engaged in the treatment of trauma survivors and co-founder of the Video Archive for Holocaust Testimonies at Yale, explores the shift required in the form taken by the psychoanalytic contract when the analysand is a 'survivor', in particular here, of the Holocaust: 'In psychoanalytic work with survivors, indeed, historical reality has to be reconstructed and reaffirmed before any other work can start. This primary stage of the psychoanalytic work has been described as "the phase of joint acceptance of the Holocaust reality" by both analyst and patient. The analyst must often be there first, ahead of his patient, and, once having acquired factual information, must wait with patience and with readiness for the latter to join him in that place.'

Laub's reference is to the work of Ilse Grubrich-Simitis, 'From Concretism to Metaphor' (*The Psychoanalytic Study of the Child*, 1984, vol. 39) which lays emphasis on the loss of the capacity for metaphorization which characterizes survivors of the concentration camps. To put it too crudely, if the subject's worst fantasies are concretized by appearing on the 'outside', in the absolute dereliction and destruction which characterizes 'life' in the camps, then an acknowledgement of that reality, in the form of what Laub calls nonmetaphorical statements passed between analyst and analysand, has to occur before the classical psychoanalytic work on unconscious fantasy can even start to take place. In this sense, the analytic contract suggested by Laub in his account of the analyst as listener/witness in 'Bearing Witness, or the Vicissitudes of Listening' represents something like a public acknowledgement of the Holocaust; or, to put it slightly differently, that contract suggests that, at least in its privileging of attentive listening, psychoanalysis has something specific to contribute to our response to what emerges from this book as the 'crisis' of our time: how to bear witness to the event which destroyed the capacity to witness.

That question dominates the commentaries on psychoanalysis, testimony and literature throughout the book. Felman's 'Education and Crisis, or the Vicissitudes of Teaching' mirrors Laub's concern with bearing witness to the trauma of his patients or interviewees (for the Video Archive) in its description of a graduate class on 'Literature and Testimony' at Yale in 1984. After following a series of readings of Conrad, Dostoevsky, Freud, Mallarmé and Celan, which Felman reproduces here, the class watched two taped interviews from the Video Archive at Yale and experienced what Felman describes as a crisis – a crisis intimately bound up with the loss of the capacity to represent how they felt about the interviews either to themselves or to one another. From this, Felman goes on to discuss the possible relation between pedagogy and crisis: 'In the era of the Holocaust, of Hiroshima, of Vietnam – in the age of testimony – teaching, I would venture to suggest, must in turn testify, make something happen, and not just transmit a passive knowledge, pass on information that is preconceived, substantiated, believed to be known in advance. . . .' This analysis of the juncture between psychoanalysis, pedagogy and trauma frames the book and Felman's four further chapters on Camus's *The Plague*, the Paul de Man 'affair', Camus's *The Fall* and Claude Lanzmann's *Shoah*. The rigorous close readings of literary, psychoanalytic and historical texts consistently refuse to take the obvious for granted – a refusal which makes the collection invaluable – but it remains unclear, for me, what status is being assigned to the trauma experienced by the survivors of the Holocaust and the trauma of those, not necessarily survivors, who attempt to bear witness to it (e.g. the graduate class at Yale). This problem is addressed to an extent by Laub's distinction between three types of witnessing: 'the level of being a witness to oneself within the experience; the level of being a witness to the testimonies of others; and the level of being a witness to the process of witnessing itself'. Laub occupies all three positions. But the problem that haunts this book – not least, I think, because it is itself a form of testimony – is the possibly absolute and incommensurable difference of that first position, of bearing witness to oneself within such a traumatic experience.

Both Lacan and the question of history return in Carolyn J. Dean's *The Self and its Pleasures: Bataille, Lacan, and the History of the Decentred Subject*. In her Introduction, Dean sets out the three questions which govern the book: 'Why, quite simply, has France been the home of the most influential theories of self-dissolution? How, then, is the decentred self historically and culturally specific? And how do we account for rather than just describe what Judith Butler has called the "regulatory fictions" that constitute it?' Like Felman and Laub, then, Dean is engaged with the 'relationship between texts and contexts' but, while the former argue for both, and simultaneously, a contextualization of text and a textualization of context, Dean focuses on how the relation between text and context has been formulated in an attempt to explain 'why one story was told about the self and not another'. Her explanation is organized through the figure of the criminal as a metaphor for another self, a metaphor that Dean finds running across psychiatry, psychoanalysis and avant-garde aesthetics during the interwar years. The result is a fascinating history of, or context for, Lacan's (and Bataille's) theories of the subject. In 'The Legal Status of the Irrational', for example, Dean reads Lacan's doctoral thesis on female paranoia and violence alongside both his contact with avant-garde circles – a contact that, it is suggested, 'shaped' Lacan's interest in madness – and his increasing interest in Freudian psychoanalysis which, at least until the 1920s, had a hostile reception in France. In her discussion of Lacan's early work, Dean extends and elaborates David Macey's exploration of the intellectual influences on Lacan in *Lacan in Contexts* (Verso, 1988). Always, though, Dean's question is why Lacan came to formulate the subject in the way he did – a question that Dean examines, in 'Gender Complexes', through contemporary representations of, on the one hand, the 'criminal threat to social order in terms of gender – in terms, above all, of non-conformist, "deviant" women' associated with sexual perversity and social anarchism and, on the other hand, anxieties about the declining authority of the father in both the social and familial spheres. Through a reading of Lacan's early, and relatively unknown, article, 'Les Complexes familiaux', Dean suggests that he 'did believe that the function of sublimation had to be embodied by the imago of the father', a conclusion which leads to her judgement that, while Lacan was a critic of patriarchy 'he really only quibbled with its forms rather than its necessity'.

This carefully historical reading of Lacan's relation to social, or patriarchal, 'crisis' will contribute to the ongoing debate about the more or less violating, more or less seductive relation between psychoanalysis and feminism. Balancing biographical, historical and theoretical detail, Lisa Appignanesi and John Forrester's very readable *Freud's Women* also confronts this relation head on. 'To write about the women who peopled Freud's life', the authors suggest in the opening pages of the book, '– his family, patients, friends, the early pioneers of psychoanalysis – and his ideas of the feminine is to be shadowed by the sense that Freud is on trial.' Neither dismissing nor accepting the 'prosecuting' case against Freud, and, by extension, psychoanalysis, Appignanesi and Forrester plot their way through some of Freud's most famous, and famously controversial, cases – 'Dora', 'Irma' (of the 'dream of Irma's injection' in *The Interpretation of Dreams*) – the apparent serenity, even banality, of his marriage and family life, and the affective and professional careers of some of his female patients and colleagues: Sabine Spielrein, Loë Kann, Joan Rivière, Helene Deutsch, Marie Bonaparte and, of course, the daughter, described as Freud's Antigone, Anna Freud. The many anecdotes which structure the book are always instructive, shedding light on the complex implication of biography, autobiography and psychoanalytic theory which emerges here – and particularly in the chapters on Helene Deutsch and Joan Rivière (see p. 74). Similarly, the final chapter, 'Feminism and Psychoanalysis', gives an uncompromising insight into the difference of what could be called psychoanalytic ethics. When Jeffrey Masson's critique of Freud was published by Faber in 1984 (*Freud: The Assault on Truth*), a Freudian analyst was asked for her views on sexual trauma in childhood: 'An important question', she mused, 'and one that has preoccupied me for much of my professional life. My view is that if the patient is acting out by having sexual relationships with children, then one can assume that the infantile traumas were real.' For the practising analyst, 'the ethical questions about sexual life that preoccupy so many other workers in the sphere of the sexual abuse of children do not acquire urgency'. For psychoanalysis, then, something is suspended at precisely the moment when others may, and must, act – a privilege, or abuse, that so often generates the 'trial' with which Appignanesi and Forrester start their book. That trial extends, of course, to Freud's female followers and, in particular, to Helene Deutsch, described here as 'the most reviled of all Freud's women'. Deutsch has become infamous for her analysis of women's masochism and of feminine rape fantasies – an infamy which tends to overshadow the broader context of her work. Appignanesi and Forrester's brief biography and discussion of a range of Deutsch's papers goes some way to correcting that bias. In addition, also published this year is Deutsch's *The Therapeutic Process, the Self, and Female Psychology: Collected Psychoanalytic Papers*. Edited by Paul Roazen, this collection includes a number of essays – 'Two Cases of Induced Insanity', 'On the Pathological Lie', 'The Family Romance', 'A Type of Pseudo-Affectivity' – which provide the intellectual context for, and elaboration of, Deutsch's examination of lying, fantasy and 'pseudologia' in the better-known accounts of masochism and femininity. Similarly, Appignanesi and Forrester's sketch of Joan Rivière's life and work as both Freud's translator and a prominent Kleinian frames what has become one of the most influential papers in psychoanalytically-oriented feminist film and literary theory: Rivière's 'Womanliness as a Masquerade', first published in 1929. Setting out Rivière's links with the Cambridge and Bloomsbury intellectual elites, her analysis with both Freud and Ernest Jones, the authors go on to suggest that, in 'Womanliness as a Masquerade', Rivière introduced into psychoanalysis 'a feminine character far more resonant with contemporary experience than any Freud or even Helene Deutsch had explored. Her subject is the intellectual woman. . . .' Given that prominence, the virtual eclipse of the rest of Rivière's work is troubling. The publication of her collected papers last year, in *Joan Rivière, The Inner World and Joan Rivière*, with a foreword by the prominent Kleinian, Hanna Segal, and a biographical chapter by Athol Hughes, should go some way to making her contribution both more readily available and assessable. In particular, Rivière's contributions to the Kleinian theory of primal envy can be read alongside her account of feminine masquerade as a defence against the anxiety of having stolen the father's envied penis – the feminine psyche as constituted through theft.

The juncture between psychoanalysis and femininity is also very much at issue in two books on psychoanalysis, literature and feminism. Elisabeth Bronfen's *Over Her Dead Body: Death, Feminin-*

ity and the Aesthetic ranges across literary and visual forms of representation to focus on the conjunction between feminine beauty and death. Of particular relevance here is 'The Lady Vanishes', an account of the death of Freud's 'favourite' daughter, Sophie Freud-Halberstadt – the mother of the little boy who invents the *fort-da* game of 'Beyond the Pleasure Principle'. Bronfen's interest is in the way in which the daughter's death makes itself felt in the rhetoric of Freud's text and his elaboration of the theory of the death drive in the context of a set of speculations about the relationship between loss and symbolization (the *fort-da* game, played by Freud's grandson whenever he is left alone by his mother). Bronfen concludes that 'Freud narrates the "fort-da" game in such a way that the sacrifice of the daughter ultimately represents the renunciation of the mother' – a collapsing of two feminine bodies and an erasure of the maternal that constitutes a lost paradigm for psychoanalysis and so generates a question: 'What would happen if we focused on this other narrative, on a notion of anxiety not based on sexual difference?' In a sense, this is a question about what would happen if we were able to change the rhetoric of psychoanalysis, a change that may only start to happen with an attention to, precisely, psychoanalysis as rhetoric. Rachel Bowlby's *Still Crazy After All These Years: Women, Writing and Psychoanalysis* is just such a starting-point which links feminist theory, literature and psychoanalysis as ways of asking about, and writing about, what women want: 'Here, however, the starting-point (there is no conclusive end to the trip) has to do with a question of feminist rhetoric. How do women write what they want (and what they don't want)? And how do the texts written about them construct possibilities and limits, openings and impasses, which set the terms for the ways in which we think about what a woman is, or where women might be going, whether individually or collectively?' A number of essays address psychoanalysis – or a French, 'feminist' psychoanalysis. 'Flight Reservations: The Anglo-American/French Divide in Feminist Criticism' and 'The Judgement of Paris (and the Choice of Kristeva): French Theory and Feminism This Side of the Channel' are crucial readings of the debates about 'French feminism' that have been taking place over the last ten years or so. Starting with a story of the encounter, the 'blind date', between feminism and psychoanalysis, 'Still Crazy After All These Years' plots the different ways in which feminism has welcomed or repudiated psychoanalysis as one of the primary forms of talking about what women want in our culture. 'Walking, Women and Writing' explores Freud's misappropriation of Plato's

Symposium in the *Three Essays on Sexuality* and the reductive divisions between homosexuality and heterosexuality generated by his 'solidly heterosexual' misremembering of the Greek paradigm for the origin of desire and sexual difference.

Finally, one of the most fascinating and suggestive books published this year is Frances Tustin's revision of her *Autistic States in Children*, which first appeared in 1981. Above all, perhaps, this book points to the need to develop a dialogue between 'high' French psychoanalytic theory and more obviously clinically-based work, a dialogue which seems to be lacking, at least within 'academic' psychoanalysis. In a discussion of the theoretical aspects of childhood psychosis, Tustin cites a personal communication from Dr James Grotstein: 'I believe that the concept of primary identification, described by Freud ['Group Psychology and the Analysis of the Ego', 1921; 'The Ego and the Id', 1921] but not dealt with by anyone except Fairbairn [*Psychoanalytic Studies of the Person*, 1952] constitutes a very important idea. . . . Marasmic children, those that have faced infantile catastrophe . . . suffer from a deficit of primary identification. I have the notion that the same is true for what you are stating about autistic children.' What emerges clearly through Tustin's analysis of autism – as the result of a set of processes defending against a traumatic experience of the reality of bodily separation from the mother – is the link between her work and Julia Kristeva's analysis of primary identification as a crucial defence against the abject mother who is neither subject nor object for the child (in *Tales of Love*, Columbia University Press, 1987). Tustin sums up the shift in her views on autism from the previous edition of the book at the beginning of the second chapter. Disputing the trend within psychoanalysis which views autism as an early stage of infantile development as well as a specific form of pathology, she now reserves the term for a set of 'disorders in which there is an absence of human relationships and gross impoverishment of mental and emotional life – these impairments being the result of the blocking of awareness by an early aberrant development of autistic procedures'. Her emphasis on pathological autistic procedures, rather than on autism as a regression to an earlier stage of development, does not, however, prevent Tustin from proposing more or less normal 'pockets' of autism in us all. In particular, her analysis of the lack of affect or emotional, empathetic response as a key characteristic of autism is made resonant when she reflects, briefly but intriguingly, on the possibility of a type of social autism as a pressing problem for 'our generation'. Her close analysis of the failure of symbolization and representation in autistic states suggests another way of looking at the 'borderline personality' so often used to describe contemporary psychic space as, precisely, disaffected, without feeling and overwhelmed – an overwhelming that Tustin relates to the difficult and fragile distinction between inside and outside, between 'I' and 'not I', between subject and other, so much at issue for critical and psychoanalytic theory.

Books Reviewed

Appignanesi, Lisa, and John Forrester. *Freud's Women*. Weidenfeld & Nicolson. pp. 563. pb £13.99. ISBN 1 853 81719 8.

Bowlby, Rachel. *Still Crazy After All These Years: Women, Writing and Psychoanalysis*. Routledge. pp. 185. pb £9.99. ISBN 0 415 08640 X.

Bronfen, Elisabeth. *Over Her Dead Body: Death, Femininity and the Aesthetic*. Manchester University Press. pp. 435. pb. £14.95. ISBN 0 7190 3827 8.

Caughie, John, Annette Kuhn and Mandy Merck. *The Sexual Subject: A Screen Reader in Sexuality*. Routledge. pp. 339. pb £12.99. ISBN 0 415 07467 3.

Dean, Carolyn J. *The Self and its Pleasures: Bataille, Lacan, and the History of the Decentred Subject*. Cornell University Press. pp. 270. pb. $17.55. ISBN 0 8014 9954 2.

Deutsch, Helene. *The Therapeutic Process, the Self, and Female Psychology: Collected Psychoanalytic Papers*, ed. with an Introduction by Paul Roazen. Transaction. pp. 268. hb £29.95. ISBN 0 88738 429 3.

Felman, Shoshana, and Dori Laub. *Testimony: Crises of Witnessing in Literature, Psychoanalysis, and History*. Routledge. pp. 294. pb £12.99. ISBN 0 415 90392 0.

Lacan, Jacques. *The Ethics of Psychoanalysis (1959–60)*, ed. Jacques-Alain Miller, trans. Dennis Porter. Routledge. pp. 342. pb £14.99. ISBN 0 415 09054 7.

Rivière, Joan. *The Inner World and Joan Rivière*. Karnac (1991). pp. 376. pb £22. ISBN 0 946 43994 X.

Tustin, Frances. *Autistic States in Children*. Routledge. pp. 255. pb £14.99. ISBN 0 415 08129 7.

Žižek, Slavoj. *Enjoy Your Symptom! Jacques Lacan in Hollywood and Out*. Routledge. pp. 198. pb £10.95. ISBN 0 415 90482 X.

7

Feminism

SARA MILLS WITH LYNDIE BRIMSTONE, KATH
BURLINSON, JANE GOLDMAN, VASSILIKI
KOLOCOTRONI, PAULINE POLKEY AND
ANGIE SANDHU

This chapter has seven sections: 1. General; 2. Feminism and
Psychoanalysis; 3. Feminism and Lesbianism; 4. Feminism, Race
and Empire; 5. Feminist Readings of Literatures of the Past; 6.
Feminism and Representation; 7. Feminism and Autobiography.

1. General

Feminist theory seems to be working primarily with the notion of
difference and diversity in increasingly interesting and productive
ways. This year has seen the publication of a number of books and
articles which address issues of race, sexual orientation and class,
trying to integrate these concerns into general theoretical frameworks rather than marginalizing them as minority issues.

There are now a number of excellent books providing background
reading for women's studies courses. Three of these published this
year are Maggie Humm's *Feminisms: A Reader*, Diane Richardson
and Victoria Robinson's *Introducing Women's Studies: Feminist
Theory and Practice*, and Helen Crowley and Susan Himmelweit's
Knowing Women: Feminism and Knowledge. All of these aim to
provide a wealth of reading for both students and lecturers alike.
Humm's anthology provides an excellent handbook for any women's
studies course: it contains selections from the texts which have been
important within the development of feminist theories within a
range of disciplines: sociology, history, linguistics, philosophy and so

on. The selections are well chosen and the extracts of a suitable length to encourage debate and discussion. The book contains a glossary. Richardson and Robinson's *Introducing Women's Studies* is novel in that, instead of providing an anthology of selected sections from classic feminist writing, as Humm's book does, it provides a group of newly-commissioned pieces which succeed in summing up the state of research in particular areas of feminist research. This makes the book very usable for many courses where women's studies could easily be structured around each of the chapters, for example on racism, sexuality, representation, language and so on. The best feature of the book is that all of the contributors are working with the notion of diversity and difference in positive and productive ways. As the editors state, 'Women's Studies has begun to recognise the need to work creatively with the concept of difference among women, which ensures that feminist theory is a synthesis of these differences in a dynamic sense – so we have meaningful dialogue around both differences and similarities, not guilty avoidance and angry accusation by women, or a hierarchy of oppressions, nor an undynamic plurality of positions which does not recognise power differences.' The bibliography is very full and there are useful suggestions for further reading. Another book which will prove useful on women's studies courses, and more generally, is Helen Crowley and Susan Himmelweit's excellent collection of essays entitled *Knowing Women*. Each of the essays engages with the title of the book, which the editors explain: 'Knowing women no longer just means developing knowledge about women, in which women feature as objects of knowledge. It also means understanding the subjective process whereby women understand, create and use knowledge. In other words, knowing women now also involves understanding women as the subjects of knowledge.' The book consists of extracts from well-known articles on particular subjects, for instance Susan Bordo's article on anorexia and Sandra Harding's article on analytical categories in feminist theory, together with newly commissioned pieces by a range of different authors.

Michèle Barrett and Anne Phillips's collection of essays, *Destabilising Theory: Contemporary Feminist Debates*, would also be of great use to women's studies courses, since the essays are drawn from a wide range of different disciplines and aim to provoke debate within feminism. This is a new approach, or at least an approach which has previously existed only at an implicit level. Rather than glossing over problems, the editors have decided to focus on those points of contradiction and difficulty within feminist theory:

elements such as debates about sex and gender, about the causes of
women's oppression, and the use of poststructuralist and postmodern theories. Moira Gaten's essay, 'Power, Bodies and Difference', is particularly insightful, engaging with notions of Marxist
theory and its usefulness at a conceptual level for feminist theoretical perspectives on power, and turning to Michel Foucault's work
in order to analyse more closely the way that power works on
bodies. Gayatri Spivak's essay, 'The Politics of Translation',
contains interesting points about the difficulty of translation, but
also the importance for feminists of considering the politics of
language learning. She states, 'If you are interested in talking about
the other, and/or making a claim to be the other, it is crucial to
learn other languages . . . I am talking about the importance of
language acquisition for the woman from a hegemonic monolinguist
culture who makes everybody's life miserable by insisting on
women's solidarity at her price.'

Gisela Bock and Susan James's edited collection, *Beyond Equality
and Difference*, is an immensely stimulating book. It is primarily the
proceedings of a conference held in 1988, but there are also several
new essays. These all circle around the difficult notions of equality
and difference, and after the rather pessimistic work in this area in
the last five years this collection is convincing proof that it is
possible to write feminist theoretical work at the same time as
engaging with notions of difference. This book is novel in that the
concern with difference does not entail a retreat into context and
specificity but, drawing on Italian feminist work, opens up an array
of other possibilities for feminist work: questioning the usefulness of
equality on men's terms and discussing the notion of female distinct-
ness without lapsing into banal essentialism. The book contains
essays by Carol Pateman, Rosi Braidotti, Jean Bethke Elshtain, and
Jane Flax on issues such as motherhood, power, citizenship and
justice.

Several books engage with Michel Foucault's work and its usefulness for feminist theory. Jana Sawicki's *Disciplining Foucault:
Feminism, Power and the Body* is one of the least successful,
although I am sure it will prove useful for students who would like
an introduction to Foucault's work from a feminist perspective. It is
a slight book (109 pages of text), consisting largely of essays which
have already been published elsewhere and a chapter which is
headed 'Personal Reflections'. It is difficult to keep patience with
this type of feminist self-indulgence. Sawicki confidently recounts an
anecdote of having met Foucault and told him about her work. He

suggested that she did not spend time writing about him but concentrate on writing genealogies – 'the essays here collected are evidence that I did not entirely abide by his advice'. I would suggest that Foucault was right. Lois McNay's *Foucault and Feminism* is a more successful engagement with the difficult liaison between Foucault's theoretical work and its possible uses for feminism. McNay focuses primarily on Foucault's work on the self and the body, and it is interesting that most feminists when using Foucault have found his later work more usable than his earlier work. McNay's book is a significant attempt to appropriate elements of Foucault's work for feminist theory.

Isobel Armstrong's edited collection, *New Feminist Discourses: Critical Essays on Theories and Texts*, is a wide-ranging survey of essays by young feminist academics on the implications of feminist theoretical work on the practice of feminist criticism. There are sections on knowledges, subjectivities, language, representation and Others, and the essays as a whole are an attempt to interrogate the notion of gender and its impact on existing bodies of knowledge as well as the new knowledges produced by feminism. Central to all of the essays is a concern with engaging in current feminist debates.

Also of importance in literary criticism is Josephine Donovan's *Feminist Theory: The Intellectual Traditions of American Feminism*. Donovan has updated her 1985 ground-breaking study of the origins and history of American feminist thought to include consideration of the recent developments in feminism and postmodernism, multiculturalism and environmentalism. This is an impressive and useful guide.

Building on the achievements of influential works such as Genevieve Lloyd's *The Man of Reason: 'Male' and 'Female' in Western Philosophy* (Routledge, 1984), Sandra Harding's *The Science Question in Feminism* (Bowker, 1986) and Carol Gilligan's *In a Different Voice* (Harvard University Press, 1982), *Women and Reason*, edited by Elizabeth Harvey and Kathleen Okruhlik, is an interdisciplinary collection of essays examining the status of femininity in relation to reason in a range of contexts from the seventeenth century to the present, arguing in general, as does more specifically Susan Bordo's key essay, 'Feminist Skepticism and the "Maleness" of Philosophy', for women's engagement with and participation in 'rational discourse', rather than its rejection as an irredeemably masculine construct. The collection opens by addressing the seventeenth-century origins of the debate on rationality and femininity: Hilda Smith, in 'Intellectual Bases for Feminist Analyses: The Seventeenth

and Eighteenth Centuries', argues against the orthodox feminist
position on reason as always and already masculine, suggesting that
women's exclusion from reason amounted to their exclusion from
the means to their own emancipation; she focuses on the ideas of
Mary Astell, who in *A Serious Proposal* (1697) systematically criticized the inferior education of women in the seventeenth century
and proposed a much more challenging Cartesian-based curriculum.

Thomas M. Lennon, in 'Lady Oracle: Changing Conceptions of
Authority and Reason in Seventeenth-Century Philosophy', also
looks at the attractiveness of Cartesian principles for women. He
suggests that seventeenth-century oracular discourse was condemned
as feminine precisely because it was understood as a challenge to
reason and truth: 'The charge of oracularity as enigmatic, vehicular,
feminine discourse', he contends, 'is a historical continuation of the
charge of diabolical possession', and the epistemological project of
Cartesianism thus becomes 'an effort at exorcising universal diabolical possession'. Kathleen Okruhlik's 'Birth of a New Physics or
Death of Nature?' returns to the seventeenth-century doctrine of
primary and secondary qualities as the basis of feminist critiques of
modern science and seeks to rescue the notion of objectivity from
orthodox feminist rejection, identifying a methodological sense of
objectivity as 'indispensable to feminist theory and practice', and
bringing critical insight to the failings of Bacon's universalist vision
of science. Julie Robin Solomon, in 'From Species to Speculation:
Naming the Animals with Calvin and Bacon', examines Calvin's and
Bacon's commentaries on Adam's naming of the animals in *Genesis*,
tracing in Calvin a recognition of rationality as bound up with
desire, and exposing in Bacon the class and gender origins that form
the (elided) basis of his vision of genderless rationality.

Alison Jaggar, in 'Love and Knowledge: Emotion in Feminist
Epistemology', examines the historical development of the opposition of reason to emotion and seeks to reclaim emotion as vital to
systematic knowledge. This is not to abandon dispassionate investigation in favour of uncritical feeling, but to recognize that emotions
are socially constructed and 'although . . . epistemologically indispensable, they are not epistemologically indisputable'; from a
feminist perspective Jaggar suggests that 'the growth of knowledge
may contribute to the development of appropriate emotions' and
vice versa. Patricia Matthews, in her essay 'The Gender of Creativity
in the French Symbolist Period', explores the gender-based paradox
of the belief in passion as the foundation of creativity: 'For males,
ecstatic, passionate suffering was the avenue to the sublime revela-

tion of ultimate truth and creativity, whereas for women, such states were seen as feeble-minded manifestations of mental illness.' Mark A. Cheetham's essay, on the other hand, looks at the theories of the Dutch painter Piet Mondrian and their masculinist legacy, and compares the work of two painters (one male, one female) who in the 1980s have responded differently to this abstractionist tradition. Kristin Brady returns to the nineteenth century for her fascinating analysis of a highly influential text in the canon of George Eliot criticism: a phrenological reading of her skull. This is ripe material indeed for a study of patriarchal 'objectivity' as instrumental in the silencing of women. Marie Fleming's impressive essay on the feminist potential of Jürgen Habermas's notoriously ungendered theory of communicative reason offers another stimulating perspective on the relation of the feminine to rational discourse. The collection as a whole is valuable testimony to feminists' increasing and challenging participation in a tradition which, as they are well aware, still seeks their silence and exclusion. The book is highly recommended.

Published in Linda J. Nicholson's 'Thinking Gender' series for Routledge (which also includes Nicholson's *Feminism/Postmodernism* and Judith Butler's *Gender Trouble*), Sandra Bartky's essay collection, *Femininity and Domination*, represents one woman's engagement with feminist philosophy over a fifteen-year period, and it reflects the shifts in this area from the 1970s preoccupation with the pitfalls and potentials of Marxist feminism to more recent debates on postmodernist feminism. Bartky declares herself 'disheartened by the decline of interest among feminists in Marxist theory' and confesses that her 'choice of topics has been controlled, far more than I realized and more than I wished, by an anticipation of what would interest my audience'. Although critical of its orthodoxies, she nevertheless argues persuasively for the reconsideration of Marxism as a powerful tool for feminism. 'Women's joys and triumphs are not my theme,' she warns; and, indeed, hers is a disturbing and challenging investigation of feminine experience and consciousness, probing women's complicity in their own subordination in the most 'innocent' areas of life while also exposing women's 'internalization of pervasive intimations of inferiority' in the most intimate of social practices. Bartky draws on and adapts recent and traditional philosophy to investigate the politics of the personal – from women's fraught relations with beauty and narcissism to their professional and personal status as emotional carers.

One of the outstanding books of feminist theory in 1992 is *Over*

Her Dead Body: Death, Femininity and the Aesthetic by Elisabeth
Bronfen. Bronfen takes as her starting-point the conjunction of
Otherness found in the figure of the beautiful dead woman, where
the mystery of sexual difference is combined with that of mortality.
In all Western cultures, argues Bronfen, femininity and death are
unique in having no fixed place in the symbolic order – both are
unrepresentable, yet incessantly represented in art and literature.
The feminine corpse, Bronfen suggests, is a reassuring sight for the
survivors and becomes a site at which cultural norms may be
debated by a masculine creative community that constitutes itself
through, over and against femininity. In Bronfen's detailed readings
of eighteenth-, nineteenth- and twentieth-century cultural texts by
Richardson, Poe, Hawthorne, Brontë, Hardy, Rossetti, Dickens,
Nabokov, Hitchcock, Atwood, to name but some, the multiple reso-
nances of the figure of the feminine corpse are revealed with subtlety
but with unwavering insistence. The scholarship of the work is
indisputable, while Bronfen also demonstrates her acumen as a psychoanalytic textual analyst in her re-readings of Freud's notions of
the pleasure principle and the uncanny. This is psychoanalytically
informed cultural criticism of a very high order that will undoubtedly prove influential for theories of representation.

Susan J. Hekman's *Gender and Knowledge: Elements of a Postmodern Feminism* is a survey of theories of postmodernism with
reference to feminist theory. Hekman believes that feminism must
embrace postmodernism because the latter's critique of Enlightenment thought is essential to undermine the dichotomies that construct contemporary Western cultures. This is a familiar argument,
and Hekman adds little innovative thought to the discussion other
than to give Gadamer more critical attention than Lacan or
Kristeva. Hekman will not persuade those who are suspicious of the
postmodern project, but her book is a user-friendly and clearly-
written introductory guide to the debates. James A. Winders's
Gender, Theory and the Canon re-reads five 'canonical' texts by
Descartes, Marx, Freud, Nietzsche and Flaubert from a perspective
informed by poststructuralist feminist, critical and cultural theory.
His readings of texts ranging from 'Beyond the Pleasure Principle'
to the first of Descartes' 'Meditations' focus on the ways in which
unstated gendered assumptions and/or questionable constructions of
femininity inform such writings. Winders writes with energy and is
genuinely interdisciplinary and non-hierarchical in his approach; he
ranges comfortably between psychoanalytic, philosophical, Marxist
and literary fields as well as peppering his study with references to

popular culture (especially songs). Yet his book seems to be addressed less to readers schooled in feminist and theoretically-informed inquiry (for whom many of Winders's general points, if not his close readings, will appear extremely familiar) than to conservatives wishing to defend (or reinstate) a history of ideas in which issues of gender, race or class are deemed irrelevant. Since it seems unlikely that the latter will concern themselves with this relatively 'lightweight' study, its usefulness lies in its local observations rather than its overall thesis.

There are several books which analyse masculinity and the role of men who are working with feminist theory. Peter Middleton's *The Inward Gaze: Masculinity and Subjectivity in Modern Culture* attempts to analyse fantasies and male self-images from a range of texts representing both high and popular culture. Some of the book is good in its attempt to deal honestly with the conflicts and difficulties for men in constructing self-images, but some of the analyses of Superman, stamp-collecting and train-spotting could have been more sufficiently theorized. The book as a whole does at least pose interesting questions for men working in this area, for example: 'If men still have power denied to women how can these male oppressors produce an emancipatory political discourse on masculinity? Isn't this more likely to be some kind of face-saving exercise than a radical political project?'. This book tries earnestly to avoid the latter possibility, and by and large it succeeds in its objective.

Jeff Hearn is editor of the Routledge series of critical studies on men and masculinities, investigating the implications for men of the feminist identification of gender as socially constructed, and its focus is not men's critique of feminism but the critique of men and masculinities. His book *Men in the Public Eye* investigates the period 1870–1920, a time of expansion and transformation in the public domain, and as such an important point of reference for his analysis of the gender relations of patriarchy in the light of postmodernist theories.

2. Feminism and Psychoanalysis

Within the discipline of psychology, the term 'power' has been used in a naïve or unproblematized manner, according to Celia Kitzinger in 'Feminism, Psychology and the Paradox of Power' (*Feminism and Psychology* 1:i.111–29). Even feminist psychologists, Kitzinger argues, have avoided analysing the term, both because the discourse of academic psychology shies away from overtly political language and because of a 'profound ambivalence' about power within feminist theory in general. Kitzinger's lucid exploration of recent feminist accounts of power highlights the inadequacy of both positivist and subjectivist interpretations, where the former tends to construct women as powerless while the latter reverts to an internalized and sometimes utopian notion of 'Womanpower'. Kitzinger also considers Foucault's analysis as contributing valuably to interdisciplinary debate, although she is sceptical about the tendency of poststructuralist thought to turn our attention away from material realities.

Luce Irigaray's *Passions élémentaires*, first published in France in 1982, appeared this year in English translation as *Elemental Passions*. Irigaray describes the essay as 'fragments from a woman's voyage as she goes in search of her identity in love'. For the majority of the essay a female speaker addresses a male other, meditating on her desire, his expectations and limitations. The impossibility of escaping a maternal paradigm of relations is a dominant preoccupation: Irigaray suggests in the Foreword that the mother is a figure as transcendent to the man as his God, but that her divinity is forgotten as she is constructed as nature/earth. Throughout the essay (which is written in characteristically elliptical and fluid Irigarayan style), there is a sense of the woman straining to be released from constricting patterns, to imagine and represent new sexual identities and to attain 'her humanity and her transcendency'. Fundamental to this process, Irigaray suggests, is exploring the relations between women and redefining these apart from male/female relations. There are echoes throughout the essay of earlier Irigarayan perspectives, but *Elemental Passions* is nevertheless valuable as an imaginatively haunting and controversial meditation on sexual politics. While some feminist readers will find its dreamy and utopian formulations risible – 'And I was changed into a cloud' – the piece also asks hard and painful questions about amatory relations that are far from being resolved in feminist theory or practice.

Teresa Brennan's *The Interpretation of the Flesh: Freud and Femininity* is a major re-examination of the processes by which a 'feminine' identity is psychically established. Unlike many contemporary feminist theorists, Brennan accepts Freud's description of the characteristics of femininity as passivity, masochism, vanity, a weaker sense of justice, and so on, believing that a 'disabling femininity' exists and that it can affect both women and men. Brennan's meticulous re-readings of Freud on hysteria, repression, the ego and superego, masochism and penis-envy explore the construction of femininity by attending especially to the spatial and temporal models that underpin psychic formation. She challenges the notion of an energetically self-contained subject, redefining Freud's understanding of psychic economy and the drives and suggesting that intersubjective relations may be thought of in terms of energy. Thus throughout the study the questions of where, how and when psychic energy is directed are vital, for femininity is above all created (as Freud suggested) through a turning back or against the self, creating a disabling inertia and lack of a stable sense of identity. Brennan's line of argument attempts to sort out the confusions in Freud's writings as well as to steer a path through Kleinian object-relations and Lacanian perspectives, offering new ways of conceiving of the relation between psychical, physical and material realities with reference to feminine identity. The book is undoubtedly a significant and original contribution to current psychoanalytic debate: Brennan's argument is complex and manifold, but she is never less than lucid in exposition and careful in her conclusions. Her methodical and rigorous re-examination challenges recent valorization and mystification of the feminine and instead calls for further exploration of the 'pathology' of femininity.

In an attempt to increase the interdisciplinary content of *Signs: Journal of Women in Culture and Society*, the editors asked literary critic Judith Kegan Gardiner and sociologist Michèle Barrett to write review essays of the same books (including Jane Flax's *Thinking Fragments: Psychoanalysis, Feminism, and Postmodernism* (1990), Nancy Chodorow's *Feminism and Psychoanalytic Theory* (1989), Marianne Hirsch's *The Mother–Daughter Plot: Narrative, Psychoanalysis, Feminism* (1989), Elizabeth Abel's *Virginia Woolf and the Fictions of Psychoanalysis* (1989) and Jessica Benjamin's *The Bonds of Love: Psychoanalysis, Feminism, and the Problem of Domination* (1988)). Gardiner observes four major strands of current interest in feminist psychoanalytic studies: attention to the role of mothers and fathers, to sexuality and the body, to psychoanalytic dialogue and transference as models for other encounters, and to historical and cultural contexts. Barrett's analysis, by contrast, is based on her observations of three dominant trends: psychoanalytic fundamentalism based on drives and instincts, object-relations concerned with the interaction of the self with others, and psychoanalysis used as a tool for cultural interpretation. Barrett's essay is considerably more hard-hitting and tenacious than is Gardiner's, who tends to summarize the books under discussion rather than engage in a sustained analytical debate. Areas of agreement emerge, however, as both critics express ambivalence about the current psychoanalytic trend towards literary and cultural studies at the expense of wider social and intellectual concerns. For Gardiner, if psychoanalysis is to be useful to feminism, the boundaries between it and other disciplines such as sociology, economics and medicine must be breached. For Barrett, pressing psychosocial issues related to ethnicity, the resurgence of religious beliefs and the crisis in genetic parenting should be high on the psychoanalytic agenda. Barrett is also concerned that the therapeutic dimension of psychoanalysis is often ignored by feminists working in academia, again an indication of the tendency to divorce theory from practice. The two essays, 'Psychoanalysis and Feminism: An American Humanist's View' and 'Psychoanalysis and Feminism: A British Sociologist's View', appear in *Signs* (17:ii.437–66).

In *Theatre Journal* (43:iv.507–16), Marc Silverstein examines the relation of the female spectator to the stage in 'Body-Presence: Cixous's Phenomenology of Theatre', arguing that Cixous's writings on and for the theatre problematically maintain a metaphysics of presence that undermines her attempt to construct a new feminist theatre/spectator. Although this line of criticism of Cixous's metaphysical tendencies is fairly commonplace, it is rarely applied specifically to theatrical practice and to the special issues of representation and presence that occur therein. Silverstein's gender-conscious argument is carefully constructed and properly locates Cixous within the theatrical tradition of Artaud and experimental practitioners such as Grotowski. Pamela Banting's closely-argued and scrupulous essay, 'The Body as Pictogram: Rethinking Hélène Cixous's Écriture Féminine' (*Textual Practice* 6:ii.225–46), begins with a summary of recent feminist debate around French feminism and the charge of essentialism. Following in the footsteps of critics such as Diana Fuss and Margaret Whitford, Banting takes issue with the too-easy dismissal of Cixous on essentialist grounds. Banting is concerned with the relation between bodies and texts, with how they 'permeate one another's membranes' and how a 'mother tongue' might find its way to the page. To this end she rejects the poetics of representation (that banish the body) in favour of a poetics of translation drawn from Jakobson and Merleau-Ponty, among others. Reconceptualizing Cixous's project of *écriture féminine* in this way provides suggestive ways of reading the 'intersemiotic, interlingual and intralingual' relationships between the body and language that, according to Banting, move beyond the essentialism/anti-essentialism debate and beyond a spurious pluralism that merely masks essentialist assumptions. Banting's tenaciously argued essay contributes valuably to this ongoing and heated debate within feminist theory, as well as shifting focus to a different theoretical arena with reference to *écriture féminine*.

Karen A. McCauley's meticulous and suggestive essay, 'Lacan and Questions of Desire in Psychosis and Feminine Sexuality' (*Literature and Psychology* 37.47–62), explores the charged issue of the relationship between femininity and psychosis through a re-reading of Lacan's 1955–6 seminar. McCauley charts the correspondences between Lacan's interpretation of psychosis as presenting itself as the mystery of the Other and his conception of femininity as related to mystery and masquerade. While significant links emerge between the two, particularly with reference to language, McCauley is also keen to emphasize that psychosis and feminine sexuality are not interchangeable concepts in Lacan's thought but need to be interrogated in relation to his use of the concepts of the Other, the *point de capiton* and the Name of the Father. Although ultimately Lacan is criticized for failing to move beyond Freud's analysis of the relation between madness and the feminine, and for reverting to a romantic conception of woman as 'a type of psychotic externalization of absence and loss', McCauley concludes that new perspectives on desire may emerge if Lacan's early work on psychosis is juxtaposed with his later comments on feminine sexuality.

Georgia Johnston's 'Exploring Lack and Absence in the Body/ Text: Charlotte Perkins Gilman Prewriting Irigaray' reads *The Yellow Wallpaper* alongside Irigaray's theories of women's writing on the female body (*Women's Studies* 21.75–86). Gilman's text, argues Johnston, figures doubleness, multiplicity and reflection as it articulates its protest against contemporary psychological treatment of women. These strategies are interpreted as incorporating the hysteric into the text of the woman within patriarchy, thus creating a new and powerful self that 'merges with the linguistic self that perceives the absent/unimaginable self'. Gilman's novella is, of course, amenable to this kind of reading, yet Johnston's argument becomes more strained and contentious when she states that the woman writer must reverse herself from 'normal' to hysteric in order to escape patriarchal signifying practices.

In *Textualizing the Feminine: On the Limits of Genre* Shari Benstock explores the representation of the feminine in texts by considering not metaphoric or tropological practices so much as punctuation and grammar, believing that 'apostrophes, ellipses, footnotes, and certain epistolary forms, orthographical conventions, and alphabetic signifiers occupy a textual space of loss or oversight'. While Benstock does not propose that grammar or punctuation are inherently 'feminine', she aligns the textual space they occupy with the cultural space that is termed 'feminine' within poststructuralist theory. In readings of Joyce's *Finnegans Wake*, Woolf's *Three Guineas*, H.D.'s *Helen in Egypt* and Derrida's *The Post Card*, Benstock practises what she terms 'psychogrammanalysis', where textuality is read psychoanalytically and the psyche read textually. While Benstock's readings are scrupulous and inventive and her use of Lacan, Kristeva and Derrida is consistently interrogative rather than unquestioning, her study is nevertheless heavy-going at times. Paradoxically, Benstock's efforts to read the unreadable are thwarted by her use of a composite theoretical discourse (deconstructive/psychoanalytic) that sometimes produces the very effects she sets out to explore.

3. Feminism and Lesbianism

In her introduction to *New Lesbian Criticism*, Sally Munt discusses the 'anxiety' and the 'insecurities' evident not only in this commendable collection but in a significant number of lesbian studies published this year. Lesbian theorists, she says, 'are acting under a compulsion to tell the truth, to record, to evangelize, and to be politically correct' whilst simultaneously recognizing (if not wholeheartedly believing) that the 'I' of experience 'is now intellectually discredited as a voice'. Bonnie Zimmerman, in the chapter that follows, 'Lesbians Like This and Like That', describes this dilemma in relation to her 1991 study of lesbian fiction, *The Safe Sea of Women*. Pulled between 'the desire to affirm a historical lesbian collectivity' and the desire to 'destabilize . . . that identity by introducing the discourses of differences within', Zimmerman frankly admits that she could not satisfy either. The editorial decision to start *New Lesbian Criticism* with so much angst did not, perhaps, sufficiently take into account the difficulties faced by new lesbian students trying to get a foothold. However, what is being acknowledged is a complicated relationship between lesbian experience (the various implications of living as a lesbian, in public and in private) and the role of the theorist as an analyst of cultural experience. The demands of subjective presence (lesbianism) and 'objective' critical distance (theory) can and often do conflict. The irony of being included in this collection precisely because she *is* lesbian provides the starting-point for Reina Lewis's 'The Death of the Author and the Resurrection of the Dyke'. For students new to postmodernist thought, Lewis provides a clear explanation of the dangers of both 'the desire for an inflated sense of identification' and continued reinforcement of the hetero/homo binary opposition that locks us into eternal 'combat with patriarchal straightdom'. Aware of the hostility to poststructuralism and postmodernism expressed by lesbians who, not unreasonably, fear a patriarchal plot to erase lesbian presence yet again, Lewis, too, highlights the 'angst which emerges from trying to validate both the field and oneself in academia whilst retaining grass-roots support and involvement'.

The essays by Katie King and Anna Wilson, who take distinct and equally productive approaches to Audre Lorde's *Zami*, are notable for their angst-free, confident engagement with black and lesbian historical context. Angela Weir and Elizabeth Wilson reassess 1950s lesbian romantic fiction and butch/femme themes in the light of 1990s postmodernist thought (in which 'dusty answers have replaced former certainties and force us into a greater recognition of complexity') and conclude that this was a far more radical period in lesbian history than has hitherto been granted. Drawing on her own experience of having been brought up within a traditionalist Christian subculture, Gillian Spraggs offers considerable critical insight into the lesbian love story with 'Hell and the Mirror: A Reading of *Desert of the Heart*' and demonstrates, as does Hilary Hinds with her astute contextualization of the BBC dramatization of *Oranges Are Not the Only Fruit*, that lesbian success in the mainstream should always alert us to look again. Sonya Andermahr, who like Lewis rejects the confines of gender binarism, presents a forceful argument against the collapsing of the sexual and the political, while Lisa Henderson challenges 'feminist certainty in which some women seek to save others from themselves and their dubious sexualities' and suggests that *On Our Backs* and *Macho Sluts* can be read as both 'culturally transgressive' and 'sexually demystifying'. Being both provocative and accessible, these latter two essays would provide good starting-points for seminar discussion.

The careful separation of *Lesbian Theories, Gay Theories* in Diana Fuss's *Inside/Out*, with this subtitle, and Joseph Bristow's acknowledgement of the potentially controversial 'and' in *Sexual Sameness: Textual Differences in Lesbian and Gay Writing*, are confusing and even disingenuous given the commitment to the deconstruction of rigid gender and sexual identity categories, i.e. queer theory, evidenced throughout both collections. This said, the range of essays contained in each is impressive and a number will appeal to feminist readers not tempted by the Fool's free fall beyond the bounds of, albeit constructed, realities. Included here would be Patricia White's 'Female Spectator, Lesbian Spectre: *The Haunting*' and Michele Aina Barale's 'Below the Belt: (Un)Covering *The Well of Loneliness*' in *Inside/Out* and Liz Yorke's 'Constructing a Lesbian Poetic for Survival: Broumas, Rukeyser, H.D., Rich, Lorde' in *Sexual Sameness*. One of the most persistent difficulties with postmodernist thought is that it remains just that: thought. Despite the pleasures it undoubtedly offers and the sensation of freedom it evokes, it is hard to know what to do with it out on the street, in the Women's Studies classroom or when reading books such as *What a Lesbian Looks Like: Writings By Lesbians on their Lives and Lifestyles* (by the National Lesbian and Gay Survey). There is something appalling, too, about the way that theory can make lived experience appear so dull, so pedestrian, so unimaginative, so readable in a single sitting, and so expendable. Drawing on the mass-observational material of the National Lesbian and Gay Survey, this anthology includes thematically organized testimonies from more than fifty lesbians between the ages of twenty and sixty living in Britain. They speak about their identity formations, their 'coming out' experiences, first loves, communities, etc., and no two sets of experience are the same. In the absence of comment, though, never mind theory, the overwhelming impression is of being in an anonymous supermarket anaesthetized by piped music and fluorescent lights and over-burdened with carrier bags. It's certainly very difficult to relate these 'real-life' stories to the radical, transgressive, cutting-edge visions in the texts so far discussed, or, indeed, in Monique Wittig's *The Straight Mind and Other Essays*. These nine influential and eminently readable essays published during the 1980s and collected here for the first time, will be welcomed by many. The trick is to read them in an isolated space because the vision of the lesbian warrior free from the 'category of sex' that caught the imaginations of a generation of lesbian feminists has certainly not found its way into *What a Lesbian Looks Like*.

4. Feminism, Race and Empire

Third World Women and the Politics of Feminism edited by Mohanty, Russo and Torres is an excellent collection of essays

examining 'Third World' feminism. The contributors explain that
the collection originated in a conference initiated by Chandra
Mohanty in 1983 entitled 'Common Differences: Third World
Women and Feminist Perspectives'. The essays represent the aim of
the editors to analyse and map out the field of Third World
feminism. In her introduction Mohanty notes the difficulties
involved in defining Third World women and feminism. Mohanty
uses the concept of 'imagined community' to suggest potential alliances and collaborations across diverse boundaries, and alludes to
Benedict Anderson's idea of nation as 'horizontal comradeship'. She
adds that this concept is also useful for avoiding essentialist notions
of Third World feminist struggles, suggesting instead political and
cultural bases for alliance. She then provides a clear summary of
what Third World women's writings on feminism have consistently
focused on. Mohanty concludes this by noting that the major analytical difference between white Western liberal feminism and the
feminist politics of women of colour, in the United States, is 'the
contrast between a singular focus on gender as a basis for equal
rights and a focus on gender in relation to race and/or class as part
of a broader liberation struggle'. Mohanty observes that citizenship
and immigration laws are crucial to feminism because their principal
concern is with 'defining insiders and outsiders'. In this sense questions pertaining to the social agency of Third World women workers
is a particularly good area for feminist organizing.

The book is divided into four sections. The first one, 'Power,
Representation and Feminist Critique', discusses how 'Third World'
feminism has been articulated by contemporary Western commentaries. Mohanty, in 'Under Western Eyes: Feminist Scholarship and
Colonial Discourses', analyses the production of 'the' Third World
woman as 'singular monolithic subject in some recent (Western)
feminist texts'. Mohanty observes that the distinction between
Western feminist representation of women in the Third World and
Western feminist self-presentation corresponds to the distinction
made by some Marxists between the 'maintenance' function of the
housewife and the real 'productive' role of wage labour. Or, put
another way, to the difference asserted by some developmentalists in
the lesser production of 'raw' material as opposed to the 'real' productive activity of the First World. This, as Mohanty comments,
aids the construction of Third World women as a 'homogenous
powerless group'. She urges the need for 'careful, historically specific
generalizations responsive to complex realities'. Moreover, as she
points out, the notion of Third World women as forming a homo-

genous entity 'colonizes and appropriates the pluralities of the simultaneous location of different groups of women: it ultimately robs them of their historical and political *agency*'. In 'Violence in the Other Country: China as Crisis, Spectacle and Woman', Rey Chow discusses how the marginalization of the 'Middle' Kingdom to the 'Far' East makes us think of China as the 'other country'. Chow notes that China is studied as a spectacle for the West, with the two main spaces for Chinese studies of women occurring in the 'case' study and the historical 'cultural garden'. As Chow points out, the refusal to acknowledge the presence of forcible Westernization of the Chinese people has meant that 'even as it is inextricable from the daily experience of Asian peoples, the materiality of Westernization as an irreducible part of Asian modern self-consciousness remains unrecognized and inarticulate in the paradigms set down by China specialists'.

The second section of the book, entitled 'Public Policy, the State and Ideologies of Gender', begins with Jacqui Alexander's essay, 'Redrafting Morality: The Postcolonial State and the Sexual Offences Bill of Trinidad and Tobago'. In it, Alexander notes that in contemporary society morality has become an important mechanism for disciplining and regulating the social. Moreover, as she points out, 'the very identity and authority of the colonial project rested upon the racialization and sexualization of morality'. The relevance of this for feminism is, as Alexander emphasizes, clear: 'Morality is a feminist issue not only because women who are "wives" become the ground on which some very narrow definitions of womanhood are redrawn, but also because the formulation of morality is underwritten in fundamentally gendered terms assigning women to a subordinated position while invoking some higher religious or natural principles in order to do so.' In 'Building Politics from Personal Lives: Discussions on Sexuality Among Poor Women in Brazil', Carmen Barroso and Cristina Bruschini discuss how, since the Kennedy administration of the 1960s, there has been a concerted effort to link economic aid to Latin America with policies aimed at checking the so-called demographic explosion. As Barroso and Bruschini demonstrate, this has been on the whole unsuccessful, despite the support of the Brazilian ruling class. In 'Women in Jamaica's Urban Informal Economy: Insights from a Kingston Slum', Faye Harrison discusses the poverty that the West has inflicted upon the economies of the Third World. As Harrison points out, 'the problem of sexual inequality as it obtains in Jamaica today is integrally related to the broader processes of uneven development within the

Caribbean periphery of the world capitalist systems'. In the final essay of the section, Juanita Diaz-Cotto discusses the significance of the increasing number of female arrests in the United States since the 1960s. She shows how the available data contradict the argument that women are committing more violent crime and reflect instead a rise in economic crime. As Diaz-Cotto points out, this means that women in local jails are 'predominantly single, poor, and working class white or minority women under the age of thirty'.

The third section, 'National Liberation and Sexual Politics', starts with Angela Gilliam's discussion of 'Women's Equality and National Liberation'. In her essay, Gilliam contends that the consequences of 'sexualism' are that it endorses right-wing women and allows the Far Right to appropriate concerns about the family. Gilliam argues that 'global class', not sexuality, should be central to feminism. Moreover, sexualism is, she insists, part of bourgeois ideology, focusing on the individual rather than the collective. Ultimately, 'sexualism becomes the new elitism, the new expression of class struggle within the movement'. This charge is taken up in the next essay by Evelyne Accad, who discusses 'Sexuality and Sexual Politics [Conflicts and Contradictions for Contemporary Women in the Middle East]'. Unlike Gilliam, Accad maintains that there is a particular need to foreground sexuality in Third World feminism. She points out that nationalism has never served women well, with women being sent back to the kitchen after the independence wars in Algeria, Palestine and Iran. Moreover, Accad argues, a 'blending' of feminism and nationalism has never, in fact, been tried out, 'since sexuality has never been conceptualized as being at the centre of the problems in the Middle East'. Her observation that it is, all too often, Marxist women speaking in the name of '*all* third world women' who are the ones to pronounce upon the primary importance of economic issues is, I would agree, a valid point. However, I am less convinced by her suggestion that what is needed is nationalism without sexism. Accad's vision of a nationalism that could 'unite all the various factions fighting each other under a common aim and belief' seems unlikely, given the reliance of a conception of outsiders in a nationalist ethos. In 'Gender and Islamic Fundamentalism [Feminist Politics in Iran]', Nayereh Tohidi provides a lucid and comprehensive criticism of the repression of women in Iran following the 1979 Iranian revolution. Tohidi combines her historical account of the revolution and its aftermath with an analysis of why so many Iranian women took part in the struggle. She documents how Western imperialism and Islamic culture created the right conditions for fundamentalism. As she observes, 'Fundamentalists in countries such as Iran, Lebanon, Morocco and Pakistan gain control by channeling people's frustration and anger into a familiar language, ideology, and value system.' Moreover, as she concludes, the Islamic fundamentalist revival in the Middle East redirects and divides people, building a strong and stable 'barrier against communism'.

The final section of the book is entitled 'Race, Identity and Feminist Struggles'. Lourdes Torres begins the section with her essay, 'The Construction of the Self in US Latin Autobiographies'. Torres discusses texts by women of colour and demonstrates how they are characterized by a radical, innovative mixture of genres that reflects the need for women of colour to find new forms of expression. Nellie Wong follows this with a call for the common concerns of socialism and feminism. The anthology closes with a gesture towards the need for alliances and 'community' set out in the introduction. Ann Russo, in 'We Cannot Live Our Lives: White Women, Antiracism and Feminism', signals her agreement with bell hooks that there is a need for an analysis of 'white supremacy' alongside discussions of racism.

Women and Islam: An Historical and Theological Enquiry by Fatima Mernissi is a detailed historical challenge to readings of Islamic culture. Mernissi is chiefly concerned to reinterpret the teachings of the Koran and 'to recapture some of the wonderful and beautiful moments in the first Muslim city in the world'. She is meticulous, but the text is a little repetitive and quite heavy reading. The consciously epic narrative style also tends to homogenize 'the' Muslim mind and imagination in order to authorize this narrative voice. *Slave Women in Caribbean Society 1650–1838*, by Barbara Bush, is a competent study of slave women. As Bush comments, it is a subject that remains largely unexplored. Bush, like hooks, points to the ongoing need for an understanding of slavery, since women are still burdened by a legacy of destructive stereotypes. The text is full of detailed and interesting historical evidence of the lives of slaves. Bush is concerned to excavate between the statements of the abolitionists and the plantation owners to find a more 'authentic' history. As she says, 'the abolitionist image of the black woman as a potentially "good" Christian wife was no less unrealistic than portrayals of her as a fallen woman'. However, in doing this, Bush tends towards a notion that somewhere in between these two conflicting viewpoints we are likely to find the truth. This has serious consequences for her overall study, as it seems that, at times, the specific experiences of slavery are being subordinated to a detached and 'neutral' observer who, for that reason, is more likely to uncover the 'truth'. In this respect, a wholesale critical rejection of slavery is liable to miss the complexity of it, providing the final insult to slave experience: 'Slave society was, in effect, a dynamic and complex entity which had a positive and creative identity.' More problematically, when Bush discusses the question of slavery and punishment it leads her to conclude that the 'Middle' ground must possess the truth. Thus, Bush cites the observations of Sir Hans Sloane, 'a relatively detached observer' who wrote that the floggings and torture of slaves 'were sometimes merited by the Blacks, who are a very perverse Generation of people, and though they appear harsh, yet are scarce equal to some of their crimes'. Given that slavery is an influential part of contemporary race relations, 'we' should be particularly careful as to how 'we' approach, and use, historical material.

Refusing Holy Orders, a collection of essays edited by Gita Sahgal and Nira Yuval-Davis, is mainly written by members of Women Against Fundamentalism and is dedicated to its cause. The editors describe the features common to all fundamentalist religious movements as 'one, that they claim their version of religion to be the only true one, and feel threatened by pluralist systems of thought; two, that they use political means to impose their version of the truth on all members of their religion'. The contributors (Sara Maitland, Elaine Foster, Ann Rossiter, Yasmin Ali, Saeeda Khanum, Maryam Poya) reflect on the diversity of 'Holy Orders' in Britain – Christian, Jewish, Muslim, Hindu – and their significance in the lives of women. Nupur Chaudhuri and Margaret Strobel's *Western Women and Imperialism: Complicity and Resistance* is a long-overdue engagement with colonial discourse and feminism. The editors state: 'Recent colonial nostalgia is notable in its efforts to co-opt feminist consciousness and activism. In an increasingly conservative political climate, it is hardly surprising to find feminism manifested as an interest in famous "heroic" white women in colonial settings.' The book aims to overturn this tendency to pose women as saintly figures in the colonial discourses. It contains excellent essays on women's travel writing and literary writing, women and moral crusades within the empire, women missionaries, and women and racism.

In *When the Moon Waxes Red*, Trinh T. Minh-ha provides an acute and stimulating reappraisal of the current debates centring around 'difference' and the 'Other'. Minh-ha produces a lucid challenge to discussions of difference which fail to perform a critical role on their own implicit position as not 'Other'. Her crucial point is that we should be challenging the Western context of rationality and knowledge that permits marginality an existence that is wholly dependent on the assumption that there is a unified central referent. As Minh-ha comments, 'The center itself is marginal . . . marginality is the condition of the center.' In her introduction, she notes that 'the function of any ideology in power is to represent the world positively unified'. It is this that she takes to task, and attempts to unravel, in her book. Using the Moon as a starting-point, Minh-Ha points out that it, like the colonized 'Other', is characterized by its lack of a fixed territory, and it is precisely this that gives it its trans-formative power. As she emphasizes, the task in hand is to confront 'the limits of centralized conscious knowledge'. Throughout the text, she reassesses imagination and beauty within their traditional place in Western aesthetics. Minh-ha argues that it is imagination that should be valued for its ability to transcend a merely oppositional way of thinking. For as she points out, if a previously powerless group attains power and proceeds to represent its concerns as a unified entity, then this merely reiterates the ideology of the powerful. Instead, Minh-ha asks: 'How can one recreate without re-circulating domination?' Moreover, she stresses that the closure that takes place in the event of a shift in power relations could be viewed more productively as a way 'of letting the work go rather than sealing it off'. Minh-ha turns on its head the discussions of margin-ality as only being of pressing concern to the marginal themselves, noting that 'the war of borders is a war waged by the West on a global scale to preserve its values'. In chapter 2, she explores discus-sions of the genre of documentary in order to emphasize how inade-quate notions of authenticity are. As she points out, it is significant that it is through genres such as the documentary that the masses and the indigenous subjects of anthropological films are *produced* as 'real' subjects: 'The silent common people – those who "have never expressed themselves" unless they are given the opportunity to voice their thoughts by the ones who come to redeem them – are con-stantly summoned to signify the real world.' The artificial eye of the camera corresponds to the all-knowing Western eye, both of which should be challenged, no matter how 'truthful' the resulting view is said to be: 'The tyranny of the camera goes unchallenged.' Minh-ha's objection to anthropological and documentary 'evidence' of how 'real' lives are lived is that representation *cannot* demonstrate reality as an objective truth: 'Society cannot be experienced as objective and fully constituted in its order; rather only as incessantly recomposed of diverging forces wherein the war of interpretations reigns.' Moreover, as she comments, the underlying desire to present experience in a coherent form expresses a trait that 'intimately belongs to the man of coercive power' who has no time for difference or the unfamiliar. Minh-ha rejects the idea of problematizing 'differences', suggesting instead that 'perhaps life would appear less agonizing when decentralization (and de-centering) are no longer understood as chaos or absence – the opposite of presence – but as a marvelous expansion, a multiplicity of independent centers'. In the earlier chapters of the book she provides examples and arguments that are intended to show that marginality is redundant as a critical term unless it is discussed alongside the illusory centrality that reflects mainstream Western thought. She stresses that 'marginality' should not remain within the oppressive parameters of Western philosophical knowledge systems. In the later chapters of the book, she challenges the regular equation that is made between difference and conflict, showing how this sometimes suppresses the creative and positive traits within difference. Minh-ha relates how her films are often criticized for their lack of conflict. This charge, she comments, reflects the concerns of Western cultural critics to retain explorations and representations of 'difference' within 'their' own designated boundaries: 'Conflicts in Western contexts often serve to define identities. My suggestion to this so called lack is: let difference replace conflict.' Noting the current 'centrality' of discussions of racial and sexual 'Otherness', Minh-ha urges her readers not to focus solely on 'the' difference as a fixed and identifiable entity but to pay attention to the ongoing state of becoming, of moving between identities and positions. She describes her own sense of self in these terms: 'the becoming Asian-American affirms itself at once as a transient and constant state: one is born over and over again as hyphen rather than as fixed entity'.

Laura Donaldson in *Decolonising Feminisms: Race, Gender and Empire-Building* performs feminist readings of classic and contemporary film and literary texts. Donaldson, like Minh-ha, locates the radical interpretation of representations as the proper ground for feminist critical work. Like Minh-ha, she wants to avoid the imperialism that lies within the expectation of recovering 'a' Truth. In this sense, her text 'attempts to counter feminism's imperialist tendency to dive deep and surface with a single hermeneutic truth'. It is through this practice that Donaldson hopes to 'empower the postcolonial reader'. In this sense, Miranda and Caliban should be viewed as both oppressed and oppressive subjects within colonialism and patriarchy. Throughout her discussion, Donaldson draws her readers' attention to the different sites in which this complexity is not recognized. Thus Spivak is quick to miss the effects of colonialism upon the white woman, and Gilbert and Gubar, from a white perspective, set off on the regressive journey towards 'an' authentic voice. Donaldson provides excellent readings of *The King and I* and *Uncle Tom's Cabin*. In chapter 3, she tackles the question of 'context' and 'textuality', and argues that despite the emphasis that critics, such as Elaine Showalter, place upon history and context, it remains an irony that so much traditional feminist theory 'seems only too little aware of history'. Donaldson argues that the subordination of context to text is essentially a 'con' which 'distorts the relationship of a literary work to its sociocultural production'. Instead, she argues, there is a need for readings that are contextual, textual, ideological and semiotic. In keeping with her attempt to produce such a reading, Donaldson in chapter 4 emphasizes the importance of recognizing that discourse cannot be viewed either as 'a simple reflection of an economic base' or as 'only fictional constructs of the bourgeois imagination'. She challenges this with a reading of the film *We of the Never-Never* and its textual source, which was a year from Mrs Aeneas Gunn's diary of life in the Australian outback. Donaldson's reading explores beyond oppositions to look also at 'the multiplicity of positions and contradictions of responses generated by the communicative interaction of the bush'.

Chapter 5 is concerned to demonstrate how films such as *A Passage to India* preserve the omnipotence of the Western eye: 'We are never allowed to perceive India through non-Western eyes.' In chapter 6 Donaldson draws upon Zora Neale Hurston to explore notions of identity. Hurston's antipathy towards 'race pride' was, as Donaldson elaborates, drawn from her distrust of the concerns of any form of nationalism. She discusses in particular *Moses, Man of the Mountain*, written by Hurston in 1939, which reformulated Moses as someone who rejected all forms of domination. Donaldson contrasts this portrayal with the pan-Africanism of Marcus Garvey, himself known as the 'black' Moses. However, as Donaldson comments, such radical pluralism is not an easy position; a point ably expressed by Karen McCarthy: 'Radical pluralism is not an easy stance toward the world, for there is no place to go "home" when the crises of one's life demand such security before anything else.' Chapter 7 explores 'the postmodernist constructs of Woman' and concludes that there is a worrying similarity of ' "Woman" within postmodernism to women as commodities within capitalist patriarchy'. Donaldson points to the 'indivisible tie binding women as social commodities to "women" as discursive commodity' and contends that 'the separation of natural and social interaction . . . is the distinguishing characteristic of the postmodernist "Woman"'. She emphasizes that we must ensure that women's lives are not lost in postmodernist scepticism, whilst at the same time insisting upon the 'production of contradictory points of identification, an elsewhere of vision'. She concludes with the advice that feminism 'must accomplish an extremely difficult task; for it must discern the experiential connections that surely exist among women and simultaneously refuse to privilege any particular connection as that which subsumes the rest'. The problem with Donaldson's argument, I would suggest, lies in a certain mystification of the world picture. Her constant reminders that we must not privilege any one oppression over another because it then distorts the world picture erases the very anger and resistance of oppressed and colonized people *to* that world picture. This is not to suggest that *only* people of colour or gay people or workers are *really* oppressed but to suggest rather that an aspect of articulating oppression lies in targeting its various sources and practices. The question then becomes, 'in what ways are oppressed people to articulate their oppression without risking the charge of "privileging" their oppression over others?'. Whilst I would not question the need for a view of identity as a fluid and at times interchangeable form, I would suggest that there is a problem when such discussions begin to downplay the different effects of different oppressions.

This is, I would argue, also of relevance to Jane Gallop's *Around 1981: Academic Feminist Literary Theory*, in which 'the Other' (in this case the lesbian) is both redefined as not really other, because after all the centre is only central because it has the economic and cultural power to look that way, and, less productively, robbed of her specific voice: 'Are lesbian critics truly faced with "a special question" or are lesbians, precisely in as much as they are located at the point where certainty hesitates, forced to articulate questions crucial for us all that the enfranchised may be allowed to overlook?' I would add that a crucial aspect of the question is how and in what way are the enfranchised in a position to overlook this question? There is a misleading sense here that the question *applies* in the same way to women once we have recognized that it is important for us all. The fact that the enfranchisee did not find it a special question is left unremarked upon. The mistrust that women of

colour may have when confronting such demonstrations of incorporating difference and resisting coherence becomes unsurprising.
For Gallop is soon informing 'us' that she has undermined coherence by including 'difference', namely by supplementing her discussion of American and British feminist theory with French feminists
such as Hélène Cixous. This is, 'we' are to believe, a case of 'inter-
nationalism'. However, it is Gallop's discussion of 'academic' and
'popular' culture that raises the most serious questions. Gallop
asserts that since 1975 the general path of feminist criticism has been
'dodging, on the one hand, the great sexist writer and, on the other,
the popular woman writer . . . feminist critics either demonstrate
that a certain great male writer is not sexist or establish that a
certain woman writer relegated to "popular" status is in fact an
artist'. She concludes that 'the contradiction between feminism and
(academic) criticism can also be found as a contradiction within
feminism. The feminist identifies with other women but also struggles to rise above the lot of women. Feminism both desires superior
women and celebrates the common woman.' This raises a number of
problems: is feminism so easily identifiable? Is feminism 'in general'
preoccupied with great women? It is interesting that 'superior'
women are not juxtaposed with, as we might expect, 'inferior'
women, but 'the lot of women'. Gallop is in effect not voicing a
complex contradiction but an assumption that most women by
virtue of their 'lot' *are* inferior to a few individual talents. And
finally, since when did 'feminism' desire 'superior' women? I would
not read this as a problem for feminism but as an arguable assumption about 'it'.

The feminism of the 1970s, Gallop continues, was interested in
role-models, which are, she argues, unproductive. We should instead
follow the advice of Lillian Robinson: 'it is not role-models we need
so much as a mass movement, not celebration of individual struggle
. . . so much as recognition that we are all heroes'. I would counter
that perhaps we are *not* all heroes. Robinson endorses a particular
view of 'mass movement' as being the sum total of individual
heroes. This does little to displace the relevance of individual heroes
as objects of study. Instead, it retains a prioritization of concepts
such as heroes and geniuses that merely makes a concern with
human society more difficult to substantiate. Gallop's concluding
assertion effectively restores 'common-sense' to the whole complicated dilemma: 'Whether in some ideal superior version of feminism
"serious" feminists would completely shun "hero-worshipping", in
the real, "popular" form that feminism is usually found, we tend to

celebrate exceptional individual women.' What interests me about Gallop's argument, apart from its obvious questionability, is the way in which the reasons for 'feminism's concentration upon individual women' are displaced from the critical arena into the popular one. I have emphasized these points precisely because they occur in a text which Gallop assumes to be reflecting the innovative effects of the debates centring around difference and otherness. Thus Gallop cites Spivak as uttering an impulse she is confident she shares: 'However unfeasible and inefficient it may sound, I see no way to avoid insisting that there has to be a simultaneous other focus: not merely who am I? but who is the other woman?'

It is precisely the ease with which discussions of difference can take place that worries bell hooks. In *Black Looks: Race and Representation*, as in her earlier work, hooks suggests that a vital way forward lies in whites challenging their own positions in such interrogations of racial 'difference'. There is, as hooks emphasizes, both a need for blacks to intervene in the controlling systems of representation and an equally pressing need for an interrogation by whites of 'whiteness'. Like Minh-ha, hooks is not about to welcome interest in the 'Other' without first analysing in what ways the 'Other' risks remaining the object of study for Western scholarship. In her essay 'Eating the Other', hooks comments that 'the contemporary crises of identity in the west, especially as experienced by white youth, are eased when the "primitive" is recouped *via* a focus on diversity and pluralism which suggests the Other can provide life-sustaining alternatives'. Moreover, for hooks, whilst the complexity of identity offers productive ways of rearticulating social and political relations, concepts such as 'home' and black nationalism are not so easy to discard. As she points out, the current contempt for black nationalism fails to recognize that it is 'more a gesture of powerlessness than a sign of critical resistance'. hooks herself, by constantly refusing to give up on the sanctity of black community and 'home', demonstrates the fear evoked by glib discussions of how 'we' should now move beyond essentialism and identity politics to a more healthy and creative pluralism. Whilst I would certainly question her tendency to unify 'the' black community, I would not query her concern that 'cultural, ethnic, and racial differences will be continually commodified and offered up as new dishes to enhance the white palate – that the Other will be eaten, consumed and forgotten'. The remaining essays collected in the book discuss relations between black women and representations of the black female body. In particular, hooks provides an acute and entertain-

ing discussion of white appropriation and exploitation of 'black-
ness', most notably in her essay 'Madonna' and in her discussion of
Jennie Livingstone's film *Is Paris Burning?* hooks also digs deeper
into the stereotyping of black men and produces evidence to substantiate her claim that 'black sex roles and particularly the role of
men have been more complex and problematized in black life than
is believed'.

5. Feminist Readings of Literatures of the Past

Ros Ballaster, in *Seductive Forms: Women's Amatory Fiction from
1684 to 1740*, condenses into 200 pages a discussion of the strengths
and shortcomings of modern theories of the novel's genesis, as well
as overviews of both the seventeenth-century French roots of eighteenth-century British erotic fiction and modern arguments concerning women's reading of romances. She includes some stimulating
analyses, drawing mainly on psychoanalytic models, of erotic fiction
by Aphra Behn, Eliza Haywood and Delariviere Manley. *Seductive
Forms* is written concisely and is stimulating to read, both for its
suggestions about the connections between party-political discourse
and the representation of seduction, and for its closely demonstrated
challenges to the schematizing tendencies of theoretical and literary-
historical accounts of the genre.

In *Ventriloquized Voices: Feminist Theory and English Renaissance
Texts*, Elizabeth D. Harvey examines 'transvestite ventriloquism', or
the use of the feminine voice by early modern male authors such as
Spenser and Donne. The centrality of the trope of voice in the
Renaissance is yoked by Harvey to recent debates within feminism
and poststructuralism concerning voice, writing and femininity;
indeed, she constantly moves between period considerations and discussions of current feminist theory in a self-conscious 'doubling'.
Thus in one of two chapters focusing on hysteria, Harvey considers
Donne's *Anniversaries* alongside Kristeva's 'Stabat Mater', while in
another concerned principally with literary property she juxtaposes
Irigaray's 'When Our Lips Speak Together' with Donne's 'Sappho
to Philaenis'. Harvey's model is not dualistic, however, for throughout she emphasizes the intertextual, dynamic relations between early
modern, classical and late twentieth-century texts, emphasizing
simultaneously the importance of historically contextualized
readings. Harvey's study is undoubtedly a valuable contribution to
Renaissance studies, notable for its subtle and lucid readings of

early modern texts, but it also contains deft analyses of writings such as Cixous and Clement's *Newly Born Woman*, illustrating how far such revisionist texts draw upon, disrupt and have continuities with early modern conceptions of femininity.

Gender and Discourse in Victorian Literature and Art is a collection of original essays edited by Antony H. Harrison and Beverly Taylor. The essays are organized into three sections related to Victorian poetry, fiction and art, and are of a high standard overall. Deirdre David's 'Children of Empire: Victorian Imperialism and Sexual Politics in Dickens and Kipling' is one of the best, examining the representation of Quilp in Dickens's *The Old Curiosity Shop* with reference to mid-century constructions of the 'savage'. David illustrates how insidious is Dickens's characterization, and constrasts this effectively, though unusually, with Kipling's *Kim*, a novel that clearly concerns itself with imperialism. David's energetic and highly readable essay exemplifies how imperialist assumptions inform and are reproduced in fiction that is ostensibly not concerned with them, and contributes valuably to the postcolonial re-reading of nineteenth-century literature. The essays on Victorian women artists are also important: their inclusion in this collection marks the increasing recognition of the interdependence of literature and art in the period (a relationship the Victorians took for granted, but which twentieth-century scholars have often ignored). Susan P. Casteras's '"The Necessity of a Name": Portrayals and Betrayals of Victorian Women Artists' illustrates the difficulties faced by women artists in all aspects of their practice and looks also at the representation of the woman artist by male and female painters of the period. The prejudices familiar in literary circles are even more in evidence in artistic spheres: Casteras ends her essay with two case-studies, of the mid-century painters Emily Mary Osborn and Florence Caxton, discussing their sometimes revisionist, sometimes conformist work with sensitivity and rigour. Late nineteenth-century sculpture is the subject of George P. Landow's essay on 'Margaret M. Giles's *Hero* and the Sublime Female Nude', which argues quite persuasively that Giles's sculpture revises conventional conceptions of the female body. Landow also discusses the boom in the number of women sculptors in the 1890s, the result of changes in technique as clay modelling replaced stone carving as the dominant practice in sculpture. Again, these essays show how much more work needs to be done on nineteenth-century women; despite years of feminist research, the surface has only been scratched.

More familiar territory is covered in other essays in the book.

Elizabeth Langland's 'The Voicing of Feminine Desire in Anne
Brontë's *The Tenant of Wildfell Hall*' uses Barthes to read the narrative structure of the novel and to argue effectively that the text is
an important representation of feminine desire in which the 'fallen
woman . . . becomes the paragon, the exemplum'. Fallen women are
also the subject of Diane D'Amico's well-researched essay 'Equal
Before God: Christina Rossetti and the Fallen Women of Highgate
Penitentiary', which details more precisely than ever before the
nature of Rossetti's involvement with fallen women at the time of
writing *Goblin Market* and many other poems dealing with untrust-
worthy men and the problem of female sexuality. A disappointing
essay on sexuality is Beverly Taylor's ' "School-Miss Alfred" and
"Materfamilias": Female Sexuality and Poetic Voice in *The Princess*
and *Aurora Leigh*', which contrasts the poems but tends to smooth
over rather than throw into relief the ideological problems of both
texts. Altogether, though, the collection is a good one, confirming
the absolutely central position of gender-based readings in Victorian
studies.

Sheila Stowell's *A Stage of Their Own: Feminist Playwrights of the
Suffrage Era* deals with 'agitprop' drama produced by members of
the Women Writers' Suffrage League (WWSL) and the Actresses'
Franchise League (AFL), c.1907–14. The book looks at works
produced by a group of writers/actresses – Elizabeth Robins, Cicely
Hamilton, Elizabeth Baker and Githa Sowerby, each one having a
chapter's worth of discussion – but there is also an additional
chapter devoted to a more generalized consideration of 'suffrage
drama'. Combining biographical details with an extremely accessible
form of literary criticism, Stowell's text is of value to undergraduates and postgraduates alike, offering a 'descriptive' rather
than theoretical analysis of suffrage drama. At the same time, the
book also considers such things as contemporary critical reviews and
publishing constraints imposed upon the writers. *A Stage of Their
Own* charts the iconoclastic effect that the WWSL and AFL movements had upon avant-garde theatre, making crucial links between
texts and historical specificity. Moreover, it is a text that teaches
feminists in the 1990s about the problems and politics faced by
women at the turn of the century. As Stowell argues, 'There is no
doubt that suffrage drama was written as part of a consciously
organized scheme to propagate political doctrine and advocate social
and cultural changes which would contribute to the dismantling of a
system based upon patriarchal oppression. To that extent, it is una-
bashedly feminist propaganda, and anticipates in some remarkable

ways the self-consciously "women's theatre" that emerged in the
1960s.' Whilst *A Stage of Their Own* could have been improved by a
more thorough problematization of 'differences' between the disparate suffrage movements – NUWSS and WSPU – it is a welcome
addition to an increasing academic interest in *fin de siècle* feminist
activism and writing.

6. Feminism and Representation

Sexuality, the Female Gaze and the Arts, edited by Ronald Dotterer
and Susan Bowers, consists of thirteen (shortish) essays culled from
presentations at a 1988 conference, and they address feminist issues
across a range of media and cultural and historical contexts: topics
go from classical myth (Ovid's Echo and Narcissus) to contemporary myth (Seidelman's Madonna). The opening essay is by
Jane Augustine: 'Bisexuality in Hélène Cixous, Virginia Woolf, and
H.D.: An Aspect of L'Ecriture Féminine'. This offers a brief
acknowledgement of the three women's bisexuality and the identification in their writing of a 'mythic twin' motif linked to their erotic
preferences; this remains undeveloped beyond very briefly sketching
out the idea in relation to H.D.'s *Helen in Egypt* and Woolf's
Orlando. Susan Bowers, in 'The Witch's Garden: The Feminist Grotesque', invokes Elaine Showalter's phrase 'the female wild zone',
Cixous's Medusa, and Kristeva's term 'the abject', not to forget
Bakhtin's Rabelais, to rehearse some useful (but familiar) observations on the feminist grotesque in relation to women's poetry
(mainly that of Anne Sexton and Cynthia Macdonald). A similar
critical arsenal (plus Laura Mulvey) is raided by Cynthia J. Fuchs,
in 'Desperately Seeking a Subject: Postmodern Sexuality, Seidelman,
and Madonna', to identify for us Seidelman's subversive cinematic
technique: masquerade, multi-voiced discourse, the shift from male
gaze to female *gazing*; but an account of the contribution made by
'Susan/Madonna's body-text' to the filmic 'collapse of subjectivity
and objectivity' seems not so much 'enabling', as it might have been
in a 1988 conference paper, but dull and unconvincing in print in
the 1990s. Similar fare is offered by Jennifer M. Green in 'Subject,
Object, Camera: Photographing Women in *The Unbearable Light-
ness of Being*', where it is provocatively argued that a scene from the
novel in which a man's wife and mistress photograph each other is
not so much male fantasy as 'a triumph of female bonding'; the
ramifications of this subversive female gaze are then explored in a

discussion of the doubly perilous (i.e. even more open to charges of voyeurism) film version of the scene. Some tricky critical manoeuvres are attempted in order to persuade us of an empowering feminist reading of novel and film. A more persuasive argument and helpful analysis comes from Debra Humphreys's comparison of two popular Hollywood films in 'The Discursive Construction of Women's Sexuality and Madness in Mainstream Cinema'. She compares the workings of patriarchal ideology in *Gaslight* (1940) and *Fatal Attraction* (1987). Mary Anne Schofield's 'Romance Subversion: Eighteenth Century Feminine Fiction' is an engaging discussion of women writers' strategies in the manipulation of romance-narrative conventions: she examines as 'euphoric' and 'dysphoric' texts Sarah Fielding's *The Cry* (1754), Charlotte Lennox's *The Female Quixote*, and a number of Eliza Haywood's works. Other essays discuss quests for personal identity/freedom in Old French literature, women in conflict in nineteenth-century German writing, the position of the feminine in Spanish romantic theatre, and images of the double in American women's poetry.

Segal and McIntosh's provocative survey of British, Australian and American feminist thought on pornography and sexuality, *Sex Exposed*, offers a range of perspectives: the political controversies of pro- and anti-censorship feminism; women's role in the sex industry; and women's use of pornography. The explosive issue of lesbian-feminist pornography is considered; pornographic portrayals and psychoanalytic accounts of female and male orgasms are investigated; there are also readings of Andrea Dworkin's novel, Robert Mapplethorpe's photographs and Mae West's films. Contributors include Elizabeth Cowie, Harriet Gilbert, Robin Gorna, Jane Mills, Mandy Merck, Lynda Nead, Carol Smart, Carol Vance, Linda Williams and Elizabeth Wilson.

Imagining Women by Frances Bonner et al. is the last in a series of four books published as a component of an Open University course, *Issues in Women's Studies* (the other three address women and knowledge, women and society, women and science and technology), but it also stands outside this context as a highly useful and informative introduction (and source book) to the field of women and cultural representation, helpfully rehearsing established arguments as well as pushing the debate further. It is organized into six chapters, each of which includes and introduces a number of key articles: chapter 1 introduces the main concerns of the book, such as representation, the gaze, women's language and so on; chapter 2 addresses literary representations and subjectivity, focusing on

women as writers, readers and critics, and ranges from Elaine
Showalter on the feminist critical revolution to Alicia Ostriker on
motherhood and poetry to Wendy Webster on British working-class
women's autobiography; chapter 3 looks at the visual arts and
addresses issues such as the politics of the gaze, black women's art,
and the status and history of women's artistic productivity (there are
several wonderful colour and black-and-white plates); chapter 4
examines popular television and film in relation to audience
position, representations of black female sexuality, women in soap
operas and game shows; chapter 5 addresses pornography, censorship and the possibility of feminist erotica; chapter 6 addresses
women and comedy. The book concludes with Alice Walker's well-
known essay, 'In Search of our Mothers' Gardens', which the
editors, somewhat paradoxically (and preciously), point out 'has not
been "situated" with editorial remarks, but rather stands on its
own'. Nevertheless, challenging and moving, it is a fitting coda to
this excellent study.

*Images of the Self as Female: The Achievement of Women Artists
in Re-envisioning Feminine Identity*, edited by Kathryn N. Benzel and
Lauren Pringle De La Vars, is a collection of essays, appreciations
and personal accounts dealing with the relationship between women
artists and the creation of a female self through art. The Introduction to the collection, a piece by Estella Lauter entitled 'Revisioning
the Self as Female: A Collaborative Project', sets the tone for an
understanding of the question of the creation and affirmation of self
through art upon which the rest of the essays in the collection are
implicitly based. That individual women have created an art which
articulates and works through this concern and challenge is the main
premise of Lauter's essay and of the collection as a whole. To
recognize, appreciate and celebrate these individual efforts, furthermore, presupposes a collective project of revaluation of women's art
which Lauter defines as 'the enterprise of re-envisioning woman as
subject and not as the other in cultural discourse'. In this introductory piece, Lauter asks the crucial questions: 'What is it like to
imagine a self in a culture whose dominant images portray one as
selfless . . .?', 'How does a being who has been excluded from
agency in most spheres of a culture gain enough leverage in that
culture to see herself as she is, not simply as she is expected to
be . . .?' These are necessary questions which may be answered in a
variety of ways – indeed, the aim of this collection is to illustrate
and pay tribute to this variety – but they do ultimately depend on a
concept of self or selfhood which is not adequately defined. Lauter

does seem to be aware of the complexity of the issue and she does
point out that this is not a static and transcendent concept:
'selfhood may be more process than product, dependent even for its
partial realization on successful engagement with the available
cultural opinions for conceptualizing it'. What is not offered,
however, is a theoretical framework upon which an understanding
of such a process of conceptualization depends.

The absence of a clear theoretical and critical perspective marks
the collection as a whole, making both selection criteria and the
splitting into sections of the material included seem arbitrary and
vague. The essays themselves are uneven in quality and focus, with
the single cohesive element being the authors' recurring references to
Lauter's introductory remarks. Although this is an inevitable structural weakness which any collection of essays on such a broad
subject would risk, the lack of a distinct argumentative thread in
this particular collective endeavour makes its table of contents look
too open-ended and directionless. The titles of the five parts thus
sound repetitive and unclear in intent: 'Uncovering a Woman's Perspective' includes an essay by Lauren Pringle De La Vars on the
appropriation by men and male critics of women's art, Gordon J.
De La Vars's essay on the life and art of Clara Schumann and a
discussion of the 'Necessary Dichotomy' between 'actress' and 'star'
in Hollywood by Victoria Amador. While this last essay seems to fit
the spirit of this project awkwardly (if at all), it is also the one
which most vividly illustrates the lack of a critical perspective from
which the collection suffers. When Amador concludes that '[w]e
must acknowledge above all as feminists, as scholars, as filmgoers,
that while strides have been made in moving images of women
toward positive reflections of empowerment, we still have far to go',
she gestures towards a form of cultural critique without having
examined the problem (or paradox) of discussing the images
churned out by Hollywood as if they are in some way 'accurate'
representations of a female self. Surely an analysis and a critique of
the culture industry that Hollywood dominates and perpetuates is in
order before one can assume that there are elements there of truth
about women's lives or selves that can be redeemed. Part 2 ('Reading Women's Verbal Imagery') deals with women writers (Elizabeth
Barrett Browning, Willa Cather, Marianne Moore and black women
artists), part 3 with women artists/painters, part 4 with women
artists and representation of domestic roles, and part 5 with contemporary and personal accounts of the question of 'Reconstructing
Self in Art'. This includes a panel discussion, a prose poem and a

short manifesto-like statement by two contemporary women artists followed by illustrations of their collaborative work. There is something for everyone in this arbitrary collection of material. The randomness of the selection makes for casual and easy reading with the odd moment of critical insight and some useful information about women artists whose work is very rarely discussed by the academic establishment. On the whole, however, the very important question which this collection claims to address remains unanswered and only partially illuminated. The interrelation of woman, selfhood, art and culture remains in the end unexamined and no theoretical possibility is offered for the formulation of a cultural critique. It is as if the construction (and re-envisioning) of a concept of female selfhood through art and in culture happens by osmosis, with its critical potential lying merely on the assumption of a community of sympathetic and sensitized subjects. This is not to trivialize the idea (and necessity) of a 'collaborative project', but it seems to me that the focus of such a project needs to be clearly defined and held in sight if it is to have a truly transformative effect.

In the Introduction to *The Feminist Companion to Mythology*, the editor Carolyne Larrington states that '[m]ythology, the study of myth, introduces us to new ways of looking at social structures, so that we can examine constants and variables in the organization of human society, in particular . . . women's roles across different cultures and historical periods'. There are two points in the above statement that seem to me to be problematic. First, it is difficult to see what Larrington means by '*new* ways of looking at social structures' when there already exists a huge variety of interpretations of social structures informed by mythology – in the last two centuries at least. Second, and this seems to me the most insidious problem, the implicit approach is one of unqualified and uncritical use of mythical narratives as representations of the truth about 'women's roles across different cultures and historical periods'.

Undoubtedly, the study of myth – as any epistemological scrutiny – provides the feminist critic/theorist with a great conceptual tool for uncovering and elucidating those processes which have contributed to the formulation of 'roles' for women in society throughout history. That is to say, however, that feminist critique is then called to *demystify* those processes rather than to validate them by reiterating their constraining effect on the understanding of women's position(s). Instead, the feminist project sketched out here purports to celebrate mythmaking about women both by reading and contextualizing various mythological traditions and also by 'bring[ing] to light . . . myths neglected, overlooked or subjected to inflexible and misogynist interpretation'. Thus myth is seen as a complex but ultimately *reflexive* narrative device and the pursuit of its original meaning a redemptive and enabling strategy. To argue that not all myths are false representations of women's roles in different societies or that there is a critical potential in the rediscovery of women's myths about themselves is an interesting – though far from immediately acceptable – issue for debate. There is no sign of a debate here, however, either in Larrington's Introduction or in the essays which constitute this *Companion*. There are only gestures towards a problematization of the question of the validity and truth-content of mythology, and these are stated in an awkwardly common-sensical manner, as in Larrington's remark that 'myths about women are not necessarily women's myths'. While this stating of the obvious may be an expression of the editor's intention to produce an accessible and thus untheorized guide to myths about women, it still seems to underestimate (and thus obscure) the complexity of the matter in question.

The compilation features different contributors' presentations of the mythologies of the Near East, Europe, Asia, Oceania and America, as well as a section on 'Goddesses in the Twentieth Century' with essays on witchcraft, feminist mythmaking and rewritings of myth. It would take an expert on world mythology to assess the various entries; it seems to me, though, that the occasional weaknesses in this collection of (very interesting and informative) material about myth result from the lack of a theoretical and critical perspective. Barbara Smith's account of ancient Greek mythology, for example, is written in a story-telling manner, which makes for easy reading but illustrates the same problematic assumption about the reflexive character of mythmaking on which Larrington's introduction is based. How else can one justify Smith's rendering of the status of 'magical women' in ancient Greek mythology when she speculates in the following terms: 'Perhaps a little surprisingly, there are few witches or otherwise magically endowed women in ancient Greek myth, the most famous being Medea. It could well be, though, that ordinary ancient Greek women were felt to be sufficiently bewitching and powerful already not to require the assistance of any arcane or supernatural powers.' Not only is Smith wrong in finding very few witches in ancient Greek mythology, but her attempt to justify this by invoking the status of everyday women in ancient Greece can only be taken as an awkward attempt at authorial humour. The pervasiveness of mythical images of women is such, however, that any feminist-inspired project of critical intervention and reinterpretation should find very little to joke about. The significance of this project is better served in this anthology by the final section, which examines some of the imaginative strategies women have employed to counteract and reclaim the potentially repressive power of mythical narratives. Jane Caputi's 'On Psychic Activism: Feminist Mythmaking' and Diane Purkiss's 'Women's Rewriting of Myth' are useful and lucid conclusions to this collective enterprise. Though the tone in both pieces is often too celebratory, they offer an account of how myth can be used to highlight the very process of imaginative conceptualization and its potentially liberating effect for women.

Lynda Nead begins her deft and eclectic essay 'Framing and Freeing: Utopias of the Female Body' (*Radical Philosophy* 60.12–15) with an examination of the topography of Thomas More's *The Island of Utopia*, arguing that it is analogous to particular utopian representations of the female body in Western art, where the ideal female figure is depicted as contained, ordered, symmetrical. This representation, however, necessarily occurs at the cost of repressing the disordered and uncontrolled, and it is these properties of the female body that have been posited as an alternative utopia in recent French feminist writings. Nead argues against both utopian tendencies on the grounds that the aesthetics of openness and disorder are as potentially restrictive as the more conventional aesthetics of containment.

7. Feminism and Autobiography

American Women's Autobiography, edited by Margo Culley, contains a wide range of contributions from fourteen American feminists working on women's autobiography/biography, the most outstanding of which include Janis Greve's discussion of ' "photo"-portraiture' in Mary McCarthy's *Memories of a Catholic Girl* (1947); Ann D. Gordon's analysis of two suffragist autobiographies (Abigail Scott Duniway's *Pathbreaking* (1914) and Elizabeth Cady Stanton's *Eighty Years and More* (1898)); and Arlyn Diamond's excellent 'Choosing Sides, Choosing Lives: Women's Autobiographies of the Civil Rights Movements', in which she examines Sally Belfrage's *Freedom Summer* (1965), Angela Davis's *An Autobiography* (1974), Virginia Foster Durr's *Outside the Magic Circle* (1985), Mary King's *Freedom Song* (1987), Elinor Langer's 'Notes for Next Time: A

Memoir of the 1960s' (1973), and Anne Moody's *Coming of Age in Mississippi* (1968). *American Women's Autobiography* represents a further addition to the now substantial body of feminist meta-narratives on women's autobiography from the United States. In her introductory editorial chapter, Culley summarizes previous feminist editions (Jelinek, ed., 1980; Stanton, ed., 1984; Smith, 1987; Benstock, ed., 1988; Brodzki and Schenck, eds, 1988; Lionnet, 1989), recognizing both the 'danger' of 'essentialist feminism' as well as urging the interconnectedness between '*auto*(self)/*bio*(life)/*graphy* (writing)'. Whilst avoiding 'essentialism', however, Culley plunges into 'particularism', and in offering a teleological approach to American autobiography argues that 'the dominant tradition of American women's autobiography has roots in Puritan beliefs about the self and the Puritan practice of conversion narratives; and that even in periods when autobiography has become a thoroughly secular enterprise its forms and purposes can be traced to these earlier traditions'.

Nancy Miller describes the subject of her book, *Getting Personal: Feminist Occasions and Other Acts*, as the problematics of 'self-representation' within feminist discourse. As a solution to both her desire for the specifics of difference within feminist theory/criticism and the need to tackle current 'published violence against feminist ideology', Miller's theoretical framework is soon stated: 'personal criticism', which she sees as providing feminists with an 'explicitly autobiographical performance within the act of criticism'. Indeed, her epigrammatic citation from Paul Valéry – 'There is no theory that is not a fragment, carefully preserved, of some autobiography' – has become a catchphrase amongst feminists who deem 'personal criticism' to be the answer to deconstructivist anonymity. Preferring the 'gossipy grains of situated writing to the academic sublime' – hence her subtitle 'Feminist Occasions' – Miller likens 'personal criticism' to having the impact of a nuclear eruption: 'I have also wanted to seize the fallout of event: the chance for something to happen in the wedge of unpredictability and not yet foreclosed by my own (rhetorically predictable) feminist discourse.'

Having theoretically identified herself, and her text, with 'personal criticism' in the first chapter and defended her position against the charge of being 'anti-theoretical' ('personal writing entails the reclaiming of theory: turning theory back upon itself'; 'feminist theory has always built out from the personal'), Miller devotes the bulk of her text to a series of not particularly interesting conference papers she has given within various US and European academic

institutions since 1978. True to theoretical form, her focus is self-
reflexive ('confessional, locational, academic, political, narrative,
anecdotal, biographematic'), offering a trajectory of her feminist
'journey' through academia. But, whilst *Getting Personal* provides a
useful source of reference, particularly for undergraduates new to
feminisms who wish to understand the historical-specificity of
American academic feminisms more fully, it is a disappointing text.
Devoting only one chapter to an outline of the 'personal criticism'/
'death of the author' debate before plunging into conference mode
(consisting of some seven chapters), Miller only tentatively suggests
her solution to the problems she sees facing academic feminisms,
and raises more questions than she initially claims to answer.

Liz Stanley's *The Autobiographical I: The Theory and Practice of
Feminist Auto/biography* is highly recommended. Refusing 'the conventional discipline boundaries that slice up contemporary academic
life into bite-size chunks', Stanley defines her work as coming under
the theoretical aegis of 'cultural politics'. 'Its appeal is strong,' she
argues. 'It draws on ideas and analyses from a wide range of
sources, including feminism, Marxism, literary theory, psychoanalytic theory, history, and my own discipline of sociology, and
uses them in radical and insightful ways; and, unlike other multi-
disciplinary endeavours, it does so while retaining a strong theoretical and analytic edge. . . . Cultural politics is concerned above all
to situate culture within a social and historical and thus *political*
context.' In the introduction, Stanley outlines the terms of her
analysis, arguing for strong 'ontological and epistemological links'
between biography and autobiography, hence 'auto/biography'.
Divided into two sections, the first problematizes the central tenets
of postmodernist theory. Whilst careful to point out that postmodernist ideas are 'crucial to any egalitarian impulse within
academic life', Stanley considers what the 'denial of authorship
actually *does*' for women writers and feminist theories alike. The
second section goes on to discuss the relationship between autobiography and photography, looking in particular at the ways in
which feminists have crucially redefined the discursive parameters
within which photographs of 'auto/biographical subjects' are interpreted.

The central body of *The Autobiographical I* contains three parts.
Part 1 explores the intertextuality of fictional and autobiographical
writing, critically evaluates the autobiographical canon, strongly
argues for the reinscribing of 'bio' in autography, and also contains
a chapter devoted to various kinds of biographical writing. Part 2 is

specifically concerned with biography. In refuting 'the conventional model of modern biography' – with claims to facticity and a microscopic 'focus on a single "unique" subject' – Stanley offers a feminist perspective that becomes kaleidoscopic. She asserts that 'We should ask of biography the question "who says?".'. And "who says" is someone who has produced one more interpretation from among a range of possibilities, and who has produced it from one particular angle rather than any other.' Opening up a challenge to the 'unique subject', essentialist focus, Stanley explores the notion of 'Feminism and Friendship', in which she 'combines the detailed specificity of biography with a social and indeed sociological view of individual lives connected with others, and also with a broad knowledge of the social, economic and political context in which those lives were led'. Finally, part 3 takes up the genre/gender debate, 'asking – and answering – the question of whether there is a feminist auto/biography'. *The Autobiographical I* is a compelling text: witty and hard-hitting. Although it requires at least a primary knowledge of theoretical frameworks, Stanley's book does not attempt to confound the reader, or confine its analysis to either/or solutions. This is a text that is long-overdue for feminist readers of biography and autobiography, and one that will act as a watershed for future feminist work.

Books Reviewed

Armstrong, Isobel, ed. *New Feminist Discourses: Critical Essays on Theories and Texts.* Routledge. pp. 371. $49.95. ISBN 0 415 06741 3.

Ballaster, Ros. *Seductive Forms: Women's Amatory Fiction from 1684 to 1740.* Clarendon Press. pp. 232. £8.99. ISBN 0 1981 1244 0.

Barrett, Michèle, and Anne Phillips, eds. *Destabilising Theory: Contemporary Feminist Debates.* Polity. pp. 224. £35.95. ISBN 0 7456 0795 0.

Bartky, Sandra Lee. *Femininity and Domination: Studies in the Phenomenology of Oppression.* Routledge (1990). pp. 141. £35. ISBN 0 415 90186 3.

Benstock, Shari. *Textualizing the Feminine: On the Limits of Genre.* University of Oklahoma Press (1991). pp. 229. $29.95. ISBN 0 8061 2358 3.

Benzel, Kathryn N., and Lauren Pringle De La Vars, eds. *Images of the Self as Female: The Achievement of Women Artists in Re-envisioning Feminine Identity.* Edwin Mellen Press. pp. 288. $99.95. ISBN 0 88946 122 8.

Bock, Gisela, and Susan James, eds. *Beyond Equality and Difference: Citizenship, Feminist Politics and Female Subjectivity.* Routledge. pp. 210. £11.99. ISBN 0 415 07989 6.

Bonner, Frances, Lizbeth Goodman, Richard Allen, Linda Janes and Catherine Kink, eds. *Imagining Women: Cultural Representations and Gender.* Polity/Open University Press. pp. 361. £11.95. ISBN 0 7456 0974 0.

Brennan, Teresa. *The Interpretation of the Flesh: Freud and Femininity.* Routledge. pp. 240. £37.50. ISBN 0 415 07449 5.

Bristow, Joseph, ed. *Sexual Sameness: Textual Differences in Lesbian and Gay Writing.* Routledge. pp. 262. £11.99. ISBN 0 415 06937 8.

Bronfen, Elisabeth. *Over Her Dead Body: Death, Femininity and the Aesthetic.* Manchester University Press. pp. 435. £14.95. ISBN 0 7190 3827 8.

Bush, Barbara. *Slave Women in Caribbean Society 1650–1838.* James Curry (1990). pp. 98. £8.95. ISBN 0 85255 057 X.

Chaudhuri, Nupur, and Margaret Strobel, eds. *Western Women and Imperialism: Complicity and Resistance.* Indiana University Press. pp. 276. hb £32.50, pb £11.99. ISBN 0 253 20705 3, 0 253 31341 4.

Crowley, Helen, and Susan Himmelweit, eds. *Knowing Women: Feminism and Knowledge.* Polity/Open University Press. pp. 396. £13.95. ISBN 0 7456 0976 7.

Culley, Margo, ed. *American Women's Autobiography: Fea(s)ts of Memory.* University of Wisconsin Press. pp. 329. hb £37.95, pb £13.50. ISBN 0 299 13290 0, 0 299 13294 3.

Donaldson, Laura. *Decolonising Feminisms: Race, Gender and Empire-Building.* Routledge. pp. 175. £13.95. ISBN 0 415 09218 3.

Donovan, Josephine. *Feminist Theory: The Intellectual Traditions of American Feminism.* Continuum. pp. 272. $14.95. ISBN 0 8264 0617 3.

Dotterer, Ronald, and Susan Bowers, eds. *Sexuality, the Female Gaze and the Arts: Women, the Arts and Society.* Susquehanna University Press. pp. 191. £27.50. ISBN 0 945636 32 6.

Fuss, Diana. *Inside/Out: Lesbian Theories, Gay Theories.* Routledge (1991). pp. 426. hb £40, pb £12.99. ISBN 0 415 90236 3, 0 415 90237 1.

Gallop, Jane. *Around 1981: Academic Feminist Literary Theory.* Routledge. pp. 230. £22.50. ISBN 0 415 90190 1.

Harrison, Antony H., and Beverly Taylor, eds. *Gender and Discourse in Victorian Literature and Art.* Northern Illinois University Press. pp. 273. £35. ISBN 0 87580 168 4.

Harvey, Elizabeth D. *Ventriloquized Voices: Feminist Theory and English Renaissance Texts.* Routledge. pp. 320. £30. ISBN 0 415 06732 4.

Harvey, Elizabeth, and Kathleen Okruhlik, eds. *Women and Reason.* University of Michigan Press. pp. 294. $39.50. ISBN 0 427 10220 6.

Hearn, Jeff. *Men in the Public Eye: The Construction and Deconstruction of Public Men and Public Patriarchies.* Routledge. pp. 262. £40. ISBN 0 415 07620 X.

Hekman, Susan J. *Gender and Knowledge: Elements of a Postmodern Feminism.* Polity (1990). pp. 190. £11.95. ISBN 0 7456 1048 X.

hooks, bell. *Black Looks: Race and Representation.* Turnaround Press. pp. 192. £8.99. ISBN 1 873262 02 7.

Humm, Maggie. *Feminisms: A Reader*. Harvester Wheatsheaf. pp. 420. £13.95. ISBN 0 7450 0925 5.

Irigaray, Luce. *Elemental Passions*, trans. Joanne Collie and Judith Still. Athlone Press. pp. 105. hb £19.95, pb £9.95. ISBN 0 485 11409 7, 0 485 120799 9.

Larrington, Carolyne, ed. *The Feminist Companion to Mythology*. Pandora. pp. 480. £12.99. ISBN 0 04 440850 1.

McNay, Lois. *Foucault and Feminism: Power, Gender and the Self*. Polity. pp. 217. £39.50. ISBN 0 7456 0939 2.

Mernissi, Fatima. *Women and Islam: An Historical and Theological Enquiry*. Blackwell (1991). pp. 294. £12.99. ISBN 0 631 16904 0.

Middleton, Peter. *The Inward Gaze: Masculinity and Subjectivity in Modern Culture*. Routledge. pp. 250. £12.99. ISBN 0 415 07327 8.

Miller, Nancy. *Getting Personal: Feminist Occasions and Other Acts*. Routledge (1991). pp. 164. £35. ISBN 0 415 90323 8.

Minh-ha, Trinh T. *When the Moon Waxes Red: Representation, Gender and Cultural Politics*. Routledge (1991). pp. 240. $45. ISBN 0 415 90431 5.

Mohanty, Chandra Talpade, Ann Russo and Lourdes Torres, eds. *Third World Women and the Politics of Feminism*. Indiana University Press (1991). pp. 352. $39.95. ISBN 0 253 33873 5.

Munt, Sally. *New Lesbian Criticism: Literary and Cultural Readings*. Harvester Wheatsheaf. pp. 207. £10.95. ISBN 0 7450 1167 5.

National Lesbian and Gay Survey. *What a Lesbian Looks Like: Writings by Lesbians on their Lives and Lifestyles*. Routledge. pp. 166. £9.99. ISBN 0 415 08100 9.

Richardson, Diane, and Victoria Robinson, eds. *Introducing Women's Studies: Feminist Theory and Practice*. Macmillan. pp. 421. £10.99. ISBN 0 333 54197 9.

Sahgal, Gita, and Nira Yuval-Davis, eds. *Refusing Holy Orders: Women and Fundamentalism in Britain*. Virago. pp. 244. £8.99. ISBN 1 85381 219 6.

Sawicki, Jana. *Disciplining Foucault: Feminism, Power and the Body*. Routledge. pp. 130. £10.99. ISBN 0 415 90188 X.

Segal, Lynne, and Mary McIntosh, eds. *Sex Exposed: Sexuality and the Pornography Debate*. Virago. pp. 344. pb £8.99. ISBN 1 85381 385 0.

Stanley, Liz. *The Autobiographical I: The Theory and Practice of Feminist Auto/biography*. Manchester University Press. pp. 298. £19.95. ISBN 0 7190 2980 5.

Stowell, Sheila. *A Stage of Their Own: Feminist Playwrights of the Suffrage Era*. Manchester University Press. pp. 170. £35. ISBN 0 7190 3677 1.

Winders, James A. *Gender, Theory and the Canon*. University of Wisconsin Press (1991). pp. 149. £37.50. ISBN 0 299 12924 1.

Wittig, Monique. *The Straight Mind and Other Essays*. Harvester Wheatsheaf. pp. 110. £9.95. ISBN 0 7450 1278 7.

8

Historicism

TONY PINKNEY

Marxism is sometimes accused by its enemies of being a political and theoretical dinosaur, lumbering obsoletely around the post-modern landscapes of the late twentieth century, a grand but irrelevant survivor from the nineteenth. The appearance of a handsome hardback edition of Antonio Gramsci's *Prison Notebooks*, the first of a five-volume set, does little to dispel that impression. Indeed, it gives one the sense of having wandered into some Jurassic Park of political and cultural theory where this formidable beast of a book, sumptuously annotated by Joseph A. Buttigieg, has been cloned up from the DNA of Gramsci's fragmentary originals. Authoritative though this weighty tome (and its four successors) will surely be, Buttigieg notes in his long Introduction that 'even the most conscientiously accurate and complete reproduction of Gramsci's manuscript will not settle the polemics, or still the urge to reconstruct the "true" Gramsci'. Moreover, one wonders about the very rationale of this volume: surely anyone who plans to work on Gramsci's text in this sort of depth could not rely on a translation anyway, however meticulous, but would have to go back to the Italian original itself?

Fortunately, not all the Gramsci publications this year have such a whiff of the museum about them. Paul Ransome's *Antonio Gramsci: A New Introduction* lives up to its subtitle and is a useful student primer, lucidly covering such predictable topics as ideology, hegemony, intellectuals, political education, and the nature of the Communist Party. A more exciting study is Renate Holub's *Antonio Gramsci: Beyond Marxism and Postmodernism* in Christopher Norris's 'Critics of the Twentieth Century' series. Holub aims to break with conventional accounts of Gramsci as social and political thinker, one of the triumvirate of 'founders of Western Marxism' (along with Karl Korsch and Georg Lukács); 'what attracts me more is to place Gramsci next to Lukács in the context of literary criticism, and in the context of Marxist aesthetics'. The prison meditations, she argues persuasively, gravitate in part around the problems of realism and modernism that occupied exiled Marxist intellectuals in the 1930s. Only, whereas Lukács concentrates on the realist author, Gramsci's stress on the reader and literary reception, on 'the modes of consumption of a stratified reading public', leads to a theory of 'modernism in the context of modernity' which is much closer to the Frankfurt School in its emphasis on the 'potentials and dangers alike in the gradual technologization and industrialization of culture'. Reminding us that Gramsci was a student of linguistics at the University of Turin, Holub also evokes the ways in which his work goes 'beyond modernism' in its attention to communicative processes. From this standpoint, he becomes 'an early master, or an anticipator of a dialectical-structuralist merger' with which we are now more familiar from Mikhail Bakhtin or V. Volosinov. Later chapters of the book rework Gramsci's varied models of intellectuality into a 'contemporary theory of the intellectual' fit for a postmodern, transnational and 'informational' global order. Finally, Holub sketches the 'minimal contours of a new critical project' which she terms – ringing the changes on Jürgen Habermas – 'differential pragmatics': an investigation of 'the possibility of telecommunicatively and electronically mediated dialogic interactions and negotiations not exclusively between individuals and groups in the western world'. This is a rich study, which articulates Gramsci's cultural theory to that of both his contemporaries and their postmodern successors in constantly stimulating ways.

Holub's book might be viewed as a possible riposte to Paul Piccone's 'Gramsci's *Prison Notebooks* – The Remake' in *Telos* (90.177–83). For this extended hostile review of Buttigieg's new Gramsci edition opens into a general, and damning, assessment of Gramsci himself as 'an Enlightenment thinker for whom even the highest human longings for universality ultimately entailed, as their necessary underside, the obliteration of that particularity and specificity constituting human identities'.

Georg Lukács is reinstated as a powerful theorist of the novel in Susan Derwin's *The Ambivalence of Form: Lukács, Freud and the Novel*. In *Theory of the Novel*, she suggests, Lukács 'challenges the literary-historical practice of defining mimesis in terms of its object'; instead, he views 'the formal totality of the novel as an effect of the subject who creates it' and thus throws the emphasis on novelistic subjectivity. A lively reading of Freud's *Totem and Taboo* as 'an efficacious translation of Lukács's *geschichtsphilosophische* discourse' leads to a stress on the role of 'formal totality in the process of identity-constitution in both writers'. The way is then clear for a reinterpretation of mimesis as a performative or enactive mode, as located in the gesture of a subject rather than in the pre-existence of the object; such, Derwin claims, is the understanding of mimesis which Walter Benjamin and Theodor Adorno derive from Lukács. Caught up in its own processes of Romantic irony, Lukács's seminal volume turns out to be more a novel in its own right than a theory of the novel, while it can simultaneously be used to show, in the case of *Jane Eyre*, that 'the conventions of Gothic literature are extreme examples of tendencies germane to the genre of the novel as a whole'. Readings of Balzac's *La Recherche de l'Absolu*, Theodor Fontane's *Frau Jenny Treibel* and Walker Percy's *The Second Coming* complete this impressive turning of mimesis on its head.

A. J. Cascardi also ponders *Theory of the Novel* in his 'Totality and the Novel' in *New Literary History* (23.607–27). He claims that the efforts of post-Lukácsean Marxists like Jay Bernstein and Fredric Jameson to historicize the volume have left its 'more pressing problems of subjectivity still very much intact', and he aims instead to reformulate the 'normative challenge set by the novel'.

Lukács has a chapter devoted to him in David Frisby's *The Alienated Mind: The Sociology of Knowledge in Germany 1918–1933*. This lucid survey of the intellectual project variously represented by Max Scheler, Karl Mannheim and Lukács has a new Afterword to the second edition which argues that 'our estimation of the significance of Georg Simmel and Max Weber should be revised . . . not only is a great deal of Simmel's cultural analysis pioneering work in the sociology of culture but also . . . some of his essays display a concern for issues that are absolutely central to the sociology of knowledge'. Frisby continues that revaluation in his *Simmel and Since: Essays on Georg Simmel's Social Theory*, which demonstrates the richness of its hero's reflections on urban existence, social space, and leisure and aesthetics in modernity. *Simmel and Culture* (Sage), co-edited by Frisby and Mike Featherstone, has not been available for review.

The Frankfurt School prompts much work, as ever. Peter M. R. Stirk's *Max Horkheimer: A New Interpretation* construes its subject's intellectual career within the overarching framework of his 'history of bourgeois society'. It is a lucid but distinctly low-key book, concluding wanly that Horkheimer was 'not always successful or even especially innovative' in his reflections upon these themes. Peter Uwe Hohendahl's *Reappraisals: Shifting Alignments in Postwar Critical Theory* is a late arrival from 1991 and comprises a set of trenchant studies of both Georg Lukács and the Frankfurt School. Hohendahl is a companionable, immensely conscientious explicator of ideas rather than a major innovative theorist, and his long chapter on 'Neoromantic Anticapitalism: Georg Lukács's Search for Authentic Culture' epitomizes the book's method; it powerfully challenges contemporary theoretical clichés and misrepresentations by a sustained return to the textual and historical record. In the hothouse of high theory, Hohendahl's is an eminently salutary intelligence to have around. Romantic anticapitalism affords a context in which fleetingly to note the one article devoted to Lukács's friend and contemporary Ernst Bloch this year. For in 'Philosophy and the Fairy Tale: Ernst Bloch as Narrator' in *New German Critique* (55.21–43), Liliane Weissberg seeks to 'follow a line from Herder to Bloch' by analysing the Romantic investment in such archaic modes of narrative as fairy tale. She shows convincingly that fairy tales are a structuring formal principle as well as a thematic concern in Bloch's thought: 'Bloch's stories *are* themselves philosophy.' In an analogous argument in 'Ludwig Klages (1872–1956) and the Origins of Critical Theory' in *Theory, Culture and Society* (9:iii.45–63), Georg Stauth and Bryan S. Turner suggest that 'the Frankfurt School was closer to the tradition of Nietzsche and *Lebensphilosophie* in their cultural critique than to Marxism (of whatever variety)'.

Translations of the work of the finest of Frankfurt theorists, Theodor Adorno, continue to pour from the presses. In the field of music criticism, we now have *Mahler: A Musical Physiognomy*, which examines the work of a proto-modernist composer who is 'particularly resistant to theorizing because he entirely fails to acknowledge the choice between technique and imaginative content', and *Quasi Una Fantasia: Essays on Modern Music*, which is Adorno's own selection from his musical articles and journalism. 'There is still room to inquire why Vienna should have been singled out as the birthplace of the modern movement,' writes Adorno in an essay titled, simply, 'Vienna'; and it is a set of meditations on the musical modernism of Schoenberg, Berg and Weber which constitutes the core of this volume. Other pieces then orbit meaningfully around this centre: 'Stravinsky: A Dialectical Portrait' reconsiders and refines the negative assessment of the composer that Adorno developed in *Philosophy of Modern Music*; 'Commodity Music Analysed' addresses the mass-cultural challengers to an austere musical avant-gardism; and so on. The second volume of the English *Notes to Literature* represents volumes 3 and 4 of Adorno's *Noten zur Literatur*. As with the first English volume, it is the range and nimbleness of Adorno's dialectical intelligence that impresses and delights here: well-known essays on commitment, on Walter Benjamin and Siegfried Kracauer, on parataxis in Hölderlin's late poetry sit alongside less familiar lucubrations on literary titles, the crisis of literary criticism, Dickens's *The Old Curiosity Shop*, 'physiological romanticism', and the use of foreign words. Within whatever detail or marginal aspect of a text Adorno starts out from, he compellingly demonstrates the unexpected presence of the social totality 'in monadological abbreviation' (to borrow Susan Buck-Morss's fine phrase).

New German Critique has a special issue on Adorno's work which offers rich pickings indeed. Peter U. Hohendahl, in his 'Introduction: Adorno Criticism Today' (56.3–15), welcomes the 'return of Adorno' in recent years and suggests that 'Adorno criticism stands at a crucial turning point'. One of the factors that contribute to this sense of urgency is the dire need for new and sounder translations of the master's works; and Robert Hullot-Kentor begins that project here in his 'Notes on *Dialectic of Enlightenment*: Translating the Odysseus Essay' (101–8), followed by the new translation itself, 'Odysseus or Myth and Enlightenment' (109–41). The second factor is a current impulse towards powerful new revisionist readings, represented in this collection by Andrew Hewitt's 'A Feminine Dialectic of Enlightenment?: Horkheimer and Adorno Revisited' (143–70), which argues that the 'very rethinking of power as representation is inextricable from the thematization of woman in *Dialectic of Enlightenment*'; and Miriam Hansen's subtle analysis of 'Mass Culture as Hieroglyphic Writing: Adorno, Derrida, Kracauer' (43–73), which aims to challenge kneejerk postmodern dismissals of Adorno as cultural elitist. The third factor in the revaluation of Adorno is a shifting sense of the historical contexts in which his work may be situated. Hohendahl's own essay on 'The Displaced Intellectuals?: Adorno's American Years Revisited' (76–100) is exemplary here. The special issue is completed by Michael P. Steinberg's 'The Musical Absolute' (17–42), which intends 'to draw the question of musicality into the ongoing debate about the nature of modernity and subjectivity', and Peter Osborne's important 'A Marxism for the Postmodern?: Jameson's Adorno' (171–92), which is a hard-hitting critique of Jameson's reworking of Adorno in *Late Marxism*. That book is, in Osborne's view, 'characterized, methodo-

logically, by two main features: the displacement of philosophical by
rhetorical analysis and an associated pragmatic reduction of judgement to the parameters of a conjuncturalist conception of hegemonic intervention into current theoretical debates'.

In a later issue of *New German Critique*, Michael Sullivan and
John T. Lysaker's 'Between Impotence and Illusion: Adorno's Art
of Theory and Practice' (57.87–122), tackles the old accusations of
political quietism levelled at their hero. They suggest that 'Adorno's
turn to aesthetic theory is a turn to a certain kind of thought
experiment, one in which we might envision how the tension
between subject and object could be maintained', and that this could
have significant consequences for a (loosely defined) emancipatory
'practice'. In 'Image and Chatter: Adorno's Construction of Kierke-
gaard' in *Diacritics* (22.100–14), Peter Fenves analyses the concept
of 'critique' at work in Adorno's study of the Kierkegaardian
aesthetic.

The centenary of Walter Benjamin's birth, in 1992, was honoured
by a whole series of international conferences which testify to the
remarkable diversity of his current influence. Gershom Scholem's
*The Correspondence of Walter Benjamin and Gershom Scholem,
1932–1940* now makes a welcome appearance in paperback, and
provides rich insights into that unique fusion of Jewish theology,
aesthetic modernism (Kafka above all in these letters) and historical
materialism which constitutes Benjamin's suggestiveness for us
today. On a very different tack, *Performing Arts Journal* contains
'Walter Benjamin's Lichtenberg' (42.33–56). This radio play based
around the eighteenth-century German physicist and astronomer,
Georg Christoph Lichtenberg, reminds us that Benjamin was to a
degree a practitioner as well as a theorist of the mass media – even
if the Nazi takeover meant that in the event the piece was never
actually broadcast.

Benjamin is everywhere in the journals this year. *Diacritics* has a
massive double issue 'Commemorating Walter Benjamin'. Among its
highlights are Fredric Jameson on 'Benjamin's Readings' (22:iii/
iv.19–35), which moves out from Benjamin's self-assembled literary
'tradition' (Leskov, Kafka, Brecht, etc.) to general problems of
modernism and of the relation of Marxism to narrative; Carol
Jacobs's intricate 'Benjamin's Tessera: "Myslowitz-Braunschweig-
Marseille"' (36–47), which deconstructively ponders the complexities
of authorship and drug experience in Benjamin's work; Rainer
Nägele's 'The Poetic Ground Laid Bare' (149–59), yet another
meditation on Benjamin's reading of modernity in and through

Baudelaire; Irving Wohlfarth's 'The Politics of Youth: Walter Benjamin's Reading of *The Idiot*' (161–71), which traces the intersection of a 'metaphysics of youth' with Benjamin's deeply enigmatic early philosophy of language in his reading of Dostoevsky; and Samuel Weber's 'Taking Exception to Decision' (5–18), which constellates classical tragedy, Benjamin's theory of baroque theatre and the 'Schmittian theory of sovereignty'. Articles by Anselm Haverkamp, Eduardo Cadava, Christopher Fynsk and Elissa Marder also grace a powerful collection that any serious student of Benjamin will simply have to equip him- or herself with. The issue also contains a helpful review-article by Fritz Gutbrodt – 'Poedelaire: Translation and the Volatility of the Letter' (49–68) – on Bettine Menke's *Sprachfiguren: Name, Allegorie, Bild Nach Benjamin* (1991), which looks (on the evidence presented here) to be one of the most important recent German studies of his work.

Modern Language Notes also has its special issue (107) on 'Walter Benjamin: 1892–1940'. Close textual readings are provided by Eva Geulen's 'Zeit zur Darstellung' (580–605), which examines the elusive concept of *Darstellung* or 'presentation' in Benjamin's great 'Work of Art' essay, and by Beryl Schlossman's 'Benjamin's *Uber Einige Motive bei Baudelaire*: The Secret Architecture of *Correspondances*' (584–79), which tracks the relationship between 'correspondence' and modernity in Baudelaire, Proust and Benjamin himself. Helga Geyer-Ryan studies 'Effects of Abjection in the Texts of Walter Benjamin' (499–520), evoking the work of Julia Kristeva to examine the project of 'resurrecting the body into the machinery of the sign' in both Paul de Man and Walter Benjamin. De Man is also an important point of reference in Arne Melberg's 'Benjamin's Reflection' (478–98), which unties a complex conceptual knot around the terms 'reflection', 'romantic irony', Fichte's '*setzen*' and 'style' in and out of Benjamin's work. I was more struck by the *lack* of de Man in Hent de Vries's interesting 'Anti-Babel: The "Mystical Postulate" in Benjamin, de Certeau and Derrida' (441–77), which examines the role of Judaic philosophies of language in recent cultural theory. Finally, in 'Theater and *Agon/Agon* and Theater' (606–24), Carrie L. Asman reconstructs Benjamin's relationship with Flores Christian Rang and its implications for his notion of *Ursprung* as 'originary break or rupture' rather than organic unfolding.

In slightly more specialist vein, *Studies in Romanticism* has its own special issue (31) on 'Walter Benjamin on Romanticism'. Philippe Lacoue-Labarthe's 'Introduction' to the French translation of *The*

Concept of Art Criticism in German Romanticism leads off the collection (421–32), and it is Benjamin's dissertation – of which, incredibly, we still lack an English translation – that forms the centrepiece of this issue. In ' "Truth is the Death of Intention": Benjamin's Esoteric History of Romanticism' (455–80), David Ferris gives a thorough survey of Benjamin's tangled attitude to Romanticism in his early writings, while Rodolphe Gasché, in his characteristically subtle 'The Sober Absolute: On Benjamin and the Early Romantics' (433–53), homes in on the concept of 'critique' as a focus for measuring Benjamin's 'point of departure from Romanticism'. Tom McCall, in 'Plastic Time and Poetic Middles: Benjamin's Hölderlin' (481–99), suggests that Benjamin's 1914 essay on Hölderlin might afford us an alternative 'tradition of aesthetic *calculation*' to the hegemonic Coleridgean 'aesthetic tradition' in the study of lyric poetry. Carol Jacobs pops up for the second time this year, in a rich and wide-ranging essay – 'Walter Benjamin: Topographically Speaking' (501–24) – on issues of space, the city, writing and death in Benjamin's work.

Angela McRobbie writes on 'The *Passagenwerk* and the Place of Walter Benjamin in Cultural Studies: Benjamin, Cultural Studies, Marxist Theories of Art' in *Cultural Studies* (6.147–69). In this rambling but pleasant account, she proposes him as 'a model for the practice of being a cultural intellectual' to the postmodern and post-Marxist cultural studies of today. *Telos* contains a series of pieces on Benjamin, presumably as a slightly half-hearted acknowledgement of the centenary. In 'The Heroic Pedestrian or the Pedestrian Hero?: Walter Benjamin and the Flâneur' (91.108–16), Graeme Gilloch surveys one of the key modernist cultural figures in Benjamin's work (whose relation to the postmodern *walkman* of our own time would bear more thinking about than it gets here); Eva Geulen's 'Forgetting Benjamin' (151–64) is an important review-essay on Susan Buck-Morss's *Dialectics of Seeing*, which concludes that Buck-Morss's 'book's success would be Benjamin's failure to adhere to the strongest principle of his thought: the resistance to chronology'; and Gilloch's later contributions on 'Benjamin and the Architecture of History' (165–71) and 'Three Biographical Studies of Walter Benjamin' (171–78) give a useful conspectus of recent German work. Elizabeth Wilson, in 'The Invisible Flâneur' in *New Left Review* (191.90–110), engages feminist debates inspired by Benjamin's key urban motif, and suggests that Janet Wolff and others have conceded too much power to male authority and to an unproblematic commodification in their accounts of women, culture and the city. Susan Buck-Morss herself returns to Benjamin's most influential essay in 'Aesthetics and Anaesthetics: Walter Benjamin's Artwork Essay Reconsidered' in *October* (62.3–41). This powerful and learned essay regrounds contemporary Marxist debates on the aesthetic not in 'the meaning of terms, but of the human sensorium itself', or more precisely, in eighteenth- and nineteenth-century physiology and neurology. Gertrud Koch tackles the same text as Buck-Morss in her 'Cosmos in Film: On the Concept of Space in Walter Benjamin's "Work of Art" Essay' in *Qui Parle?* (2.61–2); her focus – with Jewish theology as ever in the background – is on the 'messianic-prophetic power of the camera'. Marcus Bullock returns us to the question of Benjamin on Baudelaire in his 'Benjamin, Baudelaire, Rossetti, and the Discovery of Error' in *Modern Language Quarterly* (53.201–25), which takes issue with Jerome McGann's unproblematic extension of Benjamin's analysis of commodity form in Baudelaire to the poetry of Dante Gabriel Rossetti. And finally Jeffrey Grossman offers a historical (and rather predictable) survey of 'The Reception of Walter Benjamin in the Anglo-American Literary Institution' in *German Quarterly* (65.414–28), while Alina Clej writes on 'Walter Benjamin's Messianic Politics: Angelus Novus and the End of History' in *Cross Currents* (11.23–40).

Benjamin is also a significant presence in Azade Seyhan's *Representation and its Discontents: The Critical Legacy of German Romanticism*, a study which challenges Philippe Lacoue-Labarthe and Jean-Luc Nancy by demonstrating that 'the "literary absolute" constitutes the very space where the problem of representation as mediation of presence becomes more visible in its irremediable ambiguity'; it would thus emphatically *not* be the case that the Romantics had just 'elevated the literary to the absolute'. Michael Löwy and Robert Sayre's *Révolte et Mélancolie: Le Romantisme à Contre-Courant de la Modernité* is a political rather than theoretical meditation on the legacy of Romanticism. In defence of 'romantic anticapitalism', the authors range across Coleridge, Ruskin, Marx, Lukács, Ernst Bloch and the student revolts of May 1968 to demonstrate the radical potential of the appeal to the values of a lost collective past as a critique of an instrumental or rationalized present. This is a rousing, if also repetitive, book, and it ends with a stirring claim: 'sans nostalgie du passé il ne peut pas exister de rêve d'avenir authentique. Dans ce sens, l'utopie sera romantique ou ne sera pas.' Yet I miss any substantial analysis of our postmodern present here, in which it is not at all clear that the Romantic anticapitalist legacy can successfully invoke the past, Nature or *Gemeinschaft* – all of which are now, arguably, mere images of themselves – in the ways it traditionally has done. A salutary reminder (if any were needed) of just how politically ambivalent Romantic legacies can be is afforded by the essays in *Fascism, Aesthetics and Culture*, edited by Richard J. Golsan. Studies of Emil Nolde, Gottfried Benn and Martin Heidegger, among others, remind us of the darker side of Romanticism which Löwy and Sayre are inclined to downplay. These two books together constitute, as it were, the torn halves of an integral theory of the politics of Romanticism to which, however, they do not add up.

The work of Mikhail Bakhtin receives full-scale treatment in Michael Gardiner's fine *The Dialogics of Critique: M. M. Bakhtin and the Theory of Ideology*. Dissenting from the largely literary appropriation of Bakhtin's thought to date, Gardiner sets out to approach the oeuvre from 'a different conceptual terrain: that of critical social and cultural theory'. Arguing that Bakhtin's preoccupations are 'largely congruent with those of the Western Marxist tradition', he endeavours, through a 'close or "symptomatic" reading and an extended process of conceptual reconstruction', to derive a full theory of ideology from Bakhtin's text. If for Bakhtin, as for Althusser and Gramsci, ideology is not a mere epiphenomenon but an essential symbolic medium of all social relations, it is also thought of by him in a linguistic and semiotic framework, as a signifying practice produced in specific and conflictual social contexts. Gardiner terms Bakhtin's project a 'critical hermeneutics' and, in a move which boldly displaces the Russian from the Formalist contexts in which he has usually been seen, contrasts his 'critical-interpretative *Hermeneutik*' with the work of Hans-Georg Gadamer, Paul Ricoeur and Jürgen Habermas. The problem then arises of the justification of ideological critique which, Gardiner argues, is for Bakhtin based on the normative values of a Kantian philosophical anthropology and a utopian view of the dialogic community which are simultaneously the strengths *and* weaknesses of his thought.

While on the theme of ideology, we should parenthetically note Mike Cormack's *Ideology*, a short primer for media-studies students in the 'Batsford Cultural Studies' series, and John Stephens's *Language and Ideology in Children's Fiction*, in Longman's 'Language and Social Life' series. Forging a sophisticated amalgam of ideology, critique and narratology, Stephens forcefully addresses a cultural area to which Marxist critics have given far too little attention. What his analysis of the textual object seems to require, however, is equal attention to the question of readership; for if his young readers are surely deeply socialized by the literary products he discusses, it is by no means certain that they are entirely malleable and non-resistant in the texts' hands.

Returning to Bakhtin, we have two further studies: M.-Pierrette Malcuzynski's *Entre-Dialogues Avec Bakhtin: ou Sociocritique de la (Dé)Raison Polyphonique* and a collection on *Feminism, Bakhtin and the Dialogic*, edited by Dale M. Bauer and S. Jaret McKinstry. The former effects a junction of the Bakhtin circle and the 'socio-criticism' of Edmond Cros, Claude Duchet, Marc Agenot and others, and puts the resulting concepts – *sociogramme, idéosème, hétérophonie, hétérotopie* – to work in close readings of several contemporary 'neobaroque' novels. The latter is an uneven collection of essays which occasionally waters down Bakhtinian theory alarmingly, as when the editors define dialogism as 'Bakhtin's theory about encountering otherness through the potential of dialogue'. Many of its essays are straightforward readings of texts ranging from Middleton's *The Roaring Girl* to Donald Barthelme; and on the evidence of these pieces one has to conclude that the full-scale encounter of feminism and Bakhtin is yet to come.

That indefatigable Bakhtinian, Ken Hirschkop, asks 'Is Dialogism for Real?' in *Social Text* (30.102–13). Distinguishing Bakhtin's concept from dialogue *tout court* (a conflation which he claims is rife in literary-theoretical circles), Hirschkop argues that 'dialogism describes the work of those "secondary genres" whose job it is to cite and represent the languages generated in so-called primary genres (everyday speech, etc.), and that this citation and representation is an ineluctable feature of the socio-political life of the modern nation-state'. *New Literary History* (23) contains two pieces on Bakhtin: Maria Shevtsova's 'Dialogism in the Novel and Bakhtin's Theory of Culture' (746–63) aims 'to show how some of the major aesthetic categories in Bakhtin are developed through his theory of language or, quoting Bakhtin, "translinguistics"; [and] to indicate why and how the same categories are derived from his theory of culture'; while Mikita Hoy's 'Bakhtin and Popular Culture' (765–82) applies key Bakhtinian categories to such contemporary mass-cultural phenomena as style magazines and punk rock.

Francis Mulhern's collection, *Contemporary Marxist Literary Criticism*, provides us with a useful frame for current work in Marxist aesthetic theory. Mulhern's Introduction is an excellent synopsis of developments in Marxist literary and cultural theory since the founders themselves. It sketches three phases: the classical or scien-

tific-socialist moment of the mid- to late-nineteenth century, a
'critical' phase associated with the modernist Marxism of Lukács,
Adorno, Benjamin and others, and a post-1968 'critical classicism'
from Althusser onwards. Mulhern's analysis of this third phase, and
particularly that delimited sector of it which he identifies as the
'emerging formation of (post-)literary studies', is a pungent one.
Fertile in its invention of 'an enlarged domain, new objects, revised
norms, and, framing these, new terms of identity', it was also, he
suggests, incorporated by the norms of its academic environment to
the point where 'the "political" posture of radical literary studies is,
at worst, a residual group mannerism'. A final section then seeks to
'assert the distinct identity and purposes of Marxism within radical
literary studies', displacing both traditional and literary-theoretical
notions of the individual text by sustained attention to the 'rhetorics
of history' or the social 'formations of reading and writing'. The
body of the volume assembles essays by Pierre Macherey, Terry
Eagleton, Cora Kaplan, Raymond Williams, Peter Bürger, Fredric
Jameson, Tony Bennett and others to give a thorough and
modestly-priced reader. This will be an invaluable student text, and
serves as a timely reminder, in the midst of Marxism's continuing
'crisis', of its remarkable intellectual fertility and inventiveness.

The work of Raymond Williams, whom Mulhern sees as strad-
dling his second and third phases, is the subject of a special issue of
Social Text (30). In a trenchant memorial address on 'The Legacy of
Raymond Williams' (6–8), Cornel West summarizes Williams as 'the
last of the great European male revolutionary socialist intellectuals
born before the end of the age of Europe (1492–1945)'. The other
contributors both agree and disagree with this claim, marking Williams's limits while seeking also to extend certain resources that his
work offers. David Simpson's 'Raymond Williams: Feeling for
Structures, Voicing "History"' (9–25) is a deeply ambivalent meditation on 'voice' in Williams's work; for Simpson, Williams's
account of totality belongs to 'the vitalist empathic alternative to the
more familiar theoretical-analytic paradigms of the European tradition', and this is both its glory and its limit. David Lloyd and Paul
Thomas, in 'Culture and Society or "Culture and the State"' (27–
56), effect an impressive reworking of Williams's first major book.
They demonstrate convincingly and with a wealth of historical detail
that 'the under-theorization of the state in Williams's early work
prevents him from adequately addressing either the striking parallels
between the state and cultural theory or the reasons for the gradual
subordination of the institutions of culture to the work of the state

in the period he analyzes'. Michael Moriarty, in 'The Longest Cultural Journey: Raymond Williams and French Theory' (57–77), stages a dialectical encounter between Williams and Continental theory, in the spirit of the former's own remark that 'a fully historical semiotics would be very much the same thing as cultural materialism'. Catherine Gallagher, Stanley Aronowitz and Andrew Ross, meantime, do spirited battle over the implications of Williams's work for contemporary cultural studies. Gallagher's 'Raymond Williams and Cultural Studies' (79–89) argues polemically that 'our very sense that Williams's analyses are somewhat deficient or truncated . . . is ultimately in the service of a mystique of culture that privileges an excessive particularism'. Aronowitz and Ross beg to differ: the former writes 'On Catherine Gallagher's Critique of Raymond Williams' (90–7), seeking to historicize Williams's thought on culture rather than denouncing it in the name of some 'formalist' notion of correctness, while the latter, in 'Giving Culture Hell' (98–101), claims that Gallagher depoliticizes the whole issue of culture to 'yet another academic debate about how to define a disciplinary object'. Gallagher responds sharply in a later issue ('Response to Aronowitz and Ross', 31/32.283–5), attacking 'the nationalist sentiment that already feeds cultural studies from its historical roots in nineteenth- and early twentieth-century attempts to find the "inclusive" common culture of a "people"'. Finally, Williams's work is an important reference in Peter Hitchcock's 'Cultural Studies and the Prospects for a Multicultural Materialism' in *Rethinking Marxism* (5:i.78–87). Noting the absence of race and gender in Williams's theoretical perspectives, Hitchcock notes that 'it remains to be seen whether a complete recasting of the project is possible without gravely diminishing any of the theoretical strategies employed'.

Fredric Jameson, with enviable productivity, continues to churn out a book a year. His offering for 1992 is *The Geopolitical Aesthetic: Cinema and Space in the World System*, which powerfully extends the interest in film demonstrated by *Signatures of the Visible* (1990). 'Space, representability, allegory: such are then the theoretical and analytical instruments that will be mobilized to examine a variety of filmic narratives from that new world-systemic moment . . . which can indifferently be called postmodernity or the third (or "late") stage of capitalism'. The crisis of representation at the heart of Jameson's study is built into his very notion of the 'world system' itself, which has now, he argues, exceeded all the natural and historical categories of perception with which we normally orient ourselves: neither image nor story can encompass this new reality, which exists in some altogether other, abstract and non-narrative dimension. Yet still the social imaginary presses on with the impossible and unconscious task of mapping this totality; and as Jameson shows in a fine analysis of such films as *The Parallax View*, *Videodrome* and *All The President's Men*, the 'conspiracy film' is now arguably the major genre in which cognitive mapping painfully takes place. 'Nothing is gained by having been persuaded of the definitive verisimilitude of this or that conspiratorial hypothesis: but in the intent to hypothesize, in the desire called cognitive mapping – therein lies the beginning of wisdom.' The second half of the book shifts from American materials to Soviet science fiction film, late Godard, Edward Yang's *The Terrorizer* and Kidlet's *The Perfumed Nightmare*. If such films are not engaged on that 'cartography of the absolute' that preoccupied the Western conspiratorial text, they none the less face unprecedented representational problems of their own. With the collapse of Communism, Jameson sees a cultural resurgence of that system of 'national allegory' about which he first wrote in *Fables of Aggression*, but in the postmodern that old representational system is radically reworked by 'what I will now call a geopolitical unconscious': 'This it is which now attempts to refashion national allegory into a conceptual instrument for grasping our own being in the world.' This hypothesis is then carried forward into the rich and dense studies of the individual films.

Jameson's filmic explorations are extended in 'Spatial Systems in *North by North West*', his contribution to Slavoj Žižek's lively collection, *Everything You Always Wanted to Know About Lacan but Were Afraid to Ask Hitchcock*. Jameson takes Hitchcock's film as a virtual test case for his new spatial poetics, wagering that 'in this heterogeneous system of spaces, where we learn the logic and meaning, the world-ness, of each *against* the others, it follows that some deeper "system" of these spaces is at work that might, at a pinch, be crudely and abstractly articulated'. His contribution to a special issue of *Polygraph* (5) on 'Contesting the New World Order', however, turns out, rather pointlessly, to be a reprint of the introduction to *The Geopolitical Aesthetic* itself ('Geopolitical Aesthetics', 78–83).

Warren Buckland's 'Fredric on Film Theory' in *New Formations* (6.163–70) is an extended review of *Signatures of the Visible*. It offers us, in a sense, a stern professional view of the talented amateur, admiring Jameson's undoubted theoretical flair and analytic acumen but also severely counselling the reader that 'many of [his] insights have also been made, with far more historical accuracy and theoretical systematicity, within film studies itself'. Aijaz Ahmad's chapter on Jameson in his important *In Theory: Classes, Nations, Literatures* argues that the pleas for 'a theory of the cognitive aesthetic of Third World literature' that Jameson advanced in his essay on 'Third World Literature in the Era of Multi-National Capital' involves 'a suppression of the multiplicity of differences among and within both the advanced capitalist countries on the one hand and the imperialized formations on the other'. Santiago Colas deals with related issues in his 'The Third World in Jameson's *Postmodernism or the Cultural Logic of Late Capitalism*' in *Social Text* (31/32.258–70); he explores the curious paradox whereby the Third World seems both to have disappeared *and* to constitute some sort of oppositional alternative in Jameson's construction of postmodernity. On another tack entirely, Christopher Wise writes on 'Jameson/Frye/Mcdieval Hermeneutics' in *Christianity and Literature* (41.313–33); he recommends the 'chiliastic Marxisms' of Benjamin and Bloch as suggesting 'an even greater reciprocity between the interpretive systems of Jameson and Frye than Jameson himself would allow'.

Peter Bürger's *The Theory of the Avant-Garde* made a considerable impact when it appeared in English in 1984, and the translation of two further volumes by him this year seems likely to enhance his influence on Anglo-American literary theory. The first of these, *The Institutions of Art*, co-authored with Christa Bürger, in a sense logically precedes the earlier avant-garde book. The central Bürgerian concept of an 'institution of art' could be seen as answering Francis Mulhern's call for attention to the social formations of reading and writing beyond the isolated literary text: it denotes 'the set of basic assumptions and norms in a given historical context that validate particular literary practices and denigrate others'. The early twentieth-century avant-gardes can then be seen as launching a passionate assault on that institution of literature or art – insistence on the auratic uniqueness of the work within an aesthetic of autonomy – which has been characteristic of bourgeois society from the late eighteenth century onwards. Far from concentrating on the avant-garde project to return the aesthetic explosively back to everyday praxis, Bürger here examines the historical origins of the institution of aesthetic autonomy in the transition from feudal absolutism to early bourgeois society. The accompanying interpretive essays by Christa Bürger, on works by Goethe and Kleist, aim to demonstrate that the emergent institution of literature is not just an external framework for literary production, but actually leaves its decipherable marks in the texts themselves. Many similar themes are treated in Bürger's *The Decline of Modernism*. The titles of the assembled essays ring the changes on the terms 'literary institution', 'modernism', 'avant-garde', 'aesthetics', and among the subjects of reflection are Walter Benjamin, Michel Foucault, Wyndham Lewis, Joseph Beuys and Peter Weiss.

This Bürgerian context of the institution of art is probably the appropriate place to note the paperback edition of the belated English translation of Jürgen Habermas's *The Structural Transformation of the Public Sphere* (published in Germany as far back as 1962). Terry Eagleton's nimble use of the concept of the 'bourgeois public sphere' in his *The Function of Criticism* can now be compared with Habermas's more fully documented account.

Eagleton himself is rather thinly represented in the field this year. His inaugural lecture as Warton Professor at the University of Oxford, 'The Crisis of Contemporary Culture', appears in *New Left Review* (196.29–41), and ranges schizophrenically from bold general speculations about the fate of culture under postmodern late capitalism to acerbic local polemics against the current depressing state of English studies at Oxford itself. In an earlier issue of *New Left Review*, Eagleton interviews Pierre Bourdieu on 'Doxa and the Common Life' (191.111–21); both men sensitively explore the relations between traditional Marxist concepts of ideology and Bourdieu's own notions of 'symbolic power' and 'linguistic capital'.

Eagleton condenses some of the arguments of his big aesthetics book in 'The Ideology of the Aesthetic', his contribution to *The Politics of Pleasure: Aesthetics and Cultural Theory*, edited by Stephen Regan. In contradistinction to Francis Mulhern, who argues sharply in his *Contemporary Marxist Literary Criticism* for the decisive suppression of 'literary' and 'aesthetic' concerns, Regan's lucid 'Introduction: The Return of the Aesthetic' suggests that such vexed topics as pleasure, value, perhaps even beauty, can't be abolished as simply as that. That radical criticism has had so little to say about such issues may be more of a failure than a refusal, ceding this ideologically crucial though enigmatic terrain too readily to its traditionalist opponents. Other contributors to the volume include, notably, Patricia Waugh, Steven Connor and Michèle Barrett. The book concludes optimistically, in Connor's words, that 'the aesthetic, in the enlarged form of a politics of culture, may yet become a realm in which the pleasurable renegotiation of the political value of pleasure may take place'. Martin Jay also ranges over these issues in ' "The Aesthetic Ideology" as

Ideology; or, What Does It Mean to Aestheticize Politics?' in *Cultural Critique* (21.41–61); this wide survey of work by Eagleton, Benjamin, de Man, Lyotard, Hannah Arendt and others leads to the rather tame conclusion that 'not every variant of the aestheticization of politics must lead to the same dismal end'. Kate Soper more narrowly addresses 'The Ideology of the Aesthetic' in her review of Eagleton's book of that title in *New Left Review* (192.120–32); she homes in on 'the instability of both the key concepts at work in [Eagleton's] text: that of the "body", and of "ideology"'. Eagleton's work is subject to a decidedly more aggressive critique in Dmitry Khanin's 'Will Aesthetics be the Last Stronghold of Marxism?' in *Philosophy and Literature* (16.266–78). The question is interesting, but Khanin's treatment of it isn't.

Finally, a mixed set of volumes which revolve in one way or another around the theoretical and political topics of this section. Roger S. Gottlieb's *Marxism 1844–1990: Origins, Betrayal, Rebirth* is a broad survey of the tradition, which asserts the validity of a feminized and ecologized Marxism for our own postmodern times. Stephen Greenblatt and Giles Gunn's *Redrawing the Boundaries: The Transformation of English and American Literary Studies* charts the work achieved by that post-1968 radical generation that Francis Mulhern evoked above. It contains incisive chapters on all the main literary-historical periods and many major theoretical approaches, including sketches of Marxist criticism by Walter Cohen and New Historicism by Louis Montrose. One could hardly ask for a more compact encyclopaedia of the new – or perhaps 'post-' – literary studies than this. Norman Fairclough's *Discourse and Social Change* advances a broadly Foucauldian project of discourse analysis, while David Simpson's *Subject to History: Ideology, Class, Gender* is a lively collection of materialist literary and cultural analyses. One interesting sub-theme of the book, never fully articulated within it, is that encounter of Marxism and Romanticism which we noted above as an important motif in contemporary radical culture: R. Jackson Wilson writes on Emerson, Marjorie Levinson on Keats and his readers, David Simpson himself on Wordsworth, and Frank Lentricchia on 'Lyric in the Culture of Capital'. *Is Literary History Possible?* asks David Perkins, in an attractive study of some of the constitutive dilemmas of the genre of literary history since its origins in the eighteenth century: 'the aporias of form, or . . . the insurmountable contradictions in organizing, structuring, and presenting the subject; and the always unsuccessful attempt of every literary history to explain the development of the literature that it describes'.

Books Reviewed

Adorno, Theodor. *Quasi Una Fantasia: Essays on Modern Music*, trans. Rodney Livingstone. Verso. pp. 336. £34.95. ISBN 0 86091 3600.

——. *Mahler: A Musical Physiognomy*, trans. Edmund Jephcott. University of Chicago Press. pp. 178. £27.50. ISBN 0 226 007635.

——. *Notes to Literature: Volume Two*, trans. Shierry Weber Nicholsen. Columbia University Press. pp. 320. $42. ISBN 0 231 06912 X.

Ahmad, Aijaz. *In Theory: Classes, Nations, Literatures*. Verso. pp. 358. £19.95. ISBN 0 86091 372 4.

Bauer, Dale M., and Susan Jaret McKinstry, eds. *Feminism, Bakhtin, and the Dialogic*. State University of New York Press. pp. 259. pb $16.95. ISBN 0 7914 0770 5.

Bürger, Peter. *The Decline of Modernism*, trans. Nicholas Walker. Polity. pp. 189. £35. ISBN 0 7456 0622 9.

——, and Christa Bürger. *The Institutions of Art*, trans. Loren Kruger. University of Nebraska Press. pp. 169. £29.95. ISBN 0 8032 1223 2.

Cormack, Mike. *Ideology*. Batsford. pp. 109. pb £9.99. ISBN 0 7134 6510 7.

Derwin, Susan. *The Ambivalence of Form: Lukács, Freud and the Novel*. Johns Hopkins University Press. pp. 208. $41. ISBN 0 8018 4381 2.

Fairclough, Norman. *Discourse and Social Change*. Polity. pp. 259. £35. ISBN 0 7456 0674 1.

Frisby, David. *The Alienated Mind: The Sociology of Knowledge in Germany 1918–1933*. Routledge. pp. 282. pb £12.99. ISBN 0 415 05796 5.

——. *Simmel and Since: Essays on Georg Simmel's Social Theory*. Routledge. pp. 214. hb £35, pb £10.99. ISBN 0 415 00975 8, 0 415 07275 1.

Gardiner, Michael. *The Dialogics of Critique: M. M. Bakhtin and the Theory of Ideology*. Routledge. pp. 258. hb £40, pb £11.99. ISBN 0 415 06064 8, 0 415 07975 6.

Golsan, Richard J., ed. *Fascism, Aesthetics and Culture*. University Press of New England. pp. 301. hb £30.50, pb £13. ISBN 0 87451 578 5, 0 87451 584 X.

Gottlieb, Roger S. *Marxism 1844–1990: Origins, Betrayal, Rebirth*. Routledge. pp. 248. hb £35, pb £10.99. ISBN 0 415 90653 9, 0 415 90654 7.

Gramsci, Antonio. *Prison Notebooks: Volume One*, ed. Joseph A. Buttigieg. Columbia University Press. pp. 608. $52. ISBN 0 231 06082 3.

Greenblatt, Stephen, and Giles Gunn, eds. *Redrawing the Boundaries: The Transformation of English and American Literary Studies*. Modern Language Association of America. pp. 595. hb $45, pb $19.50. ISBN 0 87352 395 4, 0 87352 396 2.

Habermas, Jürgen. *The Structural Transformation of the Public Sphere: An Enquiry Into a Category of Bourgeois Society*, trans. Thomas Burger. Polity. pp. 301. pb £11.95. ISBN 0 7456 1077 3.

Hohendahl, Peter Uwe. *Reappraisals: Shifting Alignments in Postwar Critical*

Theory. Cornell University Press. pp. 247. hb $41.25, pb $14.25. ISBN 0 8014 2455 0, 0 8014 9706 X.

Holub, Renate. *Antonio Gramsci: Beyond Marxism and Postmodernism*. Routledge. pp. 247. hb £35, pb £10.99. ISBN 0 415 02108 1, 0 415 07510 6.

Jameson, Fredric. *The Geopolitical Aesthetic: Cinema and Space in the World System*. British Film Institute. pp. 220. £30. ISBN 0 85170 311 9.

Löwy, Michael, and Robert Sayre. *Révolte et Mélancolie: Le Romantisme à Contre-Courant de la Modernité*. Editions Payot. pp. 306. No price available. ISBN 2 228 88480 4.

Malcuzynski, M.-Pierrette. *Entre-Dialogues Avec Bakhtin: ou, Sociocritique de la (Dé)Raison Polyphonique*. Rodopi. pp. 331. pb Hfl 100. ISBN 90 5183 371 7.

Mulhern, Francis, ed. *Contemporary Marxist Literary Criticism*. Longman. pp. 267. hb £25, pb £10.99. ISBN 0 582 05977 1, 0 582 05976 3.

Perkins, David. *Is Literary History Possible?* Johns Hopkins University Press. pp. 192. £18.50. ISBN 0 8018 4274 3.

Ransome, Paul. *Antonio Gramsci: A New Introduction*. Harvester Wheatsheaf. pp. 252. hb £40, pb £9.95. ISBN 0 7450 1111 X, 0 7450 1112 8.

Regan, Stephen, ed. *The Politics of Pleasure: Aesthetics and Cultural Theory*. Open University Press. pp. 225. pb £12.95. ISBN 0 335 09759 6.

Scholem, Gershom, ed. *The Correspondence of Walter Benjamin and Gershom Scholem, 1932–1940*, trans. Gary Smith and Andre Lefevere. Harvard University Press. pp. 276. pb £14.95. ISBN 0 674 17415 1.

Seyhan, Azade. *Representation and its Discontents: The Critical Legacy of German Romanticism*. University of California Press. pp. 187. hb $35, pb $16. hb ISBN 0 520 07675 3, 0 520 07676 1.

Simpson, David, ed. *Subject to History: Ideology, Class, Gender*. Cornell University Press. pp. 221. hb $41.25, pb $15.35. ISBN 0 8014 2561 1, 0 8014 9791 4.

Stephens, John. *Language and Ideology in Children's Fiction*. Longman. pp. 308. pb £12.99. ISBN 0 582 07062 7.

Stirk, Peter M. R. *Max Horkheimer: A New Interpretation*. Harvester Wheatsheaf. pp. 266. £35. ISBN 0 7450 0473 3.

Žižek, Slavoj, ed. *Everything You Always Wanted to Know About Lacan But Were Afraid to Ask Hitchcock*. Verso. pp. 279. hb £34.95, pb £11.95. ISBN 0 86091 394 5, 0 86091 592 1.

9

Colonial Discourse/Postcolonial Theory

PATRICK WILLIAMS

The most controversial book of the year – indeed, perhaps one of the most controversial books ever in the field – is Aijaz Ahmad's *In Theory: Classes, Nations, Literatures*. The controversy stems particularly from Ahmad's *ad hominem* approach. In the past – especially in his well-known onslaught on Fredric Jameson (reprinted here) – that method was applauded, or at least considered part of the process of engaged debate. However, his attacks in this collection on Salman Rushdie and, most especially, Edward Said, have been deemed unacceptable by many (not least Said himself). Most unfortunately for Ahmad, his desire to land some sort of critical knockout punch on his victims leads him to wild, inaccurate assertions and weak generalizations of a sort which are (generally) absent from those chapters not devoted to personalized abuse. In addition to the 'personalized' chapters, which account for over a third of the book, Ahmad discusses 'Indian Literature' and 'Third World Literature' (both dubious categories for him), the Three Worlds Theory and Marx's writings on India, in a series of readings which are always outspoken and thought-provoking. All of these areas are interrogated in the name of Marxism from a position which is highly sceptical of much current theoretical work. Ahmad's stated aim is to 'mark a break' with 'the existing theoretical formation, both methodologically and empirically' – no small claim in itself – and perhaps when the dust has settled. regarding his treatment of Said, attention may return to assessing his achievement here.

It is interesting and instructive to compare Aijaz Ahmad's reading of Salman Rushdie with that of Sara Suleri in *The Rhetoric of English India*. Like Ahmad, Suleri's book aims 'to question some of the governing assumptions of that discursive field' [i.e. colonial discourse analysis], but apparently in the name of a better deployment of theory, rather than, as in Ahmad's case, in the name of a Marxism sceptical of current theory. While the *aim* of Ahmad's analysis – to relate Rushdie's work to historical and social conditions in a continuous fashion – is arguably preferable to Suleri's more rhetorical/discursive focus, his desire to convict Rushdie the writer of bourgeois despair, misogynistic representations of women, and suchlike, damages his readings of *Shame*. If Suleri, on another level, is more attentive to the structures and tropes of Rushdie's writing, that by no means precludes a linkage with history.

Suleri is concerned with an idea which bell hooks and others have commented on in recent years, the perceived overprivileging of the category or concept of the Other. (Anxiety about this seems to be located very much in the United States, which might say more about how theory functions there than it does about the possible problems with the concept.) 'Alteritism', as Suleri calls it, allegedly turns the rhetoric of otherness into 'a postmodern substitute for the very orientalism that [it seeks] to dismantle'. Suleri curiously ignores much of the work of those critics who have already argued precisely what she herself does – that the idea of an absolute separation between colonizer and colonized, self and Other, is untenable and that all manner of complicities and interpenetrations occur – or even when, as in the case of Homi Bhabha and hybridity, she does mention them, that does nothing to unsettle her basic contention about theory. If the Other suffers from vagueness and conceptual inflation, the same might be said for Suleri's use of 'terror' as a founding image in her analysis. Such criticisms apart, Suleri produces a series of studies of English writing on India from Burke to Rushdie which are dense, assertive, intelligent and problematic.

Some of the problems which Suleri's study creates for itself can be illustrated by comparison of her use of a term like 'terror' with that of Vron Ware in *Beyond the Pale*, where vagueness is replaced by clarity, and rhetorical allusiveness by historical specificity. Ware uses it for the deployment of methods of oppression of black populations such as lynching. Suleri, on the other hand, seems to be using it as a marker of the instability of the colonial situation, and the resultant anxieties for both colonizer and colonized. *Beyond the Pale* is one of a small but growing number of books and articles which (like Richard Dyer's article 'White' in *Screen* and Ruth Frankenberg's forthcoming book) analyse ideologies of whiteness, and link that analysis to questions of racism, male dominance, imperialism and slavery. In particular, the inter-connections between feminism and other forms of oppositional movements – anti-imperialism, anti-slavery or anti-lynching – are brought out well in Ware's admirably readable study.

Mary Louise Pratt's *Imperial Eyes: Travel Writing and Transculturation* expands on her earlier work which dealt with the 'gaze' of European colonialism. Although its main focus is different forms of travel writing, it is very much concerned with the way in which other discourses or forms of knowledge such as natural history interact with it to describe, classify, and 'produce' the non-white/non-metropolitan world for Western consumption. Interaction is an important concept for Mary Louise Pratt – her work on the 'linguistics of contact' goes back a number of years, and now she examines '*contact zones*: social spaces where disparate cultures meet, clash and grapple with each other, often in highly asymmetrical relations of domination and subordination'. The implications of contact are pursued in another of her key terms, 'autoethnography', where colonized subjects attempt to represent themselves in a complex mode involving 'partial collaboration with, and appropriation of, the idioms of the conqueror'. This in turn is an example of 'transculturation', the process by which subordinated or marginal groups make use of materials from the dominant or metropolitan cultures. It is on the latter, however, that Pratt expends most of her energy, in a study which ranges widely in time (covering more than two centuries), and even more so in space (dealing with South America, the Caribbean and Africa). Ironically, perhaps, in view of her critique of processes of domination-through-classification, Pratt can be seen as a great classifier/categorizer herself, and some of her categories, such as 'the White Man's Lament' appear over-generalizing or essentializing. In general, though, the book is as intelligent and perceptive as one would expect from her.

John Noyes's *Colonial Space: Spatiality in the Discourse of German South-West Africa 1884–1915* examines another categorizing function and another form of colonial knowledge where once again the gaze of the colonizer is central – the organization of space, especially via writing and mapping. For Noyes, spatiality is a concept which unites colonialism, representation and social form. The book is conceived as a way out of the perceived problems for colonial discourse theory in trying to link psychological causality and socioeconomic causality, in the belief that 'the uncovering of spatializing strategies in the texts of an oppressive regime is in itself a strategic intervention'. Although the book's subtitle suggests a rather arcane or specialized study (a very small area; a very restricted time-span), in fact Noyes begins with a 100-page discussion of spatiality and subjectivity which runs from Aristotle via Kant and Hegel to Lacan, Deleuze and Guattari, and de Certeau, while in the specifically colonial section which makes up the bulk of the text, South West Africa and German writing function more as a case-study for a general inquiry into the conditions and strategies of the 'production' of space. And a fascinating inquiry it is, too.

As the subtitle to Patrick McGee's *Telling the Other: The Question of Value in Modern and Postcolonial Writing* indicates, post-colonialism is only one of the topics covered in this wide-ranging study, produced from an awareness of the problems of (inter)subjectivity, belief in the value of the other, and the responsibility of the writer/critic/teacher *vis à vis* that other (however understood or constituted). Alterity is here seen less as the Hegelian Other 'which is only a detour from the subject' than the Lacanian Other, 'the Big Other . . . radical, irreducible alterity, underpinning every position insofar as it is historical'. One chapter examines the contradictions of modernism and the (unconscious) implication of writers like Woolf in Orientalist or colonialist modes of thought and representation, as well as the more conscious relation of others such as Conrad or Forster, and two postcolonial responses in the writing of Achebe and Rushdie. Though the analysis is very competently done, the conclusions – modernism as will-to-style; postcolonialism making visible modernism's ethnocentrism or imperialism – may strike some readers as fairly familiar stuff. Another chapter uses Walter Benjamin's theory of allegory to examine the work of the postcolonial African writers Soyinka, Ngugi and Bessie Head as examples of 'allegorical realism'. In the end, the book makes better use of poststructuralist than of postcolonial critics, though its underlying aim – to stimulate a conscious, 'responsible' criticism and pedagogy on the part of Western intellectuals – is excellent.

If examining the complicity of authors in metropolitan hegemonic discourses or ideologies, as for instance Patrick McGee does, is something approaching a commonplace with regard to Forster and Conrad, it is rather more controversial in the case of postcolonial writers. One great exception to this is V. S. Naipaul, now ritually excoriated as the exemplar of co-optation, the white Western literary establishment's favourite black writer. In *London Calling: V. S. Naipaul, Postcolonial Mandarin*, an intelligent study of Naipaul's nonfiction, Rob Nixon scrutinizes Naipaul's self-arrogated status as eternal exile, dispassionate observer, and expert on the Third World. Nixon has a sharp eye for Naipaul's foibles and contradictions: 'The remark is rhetorically typical of Naipaul's penchant for presenting himself as an intrepid minority of one at precisely the moment when he is performing most conventionally.' Nixon's book wears its theory lightly, and is at its best when discussing questions such as Naipaul's use of a term like mimicry in the light of Bhabha's work on the same subject.

One of the issues which McGee mentions in relation to post-colonial texts (especially those of Ngugi) is translation, and this is the focus of Tejaswini Niranjana's *Siting Translation: History, Post-Structuralism and the Colonial Context*. In a very readable discussion which draws together both twentieth-century approaches to translation (in the shape of Benjamin's eclectic Marxism, and the post-structuralism of Derrida and de Man – and their essays on Benjamin) and Enlightenment theory and practices of translation (especially as they relate to the colonial context), Niranjana argues for a reconceptualizing of translation appropriate to the contemporary situation. As she says, 'In a post-colonial context the problematic of *translation* becomes a significant site for raising questions of representation, power and historicity.' Via her analysis of Benjamin, Niranjana links translation and history, and argues for both as disruptive practices – even *vis à vis* their own discursive predecessors: 'To read existing translations against the grain is also to read colonial historiography from a post-colonial perspective.' Although the texts analysed are colonial rather than postcolonial, the theory and practice are very much oriented towards the present and the future.

Though only partly concerned with colonial or postcolonial topics, *Nationalisms and Sexualities*, edited by Andrew Parker, Mary Russo, Doris Sommer and Patricia Yaeger, is an interesting post-conference collection. The opening section on '(De)Colonising Gender' includes essays by Rhonda Cobham on African Nationalist Fictions, Gayatri Spivak on another Mahasweta Devi short story, 'Douloti the Bountiful', and R. Radhakrishnan on nationalism and gender. Questions of bodies and maps link Cobham and Spivak, whose essays are in other respects very different. Cobham looks at African novels and national identity (in particular, Nuruddin Farah's *Maps*) in relation to crises of gendered identity. It is her contention that 'the social construction of gender roles in pre-colonial Africa must have been as problematic and provisional as would seem to be the case in all human societies', and she is critical of those novels like *Things Fall Apart* and *The River Between* which seem to accept maleness and femaleness as stable categories. Farah's complex novel, on the other hand, destabilizes gender and national boundaries, challenging nativist and nationalist myths and reductive models of African reality. Gayatri Spivak's discussion of Mahasweta Devi's short story follows her now-familiar strategy of close, almost minute attention to textual detail combined with sudden leaps to global issues, or the juxtaposition of conversational sections with passages of the dense analysis for which she is famous. The essay examines Devi's depiction of India's bonded labour system, and its lowest rung, and 'last instance', bonded prostitution, their nation-wide nature creating a paradoxical 'society' of bonded labourers. In an essay full of insights and frustrating dead ends, one of the key phrases, 'postcoloniality in the space of difference, in decolonized terrain' is important enough for Spivak to return to it several times, but unfortunately remains opaque, to this reader at least. R. Radhakrishnan's 'Nationalism, Gender and the Narrative of Identity' tackles both the difficulties posed for nationalism by 'the woman question' as symptomatic of nationalism's tendency to present itself as 'the political as such', excluding all other debates or agendas, and the correlative question, 'how is any one politics to be spoken of in terms of an-other politics?'. This is focused through an examination of the work of Partha Chatterjee on nationalism, and Kumkum Sangari and Sudesh Vaid on feminist historiography. 'If the categories of gender, sexuality, nationality or class can neither speak for the totality nor for one another but are yet implicated in one another relationally, how is the historical subject to produce a narrative form from such a radical relationality, a relationality without recourse?' – a powerful question, to which the article does not fully provide an answer.

Given the importance of Edward Said for the field of postcolonial studies, it is remarkable that there have not been a string of book-length analyses of his work. However, Michael Sprinker's *Edward Said: A Critical Reader* goes quite a long way towards remedying that. A series of chapters covers all of Said's major areas of interest or intervention, with the exception of music. Said is well known for his insistence on the 'worldliness' of the critic and the critical exercise, and several of the contributions (Barbara Harlow, 'The Palestinian Intellectual and the Liberation of the Academy'; Ella Shohat, 'Antinomies of Exile: Said at the Frontiers of National Narrations'; Nubar Hovsepian, 'Connections with Palestine') deal centrally with that in relation to Palestine, the *intifada* and the state of Israel. In 'Overlapping Territories, Intertwined Histories' – despite the political-economy-sounding title – Benita Parry engages with Said as literary and cultural critic, and points out how someone sensitive to textual silences, contradictions etc., can produce readings of Charlotte Brontë, Albert Camus, E. M. Forster and Joseph Conrad which homogenize their texts in the drive to locate them as components of 'imperial mastery'. Parry also carefully traces Said's position on resistance and the forms of identity or subjectivity which this draws upon. Like Parry, Abdul JanMohamed, in 'Worldliness-without-World, Homelessness-as-Home', looks at Said's sense of the position or role of the intellectual (and Said's own location in relation to that). However, rather than the 'postcolonial cosmopolitan' of Parry's subtitle, JanMohamed studies Said as a 'specular border intellectual'. Unlike the 'syncretic intellectual' (typified by Soyinka, Achebe or Rushdie) who is seen as quite at home in the various cultures within or between which they are located, the 'specular border intellectual' (such as Said, W. E. B. DuBois or Zora Neale Hurston), while familiar with the various cultures, maintains a critical distance from them. This is an interesting assertion on JanMohamed's part, since one of the recurrent accusations against Said is precisely his perceived lack of critical distance from 'discredited' Western categories such as humanism. Like JanMohamed, Tim Brennan, in 'Places of Mind, Occupied Lands', goes back to early Said works such as *Beginnings* for another differently-inflected analysis of the role of the intellectual. This time the focus is on Said's 'deliberately repetitive elaboration of *how* to write and speak as a public person . . . his prolonged inquiry into the mechanics of doing so' – a reminder yet again of the importance of the 'worldly' situation of the postcolonial critic.

Javed Majeed's *Ungoverned Imaginings: James Mill's 'The History of British India' and Orientalism* makes some mention of Said and Foucault, but only disappointingly dismissively in the Introduction, and extremely sketchily in the Conclusion. It remains an interesting, if otherwise untheorized, study of a series of eighteenth- and nineteenth-century writers on India (William James, Robert Southey, Thomas Moore, James Mill).

Peter Hulme's excellent *Colonial Encounters* (1986) was among other things an examination of the ways in which European representations of Carib people (especially as cannibals, thanks to Columbus) meshed with colonialist near-extermination of them. In *Wild Majesty*, he and Neil Whitehead have edited an important anthology of texts from 1490 to 1990, detailing 'Encounters with Caribs'. Although it makes no use of theory, it seemed too important a work in the colonial/postcolonial field not to mention.

Among the journals, *Social Text* devotes a special double issue (31/32) to 'Postcolonialism and the Third World'. From a selection of interesting, even impressive, contributions, one of the best is Anne McClintock's 'The Angel of Progress: Pitfalls of the Term "Post-Colonialism"' (84–98). Like articles such as Mishra and Hodge's 'What is Post(-)colonialism?' (*Textual Practice* 5:iii.399–414), McClintock engages with definitions of postcolonialism, and the inadequacies of the position of *The Empire Writes Back*. She is particularly worried by the insistent singularity of the terminology: *the* postcolonial condition; *the* postcolonial intellectual, as well as its unspoken commitment to a narrative of linear time and development. In the face of this homogenizing tendency, and the 'historically voided' nature of some concepts, McClintock reasserts the very different histories contained within 'postcolonialism'. This, and her use of political economy to support her 'theoretical' points, constitutes the particular strength of the article. In 'Notes on the "Post-Colonial"' (99–113), Ella Shohat makes a number of the same points as McClintock, though generally with less force, emphasizing the institutional acceptability of postcolonialism compared to 'the terrorising terms "imperialism" and "neo-colonialism"'. Her definition of postcolonialism contains the rather strange assertion that 'the "post-colonial" implies both going beyond anti-colonialist nationalist theory as well as going beyond a specific point in time', when one would have thought that if postcolonialism had superseded something at the conceptual level (one of the implications of 'post-') then it was much more likely to be the Eurocentric ideologies of colonialism itself – Western supremacy, and civilization, progress, etc. Shohat does, however, argue sensibly for the greater power (explanatory, political) of neocolonialism, and, linked to that, of the continuing utility of 'Third World' as a concept under erasure. Bruce Robbins's 'Comparative Cosmopolitanism' (169–86) returns to the topic which he and Tim Brennan among others have previously examined. 'The interest of the term cosmopolitan is located, then, not in its full theoretical extension, where it becomes a fantasy of ubiquity and omniscience, but rather (paradoxically) in its local applications, where the unrealizable ideal produces normative pressure against such alternatives as, say, the fashionable "hybridization".' Resistance to fashion is very much part of Robbins's approach, as he goes on to argue the need for 'difficult generalisations', rather than easy ones, 'for example, the more difficult though less pious procedure of *not* assuming agency to be everywhere present', and instead attempting to explain both its presence and its absences. A particular kind of presence is the focus of Homi Bhabha's 'The World and the Home' (141–53), which examines the question of the 'unhomely' as 'the shock of recognition of the-world-in-the-home and the-home-in-the-world', noting its importance in the creation of a postcolonial consciousness – not least in his own case. Although the unhomely appears as a paradigmatic postcolonial experience, it is also relevant to fiction which deals with cultural difference in general, and Bhabha reads its occurrence in novels by Toni Morrison and Nadine Gordimer, finding time along the way to argue for a reconstituted notion of World Literature and the responsibility of the critic towards unrepresented pasts.

In 'Postcolonialism and Globalization' (*Meanjin* 2.339–53), Simon During presents quite an elegant critique of postcolonialism, incorporating some of the points made by McClintock and Shohat but also extending the discussion, in his denunciation of its failure to account for the ways in which postcolonial societies are (internally) divided or (externally) linked by the particular rhythms of globalization, as well as the fact that 'the material limits of historical knowledge rupture the ground upon which the postcolonial paradigm rests'. In addition, postcolonialism is accused of simultaneously over-inflating the impact of Western expansion on other cultures and ignoring the extent to which that expansion fulfilled the needs and desires of the colonized peoples. (What is one to make, however, of someone who devotes two-thirds of his article to mounting this type of critique, only to 'cheerfully confess' subsequently that it had been 'something of a caricature'?) Even if, sadly, it does not have nearly as much to say about globalization as it does about postcolonialism, this remains a thought-provoking piece, simultaneously sensible and tendentious.

Homi Bhabha's 'Freedom's Basis in the Indeterminate' (*October* 61.46–57) is a typically complex (and difficult to summarize) meditation on postcolonial culture and its different/differential/'disjunctive' (a favourite Bhabha term) temporalities. Culture is viewed as both transnational and translational, and postcolonialism effects its own 'translation of modernity'. Part of the latter involves the recognition of 'colonial countermodernity', which proleptically enacts many of the issues which concern contemporary theory: ambivalence and indeterminacy, agency and intentionality. Another effect of postcolonialism on modernity is the production of a 'projective past' which slows the relentless forward motion of modernity, and in so doing reveals just what that 'progress' involves.

Contesting the universal claims of modernity is also central to

Dipesh Chakrabarty's 'Postcoloniality and the Artifice of History: Who Speaks for "Indian" Pasts?' (*Rep* 37.1–26) and, in a slightly different version 'Provincializing Europe: Postcoloniality and the Critique of History' (*Cultural Studies* 6:iii.337–57). Chakrabarty seeks to problematize the idea that Indians (or any other subaltern group or culture) could adequately represent themselves in history – history as an academic discourse originating in the West and in which ' "Europe" remains the sovereign theoretical subject of all histories, including the ones we call "Indian", "Chinese", "Kenyan" and so on'. Chakrabarty examines the way in which Western (and Indian) texts read or write Indian history as lack, incompletion or failure, especially in relation to progressivist narratives of historical transition, and calls for another type of historical project, that of 'provincialising "Europe" '. This would involve, among other things, 'a radical critique and transcendence of liberalism' and a recognition of the mutually implicated violence and idealism that are part of modernity. The production of such a form of history, however, seems 'impossible within the knowledge protocols of academic history, for the globality of academia is not independent of the globality that the European modern has created'. Whether a condition of 'not independen[ce]' should be taken as totally disempowering is an issue with which Chakrabarty does not engage.

A closely related, if less extensively articulated, argument which also deals with Indian history comes from the special issue of *Social Text* mentioned above (p. 145). In Gayan Prakash's 'Postcolonial Criticism and Indian Historiography' (*Social Text* 31/32.8–19) both postcolonial criticism and subaltern historiography are, following Spivak, seen as working 'catachrestically'; in other words, they are concerned with 'reversing, displacing and seizing the apparatus of value coding'. Although neither can escape their historical relation to Western systems of domination, they both reinscribe the historical texts produced by these systems, working, in a manner close to deconstruction, within the 'fissures' of the dominant.

If Prakash follows Spivak in his use of catachresis, others follow her – hound her might be more accurate – in their apparent obsession with the question of whether the subaltern can speak or not. The interview with Spivak by Leon de Kock (*Ariel* 23:iii.29–47), if it does not add anything to her positions elaborated elsewhere, at least finds Spivak in forthright mood. To the suggestion that she might be recolonizing the margins from the centre of European thought, she responds, 'I'm not interested in finding nativist alibis for where my thoughts come from.' On the question of universalism: 'There can be no human act without some modicum of universalising. Humanity would be completely autistic if it were not always, however incompletely, universalising.' And on the 'spurious' debate around 'Can the Subaltern Speak?': 'You don't give the subaltern a voice. You work *for* the bloody subaltern. You work against subalternity.'

Spurious or not, the question reappears in Samir Dayal's 'The Subaltern Does Not Speak: Mira Nair's *Salaam Bombay!* as a Postcolonial Text' (*Genders* 14.16 34). While Dayal's analysis makes use of a range of theorists, postcolonial and other, the film ends up being assessed, and condemned, on naïve reflectionist grounds, so that when one of the female subaltern characters does speak, what she says is deemed unacceptable because it is 'inauthentic'. Similarly, Forsterian categories of flat and round characters sit uncomfortably alongside discussions of the constitution of subaltern subjectivity. These discussions are really not helped by the sort of claim that Krishna, the young boy at the the centre of the film, 'infantilises and trivialises' the subaltern because as a child he is neither man nor woman, or that because the film ends with an image of Krishna on his own, it cannot 'take us beyond the image of the helpless subaltern'.

The phrase 'the subaltern cannot speak' also turns up as epigraph to Andrew Apter's '*Que Faire?* Reconsidering Inventions of Africa' (*Critical Inquiry* 19.87–104). Apter reviews the debates over the nature of African philosophy typified in the positions of V. Y. Mudimbe and Paulin Hountondji: whether it is an ineffable *gnosis* (Mudimbe), or critical philosophy practised by African philosophers drawing on a variety of traditions – in the main, something which has not yet been fully realized (Hountondji). Behind these obviously lie other debates about the past and future of African cultures. Apter combines the two positions to argue that the 'deep knowledge' of *gnosis* provides a space for configuring difference from which a genuine critical philosophy emerges. (Interestingly, Apter makes no real use of the epigraph, other than to voice his opposition to what he takes to be Spivak and Derrida's silencing of subalterns.)

Although its title 'The "Other" Worldliness of Postcolonial Discourse: A Critique' (*Critical Quarterly* 34:iii.74–89) promises another panoptic sweep, Madhava Prasad's article in fact limits itself to a discussion of certain critics (Said, Benita Parry, Abdul JanMohamed and David Lloyd) whom he sees as situating themselves in some sense as Fanon's heirs. Prasad works hard at his critique; everybody gets it wrong: Parry for supposedly 'draw[ing] exclusively from the messianic dimension of Fanon's thought', JanMohamed and Lloyd for 'essentialist presuppositions' in their theory of minority discourse, and Said for, among other things, allegedly misreading Gramsci on the production of individual subjectivity by the historical process. Despite the conviction with which the critique is mounted, I was not altogether convinced.

Evelyn O'Callaghan's ' "It's all about ideology: there's no discussion about art": Reluctant Voyages Into Theory in Caribbean Women's Writing' (*Kunapipi* 14:ii.35–44) is a warning that you can never assume that certain basic theoretical or political debates can be taken as read, finished once and for all. Inspired by discussion at a Caribbean Women Writers Conference, O'Callaghan finds herself required to work through all the old arguments about the relation of ideology and 'art', as well as ones about the inherently colonizing/phallocentric/Eurocentric nature of 'theory', etc. If the article suggests nothing especially new, at least it is a reminder of the continuing need for a certain kind of vigilance or polemical effort.

From Caribbean women writers to African ones: Kwaku Larbi Korang's 'Ama Ata Aidoo's Voyage Out: Mapping the Coordinates of Modernity and African Selfhood in *Our Sister Killjoy*' (*Kunapipi* 14:iii.50–61) examines Aidoo's novel 'within the rubric of a Pan-African literary nationalism' and in terms of its sceptical and oppositional relation to European modernity, Western culturalism and neocolonialist and patriarchal practices in Africa. In a manner which is now widespread in postcolonial criticism, the book is read as an exercise in 'un-forgetting' – the recovery of knowledge of history, culture and selfhood 'to promote a homegrown ethic of collectivity and survival'. I am not sure, however, that the discussion is helped by the register adopted: the eminently sensible points being made risk being diminished by the high discursive mode.

On postcolonial Africa more generally, *Public Culture* (4:ii.1–30) has an article by Achille Mbembe, 'The Banality of Power and the Aesthetics of Vulgarity in the Postcolony', which it then considers important enough to devote a special part-issue to debating (5:i). Mbembe views the postcolony as the site of improvisation, excess and disproportion, the multiplication and transformation of identities, and argues that to understand it we need to move beyond standard binaries such as state/civil society, or hegemony/counter-hegemony, in order to examine relations which are more mutual and familiar, domestic and promiscuous. Mbembe focuses on the way in which ruling class power is (literally) embodied in images of physical excess – eating, drinking, farting, fucking – as well as the laughter of the populace which this occasions, and which may be admiringly complicit or mockingly subversive, or deferential *and* oppositional. The postcolony is also the realm of the spectacle, the simulacrum and the fetish, its subjects characterized by 'ability to engage in baroque practices which are fundamentally ambiguous, mobile and "revisable" '. Appropriately enough, no doubt, Mbembe's provocative article itself embodies all manner of excess: excessive exaggeration, inattention and reductiveness – aspects of which are picked up by contributors to the special issue.

Tejumola Olaniyan, in 'Narrativizing Postcoloniality: Responsibilities' (*Public Culture* 5:i.47–55) criticizes Mbembe on the grounds that several of his central categories – for example, the 'intimate tyranny' which exists between rulers and ruled, or the constitution of subjects at the interface between subjection and subjectivity – have nothing uniquely postcolonial about them. Worse than this, Mbembe, rather than demonstrating the ineffectiveness of the binaries mentioned above, simply avoids addressing examples which might reveal their effectiveness, and replaces simplistic accounts of domination and resistance with a refusal to accept their relevance to the postcolonial context.

Fernando Coronil's contribution, 'Can Postcoloniality be Decolonized? Imperial Banality and Postcolonial Power' (5:i.89–108) provides a lengthier and more trenchant critique of Mbembe, remaining 'unconvinced by his approach and his argument'. The illustrations Mbembe uses (and to which he clearly attaches importance) are criticized for their lack of historical, social or theoretical situatedness. Coronil concedes that the range of questions he is putting to Mbembe's text about both the contexts for his examples and the meanings which are drawn from them – or not – may be 'old fashioned . . . and unfashionable' but they remain indispensable for many. Mbembe's disconcerting movement between 'fragmentary examples' and 'vast generalisations about the postcolony' is something which Coronil finds particularly unhelpful in trying to establish similarities and differences between postcolonial societies. Most damningly, perhaps, it appears that, for all his claims about doing away with binaries, Mbembe has recourse to a number of them, renamed or reconfigured. Many of the problems, according to Coronil, are the result of Mbembe's uncritical adoption of postmodern assumptions and approaches to questions of power or identity. Coronil concludes what is in many ways an impressive article with a series of comments on postcolonialism, power, knowledge, the body, and related topics. Fittingly, Mbembe is allowed the right of reply, which takes the form of 'Prosaics of Servitude and Authoritarian Civilities' (5:i.123–45). This is a more careful piece, (which is one reason why it lacks the verve of the original), as it sets out the thinking behind the felt need to produce a better understanding of the shifting dynamics of postcolonial rule than was on offer from theories such as Gramscian hegemony. Again, the explanation focuses on the complex, paradoxical, intertwined processes and practices involved. Mbembe follows that with an examination of the complex production of representations and knowledge in the way that, for example, knowledge production is 'situated', or Africa and the West are part of the terms of one another's self-definition. It will be interesting to see whether, after the original flurry of critical interest, Mbembe's article and argument remain a reference point for postcolonial discussions.

The concerns of *Diaspora* are obviously not purely, or even primarily, postcolonial, but there are important areas of convergence and overlap, and some of the contributions both challenge and enlarge the sense of what is involved in postcolonialism. A piece such as Milton J. Esman's 'The Political Fallout of International Migration' (2:i.3–41) is typical of the way in which certain major issues both are and aren't postcolonial, echoed in a very different mode by Artemis Leontis's 'The Diaspora of the Novel' (2:i.131–46). Stefan Helmreich, in 'Kinship, Nation and Paul Gilroy's Concept of Diaspora' (2:ii.243–50), bravely tackles the concept of diaspora, and probably its best-known current theorist, head on. Unfortunately, he comes off worst. There are also articles which address postcolonialism directly. Rey Chow's 'Between Colonizers: Hong Kong's Postcolonial Self-Writing in the 1990s' (2:ii.151–70), while it does not discuss questions of the 'post' as well as some other articles (McClintock, for example), has genuinely enlightening things to say on the differences represented by East Asian postcolonialism. With regard to typical markers of postcoloniality: territorial sovereignty, recovery of native cultural tradition, and neocolonialism, East Asia does not fit the standard model. For Hong Kong the central question is 'How do we talk about a postcoloniality that is a forced return to a "mother country", itself as imperialistic as the previous colonizer?' This also impacts on understandings of cultural production in Hong Kong, where the liberatory energy of self-representation becomes subsumed and recuperated by the 'greater' narrative of Chinese self-writing. Chow also examines the twin dangers of nativism and postmodern hybridism, the former seen as ignoring the necessary impurity of native origins, the latter ignoring the material realities of colonialism and its legacies of poverty and dependency. Against these, Chow reads the work of singer/songwriter/poet Lou Dayou, and the emergence of a notion of community based on cultural work and responsibility rather than blood, race and soil. In 'Inhabiting the Metropole: C. L. R. James and the Postcolonial Intellectual of the African Diaspora' (2:iii. 281–304), Anuradha Dingwaney Needham focuses on the nature of resistance, and the extent to which it could be seen as compromised by the incorporation of metropolitan theories or strategies. In a perspective which regards resistance as 'necessarily affected by that which it seeks to resist', C. L. R. James is a paradigmatic figure, and Needham provides an intelligent assessment of his importance. It is perhaps fitting to end as we began, with Aijaz Ahmad: Neil Lazarus's 'Postcolonialism and the Dilemma of Nationalism: Aijaz Ahmad's Critique of Third-Worldism' (2:iii.373–400) is both an extended review of Ahmad's *In Theory* (see p. 138) and a discussion of one of its polemical mainstays, an opposition to the Three Worlds theory. While Lazarus, in a spirit of generosity, or honesty, tries harder than some other reviewers to emphasize the positive elements of Ahmad's book, he is also forcefully – and correctly – critical of its many shortcomings. He mounts a very spirited defence of Said (though arguably Ahmad's full frontal assault self-destructs so spectacularly that Said does not need defending in this way). It is no less than just that someone who is so unsparing of what he sees as the faults of others should have his own failings subjected to rigorous scrutiny, and Lazarus goes to work on Ahmad's factual inaccuracies, cultural ignorance, interpretative weakness and polemical slipperiness. Although I began by speculating about the future standing of Ahmad's book, in some ways it is hard to see it recovering from this kind of criticism.

Books Reviewed

Ahmad, Aijaz. *In Theory: Classes, Nations, Literatures.* Verso. pp. 358. £19.95. ISBN 0 86091 372 4.

Hulme, Peter, and Neil Whitehead, eds. *Wild Majesty: Encounters with Caribs from Columbus to the Present Day.* Clarendon Press. pp. 369. hb £35, pb £14.95. ISBN 0 19 811226 2, 0 19 812274 8.

Majeed, Javed. *Ungoverned Imaginings: James Mill's 'The History of British*

India' and Orientalism. Clarendon Press. pp. 225. £27.50. ISBN 0 19 811786 8.

McGee, Patrick. Telling the Other: The Question Of Value in Modern and Postcolonial Writing. Cornell University Press. pp. 218. hb £30.50, pb £10.95. ISBN 0 8014 2749 5, 0 8014 8027 2.

Niranjana, Tejaswini. Siting Translation: History, Post-Structuralism and the Colonial Context. University of California Press. pp. 203. pb $38. ISBN 0 520 07451 3.

Nixon, Rob. London Calling: V. S. Naipaul, Postcolonial Mandarin. Oxford University Press. pp. 229. £27.50. ISBN 0 19 506717 7.

Noyes, John. Colonial Space: Spatiality in the Discourse of German South-West Africa 1884–1915. Harwood Academic. pp. 317. £17.00. ISBN 3 718 65167 X.

Parker, Andrew, Mary Russo, Doris Sommer, and Patricia Yaeger, eds. Nationalisms and Sexualities. Routledge. pp. 451. hb £40.00, pb £12.99. ISBN 0 415 90432 3, 0 415 90433 1.

Pratt, Mary Louise. Imperial Eyes: Travel Writing and Transculturation. Routledge. pp. 257. hb £35.00, pb £11.99. ISBN 0 415 02675 X, 0 415 06095 8.

Sprinker, Michael, ed. Edward Said: A Critical Reader. Blackwell. pp. 272. pb £13.99. ISBN 1 55786 229 X.

Suleri, Sara. The Rhetoric of English India. University of Chicago Press. pp. 230. pb £8.75. ISBN 0 226 77983 1.

Ware, Vron. Beyond the Pale: White Women, Racism and History. Verso. pp. 263. pb £11.95. ISBN 0 86091 552 2.

10

Art History

JONATHAN HARRIS

This chapter has four sections: 1. Introduction; 2. Books (Monographs); 3. Anthologies; 4. Journals. The books section includes 'Social Histories of Art' and 'Politics and Culture', while the anthologies section concentrates on 'Theory and Philosophy' and 'Photography and Film'. The journals section is divided between 'Academic Art and Design History' and 'Art and Design in Journalism'.

1. Introduction

It has become a truism that disciplines entrench narrow fields of study within intellectual and institutional borders and thereby impede the identification and development of connections between objects of analysis located, for historical reasons, within different academic subject areas. Although forms of inquiry characteristic of art history in the past half-century have shown a remarkable internal diversity (in large part because the subject has always been able to draw on an international range of leading scholars and intellectual traditions), certain parameters, acutely, have *circumscribed* perspectives as much as enabled creative work to go on. Some of these blocks will become evident in the review that follows. Most importantly they include: (1) an overwhelming attachment to 'high art' forms and practices and a consequent neglect or ignorance of the enormous variety of visual cultural artefacts outside the canon; (2) a very narrow sense of *historical* method, still centred on the motifs of *zeitgeist*, authorial intention and 'society as background'; and (3) a continuing dominance of unexamined sociologisms mobilized in order to account for the forms of grouping that artists and designers have established from the Romantic period to the present.

Mike Davis's *City of Quartz: Excavating the Future in Los Angeles* manages to evade all of these traps and consequently is impossible to place within the categories of review which follow. One of Davis's greatest achievements is to have avoided hypostatizing any of his 'objects of study'. Chapters consider Los Angeles suburban development, the built environment (including, but also exceeding, 'architecture'), the political struggles between 'downtown' and West Side establishments, the policing of the city, the gang cultures of the East Side and their involvement with the crack industry, the historical influence of the Catholic Church, and the industrial archaeology of the area from the 1930s to the present. *City of Quartz*, therefore, is art historical, sociological, criminological, historiographical (the first chapter deals with images of Los Angeles) and also auto-biographical, as Davis grew up in Fontana – east of Los Angeles – the 'deindustrialisation' of which occupies his final chapter.

Yet *City of Quartz* cannot be placed academically at all. It is written in a fast-paced journalistic mode, invoking all manner of 'theory' (modern and postmodern), but without ever becoming slavishly or merely fashionable. It is a *tour de force* of brilliantly-controlled invective, acerbic analysis and humane judgement. If the 'postmodern world' will look as Los Angeles looks now, Davis implies, then we must try to change the future. All of the positivities of 'postmodernist' abstract theoretical rhetoric – proliferating subject-positions, the dominance of space over time, the reorganization of life-styles, the complication of political identities and struggles, new forms of 'pleasure' – are instanced negatively in Davis's study of how Los Angeles has mutated economically, socially, politically and ideologically since the New Deal.

In some respects *City of Quartz* may be considered an 'end-of-twentieth-century' companion volume to Marshall Berman's *All That is Solid Melts into Air: The Experience of Modernity* (1991). While the latter largely dealt with a generalized late-nineteenth-century 'structure of feeling' in modernizing European culture and society, Davis presents Los Angeles as a case-study in urban industrial decay and reformation in the era of multinational capitalism. One sentence may indicate the tempo and substance of Davis's analysis: 'In a mindbending demonstration of how the new globalized economy works, California Steel Industries (as the consortium calls itself) employs a deunionized remnant of the Kaiser workforce [the company responsible for building Fontana's economy up to the 1970s] under Japanese and British supervision to roll and fabricate steel slabs imported from Brazil to compete in the local market against Korean imports.' Davis is probably best known to British academics as a historian of US labour organizations, but *City of Quartz* deserves to be read by students working in all social sciences and humanities areas. Art and Design historians, whatever the putative radicalism of their own interests and preferred designations, might stop to consider whether Davis's study suggests a wholly new form of inquiry, fundamentally detached from academic specialisms, but opportunistically able to absorb, synthesize (and when necessary, reject) the theoretical formulations bred in some of the work discussed within the categories delineated below.

2. Books (Monographs)

Social Histories of Art

Nicholas Green's *The Spectacle of Nature: Landscape and Bourgeois Culture in Ninetenth-Century France* (1990), now reissued in paperback (1993), is, finally, a disappointing study. The work of a scholar closely identified during the 1980s with the radical revision of art history and the deployment of a model of 'discourse analysis' heavily reliant on the work of Michel Foucault, Green's account promises much but is seriously deficient in a number of analytic and structural ways. One of the problems is that he may well have set himself too ambitious a project:

> This book attempts to push for a more interdiscursive approach to the visual – as part of an interlocking series of histories which involve multiple relations and dependencies across a range of social domains . . . it was in and through the type of modern urbanism crystallised in 1830s and 1840s Paris that the conditions for a new discourse on nature were laid down. *The Spectacle of Nature* weaves together those urban conditions and their ideological readings of space with the range of practices – rural visits and excursions, the diorama, country houses – through which they were played out.

Green has in his sights a form of art history identified as radical (Marxist, in fact) which, he feels, actually is very conservative in its reluctance to move beyond the study of the received selective tradition of High Art. So-called 'social history of art' discourse, identified particularly with the work of T. J. Clark (*Image of the People: Gustave Courbet and the 1848 Revolution* (Thames & Hudson, 1973) and *The Painting of Modern Life: Paris in the Art of Manet and his Followers* (Princeton University Press, 1984)) effectively reproduces, according to Green, conventional bourgeois art-historical procedures and values: specifically 'the sticking point is the retention by art history, even radical art history, of a set of texts designated *art* as the fulcrum for cultural analysis . . . we cast the net much wider than the received wisdom of art history, to draw in the state and its institutions, family patterns, professional groupings and so on'. Though his critique of 'social history of art's' reproduction of the canon of great art and great artists is accurate (and T. J. Clark acknowledged the point in his book on Manet), Green's book is weak thematically and organizationally because he fails to produce an alternative object of study which is comparably coherent and tangible. While Clark's accounts play out the usual text/context oppositions, setting up a focus and a realm of epiphenomena, Green's 'interdisciplinarity' produces, on the whole, little more than a rather flattened taxonomy of figures, codes, conventions and modes ('From cholera to crime', 'The rise of the popular press', 'The provincial audience', 'Metropolitan eyes: two case studies', etc.), with little vivid sense of their intrinsic character or practical interaction. It is a background vainly in search of a foreground. There is little definition or analysis of 'the visual' of any kind, which is a particularly serious omission, chiefly because Green establishes this issue as a key part of his study. Poor editing has also reduced the quality of the text. For instance, the long descriptive (and mundane) section on 'the Fontainebleau story' of the construction of a retreat for the bourgeoisie away from Paris comes at the end, rather than, as it should have, at the beginning of the study. The book, consequently, has a very poor ending. Green's intention in writing *The Spectacle of Nature* was partly to shift art historical attention away from France and Paris between 1850 and 1880 (a period celebrated, variously, for the emergence of Impressionism, modernism and the avant-garde and fetishized, respectively, by bourgeois, formalist and neo-Marxist art historians), towards the first half of the nineteenth century. It is then, Green argues, that the character of modern Paris and metropolitan French life really was adumbrated: social history of art's emphasis on Baron Haussmann's later rebuilding of Paris within a central State strategy for reorganizing commercial and political life in the city has been made to overshadow the crucial earlier (and entrepreneurial) phase of capitalist speculation and development in the metropolis (represented by figures such as Alexis-André Dosné and Jacques Laffitte). The point is well made, though it is more useful to bring the two historiographical periods (with their particular analytic stresses) into alignment, rather than simply reject one in favour of the other. Once again, one has the sense that Green's book is in danger of losing its poignancy due to the author's attempt to polemicize, in every direction possible, *contra* Clark.

In one important respect, however, Green affirms a theoretical and political affiliation with the 'social history of art' tradition: that is, the centrality of a Marxist analysis of social relations. Despite the cutaneous Foucauldianism of Green's prose, he claims a deeper, determining ontology. Although, he says, reductionist Marxist accounts actually have been a block on properly understanding the construction of modes of modern social identity, it is Louis Althusser's theory of interpellation which has enabled Green's study of 'social personas produced in and through discourse' to be brought into 'articulation with economic categories'. His study consists, he says, of an examination of how 'the ideology of nature was lived out at the level of personal identity. Far from being anti-Marxist, the aim is to bend the "spirit" of historical materialism in new directions.' The account that follows, though, generally tends to drift between straightforward narrative or textual analysis (interesting in isolated cases – 'The magic of the diorama' or 'Critical guides to landscape', for instance) and isolated abstract theoretical injunctions. Those passages (for instance, pp. 128–30) on discursive constructions of identity, Foucauldian and Althusserian notions of subject interpellation, are valuable in themselves, but seem to bear only tenuous relation to the empirical material Green assembles. Curious also is Green's continued unexplained use of Raymond Williams's phrase 'structure of feeling' (deliberately posed in *The Long Revolution* as an incongruity requiring clarification) and lack of reference (in footnotes or bibliography) to Williams's *The Country and the City* (1973), surely a key work for any scholar working in a sphere of cultural history relating to modern industrial societies.

The most serious weakness of the study in analytic terms is that of the value of Green's account of varying 'social-types' (see part 3: 'The Subject in Nature Experience and Social power', 'the businessman', 'the metropolitan', and so on). He appears to claim these have a 'typicality' which renders them representative of the kinds of modern social identities he says developed in Paris between 1820 and 1840. Yet he produces little evidence for this claim and one is left wondering if they rather stand for a very limited section of part of a middle class fraction. Interesting, certainly, but not necessarily indicative of the generality of social composition (if such a generality existed at all). Indeed, the issue of 'typicality' as a viable analytic tool is not discussed in any depth by Green, who lurches regularly from an anti-determinist Foucauldian 'story-telling' to a rather more familiar neo-Lukácsean economistic Marxism.

An extraordinary lapse occurs mid-way through the study when Green remarks: 'Unlike many ideological domains where we can point to materially-located institutions as the sites from which power is exercised, nature, it seems, hangs in a vacuum. Because it is to do with leisure time, because it is to do with personalized perceptions, it appears to lie outside or in the interstices of more obviously institutionalized power relations.' While clearly there were not as many working-class people involved then in forms of work relating to servicing overwhelmingly middle-class tourists as there are now, surely it could not have escaped Green's attention that the vast majority of people involved with the cultural elaboration of the metropolis/countryside dyad were involved as labourers of varying kinds (and bound, therefore, into specific and identifiable relations of economic and social production by their employers), and not as part of that relatively tiny group of tourists enjoying their 'leisure time'?

Griselda Pollock is similarly interested in the phenomenon of nineteenth-century French tourism (though in the familiar, fetishized 1850–1900 period) in her *Avant-Garde Gambits 1888–1893: Gender and the Colour of Art History*. This text, originally delivered as the Thames and Hudson Walter Neurath Memorial Lecture in 1992 and inflated into a 'book' partly through the inclusion of fifty illustrations, examines the extension of the realm of the Parisian metropolis to include, in effect, the island of Tahiti. It was here that Paul Gauguin played out his avant-garde myth of 'escaping' from the city into a putatively 'virgin' land unsoiled by the sordid relations of urban industrial capitalism. According to Pollock, Gauguin's painting *Manao Tupapau* (1892), produced during the artist's first trip to the island, and initially exhibited in Copenhagen in 1893, was Gauguin's 'big stake in avant-garde game-play'. The work shows a Tahitian girl lying naked on a bed, on her stomach, while in the background stands a hooded female figure, in black. The painting becomes the vehicle for Pollock's major theme during the essay, that is, the way in which artists who wish to see themselves (and be seen by others) as part of the avant-garde of modern painting must achieve three things:

This trilogy proposes a specific way of understanding avant-gardism as a kind of game-play. In contrast to conventional histories of modern art, which tell its story through heroic individuals, each 'inventing' his (usually) novel style as an expression of individual genius, I propose my three terms. To make your mark in the avant-garde community, you had to relate your work to what was going on: *reference*. Then you had to defer to the existing leader, to the work or project which represented the latest move, the last word, or what was considered the definitive statement of shared concerns: *deference*. Finally your own move involved establishing a *difference* which had to be both legible in terms of current aesthetics and criticism, and also a definitive advance on that current position.

Gauguin's *Manao Tupapau*, then, is his 'answer' to Manet's *Olympia* (1863), the painting normally regarded by art historians (including Marxists such as T. J. Clark) as signalling the emergence of a modernist art involved in both self- and social criticism (see Clark's essay 'Preliminaries to a Possible Treatment of Manet's "Olympia" in 1865', *Screen*, Spring 1980, pp. 18-41). Initially exhibited at the Salon in 1865, Manet's painting had received a much wider showing when exhibited in 1889 at the Exposition Universelle in Paris, an event which celebrated the Western (and specifically French) appropriation of the non-Western world through economic, political and military colonization.

Pollock's agenda in *Avant-Garde Gambits* – wholly consistent with her work during the 1980s (see, for example, her collection of essays *Vision and Difference: Feminism, Femininity and Histories of Art*, 1988) – is to undermine (or at least attempt to undermine) both bourgeois art-historical accounts of great modern art and artists and the alternative accounts provided by Marxists who neglect, marginalize or refuse to engage in issues of gender. With *Avant-Garde Gambits* this critique is extended to include questions of race and ethnicity. If patriarchy is a form of metaphoric colonization of women by men, then the racism exhibited within the art and art history of Western men since the early nineteenth century (and no doubt earlier) is one 'in which the personality and the body of one group is literally colonized by the desires and meanings of the dominating group, turning Arab and African peoples into projections of Westerners of the "Otherness of the Self" '.

Manao Tupapau, from this perspective, involves a concatenation of exploitative relations and inventions: a black woman's body presented for the consumption of white Western men. The structural homology with Manet's *Olympia* extends further: while Manet portrayed (and according to Clark et al. deliberately revealed, through a sabotaging of prevailing artistic and social conventions) a working-class prostitute for the salon-going public, Gauguin's model was, in fact, his own thirteen-year-old wife. While such a marriage was acceptable in Tahiti, Pollock says, 'from a European point of view, as this painting of her was appraised in its Parisian setting, it was not possible to read this thirteen-year-old woman of colour as a "wife"'.

Pollock's essay pursues this imbrication of gender and racial exploitation through a brief history of the 'post-Impressionist' avant-gardism of Gauguin, Bernard and Van Gogh, considers the emergent discourses on tourism (borrowing ideas from Dean Mac-Cannell's *The Tourist: A New Theory of the Leisure Class*, 1976), and concludes with condemnation of an art history which 'continues uncritically to celebrate these great masters and to affirm Gauguin's self-curating strategies – his avant-garde gambits . . . confirm[ing] its collaboration with that European project, exposing not only the gender, but also the colour of art history'. While Clark and the 'social history of art' scholars associated with a Marxist analysis of modernist art are also, implicitly, lined up with this imperializing, patriarchal art history (though Pollock also defers to Clark in two footnotes), one wonders if her motivation for continuing the feminist onslaught on 'bourgeois art and art history' is solely based on 'correcting' and challenging the 'dominant ideology'. Clark has made it fairly clear that he values the art of the modern period (let's not mess about: the art of the canonical modern masters) because he believes it is technically, cognitively, aesthetically great. He also happens to believe that it is 'socially-critical', though definitely not in any crass propagandistic or tendential way. Pollock, on the other hand, seems to make no claims for the cultural worth of the art she systematically 'deconstructs'. It appears simply to stand as part of what Walter Benjamin called the record of barbarity. This may indeed be her view. If this is the *raison d'être*, then hers probably is an arid and punishing project. And more is on its way, as she tells us in a footnote: her *The Case Against Van Gogh: The Cities and Countries of Modernism* is imminently to be published.

While certainly it is true that 'bourgeois art history' keeps on coming, oiling the wheels of the art market and validating the worth of Impressionist and Post-Impressionist work in particular, it may be the case that yet another book on Gauguin, whatever its intended critical function, also works to feed the market and the reputations. For that matter, the two effects may be inseparable. If it is the case that Pollock believes the works are 'good' or valuable (for whatever reasons she has so far decided to keep to herself) it would be intriguing, preferable, and a relief, to have them elucidated.

Andrew Hemingway's *Landscape Imagery and Urban Culture in Early Nineteenth-Century Britain*, on the other hand, won't do much for the market in Girtins, Cotmans, Cookes, Constables, Turners and Vincents. Neither will it come to occupy a position in the pantheon of 'new art history'. Pollock's genius has partly lain in writing relatively short, easily-digestible 'bite-size' feminist onslaughts, aimed at undergraduates with little time to read at leisure and with deadlines for essays and examination revision. Hemingway's study, consisting of 300 pages of dense text and forty-three pages of footnotes, is clearly the product of recycling and endlessly touching up a long-distance PhD.

While Cambridge University Press might well be congratulated for having nobly allowed Hemingway the full rein of his academic musings, a shrewder editing might have produced a slimmer, more succinct and interesting study. Hemingway, one suspects, wants this book to be considerably more momentous than he knows it has any chance of being. He associates it, directly and indirectly, with the 'social history of art' tradition, with Clark (whose books are, like Pollock's, instructively on the short side) and with sophisticated Marxist analysis, yet because of its size and its rambling organization, it is doomed to remain stuck in the long-loan section of the academic library.

Hemingway's use of 'theory' exhibits a coyness around the issue of mapping a Marxist position on to what he regards as a broadly 'Foucauldian' framework. Hemingway is aware, as Green and Pollock also are, that the term 'discourse' has been subject to a gross promiscuity of usage and states 'the term is not used here with reference to the specialized models of linguistic analysis, but instead in a loose Foucauldian sense, to refer to the "body of anonymous historical rules" which governs what can be said within a particular category of knowledge within a specific historical context'.

Putting aside the issue of whether this is so loose as not to be Foucauldian in any significant sense at all, it is clear that Hemingway wants to have his Marxist logocentric cake and eat it. While this notion of discourse is useful to his consideration of philosophical criticism, academic art theory and art criticism in the eighteenth and nineteenth centuries, he clarifies for us that his 'general approach' to understanding the social function of knowledge is predicated on the concept of ideology, and not on Foucault's discourse model. A footnote to this adds that Foucault 'made little use of the concept of ideology, which he seems to have equated with its vulgar Marxist version'. Foucault, I would have thought, saw Marxism *tout court* as a reductionism, vulgarity being its defining character. Althusserian structuralist Marxism probably represented the last serious attempt to make theoretical space for what was called 'relative autonomy' at political and ideological 'levels' in the social formation.

It is because Hemingway attempts intelligently to articulate economic, social and aesthetic categories that parts of *Landscape Imagery and Urban Culture* are interesting and push 'British nineteenth-century art studies' towards the kind of systematic and reflexive theorization that work on French visual culture in the same century has achieved over the last thirty years or so. In his second chapter, 'Ideology and Naturalism', it becomes obvious that Hemingway wants to make an alliance not just with Clark's work on the nineteenth century, but also with *de rigueur* debates on modernism and twentieth-century art. Coded terms like 'cognitive effects', 'value' and 'innovations in pictorial practice' indicate that Hemingway (now researching early-twentieth-century US art) wants to tango with the likes of Charles Harrison, Tom Crow and others who have attempted to colonize the so-called 'critical-modernist' debate of avant-garde art and art theory:

> While this book is concerned primarily with larger ideological structures and systems of imagery, it also gives certain images more sustained consideration than others. Underlying this distinction is a concept of value which appraises art objects in terms of their cognitive effects. Value is measured both in terms of the acuity and depth with which objects engage with the historical development of the forms of representation involved ['critical-modernism'], and with contemporary beliefs and social phenomena.

This eventually devolves (after about a hundred pages of 'background' to the art) into claims that various landscape paintings, exhibiting relative degrees of 'sketchiness of composition', show aspects of modern British economic, social and cultural life, and therefore come close to being legitimately described as 'modernist' or near to it. For instance, Hemingway argues:

> Vincent's *Dutch Fair on Yarmouth Beach, Yarmouth Quay,* and *View of Yarmouth* represent an attempt to render the modern picturesque, while yet remaining authentic to the character of a bustling modern

port, which bore only lightly the marks of its development as a resort. In this respect these pictures stand comparison with Chalon's *View of Hastings* and Constable's *Beach at Brighton*, although only the *View of Yarmouth* suggests some of the tensions of the latter.

In the end, Hemingway seems to be saying, most British artists bottled out of shifting into proto-Impressionist mode, apart from Constable who occasionally, as with his *Beach at Brighton, the Chain Pier in the Distance*, represented something of the tensions in English seaside industrialization. This is a disappointing, though rather inevitable conclusion, given the very different traditions of visual representation available to British as opposed to French artists working in the early- and mid-nineteenth century, along with the contrast in national political and social histories.

Landscape Imagery and Urban Culture lingers too long over setting up the historical 'discursive context' in which the art eventually is discussed by Hemingway, with preliminary chapters on the sociology of British artists, taxonomies of contemporary critical forms, and a rather laborious account of 'naturalism' and academic art philosophy. By the time we get to the substantive discussion of the works (chapter 8: 'The Imagery of Seaside Resorts and Modern Leisure', and chapter 9: 'The Contradictions of Progress: Imagery of Rivers'), we are looking forward to something more than being told that most of the art more or less avoided the issues of the modern. I suspect that Hemingway is himself rather sad that this was the case. He has to report, in his conclusion, for example, that 'critical responses to landscape painting suggest that there was no struggle over their meanings as social representations', and that the 'social infrastructure which would support a vanguard practice in later nineteenth-century France did not exist in Britain at this time, and the model of artistic personality crucial to such a practice was not available yet to painters'. Finally, and rather dismally, Hemingway tells us in his last sentence: if 'British landscape painters of that period deserve any credit, it is for their short-lived attempt to develop types of imagery which could comprehend some aspects of that world'.

If we are not to be satisfied with the knowledge that the lack of phenomena in certain historical and social formations may be as significant (and interesting) as their presence in others, then we could draw the lesson from Hemingway's study that one must be very careful in choosing the vehicles for arguments and debates with which we want to engage. In this case, however, it is to be suspected that Hemingway has only relatively recently formed his attachment to modernist debates and art practices, and that *Landscape Imagery and Urban Culture* is largely (and, sadly for Hemingway, irredeemably) the relic of earlier academic interests.

Politics and Culture

Timothy W. Lukes's *Shows of Force: Power, Politics and Ideology in Art Exhibitions* promises more than it delivers. A lecturer in 'political science', rather than art history or art theory, Lukes's interest is in how recent exhibitions (of old and contemporary) art embody, represent or animate facets of North American political and social organization. Yet, on the whole, these generally short essays (seventeen in all) involve no detailed research into the motivations and planning of specific exhibitions. Such work is notoriously difficult and time-consuming, not least because museums and art galleries are very careful about releasing information to scholars who may prove to be critical of their policies or selections. Instead Lukes presents interesting (sometimes slightly off-the-wall) accounts of how the choice of a particular artist or group, or style, resonates with what he sees as a particular aspect of contemporary American capitalist polity.

The essays are written in a kind of middle-brow journalistic style (which is not intended as a criticism) and many pieces were originally published in *Art Papers*, a magazine originating in Atlanta, which, Lukes is keen to tell us (perhaps too keen) 'is a nationally recognized, regionally based journal of contemporary art'. It would not be surprising (rather a compliment, considering the US media's attempted blacklisting of Edward Said and Noam Chomsky) if the kind of connections and overlappings of 'aesthetic' and 'political' interests which Lukes attempts to identify were a source of embarrassment for the establishment which resulted in his work being held on the margins of supposedly 'national' or 'mainstream' art journalism.

His introduction doesn't toy with academic niceties:

> This book is a collection of politically grounded critiques about art. It refuses, however, to fool around in polite metatheoretical terms with abstract questions surrounding 'the politics of aesthetics' or 'the aesthetics of politics'. Instead, it subversively reexamines how cultural mythologies and political power are expressed in the showing of artworks by museums. Hence, these studies relentlessly ask how parti-

cular displays of artwork can be seen as political texts rife with conflicted rhetoric about the ideologies of the present.

Although he doesn't like the formulations mentioned above, his book actually is a set of accounts of how notions of aesthetic character and worth have had specific (and sometimes changing) social and political dimensions. The first section, 'Envisioning a Past, Imagining the West', considers seven US artists or groups of artists dominantly seen as embodying the North American 'West': these include the landscape paintings of George Caleb Bingham and Frederick Edwin Church, the cowboy genre paintings of Frederic Remington (examples of which used to feature on the walls of the sets in *Dallas* and *Dynasty*, television soap operas during the 1980s), Georgia O'Keeffe's 'abstract' paintings based on desert motifs, and so-called 'American Impressionist' works of the California School.

Mostly written during the 1980s, these essays portray America under President Reagan as a continual theme. Nineteenth-century paintings of the settled mid-West and the American wilderness, soon to be mastered by those carrying out the 'Manifest Destiny' of US citizens, incorporate and give visual form to 'the old mythologies of expansionistic Anglo-Saxon power, so cherished during much of the Reagan-Bush era, [which are] easily . . . recharged from ideological batteries like these Bingham paintings'. This kind of summation of the import of paintings tends to become rather repetitive, and Lukes is more interesting when discussing specific links between museum, artist or artwork, and local patron. In relation to Bingham, we hear, for instance, it was Boatmens Bancshares, Inc. Bank of St Louis, Missouri, collaborating with the St Louis Art Museum, the May Department Stores Company and the Monsanto Company which organized the show of works including *The Concealed Enemy* (1845) and *Captured by the Indians* (1848), both members of the cowboy genre which Bingham's work exemplified and elevated.

Nor is Lukes oblivious to the quality of technique and finish which many of these artists attained (their works now being worth hundreds of thousands of dollars). Remington's paintings, such as *The Old Stagecoach of the Plains* (1901) or *Fired On* (1907), Lukes marvels, 'use just a handful of colors – dark blue, green, brown and hints of intense yellow – to create moonlit nocturnal scenes with incredible suggestion and symbolic force'. This recognition is not diminished by knowing, as Lukes points out, that the show of Remington's work is sponsored by Merrill Lynch, 'the financial services giant', which seeks to mobilize these works in its continued drive to appear also 'on the frontiers' of financial services providing 'professionally planned economic expansion'. It's unlikely, I would have thought, that Merrill Lynch would mind the symbolism being pointed out by Lukes. This is quite overt cultural sponsorship, after all, and the success of the endeavour is based on the relationship being recognized.

Some of the essays concentrate more on the art museum than on the works displayed, and this is the case with Lukes's interesting discussion of the new Fleischer Museum of California Impressionism, situated within the grounds of the Franchise Federated Financial Corporation on the outskirts of Scottsdale, Arizona. 'It is an art space, but with a decidedly grandiose aura and assured corporate feel of flat-out self-importance – fine marble, shiny brass, thick carpets, glossy woods, chic furniture, sassy design. Viewing the show is all free, because the museum itself is always open as "a public service".' Lukes's essay on Hans Haacke in the second part of his book 'Developing the Present, Defining a World', moves to consider contemporary artists who have made the art gallery or museum itself the subject-matter of their work. Haacke's work has long been critical of the relations between corporate capitalist sponsorship, central state cultural patronage and the agendas of major national or international art institutions. Haacke's show, a survey of work going back to the early 1970s, travelled from New York to the Knight Gallery in Charlotte, North Carolina, in 1988, a town 'adorned with many signs of the same cultural, economic and political trends that Haacke's art imitates'. Perhaps curiously, Lukes is implicitly critical of Haacke's work, in comparison with his (qualified) approbation for nineteenth-century painters: 'Haacke's critique uses the same language and communication style as corporate advertisers to make his political points, remaining trapped to some extent within their outlooks and assumptions. And, on another level, Haacke's critical installations, which relentlessly indict the cultural cost of state and corporate funding for the arts, continue on their nationwide road trip courtesy of generous funding from the state and corporate sector.'

Lukes's attempts to muse over these contradictions are less satisfactory than his accounts of individual shows and artworks. This may be because Jean Baudrillard seems to be Lukes's guiding theoretical mentor, a state of affairs which leads Lukes continually to wring his hands with phrases denouncing the 'media-driven culture' or the evils of living within 'the shadow of the silent majorities'. Lukes's final essay, attempting to summarize his findings, entitled

'The Politics of Images' is the least engaging of any of his pieces. This is based on recycling the tenets of what stood for 1970s artistic radicalism – chiefly Victor Burgin's 'end of art theory' rhetoric – and connects rather poorly to the best of Lukes's specific analyses.

While Lukes's study is concerned specifically with the contemporary relationship between private corporate capital and art exhibition sponsorship in the United States, David Crowley's *National Style and Nation-State* and Michèle Cone's *Artists Under Vichy* set out to examine the historical development of cultural practices within particular political and national conditions. Crowley is interested in the origins and forms of Polish cultural design, roughly from the end of the nineteenth century to the 1930s, while Cone's study concentrates on the status of the visual arts under both Vichy government and direct German dictatorship in France between 1939 and 1945. Both books tell us more, and more interestingly, about the role of visual cultural production in modern societies than Jeremy Howard's disappointing *The Union of Youth: An Artists' Society of the Russian Avant-Garde*, which manages to turn examination of a potentially fascinating moment in pre-revolutionary Russia into a dull recounting of standard modernist history.

Cone's *Artists Under Vichy: A Case of Prejudice and Persecution* is the best of the three, although it too contains a mixture of gripping historical narrative with rather poor theoretical and analytic insight. Her main point, though, which she makes well, is that many artists carried on producing their art, and trying to exhibit and sell it, under the rule of French collaborationist leaders and then the Nazis themselves. While histories of mid-century modern art usually focus on the emigration of avant-garde artists from Paris to London and New York, Cone wishes to retrieve the histories of the many who could not or did not leave France in July 1940. What, she asks, 'are the moral options open to artists under authoritarian regimes, given that a policy of silence signifying disaffection with the state and sympathy with the outcasts is financially disastrous, while exile is practicable only in a few exceptional cases?'

Her answer seems to be, on the one hand, either a clear, unambiguous collaboration with the imposed regime or, on the other, involvement with forms of artistic production which, in varying ways and to varying degrees, implied opposition to it. An example of the former path was 'Le voyage', as it became known, by a group of French artists to Germany in October and November 1941. Thirteen artists, all named by Cone, along with the German officers who accompanied them, went on the trip, visiting hallowed shrines of Reich cultural achievement. Other artists found excuses to avoid this package deal, while those who signed on are photographed at the Gare de l'Est in Paris, between their German minders, before setting out, looking extremely uneasy. Cone observes that this group included artists associated with a variety of styles – some neo-Fauvists, two or three figurative sculptors, painters of 'poetic reality', and one or two academicians from the Ecole des Beaux Arts. Thus, nominal 'modernists' seem to have been as seduced (or scared into attendance) by the steel hand of 'cultural friendship' as the institutional conservatives.

Other artists, including Picasso, who stayed in Paris during the war, sublimated their feelings about the occupation into three or four genres of representation which, Cone argues, signalled either their detachment from (and therefore 'rejection' of) the social world, or a kind of coded form of resistance to the Nazis and their French cronies. Interpretation here becomes strictly untestable, in claims such as that Georges Rohner's *Still Life with Skull* (1942) was a comment on living under the German yoke, that Alfred Manessier's *Fighting Roosters* (1944), using red, white and blue paint, was an example of 'patriotic abstraction', or that Picasso's *Tomato Plant* (1944) showing ripe tomatoes about to fall was a visual symbol for the coming of D-Day. Cone goes some way towards defending Picasso's range of contacts with Germans and French collaborators in Paris during the war, who variously tried to arrest, ridicule or buy pictures from the man.

Artists Under Vichy undoubtedly is a valuable study particularly because the period and the subject have received comparatively little attention within art history: wars are usually posed as *interruptions* to the teleology of modernism, or as corruptions of it. Cone's data establishes that many modern artists saw little intrinsic connection between 'their art' and social or political radicalism. There was also enough of a tradition of French (and specifically Parisian) anti-Semitism and national chauvinism for the Nazis to exploit, and recruit, by permitting some institutions and some exhibitions (such as those of the Salon d'Automne and the Salon des Indépendants) to continue, thus enabling the occupiers to appear relatively liberal and respectful of some forms of French culture.

Crowley's *National Style and Nation-State: Design in Poland from the Vernacular Revival to the International Style* does not have the degree of focus that gives Cone's book intrinsic integrity. It also lacks the implication of moral and political urgency that a study of tyranny and occupation necessarily entails. More significantly, however, Crowley's study fails as a piece of rigorous historical and critical analysis. It neither constructs theoretically-cogent notions of the 'nationalism' and 'patriotism' it seeks to examine through cultural materials, nor is able to sustain a systematic and connective examination of the components of this putative national culture. On many occasions it begins to sound like a piece of (post-Soviet Bloc) Polish tourist guide prose: 'Unlike most other marginalized and suppressed peoples seeking national consciousness and expression in the nineteenth century, the Poles sought to return to the condition of statehood . . . the Poles possessed an increasingly distant, though actual memory of 'golden ages'; times in which Poles had controlled their own national destiny. . . .' Which Poles? Whose memories? What kind of 'statehood'? Crowley effectively evacuates any specificity of analysis relating to social class or regional identity, never mind questions of gender or the possibility of forms of alternative political and social struggle within the Polish population. Such nationalist sentiments are always purer and more romantic when the nation does not yet exist (black 'nationalism' in South Africa and Irish 'nationalism' in the north of Ireland are two contemporary examples). Crowley's dilemma is probably that Poland has been divided and reorganized so many times since the eighteenth century that memories and histories of the 'myth of Poland' are stronger than those of any of its actual political forms.

Chapters 2 and 3, 'In Work Consoled' and 'In Dreams Consoled', examine the cultural practices within which this supposed collective and unified Polish yearning for national identity and integrity were embodied: in cultural institutions such as the museum Adrjan Baraniecki established in Cracow in 1868, which exhibited products from manufacturing industry, home industry and farming; in the ideology of a specifically Polish architecture associated with the architect Szymon Szyller; in the concerted study by Stanislaw Witkiewicz and others of forms of popular dress, tradition and possessions held to be essentially Polish; and in the celebration of the Zakopane Style, or vernacular Polish interior and exterior housing design. On these subjects Crowley is interesting and informative, but he never pursues the analysis into questions of the relationship between these putative 'national' cultural forms and other aspects of the lives of the people who inherited and adapted them. They remain, instead, the abstractions of 'the Poles' and 'the people' whose destiny is, apparently, simply to found a nation.

Crowley is most acute in his discussion of the shift from forms of 'art nouveau', present in Polish cultural life around the turn of the century, to the dissemination and adaptation of 'modernisms' from outside Poland (chapters 5 and 6: 'Questioning Parochialism' and 'Modernism Revised'). The issue of 'national' and 'international' cultural forms and meanings here becomes unavoidable and Crowley recognizes 'hybridization' and eclecticism as inevitable features of design practice and value formation. This subtler language of critical identification and analysis could usefully be taken as a model for developing a vocabulary of political and sociological discriminations able to push questions of 'national identity' and culture beyond simple Hegelian teleologies and idealist abstractions. Studies published recently by authors as diverse as Homi Bhabha, Eric Hobsbawm and Terence Ranger, Paul Gilroy and Edward Said all provide elements which enable the problematics of 'nationalism' and 'patriotism' to be recast, both theoretically and historically. As an advertisement for the fledgling discipline of 'design history', *National Style and Nation-State* articulates the weaknesses of the academic terrain much more clearly than its strengths.

Placed beside Howard's *The Union of Youth: An Artists' Society of the Russian Avant-Garde*, however, both Cone's and Crowley's books appear relatively reflexive and critically adept. Howard's study, largely based on archival resources recently opened to academics from outside Eastern Europe, assembles a mass of extremely interesting data relating to the status of modern art and artists in St Petersburg around 1910–13, but uses it to regurgitate the worst kind of modernist historiography. It is particularly sad to see such a fount of new information arranged in such a way as to negate the advances in critical studies of 'avant-garde' formations made, for example, by Peter Bürger (*Theory of the Avant-Garde*, 1984) and Raymond Williams (*Culture*, 1981, and *The Politics of Modernism*, 1989).

Howard refuses to define any of his key terms and consequently is unable to engage with the now longstanding and complex debates over the historical and formal taxonomy of 'early modernist' art production in Western and Eastern Europe before the First World War. 'Modernism', 'idealistic', 'realistic', 'modernization', 'Cubist', 'Futurist', 'neo-Primitivism', are words fraught with intense internal ambiguities and symbols of arguments over meaning and value with roots in the critical discourse of the period itself. Howard's introductory qualification over his use of such terms merely indicates the degree of confusion his account will exhibit: 'A capital letter is used for Impressionism, Cubism and so on, when it signifies the specific artistic movements; lower case letters denote practices divorced from the original movement.' Surely it can not have escaped Howard's notice that precisely these terms were not used by the artists themselves (as 'Surrealism' was), but are the result of contemporary critical nominations upon which have been layered decades of wrangling over the content and value of the labels. 'Impressionism', for instance, was the subject of Stephen Eisenman's recent essay 'The Intransigent Artist or How the Impressionists got their Name' (in Charles S. Moffett, ed. *The New Painting: Impressionism 1874–1886*, 1986). At times, Howard's prose is simply a litany of art-historical 'isms':

> By analysing the sequence of events concerning the Union of Youth, the transformation of painterly styles in Russia between 1910 and 1914 is more clearly identified. This period is shown to mark the transition from fin-de-siècle symbolism via Neo-Primitivism to Cubo-Futurism, with the reception of Fauvist and Cubist principles and Futurist ideas playing a fundamental role. . . .

This is vacuous taxonomy at its worst, clarifying nothing and reducing everything to chronological location within a version of 'history' that apes A. H. Barr's infamous 'diagram' of modern art development from 1936.

Howard's use of the term 'movement' is similarly naïve: in what sense were Picasso and Braque (the two original 'Cubists'?) a 'movement'? The term is intolerably imprecise and admits all kinds of abuses – was the Union of Youth (a formal organization, with elected members and a code of activities) a 'movement' in the same way that Russian futurists (lower case) were a 'movement'? Howard's organization and dissection of material relating to 'avant-garde' groupings in Russia before the First World War has little or no sociological structure: it neither understands the internal formal variety and complexity of these groupings nor is able to relate these at all to the rest of Russian society. Instead, as is conventional with this kind of modernist hagiography, events such as the October uprising appear simply to 'happen' around the art and artists. Howard makes no attempt to examine what kinds of people formed or joined organizations such as Dr Nikolai Ivanovich Kul'bin's Triangle (which immediately 'preceded' the Union of Youth, like the 10.25 express precedes the 11.00), nor to assess how their social, regional or educational backgrounds may have contributed to their understanding of the role of art in contemporary society. Why was it, for instance, that artists in the Union of Youth were 'inspired by

Kul'bin's ideas and developed his call for a synthetic and psychological art'?

What becomes clear from Howard's account is that many artists apparently saw art and art organizations as socially-enclosed cells in which they could effectively *detach* themselves from the practical politics of Russian life, in a period of extreme economic and social dislocation. In this regard, the Russian 'avant-gardists' were reproducing the extreme subjectivism (and even solipsism) characteristic of those Howard would call the 'Post-Impressionists' (a label invented by Roger Fry around 1910) – Paul Gauguin, Van Gogh and later Paul Cézanne. Howard's material could be used to bolster the argument that a continuum actually exists between putatively separate 'romantic' and 'modernist' artistic forms and intellectual rationalizations. Kul'bin, we hear:

> grounded his theory in a mechanistic worldview, asserting, as in 'Colour Music', that sensations of light are provoked as aural phenomena – in other words, sounds in the ears may simultaneously stimulate a perception of light in the eyes (closed or open). He emphasized that it was important to communicate the basic traits of objects and phenomena, but to omit details – the work of art being supplemented by man's inner experiences. These ideas have implications for Larionov's subsequent development of Rayism, which claimed to depict the immaterial matter between objects, and Malevich's and Kruchenykh's art of *zaum*, which expressed the perception of the world according to an altered state of consciousness.

This passage gives an accurate flavour of Howard's style and attentions throughout the study – a kind of vapid and uncritical 'history of ideas' approach to the unearthed documentation of exhibitions, manifestoes and correspondences between involved parties. Howard never attempts to question the meaning of the apparent intentions, ambitions and values of those artists and critics whose actions he recounts. Yet the data provide all kinds of clues as to the situated nature of these organizations, exhibitions and statements of belief. The Union of Youth was a formal society, with members elected to it, and members subscribed to a formal statute of intentions and values, and 'a new sense of individuality or a new common movement' (A. Rostislavov, 'Soyuz Molodezhi', *Rech'*, 8 January 1910, quoted by Howard, p. 42). Howard's documentation enables us to mobilize Raymond Williams's two-part classification of artists' formations, relating to (1) orientation toward the wider society, and (2) internal organization. The Union of Youth was, it seems, an *alternative* grouping, perhaps critical of society, but not formed to intervene in a direct way against elements of it (unlike the Surrealists in the 1920s); it was, moreover, limited to a relatively conservative interest in culture and the arts (albeit 'modern' arts), and in this respect may be identified as specialist in Williams's terms. Its 'official' organizational arrangements were similar to those of traditional established societies, such as the Russian Academy of Arts in Moscow, and this perhaps indicates something else that was relatively conservative about its intended form and function. Whatever its vaunted artistic or aesthetic radicalism (described and celebrated in standard modernist histories), it seems reasonable provisionally to see the Union of Youth, along with many other avant-garde groupings in Russia before the 1917 Revolution, as a detached social and cultural form, alarmed at the developments in Russian society, but with no interest in bringing about practical changes or in actively (and formally) supporting any political and ideological programmes.

Guy Debord's film *In Girum Imus Nocte et Consumimur Igni* (1978), the script for which has been translated ably by Lucy Forsyth, and published along with captions for the visual imagery, is predictably apocalyptic on the subject of the fate of culture in societies where 'the spectacle' has become predominant. Here he could be commenting on popular film in the 1920s or now:

> The manipulators of advertising, with the traditional cynicism of those who know that people are inclined to justify insults which they do not avenge, calmly announce today that 'when you love life, you go to the cinema'. But this life and this cinema are equally paltry, and this is why you could actually exchange one for the other with indifference.

Debord's exhausting cultural pessimism, a feature of his *The Society of the Spectacle* (1967) and his later addendum *Comments on the Society of the Spectacle* (1990, translated by Malcolm Imrie), is unrelieved in the film-script, the title of which is the Latin palindrome 'we go round and round in the night and are consumed by fire'. It is somewhat of an irony that a veritable Situationist Industry has recently been built up from the Debord *oeuvre*, developing its own spectacularity in the outpouring of academic and 'cultural studies' texts citing strategies of *détournement* as founding influences. Debord's photograph on the back cover of *In Girum*, however, suggests he knew all along what was likely to happen to his contribution to critical theory.

Wayne Bragg's *Sandino in the Streets* (1991), a book of photographs and short textual excerpts from the writings of Augusto
Cesar Sandino, the Nicaraguan revolutionary, possibly stands as a
new method of presenting the history of social and cultural uprising:
the silhouette of Sandino, reduced to an outline of a sombrero,
boots and jeans, still functions as an image of history-remembered
and present-day resistance in Nicaragua. The montage-like format of
the book short-circuits the tedium of some kinds of academic
history-writing discussed above, institutes a form of hope for change
dismissed by Debord, and directly connects the visual image to the
possibility of contemporary social struggle. *Sandino Vive!*

3. Anthologies

Theory and Philosophy

Francis Frascina's and Jonathan Harris's *Art in Modern Culture: An
Anthology of Critical Texts* is the reader for the Open University's
third level arts course 'Modern Art: Practices and Debates', which
began its academic life in 1993. The course material primarily
consists of four books, co-published by Yale University Press (which
will be reviewed here next year), along with a number of television,
radio and audio-cassette programmes. Another course reader, *Art in
Theory, 1900–1990: An Anthology of Changing Ideas*, edited by
Charles Harrison and Paul Wood, was published by Blackwell. Originally it was planned that two readers would be co-produced for
the course, tailored directly to the needs of Open University
students. This became impossible because of financial limitations
(the number of audio-visual programmes was also reduced
compared with those produced for the previous course, *Modern Art
and Modernism*, 1983). The four books constituting the course, each
written by three or four academics, were also prepared and
packaged by Yale University Press as volumes that could stand as
commodities autonomous from the Open University teaching programme. The financial reductions and rationalizations carried out at
the Open University have thus resulted in a 'course' which looks
very different from those previously produced and controlled entirely
by University academics and managers. *Art in Modern Culture* and
Art in Theory represent very different projects, collaborations and
ambitions. Literally black and white. Co-published with Phaidon,
Art in Modern Culture is a manageable 352 pages, divided into 5

sections, with 32 texts in all, along with a general introduction and a shorter introduction for each of the five sections: 'Introductory Texts', 'Capitalism and Culture', ' "Gender" ', ' "Race" and the Politics of Representation', 'Historical Methods and Critical Perspectives' and 'Aesthetic Theory and Social Critique'. *Art in Theory*, on the other hand, is more of a filing cabinet than a book (no doubt the idea of the use, in installations, of filing cabinets by the members of the collective 'Art and Language' in the early 1970s, whose membership then and later included, if tenuously, the two authors, served as an important 'resource', as they would say, for planning this compendium). Consisting of 1189 pages, with 8 major sections and 24 subsections, along with a general introduction, section introductions and prefaces for each extract, *Art in Theory* resembles more a telephone directory or British Rail timetable than an anthology. Acclamations from Professors Tom Crow and Michael Fried on the back cover, identifying its function as 'an unequalled resource' and requiring the 'gratitude of everyone seriously interested in modern art', indicate also the seriousness of the play for a place in the market which Harrison and Wood have made.

Compared with *Art in Theory*, Hershel B. Chipp's *Theories of Modern Art* (1968) – the anthology the editors set out to make obsolete – is a mere laundry list of items, an anorexic mouse next to this elephantine creature now straining the bookshelves of shops catering for the 'serious' scholars of modern art.

Art in Modern Culture opens with four texts designed to stake out the theoretical and political parameters of the kinds of inquiry which most of the extracts in the volume exemplify. These essays by Anthony Giddens, Raymond Williams, Griselda Pollock and Noam Chomsky adumbrate, respectively: a social theory and historical sociology of modern societies (extract from *Modernity and Self-Identity: Self and Society in the Late Modern Age*, 1991), a critical historiography of Modernist culture (extract from 'When Was Modernism?', *New Left Review* 175, May/June 1989), a social-historical feminist critique of art history (extract from 'Vision, Voice and Difference: Feminist Art History and Marxism', *Block* 6, 1982) and the outline of a critical theory of the role of intellectuals in modern industrial societies (extract from *Language and Responsibility*, 1979). The sections that follow contain texts which develop and extend the kinds of critique broadly covered by the key texts. Shrewd users of the anthology could put together short reading programmes consisting of three or four texts which bring together relatively abstract theoretical discussion with historical case-studies: for instance, Williams's 'When Was Modernism?', followed by Barbara M. Reise's 'Greenberg and the Group: A Retrospective View' and Dick Hebdige's 'Postmodernism and the "Politics" of Style'. This line of examination could then be recomplicated by turning to another, complementary (or perhaps contradictory) theoretical text, such as Pollock's or Anna Chave's 'Minimalism and the Rhetoric of Power'. On the whole, the editors of *Art in Modern Culture* were happy with the range of pieces included (though they were forced to leave much interesting material out), while certain texts received a place only because they had been required by academics writing for the course: extracts by Richard Shiff, Stephen F. Eisenman, Philip Leider and Yve-Alain Bois were included on this basis. The anthology strikes a reasonable balance between historical and contemporary material, and between British and North American authors. Perhaps the most significant line of demarcation within the array of texts is between those who adhere (explicitly or covertly) to a defence of 'high art' and the remnants of 'modernist' theories of art and those who refuse the dichotomy of 'high/low' and instead begin from sociocultural principles of analysis and evaluation. It is significant that this division doesn't reflect straightforwardly political 'left' and 'right' positions. Included extracts by Theodor Adorno, Hal Foster, Rosalind Krauss and Benjamin Buchloh (the latter trio associated closely with *October* magazine) tend toward qualified defences of 'autonomy of the aesthetic' arguments, despite the critiques of forms of art and art writing which characterize their essays. Whatever its weaknesses and omissions, *Art in Modern Culture* attempts to offer an outline of modes of analysis and evaluation consonant with a framework of political positions which are anticapitalist, antisexist, antiracist, and which support diversities of cultural production and radical cultural critique. All of which is part of what Harrison and Wood, it is to be presumed, call 'soft totalitarianism'. The quality of innuendo characterizing their introduction makes it difficult firmly to identify those indicted by the editors for a variety of sins associated with not loving Art enough or not believing in its (obscure) redemptive powers. Certain pivotal but opaque terms and phrases litter Harrison's and Wood's prose (probably familiar to those who know the writings of those associated with 'Art and Language'), acting like coded messages for those with the appropriate 'cognitive' (another key-word) equipment to sort out who has been demonized and why. The following serves as a useful example:

The determined defenders of the autonomy of art were at least proof against one distinctive form of twentieth-century malaise: that species of soft totalitarianism which has a way of creeping to the fore when there is little that is culturally vivid to disqualify and displace it.

One must reconstruct the intended sense of this by placing it in context, alongside other remarks indicating the eucharistic value being attached by the editors to Art:

The awareness of history animates the understanding of art, just as the critical experience of art sophisticates the understanding of historical process.

In attempting . . . to review the historical narratives of art in theory, we have sought on the one hand to resist the adoption of pluralism as an alibi for confusion, on the other to avoid that species of correctness which would require nothing so much as the abandonment of autonomy at all levels.

. . . the possible survival of art as a morally independent cultural practice.

It is art we are concerned with, and the theory it is made of; not the culture it is made of, nor the theory of the culture.

All this may seem fairly obscure to most of the readers of *Art in Theory*, who probably dip in for just a look at one of the 300 or so pieces included, yet it should indicate to Open University students at least that a major ideological, political, social and academic division opened up between collaborating academics during the making of 'Modern Art: Practices and Debates', and that the anthologies are one site in which this division is played out. Harrison and Wood's pretensions to dominating the global market for 'art theory' aside, *Art in Theory* is a vehicle for setting out what they call a selection which 'stands as an accurate product of our intentions'. This selection is, they say, 'a substantial and representative collection of relevant texts, drawn from a wide variety of sources'. Well, it certainly is wide. Whatever earlier plans they may have had to limit the collection to texts concerned specifically with 'high art' and 'authentic' art criticism were thrown out of the window, presumably when it was realized that they had a chance here to anthologize whatever they thought might flog a few more copies. This is why the latter sections, particularly 'Institutions and Objections' and 'Ideas of the

Postmodern' contain all the silly political, feminist, structuralist and poststructuralist twaddle that Harrison and Wood detest so much. It is hard to believe that the editors really believe that reading Julia Kristeva's 'Powers of Horror' (1980) is going to be a useful 'accompaniment to the first-hand experience of modern art'.

Any collection of texts has a use-value. The bringing together of disparate materials will always enable people to read (edited) pieces which they would otherwise not be able to see. *Art in Theory* will succeed for this reason. It would be interesting (but probably impossible) to monitor which texts are read regularly and which aren't. The range of materials included concerned with post-1945 art is such that much will be unfamiliar to readers. In this sense anthologies can work to constitute a history, as well as claim simply (and disingenuously) to reflect an existing tradition and culture. 'Art and Language' texts will attain a status they never had before, their place in this 'history' of modern art 'performed' by their inclusion in the anthology: generations of readers may come to believe, however, that *Art in Theory* simply reflected the already-confirmed status of 'Art and Language'.

Despite the vaunted radicalism of much of the material included, the 'histories' of art presented in the introductions to each section are highly orthodox accounts: Realism and Abstraction, Modernism to Postmodernism, the shift from the 'social' to the 'self-critical' in painting, etc. Harrison and Wood use the Western term 'art' as a catch-all label half the time – they talk casually of 'the art of the colonized cultures' – and as a marker for aesthetic Greatness and Autonomy the other half. Considering Harrison spent much time on course material for 'Modern Art and Modernism' explaining the difference between the terms 'representation' and 'resemblance', clarifying that 'abstract' art also 'represents' the world in a number of ways, it is disappointing to read him effectively (if implicitly) collapsing the distinction with the claim that 'Cubism was always at bottom a representational art'. It's entirely typical, though, to read once again that the measure of art for critics in the modernist tradition lies in 'a level of quality [undefined] for which previous art furnishes the *only* [my italics] meaningful standard'. It may be *Art in Theory*, but it certainly isn't art in reality.

Neither is it *Art After Philosophy and After* (1991), the title of Joseph Kosuth's collected writings between 1966 and 1990. Kosuth was closely involved with 'Art and Language' in its early collective (and Anglo-American) years, before its relatively varied critiques of institutions, art histories and theories, and art practices had settled down into its present Michael Baldwin and Mel Ramsden duo arrangement (with Charles Harrison as bolt-on art historian).

Art After Philosophy and After contains around fifty pieces – some very short, manifesto-like, and others lengthy and perhaps overly academic – linked by a concern to excavate the diverse uses of language in forms of explanation. The collection stands as an important resource for those interested in trying to reconstruct the early days of 'minimal' and 'conceptual' art in the mid- and late 1960s. Kosuth's two-part essay 'Art After Philosophy' (1969) is particularly important in this regard. But his 'Statement for Whitney Annual Exhibition, 1969' neatly encapsulates the collection's relationship with (and intended dislocation from) the 'art world':

> While my work is in an area which could be considered the heir to Western painting and sculpture, I do not consider it either 'painting' or 'sculpture' but rather an 'art investigation' . . . the word art denotes the general context of my activity, while the words 'painting' and sculpture ascribe particular qualities to the materials used within my art investigation in such a way as to imply a relationship between my art and earlier art on morphological grounds . . . one of the further disadvantages of specific terms such as painting and sculpture is their 'defining' character, and the subsequent limitation of the area of consideration. This limiting would seem to me to be contrary to the nature of art in our time.

Certainly *Art After Philosophy and After* makes sense (as a theoretical and historical text) without having to be read in relation to the products of his own art practice (which are illustrated at the end of the volume). This is more than can be said for the Foreword to the book by Jean-François Lyotard. This borders on the incomprehensible; not, as in the case of much early 'Art and Language' work a deliberate, canny kind of obfuscation designed to reveal the opaqueness of language and its constitutive role in meaning, but a straightforward daft French incomprehensibility which has no appealing characteristics, and which, in the end, has little in common with the intentions of Kosuth's writings and art work over the past twenty-five years.

Some of the essays in *Art After Philosophy and After* were originally published in the journal *Art-Language* in its early phase, such as 'Introductory Note to Art-Language by the American Editor', while others, including '1975' appeared in the short-lived American magazine *The Fox*, a kind of disgruntled offshoot of *Art-Language*, brought into being when the disputes between putative co-art

workers made joint publication impossible. '1975' contains not only
an acute critique of post-1945 formalist art criticism, and centrally
of its Greenbergian moment in the early 1960s, but also a statement
of the bases of his dissatisfaction with aspects of 'Art and Language'
(GB). Most significantly, in a footnote, Kosuth states:

> Art-Language . . . allowed for individual effort as part of a collective
> ideological front which it constituted as the 'party organ'. The Art-
> Language which has reappeared more recently has been victimized to
> some extent by the 'social problems' similarly manifested as well as
> acerbated by the group's participation in the gallery and museum
> system.

Kosuth's *Art After Philosophy and After* contains many essays which
detail and examine the social use of language as a form of authority
(and power) and offers through this analysis a version of art and
'art theory' as a means to unmask power relations within cultural
and social organization (including within putatively radical groupings such as 'Art and Language'). It is a valuable collection of
essays both in terms of constituting a history of Kosuth's own work
and in offering a sample of relatively user-friendly neo-Wittgen-
steinian 'language-critique'. Philosophical aesthetics features as a
putative organizing principle in two other anthologies: *A Companion
to Aesthetics*, edited by David Cooper, and *Philosophical Aesthetics:
An Introduction*, edited by Oswald Hanfling. The latter was co-published by the Open University and Blackwell (again), as a reader for
the 'Philosophy of the Arts' course, and consists of articles commissioned as synoptic overviews of issues featuring in the curriculum.
The eleven essays included were written by Oswald Hanfling, Diane
Collinson, Robert Wilkinson, Rosalind Hursthouse, Tom Sorell,
Colin Lyas and Stuart Sim.

No doubt suitable (and valuable) for undergraduates, the texts, on
the whole, are rather plodding surveys and evaluations of old
debating chestnuts in the philosophy of aesthetics. Disappointingly,
and following Harrison and Wood's usage, the term 'art' is bandied
about as a descriptive label for all kinds of specified and unspecified
kinds of representation (although it is fairly clear that the usual
implied range is restricted to 'fine' or 'high arts' – painting, sculpture, music, drama, literature). This results in a characteristic historical illiteracy of philosophical ponderings:

> The activity of art is much older than philosophical reflection about
> the arts, and artistic objects and activities can be found in almost

every society, including those in which there is no explicit concept of
art.

Apart from what could be construed as the logical absurdity of this
sentence, Hanfling shows a blithe disregard for the specifics of ety-
mological usage and development: the word 'art' only came into
English in the thirteenth century, when it meant 'skill'. What this
blindness presages, though, is a consistent ahistoricism of analysis
and evaluation which renders most of the essays worthless except as
exercises in what might be defended as 'rational' discussion (that is,
represented in terms of 'learning how to "think" and "talk" as a
philosopher'). The value of this kind of activity seemingly has little
or nothing to do with accounting for historically specific practices,
ideas and values. The first two parts of the book, 'What is Art?' and
'Art and Feeling' rehearse and reproduce the forms of tedious conundrum and ineffability characteristic of early-twentieth-century
'modernist' thinking about 'aesthetics', mainly in the Bloomsbury
mould of Roger Fry and Clive Bell (the latter tradition combining
ineffability with stupid upper-class English anti-intellectualism).
Sections 3 and 4, 'Art, World and Society' and 'Art and Value'
become more interesting because historical and social specificity are
implicated intrinsically in the debates – especially in the essays
'Structuralism and Post-structuralism' and 'Marxism and Aesthetics'
(both by Stuart Sim).

David Cooper's *A Companion to Aesthetics*, despite the title, has a
much stronger historical and social emphasis. This book is more of
an encyclopaedia of issues in 'art history and philosophy of aesthetics' than a straightforward collection of essays on doxological
subjects. Despite the conservatism of Cooper's own interests and
outlook – he also warbles on about 'art' without making any serious
attempt to define his terms – the sheer range of contributors and
subjects included in this volume escapes narrow circumscription.
Although his Introduction claims that 'a more or less arbitrary line
had to be drawn between those who should count as philosophers of
art and those who had to be excluded as "mere" critics, historians
or men of letters [!]', the volume includes some writers whose interests and values are clearly antagonistic to traditional 'philosophy of
aesthetics' formulations. Entries by Patricia Waugh ('The Canon'),
Steven Connor ('Modernism and Postmodernism'), and John
Sturrock ('Narrative'), alleviate the mundanities of most of the
material which, although probably useful to undergraduates with an
essay to write, renders the volume more of a textbook *lisable* than a

text *scriptible*. Cooper's own doubtfulness about the way the project turned out is perhaps registered by his remark that the 'intimate knowledge' of his two editorial advisers in the United States 'helped guarantee that, on their side of the Atlantic *at least*, the right people were commissioned for the right jobs' (my italics)! Given that the interest-value of the entries is inseparable from the intellectual perspectives of the writers, it would have been useful (and time-saving) for Cooper to have included an index of which author produced which entry.

Edward Lucie Smith's *Art and Civilization* purports to be a kind of encyclopaedia of 'world cultural history' ('. . . [O]ne of the fascinating aspects of the human quest for creative achievement and self-improvement is the enormous varieties of ways of thinking it has produced . . .'), though, predictably, it reproduces the standard Western European post-Renaissance concepts of chronology, 'progress' and style-development. The non-European world is ejected around 500 BC (after a brief nod to the Egyptians) and the remaining 500 pages are taken up with the glories of artistic progress up to and including postmodernism (now a staple ingredient of even the most toe-achingly boring conservative accounts, such as this one). This type of book must find its readership in schools and the 'general public', I imagine, as its utility within any serious university curriculum is almost zero.

The best thing about *The Language of Art History*, edited by Salim Kemal and Ivan Gaskell, another anthology dealing with issues in 'philosophy of the arts', is the cover, which contains an illustration of Barbara Kruger's well-known photomontage *Your Gaze Hits The Side Of My Face*. This image connotes a radical, politicized perspective on visual cultural production which, unfortunately, is scrupulously absented from most of the ten essays collected here. Not one of the pieces included discusses the issues of gender, feminism and representation imbricated within Kruger's work. Kemal and Gaskell have managed to solicit 'keynote' essays by Jean-François Lyotard, Richard Wollheim and Michael Baxandall, but these are, respectively, unintelligible, mundane and critically modest. The editors' introductory essay 'Art History and Language: Some Issues', which contains summaries of the pieces to come, is more readable, succinct and clarificatory than most of the texts by other contributors. It is plodding, certainly, but at least sets out the gamut of concerns long associated with philosophical habits of puzzling over 'the aesthetic'. It might keep you occupied for one wet afternoon. They conclude with the banality that one needs language to talk about 'the visual' and propose that the value of the collection lies in terms of the need to 'encourage art historians and critics to measure the meaning, accuracy, and coherence of their language [and] . . . to question the reliability of concepts imported from semiology and other totemically treated terminologies'.

Lyotard's essay 'Presence' boils down to being a defence of the quotidian notion that visual art has an ineffable quality somehow to do with it *not being language*, while Wollheim's piece, 'Correspondence, Projective Properties and Expression in the Arts', rambles on for fifteen tedious pages, concluding with the less than novel insight that art works should be understood in terms of the intentions of the makers ('The artist intended the work to have this property so that it can express some internal condition that he had in mind'). Baxandall's 'The Language of Art Criticism' (written in 1979) mostly amuses because he reveals how bored he has got with having to write the essay at all – '. . . If I apply half-a-dozen simple terms of visual interest (a phrase I am not going to define) to the pencil I am writing with – "long", "thin", "shiny", "green", "of hexagonal section", "with one conical end". . .', etc. Less than stunning stuff. David Summers's essay 'Conditions and Conventions: On the Disanalogy of Art and Language' is probably the most interesting piece because he claims philosophers must abandon their usual ahistoricism and try to engage with historical and social phenomena outside of the realm of 'rational' debate:

> It is the spaces and uses we do not know that finally explain why these works were made the way they evidently were; at the same time, we must understand our own institutional spaces and uses, and the historical contingency of our own institutional spaces and uses, in order to try to understand the art of other times and places.

It may not be pretty, but it achieves a kind of breakthrough for someone trained in the tortuous empiricist rigours of the Anglo-American analytic philosophical tradition. The examples of philosophical speculation contained in *The Language of Art History* generally fall far short of the quality of work undertaken in empirical studies of visual culture, which can bring into alignment the stringencies of categorical analysis ('visual'/'verbal', etc.) with extended investigation of specific visual representations. Two studies are particularly noteworthy in this respect: Mieke Bal's *Reading Rembrandt: Beyond the Word–Image Opposition* (1991) and Michael Camille's *The Gothic Idol: Ideology and Image-Making in Medieval Art* (1989), now available in paperback. While Bal's essays on Rembrandt are heavily reliant on 'interpretative modes' (especially psychoanalytic schemas) derived from literary studies, and generally ignore historical issues, the poignancy and interest of the analyses lie in her treatment of actual visual representations. One can appreciate the kinds of arguments she tries to make because they are made vivid through exemplification. In comparison, standard philosophical essays, like those contained in *The Language of Art History* usually remain at an untenable level of abstraction and idealization. Camille's study of mediaeval illustrated manuscripts and other forms of visual representation marries the kind of 'close reading' skills one would expect of a Cambridge English graduate with a formidable knowledge of ecclesiastical social history. Once again, it is the wealth of specific visual examples which makes his arguments about the inter-relation between image and text in *The Gothic Idol* so compelling.

Richard Shusterman's *Pragmatist Aesthetics: Living Beauty, Rethinking Art*, a collection of related essays by the author, rather than an anthology, is similarly – but much more successfully – concerned with combating the 'analytic aesthetics' of G. E. Moore, Bertrand Russell, and Ludwig Wittgenstein with the outline of principles for a historical and social understanding of cultural production. This is orchestrated through an account and elaboration of the work of John Dewey (particularly of his *Art as Experience* (1934), an extremely influential book during the 1930s in the United States, but neglected since), and by modernizing these ideas via a consideration of Richard Rorty (the chief self-declared pragmatist of the 1980s), and the 'revisionist' analytic thinking of W. V. Quine, Nelson Goodman and Donald Davidson. Shusterman's essays grasp at points made long ago by those working in the 'cultural studies' veins of art history and literary studies, as well as in studies of popular and folk cultures (for example, by the so-called Russian Formalists, members of the Frankfurt School, and the Raymond Williams/Stuart Hall/Richard Hoggart wave of British cultural studies in the early 1960s). Nevertheless, he makes his arguments as straightforwardly and accessibly as is possible within institutional philosophical discourse and, refreshingly, his examples include poetry and painting, but also rap music and forms of popular dance.

Two much more interesting anthologies dealing in 'theory' (as opposed to 'philosophy') of art and historical analysis are *Zeitgeist in Babel: The Postmodernist Controversy*, edited by Ingeborg Hoesterey and *The Critical Image: Essays on Contemporary Photography*, edited by Carol Squiers (both 1991). The former brings together issues at the political end of 'philosophy of culture' (Richard Rorty, Martin Ray, Jürgen Habermas) with analyses of particular cultural forms. The theoretical formulations are much crisper (even if doubtful, politically and intellectually – for instance Clement Greenberg's attack on postmodernism in his essay 'The Notion of "Postmodern"' and Rorty's 'Habermas and Lyotard on Postmodernity'). Whatever his weaknesses and arrogances, Charles Jencks's written style, exemplified here in his essay 'Postmodern vs. Late-Modern', is great teaching material and engaging for scholars.

Photography and Film

The Critical Image is a collection of essays elaborating and investigating something of the full range of photographic practices, an examination which John Tagg had argued for during the 1980s, most notably in his book *The Burden of Representation: Essays on Photographies and Histories* (Macmillan, 1988). According to Squiers, this would entail:

> an examination of all institutional production of photography, from newspaper and magazine photojournalism to images taken for purposes of surveillance to commercial wedding photography and amateur snapshooting.

Essays included discuss, for instance, representations of AIDS sufferers (Simon Watney), the use of photography in promoting 'green' corporate identities (Kathy Myers) and the use of computers in image-generation (Fred Ritchin). Highlights of the collection are Carole S. Vance's 'The Pleasure of Looking: The Attorney General's Commission on Pornography versus Visual Images' and Joanne Lukitsch's 'Practising Theories: An Interview with John Tagg'. The former describes the extensive use of photographic imagery in the campaigns organized in the United States to attempt to ban pornographic visual materials (see the interesting debates around this question for feminists examined in *Pornography and Feminism: The Case Against Censorship*, edited by Gillian Rodgerson and Elizabeth Wilson, 1991). One drawback to this interesting account, however, is Vance's continued description of anti-censorship activists as 'recognized experts' on visual representation, who were denied the right to give evidence in the rolling US government inquiries held in various cities between 1985 and 1986. By crediting such people with the title 'expert' she effectively reproduces and validates the technicisms of knowledge organized and mobilized by central state organizations which John Tagg has spent years identifying and correctly attacking. The interview with Tagg that concludes the volume indicates something of the status (in America at least) which he has achieved. The conversation is mostly backward-looking (recorded in 1988), however, and rather too celebratory. The danger of Tagg's elevated position is that he stops doing the kind of novel research which constituted his important work during the early and mid-1980s. His value as a theorist and historian of the varying modes in which photographic technology has been deployed is undoubtedly great, but it is an open question whether his Foucauldian ' "micro-physics" of power' position, antagonistic to holistic accounts of contemporary social formations, is an impasse or a possible route to further innovative research. *The Critical Image* collection, however, is a tribute to his influence and originality as a theorist of 'the photographic' as a realm of diverse social practices.

Tagg's own *Grounds of Dispute: Art History, Cultural Politics and the Discursive Field*, largely a collection of essays written between about 1985 and 1990, is a rather poor companion to *The Burden of Representation*. This judgement might be a little unfair, though, because it is probably wrong to believe that the two volumes were intended to share a similar purpose or reflect the same concerns. *Grounds of Dispute* is much more like many quotidian anthologies of essays by academics working (broadly) in Art or Design History, or in Cultural Studies. The essays tell you about the themes and arguments mounted by X or Y over a number of years, and are more or less satisfying as a collection. In contrast, *The Burden of Representation* was much less about Tagg and much more about the problem of photographies and ways of thinking them through – historically, theoretically, politically. The second collection emphatically is about Tagg as a northern British academic now resident in North America. This is signalled partly by the notes on the back cover which tell us that Tagg 'is now a permanent resident of the USA'. What does this mean exactly? That Tagg intends never to live in England again? That he has a green card? That he has taken up US citizenship? As essays in the collection make clear, I think, it really tells us that Tagg feels that America is his home now. More interesting than this, though, is Tagg's need to tell us. Many moments in the essays reinforce this confidence, including a paragraph in his rather irritating 'Introduction/Opening' (the only piece written for the book), when Tagg, in a drippy postmodernist, poststructuralist kind of way explores his sense of being 'different':

> Where am I now? A body that wants to sleep. With my pale, white,
> northern English skin. In a shirt and tie and well-creased pants. In an
> executive armchair. In an office closed to 'the public'. . . .

Later in the same piece this highly self-conscious 'discourse of biography' enters a social-historical phase:

> We are compelled to migrancy by the very relations that punish our
> vagrancy. In 1967, for some the summer of flower power as I recall, I
> left Tyneside to go South to the University of Nottingham. At the
> same time, the working populations of entire pit villages in the North-
> umberland coalfield were being transported to the 'modernized' mines
> of Nottinghamshire and Derby . . . the Miners' Strike of 1984–5 . . .
> was still being fought as I left unemployment in Leeds and – following
> so many forgotten generations of Geordies and Scots [forgotten by
> whom it might be asked] – took the train to London, then flew across
> the Arctic to Los Angeles.

Finally, the references become 'political' and apparently bitter, in
Tagg's 1985 essay 'Art History and Difference':

> I came to Leeds [University] in 1979 when Tim Clark left for Prince-
> ton. I came for one year but he did not come back, so I stayed on five
> years on one-year contracts without the tenure which would have
> guaranteed my intellectual freedom and integrity. . . .

These extracts might serve an allegorical purpose: that of document-
ing the intellectual self-inspection (bordering on self-concern) which
can occur when academics are lionized. This can become fatal when
such self-regard dovetails with the current popularity of 'poststructuralist' musings on 'the body' and 'personal biography', à la
Barthes, Deleuze and the rest. Reprinting interviews with yourself
('Practising Theories: An Interview with Joanne Lukitsch') and
quoting your own famous and wise pronouncements ('as I said in
my earlier essay'. . .) are other signs of this malaise. Tagg manages
to avoid slipping too far down this chasm, and, of course, there is
other purpose and value in reinstating accounts of individual lives
and histories within wider histories, but if this 'discursive mode'
takes over it can rapidly become tedious and vacuous. The substantive essays in *Grounds of Dispute* roughly fall into categories: on
the one hand, pieces concerned with the state of art history,

'engagement' within academic institutions, and debate over 'post-modernism'; and, on the other, work on forms of visual representation (mainly photographic) and cultural display. The last included essay, 'The Pachuco's Flayed Hide: Mobility, Identity and Buenas Garras', concerned with the place of Latin-Americans in US culture, co-written with Marcos Sanchez-Tranquilino, will be least familiar to British readers. It is Tagg at his most Dick Hebdige-ish and quite unfamiliar in terms of theme and style. Once again, however, it also tells us about Tagg's new-found affiliations: this time to what may be an equivalent for his displaced Northumbrian miners. 'Art History and Difference' and 'Postmodernism and the Born-Again Avant-Garde', both published during the 1980s in *Block* magazine, represent Tagg at his most incisive in discussing the production of theory within institutions like universities and museums. This question has all but dropped out of contemporary debate – partly because of a general sense of helplessness regarding the all-too-obvious impotence of academics within *Thatchered* institutions – but the need to see 'new art history' as a necessarily situated practice, dependent on the specific relative autonomies of universities and museums as well as on the relations of the book and journals market, is important. Indeed these sites and relations exert pressures and effect determinations which Tagg must know limit and direct even his 'intellectual freedom and autonomy'.

Two or three essays in *Grounds of Dispute* are very slight and give the impression that a certain amount of barrel-scraping has gone into producing this volume: notably 'Should Art Historians Know Their Place?', 'Globalisation, Totalisation and the Logic of Discourse', and 'Occupied Territories: Tracking the Work of Rudolf Baranik'. Other pieces, including 'The Proof of the Picture' and 'Totalled Machines: Criticism, Photography and Technological Change', either repeat themes elaborated more satisfyingly in other, longer essays, or appear as mere footnotes to his mid-1980s work on photographic history and theory.

Nevertheless, *Grounds of Dispute* will be a valuable teaching resource for undergraduates, postgraduates, teachers and others involved in the broad areas of art and design history, cultural theory and what might be called 'photographic studies'. Indeed, Tagg's work over the last fifteen years has helped fundamentally to redefine such a terrain of inquiry, suggesting a major shift in focus and method away from the previous ragbag of ill-defined 'theories' and unacknowledged assumptions. The challenge for Tagg, however, is to resist the attractiveness of resting on his present laurels and to produce another body of work with comparably radical ambitions and consequences.

Studies of nonfiction film and debates relating to definitions of 'documentary' and 'truth' in film have also moved some way towards the premises of Tagg's work on still photography. Bill Nichols's *Representing Reality: Issues and Concepts in Documentary* (1991) and Richard Barsam's *Nonfiction Film* are two cases in point. Although the latter is a reprint of a study originally published in 1973, the author has revised and expanded his study in order to catch up with (and no doubt attract) the current 'theory-oriented' market for such a sub-terrain of film studies. A concluding chapter on 'New Voices of the 1980s', concentrating on feminist, lesbian and Third-World nonfiction film, is particularly welcome.

Although Barsam sees the political and cultural value of this inclusion, his general theoretical premises have remained rather more unexamined: his introduction leaves key terms like 'actuality', 'reality' and 'factual reality' more or less unproblematically in place. While his chapter on 'American Nonfiction Film: 1930–1939' is informative and historically located, his accounts of films – for example, Robert Flaherty's *Man of Aran* (1934) or Pare Lorentz's *The Plow That Broke the Plains* (1936) – beg many questions relating to audience, consumption, and 'reception aesthetics'. Barsam's method is squarely *auteur*-based, despite his recognition of historical issues, and leaves the whole field of questions relating to *whose* reading, *whose* values, *whose* interests untouched. The range of reference in *Nonfiction Film*, though, is highly impressive. Barsam deals with the history of early film-making; the First and Second World Wars and film; exploration, romantic and Western avant-garde film; Russian, British, continental European and American documentary film before the Second World War; British, continental European and North-American nonfiction film after the Second World War; American *cinéma vérité* in the 1960s; and then the developments in 1970s film and political movements mentioned above. It is a very useful reference source and outline guide to historical developments in nonfiction film-making.

Nichols's *Representing Reality*, a kind of delayed sequel to his *Ideology and the Image* (1981), examines the genre of 'documentary' film through a series of thematic studies. Barsam's and Nichols's books, perhaps, are most valuable when used together, adding up to a critical, historical account of nonfiction film, the latter problematizing the vast range of important materials contained in the former. Nichols claims to have identified four kinds of documentary mode in film: expository (classic 'voice-of-God' commentaries), observational (which appear to minimize the film-maker's presence), interactive (where film-maker and 'social actors' acknowledge each other in various explicit ways), and 'reflexive' (where the film-maker draws the viewer's attention to the form of the work itself). Later chapters deal with the relationship between documentary film and social democratic politics (a major theme in Tagg's *The Burden of Representation*); the issue of ethics in film-making, with studies of pornographic and ethnographic film, which Nichols (and his co-authors for that chapter) see as similar in form; and finally a more-or-less obligatory poststructuralist chapter on film and 'the body'. For all his theoretical sophistication, however, Nichols's definition of 'objectivity', qualified and revised in his first chapter, centres on the idea of 'empathetic identification' between scene and viewer, an old definition held by, for example, William Scott in his *Documentary Expression and Thirties America* (1973). Still, *Representing Reality* is a valuable and important book, with a field of influence hopefully stretching beyond the enclave of film studies.

4. Journals

Academic Art and Design History

This year saw the continued presentation of *Art History* as the journal earnestly responsible for promoting and safeguarding the academic discipline of art history. As far as its editors are concerned, however, in institutional terms, this is almost entirely a mid-Atlantic affair, while intellectually the content seems to oscillate rather bizarrely between straightforward iconology of mainly Renaissance subjects and Norman Bryson-tinged psychoanalytic essays on modernist themes. This contrast is embodied in, for instance, volume 15, number 1, where one is confronted by Craig Harbison's pedestrian 'Meaning in Venetian Renaissance Art: The Issues of Artistic Ingenuity and Oral Tradition' (19–37) and then by David Clarke's seemingly pneumatic 'The Gaze and the Glance: Competing Understandings of Visuality in the Theory and Practice of Late Modernist Art' (80–98). The latter essay (well, the title at least) is probably good enough to have been rejected by the defenders of avant-garde radicalism camped on the other side of the Atlantic at *October*. Bryson also crops up as a guiding light of intellectual wisdom in Angela Rosenthal's piece on Angelica Kauffman

(38–59), but is subject to a few acute criticisms when his *Looking at the Overlooked: Four Essays on Still Life* (1991) is taken to task by Paul Taylor. This is refreshingly different from Lynda Nead's tactically respectful applause for Marcia Pointon's *The Naked Authority: The Body in Western Painting 1830–1908* (1990).

Art History's second number of the year dwelt further amongst the putative origins of art-historical discourse, dallying with Italian Renaissance furniture painting, Botticelli (the *Gazza* of vehicles for iconological meandering), reliquary chapels, and Albrecht Dürer (always a dependable mid-field player in this kind of outfit). Amelia Jones attempted to put the cat amongst the pigeons with her relatively critical review of Whitney Chadwick's *Women, Art and Society* (1990) and Janet Wolff's anthology *Feminine Sentences: Essays on Women and Culture* (1991). Number 3 migrated somewhat to the twentieth century with rather light pieces by Sarat Maharaj ('Pop Art's Pharmacies: Kitsch, Consumerist Objects and Signs, the "Unmentionable"', 334–50), and John Tagg's disappointing 'A Discourse (with Shape of Reason Missing)' (351–73), this latter piece further indicative of his present wandering through the well-trodden fields of poststructuralist cliché. One gets the sense that *Art History* editors are at something of a loss when it comes to 'the modern period' and choosing pieces resembles for them blindly aiming darts at a board. The final edition for the year resorted to reliable old nuggets: Linda Stone-Ferrier on Rembrandt's etchings, John Goodman on Parisian neoclassicism, and Adele M. Ernstrom's investigation of Sir Charles Eastlake's mid-nineteenth-century art collecting. These contrasted somewhat with Charles Reeve on Donald Judd's sculptures and Mary Beard's look at the culture of the museum. The effects of the change of editorship at *Art History* in 1993 will be examined here next year. Compared with *Art History* in 1992, *The Oxford Art Journal* – though sounding marginally more boring – achieved two relative triumphs of thematic unity. Four substantive articles in volume 15, number 1 dealt with late-nineteenth-century US art: Angela Miller's piece on landscape painting 'The Mechanisms of the Market and the Invention of Western Regionalism: the Example of George Caleb Bingham' (3–20), Michael Hart's ground-breaking piece on mid-nineteenth-century American sculpture and race, Timothy Rodger's 'Alfred Stieglitz, Duncan Phillipps and "the $6000 Marin"' (54–66) and J. Gray Sweeney's 'Racism, Nationalism and Nostalgia in Cowboy Art' (67–80), which dealt with the contemporary status of such folk myth as much as with examples of artists working in the genre in the late nineteenth and early twentieth centuries. The second and final number of the year rather more predictably 'themed' gender and visual representation, with essays by Ann Pullan on female viewers, Alex Potts on 'Male Phantasy and Modern Sculpture' (38–47), Robin Adele Greeley on Magritte's depiction of the female body, and Whitney Davis's 'Sigmund Freud's Drawing of the Dream of Wolves' (70–87), which, no doubt, will be lapped up by the Bataille-Lacan fanclub operating on an axis from Ohio to Bloomsbury. The *Journal of Design History* came in a long way behind the *Journal of Decorative and Propaganda Arts*, reviewed here for the first time. Published in Miami and sponsored by the Wolfson Foundation of Decorative and Propaganda Arts, this sumptuously illustrated journal ran its one 1992 issue on Argentina, and included a wide diversity of subjects and authors. Beside this, *Journal of Design History* volume 5, number 3's slim, black-and-white, two columns of type format seems moth-balled both as an intellectual project and as a 'design' itself. Apart from Alan Wallach's intelligent essay on 'The Museum of Modern Art: The Past's Future' (207–16), the *Journal of Design History* ran essays with titles which instantly put the reader off, whatever the merits of the essays themselves: for instance, 'Representations of Plastic Materials, 1920–1950' (Jeffrey L. Meikle). In contrast, the *Journal of Decorative and Propaganda Arts*, number 18, quite heavily funded through advertising, it would appear, ran well-illustrated pieces on theatre and stage design, Argentine architecture in the 1930s, urban art in Buenos Aires, Argentinian Social Realism, fashion, public sculpture, Art-Nouveau and many other facets of Argentinian culture in the twentieth century.

The new *International Journal of Cultural Property*, published in New York and Berlin, potentially offers much more than its first number delivered. At present it consists of essays on: particular subjects currently at issue in legal disputes over cultural artefacts; a chronicle of events; a large section of case-notes on particular court-room debates involving cultural property; information on international legal treaties; conference reports; documents; and book reviews. A lot of this material is actually very interesting, despite one's initial sense that it may be arid or arcane. Once one enters the jargon (far less obscure, it should be said, than that operating in academic 'cultural theory'), the journal becomes a dense site for exploring how discourse on 'culture' and 'law' functions in this country and abroad. The journal could become essential reading for those interested in cultural history and theory if the editors embraced traditions of *critical* legal studies mostly developed outside of Anglo-American philosophy of law and case-history. This would involve, centrally, the development of historical perspectives on law as a system of statutes, institution of arbitration, and mechanism of social reproduction. Equally importantly, the journal should move to consider 'culture' critically: at the moment the term is being used in a pseudo-open sense largely synonymous with the usual meanings for 'art'. 'Culture' is preferred by the editors because the most salient legal wrangles recently involving 'art-works' have been over artefacts whose historical and contemporary value have been disputed by people from different countries or forms of social life (e.g. the Elgin Marbles controversy, or the spate of cases in Australia where courts have required museums to return objects to aboriginal tribes). 'Culture' is deployed, therefore, in a still-weakly defined anthropological sense which has a kind of Political Correctness to it but lacks any sophisticated reasoning. A cursory glance through the case-notes section to the journal reveals that all of the artefacts referenced would come under a traditional (narrow) 'high art' category: paintings, altarpieces, religious icons, etc., although many of these items have been appropriated to a Western 'high art' notion far removed from their original non-Western function. While clearly it would be wrong to prejudge future numbers of the journal, the test of the real openness of the examination may well be over whether stolen and repainted Ford Escorts or bootlegged Beatles songs make the pages in the coming years.

Two journals, both published by Taylor and Francis, continued to produce perhaps the most sustained examples of study in highly specialized areas: *Word and Image* and *Journal of Garden History*. Of the two, the latter is probably more innovative. The 'field' of garden studies has only comparatively recently been taken up by British universities (Middlesex University now has a Chair in Landscape Gardening). *Word and Image* also suffers from something of the *Art History* malaise – concentration on Renaissance-up-to-nineteenth-century subjects, along with random spatterings of modernist topics, with Cubism as a constant favourite. Also like *Art History*, *Word and Image* largely neglects anything except the 'high culture' portion of the cultural terrain. A notable exception to this is Peter R. Sattler's 'Ballet Mechanique: The Art of George Herriman' (8:ii.133–53), in which cartoon articulations of image and text are discussed.

As with the *International Journal of Cultural Property*, one waits to see a *Word and Image* themed-issue on Madonna pop videos (the editors have seemingly bracketed the Derridean word-as-voice) or the use of 'image and text' in various television programmes such as *The Rough Guide* or *The News with Subtitles*. Two US publications attempt to deal with some aspects of popular cultural visual representation, yet do so in very excluding academic language: these are *Discourse:Journal for Theoretical Studies in Media and Culture* and *Differences: A Journal of Feminist Cultural Studies*. Kaja Silverman's interview with the film-maker Harum Farocki, director of 'Images of the World and Inscription of the War' (*Discourse* 15:iii.57–75), along with commentary and still photographs from the film (78–92), are very interesting, once one gets beyond the University of California, Berkeley lingua franca. Similarly, *Differences* (5:i) contains innovative interdisciplinary work on shop-lifting (Leslie Camhi, 'Stealing Femininity: Department Store Kleptomania as Sexual Disorder', 26–50) and on popular music (Lynne Joyrich, 'Elvisophilia: Knowledge, Pleasure and the Cult of Elvis', 73–91). Both journals, however, seem to be aimed exclusively at academic constituencies.

Journal of Garden History is yet to produce its Marxist number, but the signs are positive. Volume 12, number 1 included Joachim Wolschke-Bulmahn's and Gert Groening's interesting 'The Ideology of the Nature Garden: Nationalistic Trends in Garden Design in Germany During the Early Twentieth Century' (73–80). Both journals, incidentally, are very well illustrated and attractively presented.

Art and Design in Journalism

Eastern Art Report and *Art Business Today* indicate something of the other side of publishing in the field of art and design history and theory: that end concerned with shifting the goods. *Art Business Today*, published by the Fine Art Trade Guild, is basically a newspaper specializing in matters relating to tax, copyright and sales promotion. It could speak profitably with the *International Journal of Cultural Property*. *Art Business Today* inhabits a world untroubled by disputes over social class and representation, or taxonomic issues relating to word and image. Similarly, *Eastern Art Report*, for all its coverage of non-Western visual culture, seems mainly to be a means of flogging oriental rugs and Korean silverware. Needless to say, both these magazines are expensively illustrated with colour photographs and have hundreds of advertisers. *Museum*, published by the United Nations Educational, Scientific, and Cultural Organization, is a forum in which museum-workers from all over the world may swap details on their latest institution. Volume XLIV, number 4 contained reports from Canada, Brazil, France, Australia, the United States, Mexico, Sweden, Britain, Cyprus and Italy.

Women's Art, published by the Women Artists Slide Library in London, combines features on specific women artists, articles on visual culture and issues in women's art practice, exhibition and book reviews. Number 49 contained pieces by Lynda Nead, Alison Yarrington, Hilary Robinson and Pauline Barrie, amongst others.

Books Reviewed

Bal, Mieke. *Reading Rembrandt: Beyond the Word–Image Opposition*. Cambridge University Press (1991). pp. 495. £60. ISBN 0 521 39154 7.

Barsam, Richard M. *Nonfiction Film: A Critical History*. Indiana University Press. pp. 481. £60 ISBN 0 253 31124 1.

Berman, Marshall. *All That is Solid Melts into Air: The Experience of Modernity*. Verso (1991). pp. 384. pb £12.95. ISBN 0 86091 785 1.

Bragg, Wayne C. *Sandino in the Streets*. Indiana University Press (1991). pp. 117. £20. ISBN 0 253 35207 X.

Camille, Michael. *The Gothic Idol: Ideology and Image-Making in Medieval Art*. University of Chicago Press (1989). pp. 407. hb £42.50, pb £17.95. ISBN 0 521 34040 3, 0 521 42430 5.

Cone, Michèle. *Artists Under Vichy: A Case of Prejudice and Persecution*. Princeton University Press. pp. 264. 78 illus. $35. ISBN 0 691 04088 5.

Cooper, David, ed. *A Companion to Aesthetics*. Blackwell. pp. 466. £60. ISBN 0 631 18236 5.

Crowley, David. *National Style and Nation-State: Design in Poland from the Vernacular Revival to the International Style*. Manchester University Press. pp. 150. 40 illus. £29.95. ISBN 0 7190 3727 1.

Davis, Mike. *City of Quartz: Excavating the Future in Los Angeles*. Vintage. pp. 462. pb $14. ISBN 0 679 73806 1.

Debord, Guy. *Comments on the Society of the Spectacle*, trans. Malcolm Imrie. Verso (1990). pp. 94. pb £8.95. ISBN 0 86091 520 4.

———. *In Girum Imus Nocte Et Consumimur Igni: A Film*, trans. with preface by Lucy Forsyth. Pelagian Press. pp. 80. 24 illus. pb £6.95. ISBN 0 948688 06 8.

Frascina, Francis, and Jonathan Harris, eds. *Art in Modern Culture: An Anthology of Critical Texts*. Phaidon in association with the Open University. pp. 352. 56 illus. pb £12.95. ISBN 0 7148 2840 8.

Giddens, Anthony. *Modernity and Self-Identity: Self and Society in the Late Modern Age*. Polity (1991). pp. 256. pb £11.95. ISBN 0 7456 0932 5.

Green, Nicholas. *The Spectacle of Nature: Landscape and Bourgeois Culture in Nineteenth-Century France.* Manchester University Press (1990). pp. 238. 31 illus. hb £50, pb £12.95. ISBN 0 7190 2843 4, 0 7190 3909 6.

Hanfling, Oswald, ed. *Philosophical Aesthetics: An Introduction.* Blackwell in association with the Open University. pp. 483. pb £10.99. ISBN 0 631 18035 4.

Harrison, Charles, and Paul Wood, eds. *Art in Theory 1900–1990: An Anthology of Changing Ideas.* Blackwell. pp. 1189. pb £12.99. ISBN 0 631 16575 4.

Hemingway, Andrew. *Landscape Imagery and Urban Culture in Early Nineteenth-Century Britain.* Cambridge University Press. pp. 363. 120 illus. £65. ISBN 0 521 39118 0.

Hoesterey, Ingeborg, ed. *Zeitgeist in Babel: The Postmodernist Controversy.* Indiana University Press (1991). pp. 269. pb £11.99. ISBN 0 253 20611 1.

Howard, Jeremy. *The Union of Youth: An Artists' Society of the Russian Avant-Garde.* Manchester University Press. pp. 240. 26 illus. £35. ISBN 0 7190 3731 X.

Kemal, Salim, and Ivan Gaskell, eds. *The Language of Art History.* Cambridge University Press (1991). pp. 245. pb £12.95. ISBN 0 521 44598 1.

Kosuth, Joseph. *Art After Philosophy and After.* MIT Press (1991). pp. 289. 58 illus. £26.95. ISBN 0 262 11157 8.

Lukes, Timothy W. *Shows of Force: Power, Politics and Ideology in Art Exhibitions.* Duke University Press. pp. 250. pb $15.95. ISBN 0 8223 1123 2.

Nichols, Bill. *Representing Reality: Issues and Concepts in Documentary.* Indiana University Press (1991). pp. 313. pb £14.99. ISBN 0 253 20681 2.

Pollock, Griselda. *Vision and Difference: Feminism, Femininity and Histories of Art.* Routledge (1988). pp. 239. pb £10.99. ISBN 0 415 00722 4.

——. *Avant-Garde Gambits 1888–1893: Gender and the Colour of Art History.* Thames and Hudson. pp. 80. 50 illus. £6.95. ISBN 0 500 55025 5.

Rodgerson, Gillian, and Elizabeth Wilson, eds. *Pornography and Feminism: The Case Against Censorship.* Lawrence and Wishart (1991). pp. 79. pb £4.99. ISBN 0 85315 742 1.

Shusterman, Richard. *Pragmatist Aesthetics: Living Beauty, Rethinking Art.* Blackwell. pp. 324. pb £14.99. ISBN 0 631 18236 5.

Smith, Edward Lucie. *Art and Civilization.* Laurence King. pp. 560. £25. ISBN 1 85669 027 X.

Squiers, Carol, ed. *The Critical Image: Essays on Contemporary Photography.* Lawrence and Wishart (1991). pp. 240. pb £12.99. ISBN 0 853 15737 5.

Tagg, John. *Grounds of Dispute: Art History, Cultural Politics and the Discursive Field.* Macmillan. pp. 219. pb £10.99. ISBN 0 333 55740 9.

11

Popular Music

DAVID BUCKLEY

This chapter has four sections: 1. Introduction; 2. Biography and
Autobiography; 3. Anthologies, Collections and Encyclopaedias; 4.
History and Analysis.

1. Introduction

There is an overwhelming tendency, according to musicologist Dick
Bradley in his book *Understanding Rock'n'Roll: Popular Music in
Britain 1955–1964*, to reduce popular music criticism to a regurgita-
tion of 'hard facts', of 'dates, names and places with a vague,
decontextualized, overwhelmingly adjectival, avowedly subjective
type of description of music'. To counter what is perceived as the
tyranny of journalistic discourses, the main intellectual thrust, reflected here in many of the books and articles discussed in this essay, is
to go beyond what Barthes identified as the supremacy of the
'poorest of linguistic categories: the adjective' and to explain
popular music and its impact on contemporary culture in a much
more objective, multidimensional way. The complex relationship
between art and commerce is not an ineffable one and popular
music studies has begun to challenge assumptions and to describe
the problematic cultural terrain in a more sophisticated manner.
Bradley is undoubtedly right in identifying the semantic redundancy
of much descriptive writing. But are we then to strip popular music
writing of all its subjective power? Are 'journalistic' and 'academic'
discourses really as immiscible as they are sometimes portrayed? The
extent to which this search, by an educated, privileged elite working
in academia, actually respects and responds to the much larger com-

munity of serious-minded pop fans and practitioners both within and outside of academia is another matter. There are also definite signs of a split in popular music studies at the top. Some of the material reviewed in this book is depressingly exclusive, written for a couple of hundred (or in some cases substantially fewer) like-minded academics. That this is doubtless the case in other academic disciplines as well is cold comfort. Popular music studies is, perhaps, uniquely placed in the potential richness of approaches at its disposal. The unfortunate side-effect of this academic exclusiveness is that the healthy numbers of students taking popular music courses at various academic institutions around the world are robbed of literate but understandable reading matter. The central problem is not that academic study at the highest level should not be taking place, but that the fruits of this research are not being successfully communicated to those who need the information most: the students. Primarily with their needs in mind, the aim of this review essay is to signal some of the more usable pieces of analysis.

2. Biography and Autobiography

The poorest writing on popular music is undoubtedly in the area of biography, and there are a number of reasons for this. The popular presses are fixated with the individual, and yet almost always commission angst-ridden fan-biographies, snide insider accounts, anodyne official assessments or so-called myth-shattering 'unofficial' sensationalism. The writing is overwhelmingly descriptive, often self-aggrandizing and customarily factually inaccurate. Little attempt is made to link individuals to either the pop process or societal changes, and attempts at 'analysis' often amount to uninformed opinion. As a result of the general paucity of good coverage from journalism, academia has largely ignored biography. The result is that the academic study of music is largely, and rather perversely, devoid of accounts of individuals. Part of the reason has, of course, been an unwillingness to return to a hagiography or naïve auteurism and to a personalizing view of popular music.

Ross Benson's *Paul McCartney: Behind the Myth* is an example of what Simon Frith called the 'scoffing biography' – an attempt to retrieve the truthful authentic self behind the constructed media image, rather than an attempt to tackle the issue of how pop stars mythologize their commercially-created personae. Benson's premise that the public conception of McCartney is still that of 'the cute one' from the Beatles does not bear close scrutiny. It is stretching the bounds of credulity to believe that most pop fans are not aware of his hard-nosed commercial instincts, his soft-drug habit or his politicization as an animal-rights spokesman. With no 'myth' about McCartney to begin with, the whole rationale for the book collapses as soon as it begins. As the 1960s unwind, McCartney's avant-garde credentials are established whilst Lennon is characterized as a drug-addled wreck by the time of *Sergeant Pepper* (once again rather predictably described as 'the most important album of all time'). As a discussion of McCartney's work within the Beatles it is sketchy, muddled and littered with omissions. Here is an example of the quality of Benson's analysis: 'had he [McCartney] bothered to acquire the intellectual self-discipline necessary to complete his A levels successfully, the trite flaccidity of many of his later song lyrics might have been avoided'. This book does nothing to aid our appreciation of McCartney beyond re-telling, in tabloid style, an oft-told story.

Another biography attempting to tease out the essence of the individual is Clinton Heylin's *Dylan: Behind the Shades*. Heylin points to the inadequacies of previous Dylan biographers such as Robert Shelton and Scaduto, and promises a critical appraisal of Dylan the artist which will give due coverage to his later work. Dylan, along with Astaire, Welles and Hendrix, is painted as one of the true geniuses of popular culture in the twentieth century. In an attempt to revive him as another one of the select but growing band of 'rock chameleons', Heylin asserts Dylan's reinvention of self on record and on stage without much supporting evidence. His Dylan is an authentic survivor, a true innovator, compared to the 'regressive authenticity' of Springsteen or the 'mock artistry' of Bowie, but there is no discussion of what labels such as 'original', 'artificial' and 'genius' actually mean, and the aesthetic framework remains unproblematized. Not only are Dylan's competitors neatly dismissed, but the political and social backdrop to his songs remains undeveloped. Methodologically the book has problems too: Heylin adheres to a strict chronological approach without ever seeing any larger patterns to Dylan's work, and the interspersion of chunks of interview material as commentary reads oddly. There are moments, however, when Heylin's writing is telling: he is particularly astute in assessing the reaction to Dylan's abandonment of the didacticism of the protest song in the mid-1960s, and his description of the Newport Folk Festival has a wonderful tragicomic slant. Dylan's conversion to Christianity in 1978 is also dealt with without the condescension expressed by some other critics, and Heylin's description of Dylan's 'cinematic imagination' is helpful. He has an impressive knowledge of all things Dylan, but on the whole the book is only a partial success.

Jimi Hendrix, the most innovative guitarist of his day, is the subject of two biographies. *Hendrix: Setting The Record Straight* by John McDermott with Eddie Kramer (Hendrix's long-serving producer and engineer) argues that Hendrix's 'many achievements have been all but crushed by the trappings of psychedelia and the lurid details of the 1960's drug culture'. Rather than trying to see how Hendrix articulated psychedelia, McDermott and Kramer appear embarrassed by the period's 'excesses'. The public perception of the undisciplined drug addict is dismantled in an attempt to legitimize Hendrix's contribution to popular music. Hendrix is referred to as the 'grand gadgeteer', and his penchant for technical innovation spoken of pejoratively. The book is painstakingly thorough on the chronology of Hendrix's active working life, but makes no attempt to assess his enormous influence on the trajectory of popular music beyond a vague two-page summary. Harry Shapiro and Caesar Glebbeek's revised and updated *Jimi Hendrix: Electric Gypsy*, although a more impressive biography, still fails to deal in any convincing theoretical way with Hendrix and his work. It is vastly detailed, reproducing a number of hand-written letters by Hendrix himself, and comes with 200 pages of appendices, including a full discography and interesting material on instrumentation. Those more interested in the cultural context of Hendrix's work, rather than a Gradgrindian chronological trawl, should return to Charles Shaar Murray's *Crosstown Traffic: Jimi Hendrix and Post-War Pop* (Faber, 1989).

Elvis Presley continues to haunt the terrain of popular culture, and Dave Marsh's *Elvis* is a kindly, though critical, assessment of a mixed legacy. Originally published in 1982 as a corrective to Albert Goldman's intensely vitriolic biography, *Elvis* (McGraw-Hill, 1981), the text comes with a new introduction and some excellent photographs. Marsh argues that Presley was neither a 'savior' nor Goldman's 'junkie pervert' and that reductionist myths have vulgarized our view of a complex individual. He writes: 'those who hold these simplistic views are exempt from having to live up to the greatest challenge lives such as Elvis Presley present to us: the challenge of seizing the chance to invent ourselves and, in the process, reinvent the world'.

Morrissey, one of the most enduring (and endearing) British post-

Punk pop icons, is the subject of a major biography by Johnny Rogan. *Morrissey and Marr: The Severed Alliance* is particularly strong on the pre-Smiths Morrissey, his preoccupation with outsiders, criminals and 'monsters', and his deep and passionate understanding of pop. However, the text is constructed very firmly along traditional lines, and although this is a well-above-average biography, the attempts at contextualization sometimes read oddly. Modern biographers are at such pains to make sure that their object of study is not hermetically sealed off from externalities that often the most mundane and irrelevant of material is included as contextual. Rogan's assessment of the Smiths' canon is lucid and detailed without ever offering us any in-depth theoretical rationale for Morrissey's always problematic narrative stance. Julian Stringer's short but extremely valuable article 'The Smiths: Repressed (but Remarkably Dressed)' (*Popular Music* 11:i.15–36) endeavours to do just that. In an attempt to move away from simple reportage as a means of explaining stardom, Stringer draws upon the work of Richard Dyer and particularly the notion of the 'star text': 'All official, unofficial and semi-official publicity about a star . . . has a part to play in the building of a star image. Any publicity which seeks a caught-you-with-your-trousers-down backstage "truth" can only inflect or extend the meaning of that image. In other words, because a star is a media sign we can only "know" the person through the signifying elements of his or her star image.' Stringer convincingly shows that the Smiths' songs were written as 'star vehicles' for Morrissey, and his discussion of vocal style is astute. He concludes his analysis with several telling observations about how notions of English national identity and repressed sexuality were encoded in the Smiths' songs. Reacting to the claim that the Smiths (and Morrissey in particular) were racists, Stringer concludes: 'I see their image as being about how white ethnicity gets naturalized within a specific national context, one defined by a heritage of racism.'

One of Morrissey's idols was Marc Bolan, whose career is the subject of Mark Paytress's *Twentieth Century Boy: The Marc Bolan Story*. In this highly readable biography, Paytress shows himself adept at contextualization and at relating Bolan's iconography to the pop process. The rationale – to elevate Bolan to a position of importance concomitant with Dylan, Lennon and Bowie – at first seems misguided. Whilst Paytress is not entirely convincing, Bolan's position as the first 'Glitter Rock' idol of the 1970s is restored, and the portrayal of Bolan's slide into mediocrity from 1973 to his death at 29 four years later is in turns both critical and sympathetic. He writes: 'Inhabiting the "low" esteem cultural space of fashion and the "high" domain afforded to poets and creative artists, provides the best sense in which Marc Bolan was what he coined a "20th Century Boy".' Paytress's Bolan is obsessed with style ('I was simply knocked out by my own image') and by 1970 manages to fuse together two 1960s codes, the mysticism of Hippydom and the narcissism of the 'hipster'. However, although 'the perfect glam idol', he was unable to capitalize on his early-1970s commercial success: 'Contemporaries like David Bowie managed to stake out new territories and guises. Marc Bolan could only ever be Marc Bolan.'

Very often pop biography is concerned with the cadaveric activity of exhuming the careers of the long-dead for public consumption. *Love, Janis*, a biography of the American singer Janis Joplin by her sister Laura, has an immediacy lent to it by the incorporation of a number of unpublished letters. The biography will be of little interest to those seeking an analysis of Joplin's music or cultural significance, but as a detailed account of the life and intensely contradictory personality of one of the leading singers of the late 1960s, Laura Joplin's work, although hardly dispassionate, is of some value.

Finally, a literary curio from musician James Young: in *Songs They Never Play on the Radio: Nico – The Last Bohemian*, Young details life on the road with the ex-Velvet Underground singer. Young's insouciant style is engaging, although the author remains conspicuously, and rather unconvincingly, aloof from the degradation of his confreres. Nico emerges as capricious and obsessive, with an all-persuasive power to manipulate those around her. What makes the book valuable is that 'the characters who orbited her – the has-beens, the could-have-beens, the never-will-bes – are people whose lives are rarely sung in the deafening hyperbole of Rock History'. Young's book, like Bruce Thomas's account of touring with Elvis Costello, *The Big Wheel* (Penguin, 1991), stops well short of the kind of analysis which would be invaluable. What is needed is a systematic, dispassionate investigation of a major rock tour which seeks to bring out cultural, economic and aesthetic meanings in order to complement these journalistic, on-the-road accounts.

3. Anthologies, Collections and Encyclopaedias

I have argued that much of the most important comment on popular music comes from journalism, but this writing is diffuse and sometimes not easily accessible. In *The Penguin Book of Rock and Roll Writing*, Clinton Heylin has assembled almost 700 pages of reviews and commentary, and one would have thought that with the rich variety of styles available to him, he would have been able to cover adequately a shifting terrain. The result, however, is very disappointing. Heylin has a specific historical line to push. In his rather flippant introduction he writes: 'I consider it self-evident that rock is "a white boy's club".' From Heylin's roll-call of writers, Jon Landau, Barney Hoskyns, Tony Parsons, Charles Shaar Murray, Lester Bangs and Nick Kent are often picked to further his authenticist line. His running commentary is simplistic and self-assured (all the old popular music historical myths go unchallenged), and the 1980s and 1990s are caricatured as artistically redundant re-creations of rock's golden age of the 1960s. Heylin thus does a great disservice in suggesting that pop culture and pop writing have lost their appetite for innovation. The inclusion of writers such as Simon Reynolds or Jon Savage would, however, have cast serious doubt on the white machismo of Heylin's pop world. This anthology, simply because of its length, does contain pieces well worth investigating, but overall it reads more like a reprint of Heylin's own research material for his Dylan and American Punk rock projects.

Lester Bangs once wrote: 'I belong to the generation for whom the Velvet Underground was our Beatles and Dylan combined.' Although largely ignored by critics and the public during their active years, the Velvet Underground's impact on popular music has been profound. Mike Kostek's *The Velvet Underground Handbook* is an impressive piece of archaeology which lists all Velvet Underground recordings and films together with information on cover versions of VU songs (by over 800 artists to date), books, television appearances and bootlegs. Kostek concludes that 'they were the first rock band on a major label who made no compromises for commercial success'. Lou Reed's quest for acceptance from the *literati* goes on apace and he has some of his best lyrics reprinted in *Between Thought and Expression: Selected Lyrics of Lou Reed*. As a fan, I enjoyed reading this very much, and his lyrics have a surprising resonance when decoupled from their musical context. 'Venus In Furs' is chilling, 'I Wanna Be Black' perversely funny, and the *reportage* of the *New York* material such as 'Dirty Boulevard' and 'Last Great American Whale' compelling. The collection also boasts two interviews conducted by Reed. The interview with Vaclav Havel, a long-standing Velvet Underground fan, is quite moving, as is Reed's description of an impromptu gig backed by a Czech VU revivalist band.

The tendency to list and compartmentalize pop around the star-image nexus is catered for by the burgeoning number of popular music encyclopaedias. Irwin Stambler's up-dated *The Encyclopedia of Pop, Rock, and Soul* offers expansive coverage of individual artists, with extensive use of interview material. The coverage of British pop, however, is inaccurate and highly selective, with some serious omissions such as the Smiths, the Stone Roses, Pet Shop Boys, Happy Mondays, Erasure, Human League, Frankie Goes To Hollywood and Madness. Almost inevitably, there is little coverage of non-Anglo-European acts. *The Faber Companion to Twentieth Century Popular Music* by Phil Hardy and Dave Laing, although spending considerably less time on detailing career minutiae, is a more stylish production, and the narrative avoids the mundane prose which characterizes other encyclopaedias such as Peter Gammond's stately *Oxford Companion to Popular Music*. Unlike Gammond, however, there is no discussion of musical genres beyond a three-page glossary at the beginning. Given the excellence of some of Dave Laing's other writings, it comes as a slight disappointment that the entries, although often refreshingly critical of established acts, seldom move beyond a chronological run-through of artistic careers to make wider cultural points. And again, the list of omissions, although not as heinous as Stambler's, is disconcertingly long. That said, Hardy and Laing's effort is the best yet of what is in truth not a terribly distinguished bunch of pop encyclopaedias.

Perhaps the best current assessment of rock past and present is the highly selective, but unerringly astute, *Rock on CD* by *The Times*'s 'baby-boomer' rock critic Dave Sinclair. Sinclair has selected around 125 artists and, unlike Heylin, has kept his 'definition of rock fairly "loose", assuming the scope to cover the more obvious of the country, soul, rap and blues artists whose work has had a significant impact on the rock mainstream'. His selections are sometimes quirky (why are Jesus Jones worthy of inclusion but New Order not?) and his tone sometimes rather patrician, but at its best it is excellent. It is also refreshingly taboo-breaking: the Beatles' *Sergeant Pepper*, 'the most overrated album in the history of rock', heralded the 'otiose horrors of the rock opera'.

Academic presses have deluged the market with critical anthologies, and whilst the standard is almost always uneven, there are some very worthwhile articles hidden away.

The Adoring Audience: Fan Culture and Popular Media, edited by

Lisa A. Lewis, 'considers the relationship between fans, stars, media texts and media industries' and contains essays by John Fiske, Lawrence Grossberg and Fred and Judy Vermorel. In 'Is There a Fan in the House?: The Affective Sensibility of Fandom', Grossberg calls for a theoretical balance between the study of fans and the study of texts, and argues that 'the fan's relation to cultural texts operates in the domain of effect or mood'. As an introduction to the debates concerning fandom in general, Joli Jenson's 'Fandom as Pathology' presents the arguments clearly. Jenson writes: 'there is very little literature that explores fandom as a normal, everyday cultural or social phenomenon. Instead, the fan is characterized as (at least potentially) an obsessed loner, suffering from a disease of isolation, or a frenzied crowd member, suffering from a disease of contagion'. Jenson explores these two iconic images in the light of debates centring around modernity, and engages with the critique that fans 'seek contact with famous people in order to compensate for their own inadequate lives'. Jenson also argues that a bogus distinction has been drawn between 'aficionadohood' (an attachment to 'elite, prestige-conferring objects') and 'fandom' (the dangerous attachment 'to popular mass-mediated objects'). The result is that 'the perceived-to-be-deviant, exotic and dramatic, is studied with zeal, while the normal, everyday, and accepted is ignored'.

Present Tense: Rock and Roll and Culture, edited by Anthony DeCurtis, is an eclectic collection of writing from an almost exclusively American perspective. DeCurtis, a writer for *Rolling Stone* with a doctorate in American literature, writes: 'I have been saddened by the degree to which academic and journalistic writing has been forced apart since the late Seventies. . . . Pushed to the margins by the go-go economy of the Eighties, academics struck back by retreating into a cult of the obscure – and thereby accelerated their movement out of the mainstream. For their part, journalists allowed their writing to become increasingly ephemeral. . . .' The collection's great strength is the plurality fostered by DeCurtis. His own tone-setting assessment of the 1980s, however, is a quintessential reaffirmation of traditional rock values. Aesthetically, his judgements are highly traditional and predictable. The video age is seen as emasculating a 'rebel's world', and his critical assessment of 1980s music is bewilderingly reactionary. We are told that Sting made 'two ground-breaking albums', British synth pop was 'anaemic' and that 'most pop songs featured lyrics hardly worth any attention at all'. *Present Tense* does, however, contain some important articles. I particularly liked Trent Hill's discussion of the censorship of rock-and-roll in the 1950s and Paul Smith's 'Playing for England', a discussion of the relationship between youth culture, politics, music and football in early-1990s Britain.

The link between music, mass culture and political expression is a complex one and Reebee Garofalo has edited a collection of writings on the subject – *Rockin' the Boat: Mass Music and Mass Movements*. In his introduction, Garofalo points to the distorted views of mass culture produced by both the left and right, and specifically attacks the crude unidirectionalism of the cultural imperialism thesis. The view of a 'debased culture, produced only for profit and manipulated from above', which turns the audience for pop into mass-manipulated dupes, is a chimera. The politics of global events such as Live Aid and the Mandela Concerts are the subject of two further essays by Garofalo. This collection also reflects the growth in interest by the academic community in indigenous folk musics from throughout the world. Around half the book is allotted to an international perspective and there are essays by Peter Wicke on the former East Germany, by Joanna Ching-Yun Lee on China, by Marcus Brean on Australian Aboriginal Music and by Simon Frith and John Street on Rock Against Racism and Red Wedge in 1970s and 1980s Britain.

4. History and Analysis

The functioning of the music business is the focus of four new critical studies. Andrew Blake's *The Music Business*, written for a cultural studies market, is the most accessible, but also the weakest. Blake offers no in-depth discussion, and his narrative, in an admirable attempt at readability, unfortunately also steers clear of engaging with any of the main theoretical or historical debating points or with any of the most important popular music writers who have discussed the industrialization of music and the organization of the music business. Blake's use of rather vague and simplistic diagrammatic materials, occasional factual inaccuracies and incorporation of often superfluous photographic material make the book a disappointment, save one chapter: 'Inside the Circuit: Making Music' is noticeably more detailed and convincing than the rest of his material and provides an excellent short historical survey of the evolution of instrumentation and performance.

Although sometimes doggedly sociological in style, Keith Negus's *Producing Pop: Culture and Conflict in the Popular Music Industry* is a more important work, and must be considered a valuable contribution to popular music studies. Negus's book has a veracity absent from Blake's account, based as it is on four years of fieldwork among record company personnel in New York and London. Negus counters the theorists who have caricatured the music business as a battle between radical and sincere 'indies' on the one hand and reactive 'majors' on the other by arguing for the existence of 'webs' of interdependency on the level of distribution, marketing and artist development. He takes issue not only with the 'top-down' theorizing of Adorno, Attali and Peterson and Berger, but also with the view that 'sees changes in popular music bubbling up from below as a result of the spontaneous eruption of creative activity . . .', and suggests that 'greater attention has to be paid to the day-to-day work of the people in the industry itself'. The book is full of lucid discussions of a wide range of topics and, as an introduction for students and researchers, it is admirable. Importantly, Negus argues for the existence of two ideologies of creativity; the 'organic', a naturalistic approach by A&R staff to artists, and the 'synthetic', which Negus calls 'a combinatorial approach to both acts and material'. Negus convincingly shows that the 'organic' ideology is entrenched in the middle-class, middle-aged, white, male-dominated A&R departments and that this explains the development of guitar-based bands at the expense of pop or dance artists, who tend to develop in a more random, experimental manner.

Krister Malm and Roger Wallis's *Media Policy and Music Activity* is unlikely to have the same pedagogical spin-offs as Negus's work, but will prove valuable for any researchers interested in cultural policy and music. In part 1 of the book, Malm and Wallis outline their research methods and postulates in a rather laboured way. The music industry is seen as a 'set of systems' operating on a local/ national/international level and affected by technological, economic and organizational constraints. Malm and Wallis detail the various institutional agents of policy, such as musicians' unions and hardware companies, before, in six case-studies in part 2 of their book (in Jamaica, Trinidad, Kenya, Tanzania, Wales and Sweden), assessing their influence on grass-roots music-making. A sixty-page conclusion rounds off the study.

Finally, for those interested in a clearly-presented factual guide, Diane Sward Rapaport's *How to Make and Sell Your Own Recording: A Guide for the Nineties*, written from an American perspective, has chapters on promotion, sales, legal issues such as recording contracts and copyright, manufacturing, design, and recording technique.

Textual analysis has come a long way since the monodisciplinary sociological engagements with musical styles in the 1960s and 1970s. That most maligned musical style, heavy metal, finds its most eloquent apologist yet in Robert Walser. In his article 'Eruptions: Heavy Metal Appropriations of Classical Virtuosity' (*Popular Music* 11:iii.263–308), Walser argues that an examination of appropriation of classical music (and Bach in particular) by guitarists such as Ritchie Blackmore, Jimi Hendrix, Randy Rhoads and Yngwie Malmsteen forces us to re-evaluate the original texts themselves: 'We must ask: if we do not understand why his [Bach's] influence shows up in the music of Ozzy Osbourne or Bon Jovi, do we really understand *Bach* as well as we thought we did?' Walser's article celebrates the dialogical nature of popular culture and contrasts it with a perceived unwillingness on the part of art music aficionados to abandon their obsolete high culture aesthetic. Aaron A. Fox shares something of Walser's proselytizing zeal, and his essay 'The Jukebox of History: Narrative of Loss and Desire in the Discourse of Country Music' (*Popular Music* 11:ii.53–72) tackles the style's detractors through a remarkably astute reading of 'the true' and 'the false' in country music. Country denaturalizes '"ordinary" languages of private desire and public rationality' and in turn renaturalizes them in a performance aesthetic which distils 'the public, poetic expression back down to a one-to-one talk, addressed to the individual listener as a bar-room *confidant*'. Finally, Steven G. Smith in his rather wordy and slightly pretentious article 'Blues and our Mind-Body Problem' (*Popular Music* 11.ii.41–53) gives a philosophical rationale for the meaning of the blues, identifying, in much the same way as Fox did for country, a rich vein of irony in the style. Furthermore, 'blues undermines the leap to music, or deliberately fails to be music, in two complementary ways: by falling short of musical standards of coherence in its roughness, and by deadening the interest of musical pattern through its extreme structural simplification'.

Michael Bane, in *White Boy Singin' The Blues: The Black Roots of White Rock*, a reprint of his 1982 book with a new introduction, is rather more earthy in his description of how 'black' musical styles have been appropriated by whites. Using a mixture of flashbacks, first and third person narration and anecdotal material, Bane describes a musical 'battlefield' witnessing the 'continuous battering of black against white'. Bane is interesting on pre-rock-and-roll musics such as gospel, work songs and spirituals, and on the musical culture of Memphis, Tennessee, but his idiosyncratic and vulgarizing style soon begins to pall.

Rap, one of the most important emergent styles of popular music in the 1970s and 1980s, has in turn been on the receiving end of some of the most hostile (and fatuous) criticism, culminating in Donald Clarke's summation in *The Penguin Encyclopedia of Popular Music* (Viking, 1989): 'do you spell rap with a big or small c?' *Rap: The Lyrics*, a collection of 150 texts edited by Lawrence A. Stanley, is an attempt at legitimization. Detached from any musical context, one might have expected lyrical meaning to be emasculated, or at least deflected. However, the vocal strategies of Rap artists often show such a similarity that the nuances of vocalization which crucially determine the meaning of pop songs do not play such a big role. A short introduction by Jefferson Morley sketches in some of the historical context, but anybody interested in seeing how the style has developed in more detail must return to David Toop's *Rap Attack 2* (Serpent's Tail, 1991).

David Brackett in his essay 'James Brown's "Superbad" and the Double-Voiced Utterance' (*Popular Music* 11:iii.309–24) examines the vocal style of one of Rap's progenitors. Using the linguistic distinction between Black English and Standard English Brackett identifies an emphasis on sound, on 'the materiality of the signifier, an almost complete lack of emphasis on narrative and on syntagmatic or chain-like continuity'. Brackett uses Henry Louis Gates's notion of 'double-voiced' utterance (originally coined by Bakhtin – a theorist very much in vogue at the moment), describing 'the manner in which a word can partake simultaneously of both black and white discursive worlds', to demonstrate the semantic shifts in Brown's vocal delivery.

Although the focus is not on popular music, *Excursions in World Music* by Bruno Nettl, Charles Capwell, Philip V. Bohlam, Isabel K. F. Wong and Thomas Turino will provide some easily digestible background material on the musics of the world. The book includes a rather contracted introduction followed by descriptions of the music of India, the Middle East, China, Japan, Indonesia, Sub-Saharan Africa, Europe, Latin America and North America.

The 1960s' position as the most innovative decade in pop culture remains unchallenged, and the next part of this article looks at some of the textual and contextual accounts of the period. The Beatles' *oeuvre* has been analysed *ad nauseam* but Stuart Madow and Jeff Sobul's *The Colour of Your Dreams: The Beatles' Psychedelic Music* must be one of the most inconsequential studies yet. In a little over 100 pages Madow and Sobul discuss more than thirty songs from 'Revolver' to 'Let It Be' in an imprecise and platitudinous manner.

Behind Epstein's packaging were 'four young men of hardened steel' who created an 'entirely new and different genre of music . . . "Beatles' Psychedelic"'. About *Sergeant Pepper* we are told that 'it may also be that there is no one single "greatest album ever" musically because of differences in musical tastes'. The description of the Beatles' music is incredibly vague, even for the sort of adjectival descriptions so disliked by Barthes. Vocals are 'strange', the bass is 'penetrating', strings 'lush and full'. The 'analysis' of the creative process is ludicrous: 'John would come to Martin with a vision and Martin would produce the sound. It was all highly experimental', and attempts at sociological analysis embarrassing: 'For kids, the attitude of the time [the 1950s] was to do what their parents told them. John, a rebel since his youth, disagreed.'

Sheila Whiteley in *The Space Between the Notes: Rock and the Counter-Culture* provides a literate and astute reading of late-1960s progressive rock, and the way in which she manages to interweave musicological and contextual material is refreshingly exoteric. Whiteley examines the work of Cream, Pink Floyd, Hendrix, the Beatles and the Rolling Stones and develops a homologous theory of 'psychedelic coding' as a means of understanding how the sounds themselves articulated the psychedelic experience. She writes: 'musically psychedelic coding focuses on *alternative meanings* and involves a correlation of drug experience and stylistic characteristics'. Some themes such as the visual side of pop performance (particularly the early Pink Floyd's theatricality and Barrett's whimsical camp) remain undeveloped, and the link between progressive rock and musical innovation is unproblematized. Whiteley's book is marred somewhat by a succession of factual inaccuracies. For example, *Dark Side Of The Moon* was not number one for two years (in fact, it has never reached the top in the UK), and Whiteley states that the lead vocal on Astronomy Domine is by Syd Barrett, then by Rick Wright.

The link between hallucinogens and the counterculture is well-known, and those interested in a discussion of the history of drugs and human evolution will find Terrence McKenna's *Food of the Gods: The Search for the Original Tree of Knowledge* provocative. McKenna argues that the loss of shamanic gnosis led to the increasing use of highly dangerous and addictive drugs such as alcohol and heroin. He expertly details the morphology of addiction. LSD paradoxically created a 'community' of disconnected, atomized individuals: 'The sudden introduction of a powerful deconditioning agent such as LSD had the effect of creating a mass defection from community values, especially values based on a dominator hierarchy accustomed to suppressing consciousness and awareness.' McKenna therefore provides some much-needed contextual material, but unfortunately little analysis of the counterculture itself. For an equally idiosyncratic, though excellent, analysis of shamanism, the use of hallucinogens and popular entertainment (including a section on pop performers) see Rogan Taylor's *The Death and Resurrection Show: From Shaman to Superstar* (Anthony Blond, 1985).

In *Selling the Sixties: The Pirates and Pop Music Radio* Robert Chapman details the evolution of pirate radio. Using Radios Caroline and London, Chapman attempts to demythologize 1960s British pirate radio. The pirates did not simply represent an outlet for pop in a response to the reactionary mentality of the Establishment. He writes: 'Although the rise of offshore radio could undoubtedly be attributed in part to the low priority the BBC gave to pop music there was always a great deal of diversity in the pirates' programming.' Very often the pirates played a diet of middle-of-the road. Chapman shows that, far from there being an idealistic camaraderie and commitment to pop amongst pirate stations, the relationship was in reality marked by a hostile competitiveness. The study ends with a discussion of the BBC's response to pirate radio and an analysis of the early years of Radio 1.

Dave Harker has a debunking essay, 'Still Crazy After All These Years: What Was Popular Music in the 1960s?', included in *Cultural Revolution? The Challenge of the Arts in the 1960s,* edited by Bart Moore-Gilbert and John Seed. Harker rather cantankerously argues that the position of dominance assigned to the Beatles is hard to sustain in terms of chart performance and records sold and that the 'really hegemonic group of the decade' was 'Soundtrack, featuring Original Cast!'. Harker is wary of putting too much store by chart facts and figures, and yet his critique of our overestimation of the Beatles' importance (which may, in fact, be completely justified) rests wholly on a perceived mediocre chart performance. A glance at the *Guinness Book of Hit Singles* shows, however, that the Beatles spent 338 weeks in the top hundred in the period from 1962 to their split in 1970 – hardly lacklustre. Harker does make a very good point when he argues that the huge success of *The Sound of Music* has been struck out of accounts of the 1960s by academics because 'it does not suit their subjective, and perhaps not wholly representative tastes . . .'. Simon Frith in particular comes in for a volley of criticism: 'In seeking to elaborate a general theory of the popular in music . . . Frith begins with his own legitimate personal tastes and then (illegitimately) seeks to marginalize or even exclude much really popular music from his "definition".' Harker concludes that 'what critics and students have to acknowledge is that, so far, the musical practices and tastes of most people – the working class – are marginalized or ignored in even the better critical accounts of periods like the 1960s; most of the critics try to generalize from the experience of students and budding academics'.

Mention has already been made on p. 198 of Dick Bradley's *Understanding Rock'n'Roll: Popular Music in Britain 1955–1964*, and of his exhortation to move beyond the vagueness of adjectival subjectivity masquerading as analysis. Bradley calls this the 'descriptive-evaluative mode', typified by the writing of Charles Gillett and early Dave Laing. Such writing is 'inexplicit in its terms for musical "content" or "meaning"' and 'by virtue of this inexplicitness . . . elides evaluation and description, so that the former is able to pose as the latter'. However, Bradley's own narrative style and analytical register is problematic. Firstly, by using the first person singular so often, the text takes on, if unwittingly, a hectoring, schoolmasterly tone. Secondly, in an effort to transcend subjective responses, Bradley's narrative becomes extremely obtuse and theoretical rather too often for it to be unreservedly recommendable to undergraduates. Those reservations aside, I liked the book, particularly the chapter on 'Codes of the West' and its discussion of the differences between 'the tonal-European code' and the 'Afro-American code'. Bradley also provides an analysis of British popular music's American antecedents, a discussion of the musical codes and singing styles of rock-and-roll, and an analysis of issues such as class, ethnicity, gender and youth culture.

A considerably more straightforward, though rather simplistic, analysis of popular music is offered in Charles T. Brown's *The Art of Rock and Roll*. The book is obviously written with teaching needs in mind, and traces the history of rock from Presley to Rap. Brown is, however, unmistakably nationalistic and reduces the history of pop to the forging of the American dream. He writes, 'rock is a legitimate art form, primarily fostered in the United States'. This history is also made by a select number of great players, almost exclusively American: Haley 'started the whole thing called rock-and-roll' but was 'not a terribly good musician'. The sections on British pop are weak: the Beatles' impact is reduced merely to reflecting late-1960s American 'turmoil', and the description of post-Beatles pop, which largely includes discussions of the leading lights of the 1960s such as the Who and the Rolling Stones, confirms that,

for Brown, rock's significance started and stopped in the 1960s.
Brown does include an interesting chapter on 'The Sources of
Rock', with a discussion of slave music, jazz, country blues and vau-
deville, which students may find helpful. However, the standard of
analysis is generally vague, and omits any engagement with the
leading 'authorities' on pop, although I was intrigued to find out
that 'some people have said that he [Presley] could make women
faint simply by moving the glottal flap'.

Martin Williams in his collection of essays *Hidden in Plain Sight:
An Examination of the American Arts* shows none of Brown's love
for American popular culture. In fact Williams argues that the
notion of 'popular culture' is fallacious and has done great damage
to the prestige of American art. Americans have thus traditionally
shied away from regarding their finest musicians, playwrights, poets,
artists and authors as being on a par aesthetically with the
European greats. However, in attempting to reclaim American art,
Williams distorts its character. His arguments have the effect of
creating a parallel artistic world in which the aesthetic values of
European high culture are to be aspired to, not redefined. Thus
Duke Ellington is compared to Joseph Haydn and Greek and Eliza-
bethan dramatists. Whilst Williams's writing is sometimes good, his
judgements appear reactionary.

In *We Gotta Get Out Of This Place: Popular Conservatism and
Postmodern Culture* Lawrence Grossberg examines the link between
politics, culture and music in America. I found Grossberg was at his
most interesting when discussing the social, economic and aesthetic
contexts of Reaganite American culture, and I recommend the book
on this count alone. However, Grossberg's writing becomes increasingly abstract once the relationship between music and youth culture
is established. Early on in the book, his study of the relationship
between 'effect' and popular culture is lucid enough, but a hundred
pages later I would imagine that most readers will be in some difficulty. In a six-page section 'The Identity of Youth and the Politics
of Fun' I counted 7 invest/ments, 7 locate/d/ings, 12 contructed/ings,
5 'space's and quite a few 'placed's, 'positioned's and 'sites'. Grossberg writes: 'The articulation of rock and youth transformed a transitional culture into a culture of transitions (and the transitional
body of youth into a body of transitions).' This cultural-studies
jargon results in a narrative so abstracted, so limiting, so repetitious
and so divorced from everyday language that most informed readers
will simply switch off. Rather depressingly, I get the feeling Grossberg does not care: 'Intellectuals are laborers paid to produce some-

thing called knowledge. And like any laborer, they seek to develop skills and vocabularies which give them a privileged claim to compensation . . . status and power.'

The need for clarification and reassessment is one which will become stronger as the body of popular music writing grows. Anne Beezer provides a reading of a seminal subcultural theory text in her article 'Dick Hebdige, *Subculture: The Meaning of Style*' which appears in a collection of reassessments she has edited with Martin Barker, *Reading into Cultural Studies*. Beezer succinctly reviews Hebdige's structuralist stance in a way that students will find reads clearly, and contains sections on 'The Semiological Framework', 'Race and Subculture', 'Structural Form and Formation' and 'Reading Style'.

Jeff Pressing's enormously detailed *Synthesizer Performance and Real-time Techniques* is geared exclusively for musicians in need of a guide through the latest technological developments. Pressing describes the type of software available and details a range of performance techniques. The focus is less on popular music than on the use of the synthesizer in 'serious music' and Pressing has little or nothing to say on how the synthesizer has developed in popular music since the 1960s.

Finally, we have something of a breakthrough by musicologist Allan Moore in his article 'Patterns of Harmony' (*Popular Music* 11:i.73–106). Those who, like myself, have struggled through musicological analysis only to find the range of musics engaged with restricted to blues, jazz, Tin Pan Alley and the Beatles, will find Moore's knowledge of pop styles refreshingly catholic. His article is the first step towards what he calls a 'generative theory of rock/pop/soul harmony' and contains a 24-page appendix which groups songs into different classes of harmonic structure. Moore knows his stuff, as a cursory glance at his subject-matter (which ranges from Ray Charles to the Wedding Present) demonstrates. Moore concludes that 'contrary to received opinion, there is a great variety of harmonic patterns used along the rock/pop/soul continuum', but he also suggests that there is 'a *single harmonic language* for rock/pop/soul which, in turn, may serve to differentiate this music from jazz-derived popular musics'.

The following books, which may prove useful, were not seen: Bockris, Victor, *Keith Richards: The Unauthorised Biography* (Hutchinson); Eliot, Marc, *Down Thunder Road: The Making of Bruce Springsteen* (Plexus); Gambaccini, Paul, Tim Rice and Jonathan Rice, *British Hit Albums* (Guinness); Herman, Gary, *Rock* 'n' Roll Babylon (Plexus); Jones, Steve, *Rock Formation: Music, Technology and Mass Communication* (Sage); Larkin, Colin, *The Guinness Encyclopedia of Popular Music* (Guinness); Lewisohn, Mark, *The Complete Beatles Chronicle* (Crown); Marsh, Dave, *Louie, Louie* (Hyperion); May, Chris, *Hugh Maesekela: The Authorised Biography* (Square One); Simpson, Jeff, ed., *Radio 1's Classic Interviews: 25 Rock Greats in Their Own Words* (BBC); Tagg, Philip, *Fernando the Flute: Analysis of Musical Meaning in an Abba Mega-Hit* (Liverpool: Institute of Popular Music).

Books Reviewed

Bane, Michael. *White Boy Singin' the Blues: The Black Roots of White Rock.* New Introduction. Da Capo. pp. 269. pb $12.95. ISBN 0 306 80479 4.

Barker, Martin, and Anne Beezer. *Reading into Cultural Studies.* Routledge. pp. 200. pb £10.99. ISBN 0 415 06377 9.

Benson, Ross. *Paul McCartney: Behind the Myth.* Gollancz. pp. 289. £15.99. ISBN 0 575 05200 7.

Blake, Andrew. *The Music Business.* Batsford. pp. 128. pb £9.99. ISBN 0 7134 6662 6.

Bradley, Dick. *Understanding Rock'n'Roll: Popular Music in Britain 1955–1964.* Open University Press. pp. 191. pb £12.99. ISBN 0 335 09754 5.

Brown, Charles T. *The Art of Rock and Roll.* Third Edition. Prentice Hall. pp. 336. pb $53.35. ISBN 0 13 044892 3.

Chapman, Robert. *Selling the Sixties: The Pirates and Pop Music Radio.* Routledge. pp. 295. pb £11.99. ISBN 0 415 07970 5.

DeCurtis, Anthony. *Present Tense: Rock and Roll and Culture.* Duke University Press. pp. 317. pb $14.95. ISBN 0 8223 1265 4.

Garofalo, Reebee, ed. *Rockin' the Boat: Mass Music and Mass Movements.* South End Press. pp. 333. pb £10.95. ISBN 0 89608 428 0.

Grossberg, Lawrence. *We Gotta Get Out Of This Place: Popular Conservatism and Postmodern Culture.* Routledge. pp. 436. pb £11.95. ISBN 0 415 90330 0.

Hardy, Phil, and Dave Laing. *The Faber Companion to Twentieth Century Popular Music.* Faber & Faber. pp. 875. pb £12.99. ISBN 0 571 16865 5.

Heylin, Clinton, ed. *The Penguin Book of Rock and Roll Writing.* Viking. pp. 682. £17.99. ISBN 0 670 84559 0.

——. *Dylan: Behind the Shades.* Penguin. pp. 548. pb £7.99. ISBN 0 14 014310 6.

Joplin, Laura. *Love, Janis.* Bloomsbury. pp. 342. £15.99. ISBN 0 7475 1265 5.

Kostek, M. C. *The Velvet Underground Handbook.* Black Spring Press. pp. 221. pb £8.95. ISBN 0 948238 12 7.

Lewis, Lisa A. *The Adoring Audience: Fan Culture and Popular Media.* Routledge. pp. 245. pb £10.99. ISBN 0 415 07821 0.

Madow, Stuart, and Jeff Sobul. *The Colour of Your Dreams: The Beatles' Psychedelic Music.* Dorrance. pp. 115. $13.00. ISBN 0 8059 3261 5.

Malm, Krister, and Roger Wallis. *Media Policy and Music Activity.* Routledge. pp. 271. pb £11.99. ISBN 0 415 05021 0.

Marsh, Dave. *Elvis.* Art direction by Bea Feitler. Revised Edition. Omnibus. pp. 245. pb £12.95. ISBN 0 7119 3222 0.

McDermott, John, with Eddie Kramer. *Hendrix: Setting the Record Straight.* Little, Brown. pp. 458. £16.99. ISBN 0 316 90518 6.

McKenna, Terrence. *Food of the Gods: The Search for the Original Tree of Knowledge.* Rider. pp. 311. pb £9.99. ISBN 0 7126 5445 3.

Moore-Gilbert, Bart, and John Seed. *Cultural Revolution? Challenge of the Arts in the 1960s.* Routledge. pp. 287. pb £12.99. ISBN 0 415 07825 3.

Negus, Keith. *Producing Pop: Culture and Conflict in the Popular Music Industry.* Edward Arnold. pp. 175. pb £10.99. ISBN 0 340 51759 X.

Nettl, Bruno, Charles Capwell, Philip V. Bohlam, Isabel K. F. Wong and Thomas Turino. *Excursions in World Music.* Prentice Hall. pp. 340. pb $49.95. ISBN 0 13 299025 3.

Paytress, Mark. *Twentieth Century Boy: The Marc Bolan Story.* Sidgwick & Jackson. pp. 294. pb £9.99. ISBN 0 283 06171 5.

Pressing, Jeff. *Synthesizer Performance and Real-time Techniques.* Oxford University Press. pp. 462. £35.00. ISBN 0 19 816275 8.

Rapaport, Diane Sward. *How to Make and Sell Your Own Recording: A Guide for the Nineties.* Revised Fourth Edition. Prentice Hall. pp. 240. pb $38.95. ISBN 0 13 402314 5.

Reed, Lou. *Between Thought and Expression: Selected Lyrics of Lou Reed.* Viking. pp. 182. £14.99. ISBN 0 670 84532 9.

Rogan, Johnny. *Morrissey and Marr: The Severed Alliance.* Omnibus. pp. 352. £14.95. ISBN 0 7119 1838 4.

Shapiro, Harry, and Caesar Glebbeek. *Jimi Hendrix: Electric Gypsy.* Revised Edition. Mandarin. pp. 723. pb £12.99. ISBN 0 7493 0544 4.

Sinclair, Dave. *Rock on CD: The Essential Guide.* Kyle Cathie. pp. 416. pb £9.99. ISBN 1 85626 058 5.

Stambler, Irwin. *The Encyclopedia of Pop, Rock, and Soul.* Revised Edition. Macmillan. pp. 881. pb £14.99. ISBN 0 333 51833 0.

Stanley, Lawrence A. *Rap: The Lyrics.* Penguin. pp. 432. pb £8.99. ISBN 0 14 014788 8.

Whiteley, Sheila. *The Space Between the Notes: Rock and the Counter-Culture.* Routledge. pp. 139. pb £11.99. ISBN 0 415 06816 9.

Williams, Martin. *Hidden in Plain Sight: An Examination of the American Arts.* Oxford University Press. pp. 153. £17.50. ISBN 0 19 507500 5.

Young, James. *Songs They Never Play on the Radio: Nico – The Last Bohemian.* Bloomsbury. pp. 207. pb £12.99. ISBN 0 7475 1194 2.

12

Media Theory

Derek Longhurst

This chapter has five sections: 1. Introduction; 2. Media, Culture and Society; 3. Europe; 4. Audience Studies; 5. Conclusion.

1. Introduction

Any analysis of media theory in the early years of the decade has to register the importance of the historical context(s) of the collapse of the command economies of the former Soviet Union and Eastern Europe together with debates generated by movements towards greater political and cultural as well as economic convergence in Western Europe. This has produced, on the one hand, a resurgence of nationalism, often in tension with diversity of ethnic and religious identities while, on the other, the key questions have focused around the sovereignty of the nation-state in relation to pan-European 'cultural identity' in association with political, legal and social institutions or value-systems.

A further context emerged clearly into the light during the final stages of the GATT talks when it became clear that the French, in particular, were concerned as much about the threat of American dominance to national culture and the future of the audio–visual industries as they were about agricultural production. Often equated simplistically with Americanization, globalization has been, then, a major preoccupation within media theory of the 1990s. As John B. Thompson argues in *Ideology and Modern Culture* (1990):

> during the revolutionary upheavals in Eastern Europe, control of the means of television broadcasting became a crucial stake in the battle.

But the events in Eastern Europe also illustrate that, in the era of modern mass communication, the battlefield itself can no longer be strictly delimited in spatial and temporal terms, since the means of communication make possible forms of action and reaction which are extended or compressed in time and which transcend the boundaries of particular nation-states.

Here Thompson is clearly drawing his reference points from the Giddens–Harvey debates concerning time–space distanciation or compression. These have featured widely in media theory of the 1990s and are frequently related to arguments about the media and postmodernism. Importantly, however, there are signs in European media theory of a movement away from the simplicities represented, say, by John Fiske (always more influential in America than in Britain) towards more elaborated forms of political-economy analysis. This has been manifested in a revival of interest in Habermas's concept of the public sphere – heavily qualified by the recognition of, especially, gender and class inequalities – together with an engagement with conceptions of citizenship which move beyond consumer charters. This preoccupation may be traced, on the one hand, through significant interventions concerning the location of the media (primarily but not exclusively television) within everyday life, both in terms of domestic technologies and as forms of 'talk' or 'public address' while, on the other, convergence within corporate media industries has produced analysis of ownership, the impact of deregulation and governmental commitment to the ideology of the market. This has led, then, to a continued concern in the 1990s with how the media construct audiences and how 'audiences' make sense of media texts alongside discussion of the role of the media within state formations and as agencies within national cultures.

The most influential 'collection' of the period in question (1990–2) is *Mass Media and Society* edited by James Curran and Michael Gurevitch. Like its predecessor volume, *Mass Communication and Society* (1977), this collection of essays is aimed at students and is intended to provide them with an updated account of the field, including a reflection of, and critical response to, so-called 'new revisionist' scholarship. Curran's own contribution to the volume suggests that the old dichotomies of liberal-pluralist and radical paradigms have broken down within media theory. This was an argument Curran had previously advanced in 1990, in an article in the *European Journal of Communication* (5:ii–iii.135–64):

a major change has taken place. The most important and significant overall shift has been the steady advance of pluralist themes within the radical tradition: in particular, the repudiation of the totalizing, explanatory frameworks of Marxism, the reconceptualization of the audience as creative and active and the shift from the political to a popular aesthetic.

In the subsequent essay 'Mass Media and Democracy' Curran argues for a reworking of Habermas's concept of the public sphere in the contemporary context which he argues 'can be best realized through the establishment of a core public service broadcasting system, encircled by a private enterprise, social market, professional and civic media sectors'. Only through such a media system will it be possible to retrieve participative, representative democracy, one in which difference and sectional interests are worked through and form part of consensual agreement rather than being repressed through domination at the centres of power.

Stung into riposte by the charge that his work on audiences may be associated with a rehashing of the 'uses and gratifications' tradition masquerading as innovation, David Morley in *Television, Audiences and Cultural Studies* accuses Curran of mobilizing his own particular version of the history of audience research and one which could not have been written without the transformative impact of the 'new revisionism' he is attacking. Moreover, Curran fails to grasp fully, according to Morley, the engagement with semiology which contributed an extra dimension to the understanding of the concept of the message frequently neglected in mainstream audience research.

Where Morley and Curran are in agreement, however, is on the ambivalence of Foucauldian theory for media research. Drawing upon a partial reading of Foucault has led some critics to see power as existing only in discourse or suggesting that the role of the media can be 'reduced to a succession of reader–text encounters in the context of a society which is analytically disaggregated into a series of concrete instances . . .'. As Morley argues, this is in fact a critique which is most appropriately directed to the prolific writings of John Fiske and an emergent American cultural studies.

In his essay on 'Postmodernism and Television' in *Mass Media and Society*, however, Fiske critiques Baudrillard's theoretical position for failing to take account of the ways in which the socially subordinate do construct meanings and draw upon them as 'resources in their daily lives'. Clearly this again articulates a continuation of Fiske's populist notions of the resistances of popular culture within a 'semiotic democracy'. Here, however, he does suggest that 'bottom-up meanings are produced in a structural relationship to top-down ones'. Reviving his appropriation of Gramscian theory, Fiske does acknowledge that the subordinate can only be exerted within a struggle with the dominant. Therefore, he concludes, post-modern theory can only offer valuable insights into contemporary culture if it is grounded in 'social materialism', politicized accounts of everyday life within capitalist societies. Here, as elsewhere in Fiske's writings, it is difficult to be sure what is meant by the 'political', other than a rhetorical gesture following on from a pre-occupation with a general notion of polysemic textuality.

These are issues taken up by Todd Gitlin and John Corner in their contributions to the third section of the volume: 'Mediation of Cultural Meanings'. Gitlin in 'The Politics of Communication and the Communication of Politics' rightly critiques the fashionable conflation of consumerism and politics, while Corner's 'Meaning, Genre and Context: The Problematics of "Public Knowledge" in the New Audience Studies' emphasizes the social context of meaning-production and also that oversimplified accounts of the multiplicity of meanings take no account of the extent to which texts and genres operate closure of meaning. This final section of the volume is completed by three further contributions to audience studies. Jack M. McLeod, Gerald M. Kosicki and Zhongdang Pan in 'On Understanding and Misunderstanding Media Effects' survey empirical work on media effects, concluding that critiques originating out of critical cultural studies are often rooted in prejudice, failing to acknowledge the extent to which the effects tradition has moved on from untheorized empiricism. They urge a 'coming-together' of perspectives in the interests of knowledge and understanding of the selective and complex ways in which audiences are influenced by the media. Similarly Sonia Livingstone in 'Audience Reception: The Role of the Viewer in Retelling Romantic Drama' argues that empirical reception research 'offers an integrating, convergent approach to the television audience' in grasping the role of the active viewer in the complex dynamic between text and reader. She offers a case-study of soap opera with particular reference to *Coronation Street* in order to draw out unpredictable and often contradictory readings to set against conceptions of the ideal reader. Finally, Ien Ang and Joke Hermes explore 'Gender and/in Media Consumption', arguing for the openness of postmodern feminism in its acknowledgement of the particular, the partial, heterogeneity and difference, which would be a more politically constructive position from which to review the articulation of gender in practices of media consumption as against normative categorization of 'women' which can lead to easy and mechanical generalization. They argue, for instance, that Morley's study of the gendering of television viewing habits, in focusing upon the 'structured relational context' of the family tends to 'collapse gender positionings and gender identifications together'. Thus, articulations of gender in media consumptions can never be seen as either contextually total or final but always as diverse (e.g. variations between families) and shifting (e.g. variability of Morley's pairings of concentration/masculine, distraction/feminine practices).

Liesbet van Zoonen also addresses these issues earlier in the collection in her overview essay 'Feminist Perspectives on the Media'. She outlines a typology of liberal, radical and socialist feminist approaches, and goes on to argue against transmission models of communication associated with some feminist research (the analysis of stereotypes for instance). She concludes by raising some problems for feminist research. For instance, the concentration on constructions of femininity and on particular 'women's genres' such as soap opera has tended to leave masculinity out of account (i.e. men who take pleasure in watching soap opera?). Nor do these foci relate easily to such issues as the future of public service broadcasting, the new communication technologies or analyses of political communication. Moreover, van Zoonen expresses some concern that the particularist nature of feminist research raises some political problems. As she argues:

> If meaning is so dependent on context, can we still pass valid feminist judgements about the political tendencies and implications of texts? . . . If one interpretation is not by definition better or more valid than another, what legitimation do we have to discuss the politics of representation, to try to intervene in dominant culture?

In answering these questions she cites Mary Ellen Brown's appropriation of women's pleasure as useful in that it 'implies a conception of politics that incorporates power relations in the private domestic sphere of media consumption' (see Brown, M. E., ed. *Television and Women's Culture: The Politics of the Popular*. Sage, 1990). Warning, however, of the dangers of populism, van Zoonen proposes that feminist media research should also address relatively 'closed' genres, such as news, as social construction, while developing strategies of 'semiotic empowerment' for female media recipients as a consequence of the importance now attributed to audience–text relations.

The remainder of the volume is concerned largely with globalization and media production. Judith Lichtenberg argues in her essay 'In Defence of Objectivity' that we should not swim unthinkingly with the anti-rationalist postmodern tide and that objective interpretation of real facts and events for journalism remains an epistemological possibility. Michael Shudson reviews the strengths and weaknesses of political-economy, organizational and culturalogical paradigms for understanding news production, concluding that all three pay too little attention to historical and comparative analysis. Often there is a tendency to smuggle into debate a normative functionalism which seeks to define what the role of the media *should* be in fostering active citizenship while simultaneously *not* addressing the theorization of 'the audience' or 'the public' in any concrete way.

Clearly globalization has been a central theme of media theory in the 1990s and Annabelle Sreberny-Mohammadi's overview essay 'The Global and the Local in International Communications' outlines three stages in the 'cultural imperialism' thesis: Western media as agents of modernization and democracy for developing nations; Western media as agents of normative Western values threatening indigenous cultures; a two-way flow of communications between countries and a heightened sense of audience autonomy (see, for instance, Boyd-Barrett, Oliver, and Daya Kishan Thussu. *Contra-Flow in Global News: International and Regional News-Exchange Mechanisms.* John Libbey, 1992). Sreberny-Mohammadi, not surprisingly, concludes that the media do not have to be perceived as operating through an either/or dichotomy but can operate as agencies of social control while also stimulating local and regional identities within nation-states. Indeed, the nation-state becomes an inadequate conceptual framework through which to view the complexity and diversity of power relations interacting with centre-periphery identities.

Michael Gurevitch takes up some of these arguments in his examination of 'The Globalization of Electronic Journalism' and the ways in which new electronic technologies have impacted – and will continue to do so – upon power relations between governments and the media. Jay G. Blumler offers an analysis of the multi-channel marketplace in America, arguing strongly that there is a necessity to build a stronger public service broadcasting sector in order to provide a more mixed television economy to overcome the morass of commercial competition which is in danger of undermining both the quality of output and the dynamic of the industry. And, finally, Joseph Turow proposes that media theory should focus more specifically on defining 'entertainment' and how interrelated industries construct cultural models, with what effects and consequences.

I have concentrated on *Mass Media and Society* in such detail because it is the collection which sets out to define the 'state' of media theory in the early 1990s, especially for the student/academic market. As such, then, it is a book which can be seen in itself as a 'primary definer' of the terrain while also attempting to represent 'positions' which are developed more fully elsewhere (e.g. Denis McQuail's essay 'Mass Media in the Public Interest: Towards a Framework of Norms for Media Performance', in his *Media Performance: Mass Communication and the Public Interest*. Sage, 1992). Perhaps the volume suffers a little from the attempt to produce convergence of liberal-pluralist and radical approaches to media analysis and systems of power. Clearly the most obvious shift since the 1980s is the erosion of Marxist perspectives, here represented mainly in Peter Golding and Graham Murdock's excellent 'Culture, Communications and Political Economy' which seeks to define a political-economy perspective as against structuralist Marxism.

One indicator of the shift in debate is the virtual absence in *Mass Media and Society* of the previously central concept of ideology (indeed, the index lists only one reference in the whole collection!) which would have been unthinkable a decade earlier. The major social theorist of the current decade who has sought to review the (re)definition of the concept is John B. Thompson in his *Ideology and Modern Culture*. Thompson begins from the position that previous theorists of ideology have inadequately understood the role of mass communications in the modern world. He reviews the dominant definitions of the concept and offers a critique of 'the grand narrative of cultural transformation, on the one hand, and the general theory of state-organized and ideologically secured social reproduction, on the other'. The argument then pursues the theme of the mediazation of modern culture, exploring the concept of culture, the centrality of mass communication and new technologies to cultural transmission, their impact on social experience and interaction, and concluding with an examination of the relevance of hermeneutics for social and historical inquiry into the growing role of the media in modern culture.

One of the theorists critically addressed by Thompson is Jürgen

Habermas and while it is clear that, as I suggested earlier, Habermas's analysis of the media is heavily influenced by a debt to the Frankfurt School, his concept of the public sphere has enjoyed something of a qualified revival in media theory of the 1990s. This can be most obviously traced in *Communication and Citizenship: Journalism and the Public Sphere in the New Media Age,* edited by Peter Dahlgren and Colin Sparks. Peter Dahlgren opens the collection with a critique of Habermas's development of the concept of the public sphere but argues that the 'defence and expansion of the public sphere always remains a political accomplishment', one which must be attentive to sense-making processes in everyday life and avoid characterizing mainstream media as monolithic or homogeneous. The concept of a redefined public sphere, then, can be useful in addressing a nexus of four key contemporary issues: 'the crisis of the nation-state, the segmentation of audiences, the rise of new political and social movements and the relative availability of advanced computer and communication technology to consumers'.

James Curran follows this by arguing for a public sphere of media production which is balanced between market forces and state-subsidized public service broadcasting. As such his conclusions are not dissimilar from those of Jay Blumler in *Mass Media and Society.* In the context of the United States John Phelan's essay traces the influence of the market on TV journalism and health or public service campaigns. Colin Sparks argues that the heterogeneity of the newspaper in Britain is undermining serious journalism and the political function of the press:

> The mass circulation press is no longer concerned primarily to articulate the different opinions of competing sections of a narrow political élite but with the general maintenance of the conditions upon which the continued dominance of that élite rest. This, surely, is best seen not as the decline of the political role of the press but its adaptation to the conditions of bourgeois democracy.

Completing the first section of the book is an essay by Vincent Porter and Suzanne Hasselbach, 'Beyond Balanced Pluralism: Broadcasting in Germany', in which they investigate the economic and political struggles around regulation of public service and commercial broadcasting in former West Germany. They conclude that 'the ideal of a pluralist federal broadcasting landscape, which had inspired so much of the original broadcasting legislation, is crumbling in the face of increasingly pragmatic regulation'. This is an argument which is developed in more detail in Vincent Porter and Suzanne Hasselbach's *Pluralism, Politics and the Marketplace: The Regulation of German Broadcasting.*

The second part of the collection focuses on 'Politics and Journalism' in which Todd Gitlin argues that news management in the American context almost celebrates disempowerment of citizens, whereas Paulo Mancini demonstrates the control of the Italian media by powerful elites. On the other hand there is always the potentiality for the emergence of alternative public spheres, as occurred in Poland, according to Karol Jakubowicz, when the church and Solidarity challenged the legitimacy of the official public sphere dominated by state and party. Finally, Ann Crigler and Klaus Bruhn Jensen develop a comparative case-study analysis of American and Danish television viewers, arguing that audiences reconstruct the meanings of political and social information presented in news programmes by actively imposing thematic structures on the news stories concerned. They suggest that further research on political conceptualization and reception would be valuable and that the context in which individuals process political information is crucial. The dominant themes which emerged from their audience analyses were human impact, powerful others, economics and centre-periphery relations: the 'perspectives of control/power, personalization, social distance, money and the global roles of the two countries framed the discourse on political issues differently in the US and Denmark'.

The final section of *Communication and Citizenship* centres on journalistic practices, with Michael Gurevitch, Mark R. Levy and Itzhak Roeh exploring the internationalization of the TV news in 'The Global Newsroom'. They examine the ways in which news topics are accorded meaning within the frameworks of diverse national cultures. Liesbet van Zoonen undertakes one of the projects for feminist research she outlined in her contribution to *Mass Media and Society* in her essay 'A Tyranny of Intimacy? Women, Femininity and Television News'. She investigates the phenomenon of Dutch television news where women newsreaders predominate, but concludes that this in itself does not reconstruct the division between a public male world and a private female world and, indeed, can be seen as 'yet another articulation of traditional femininity'. The final essay by Ian Connell provides a review of the phenomenon in the tabloid press of 'news' stories about actors and presenters of television programmes, striking both in terms of their quantity and prominence. He argues that the genre is a hybrid one, fabulous and yet journalistic in its construction of the world of television, accepting the spectacular opulence of the show-business world only if it seems in line with an 'ordinary world' morality by which political and show-biz personalities are to be judged in their 'private' lives. He concludes, therefore, that the tabloid press is more complex than academic criticism often reveals, in that there is an overt ambivalence about the position of privilege in society.

2. Media, Culture and Society

The most influential journals, certainly in Britain, in the field of media analysis are *Media, Culture and Society* (published by Sage), the *European Journal of Communication* (Sage Publications) and *Screen* (BFI Publications). As the latter is a cross-media journal and still significantly concerned with film, I will concentrate here on the first two journals.

As Paddy Scannell et al., the editors of *Culture and Power*, a collection of essays first published in *Media, Culture and Society* during the late 1980s and 1990s, make clear:

> we would note that this journal has always been deeply suspicious of the retreat from reason that postmodernism represents. Within the broad spectrum of work represented in *Media, Culture and Society*, one unifying emphasis is on the possibility of rational social enquiry producing valid knowledge of the workings of the social world. This project, in line with that commitment of the Enlightenment to a critique of the present in the name of a better tomorrow, is incompatible with the philosophical basis of postmodernism.

While the emphasis in media theory over the last decade has shifted from analysis of production and institutions to consumption, its contexts, the articulation of social identities and interpretative strategies, the editors of *Media, Culture and Society*, refreshingly, hold on to a scepticism about consumer power as people power and seek to address the structures and 'conditions of existence' which constrain and limit human agency. In the *Culture and Power* reader, for instance, Philip Schlesinger, John D. H. Downing, Colin Sparks and Paddy Scannell focus on 'The Media and Public Life', clearly addressing various dimensions of the Habermasian notion of the public sphere and the involvement of the press and broadcasting in constituting politics as spectacle.

Three further essays published in the journal in 1991 offer critical perspectives on contemporary cultural studies and postmodernism. David Tetzlaff, in 'Popular Culture and Social Control in Late Capitalism', elaborates a thesis which sees commodified culture as fundamentally oppositional to all forms of collective resistance. Far from mass culture producing ideological unity, it initiates and sustains diversity and fragmentation while postmodernist celebrations of the disintegration of meaning, he argues, serve in the end to maintain capitalist social control. The collapse of the Eastern bloc Communist states has led in the West to declarations of 'the triumph of Liberalism' and 'the end of Marxism', most notably in Frances Fukuyama's *The End of History and the Last Man* (1992). Kuang-Hsing Chen, in 'Post-Marxism: Critical Postmodernism and Cultural Studies', sees cultural studies as a sphere of contradiction in that it demonstrates a residual Marxism while also drawing upon a critical postmodernism which is, however, dismissive of orthodox Marxism. He proposes some kind of reconciliation under the label of post-Marxism which draws upon similar critical perspectives around history, cultural politics and the mass media. Finally, Sarah Franklin, Celia Lury and Jackie Stacey review the interactions between 'feminism and cultural studies' (the title of their essay), especially around three areas of study: popular representations, science and technology, Thatcherism and the enterprise culture. While it is possible to trace many areas of overlap they also argue that the models of culture predominantly developed within the cultural studies tradition pose many problems for feminism in the failure to engage fully with dimensions of gender inequality and patriarchal power.

While engaging, then, with emerging contemporary debates around culture and identities of nation, class, race, gender and sexuality, *Media, Culture and Society* has continued to explore the political economy of the media, cultural policy and the new information society, the media and everyday life, the media and language. Exemplary of some of these themes is, for instance, Nicholas Garnham's collection of essays *Capitalism and Communication: Global Culture and the Economics of Information,* in which he conducts a series of trenchantly polemical arguments around media theory, methodology, politics and intellectual inquiry. Rejecting fashionable postmodernism, Garnham offers a defence of Marxist political-economy analysis which locates the media within a wider political framework which can encompass global economic restructuring and telecommunications technologies. At the heart of Garnham's series of essays dealing with public service broadcasting and the market, telecommunications policy and the cultural industries is a concern with democracy, politics and citizenship.

A second strand associated with *Media, Culture and Society*, a concern with the media and everyday life, can be traced in part 2 of *Culture and Power* (1992), which collects together the journal's contributions to audience/readership studies between 1988 and 1991. Shaun Moores, in 'Texts, Readers and the Contexts of Reading', reviews audience research since the mid-1970s, examining *Screen*'s focus upon spectator–text relations and the critique of *Screen* theory which developed out of the Birmingham Centre for Contemporary Cultural Studies. Initiated by the ground-breaking *Nationwide* project and Stuart Hall's influential essay on encoding and decoding, progress was made towards what came to be widely known as an 'ethnography of reading' (see Brunsdon, C., and D. Morley. *Everyday Television: 'Nationwide'*. BFI, 1978, and Hall, Stuart, 'Encoding/Decoding', in Hall, Stuart et al. (eds). *Culture, Media, Language: Working Papers in Cultural Studies, 1972–79*. Hutchinson, 1980). Moores concludes his review by suggesting that future study should address three principal issues – 'the interrelated questions of meaning, pleasure and taste'. This succinct account of audience research is supplemented in *Culture and Power* by five empirically-based contributions. Kay Richardson and John Corner analyse differential readings by people in Liverpool of a documentary *A Fair Day's Fiddle* (1984) about dole-fraud. They analyse a spectrum of readings by viewers in which meaning is attributed along a grid from transparent readings (accepting the programme at face value) to mediated readings where viewers display an awareness of the manipulation of discourses. Similarly, Elizabeth Frazer's analysis of teenage girls reading *Jackie* reveals a critical detachment in tension with acceptance of an agenda-setting discourse register through which real problems were conceptualized by the girls. Peter Dahlgren's 'What's the Meaning of This? Viewers' Plural Sense-Making of TV News' argues that 'meaning is negotiated . . . in the force field between the givenness of the programmes and the sense-making of the viewers'. Reflecting on reception research he argues that viewers adopted context-specific 'official' discourses in talking about the news during formal interviews, dissolving into more personal discourse afterwards. This interplay of discourses registers a spectrum of responses around dutiful and responsible citizenship through to cynicism and a sense that 'things don't work, we really are powerless in relation to the centres of political, economic and administrative command as well as to the media complex itself'. Klaus Bruhn Jensen also takes up this issue of 'The Politics of Polysemy: Television News, Everyday Consciousness and Political Action', rejecting Fiske's claim that the capacity of audiences to produce readings of media texts is politically empowering. Rather, his case-study of mainly American academics responding to television news 'poses the general implication that neither the availability of political information nor a particular level of formal education will ensure substantive social uses of news'. His respondents watched news in order 'to keep in touch' and to be able to engage in conversational discussion of events and issues but they also experienced a disempowering disjunction between the public realm of political life as represented in the media and their everyday realities.

This is a terrain explored in a collection of essays edited by Paddy Scannell, *Broadcast Talk*. Here it is recognized that:

> Radio and television mediate the public into the private and the private into the public in the manner and style of their performances in a wide range of settings and for correspondingly diverse purposes.

The main contention is that broadcast *talk* is central to this process and to the 'liveness' of the media in a way which goes beyond orthodox text–reader or encoding–decoding models of communication. It is necessary, then, to explore the extent to which broadcast talk approximates to the norms of 'ordinary, informal conversation' and becomes a central element in the routines of ordinary life. The essays which follow inquire into the institutional management of language use, early television documentaries, news and political interviews, the embedding of ideology in common-sense assumptions in the context of the 1987 general election, the radio phone-in, DJ talk, the chat show.

A concern with popular culture and its diverse forms remains central in the 1990s. Steve Neale and Frank Krutnik in *Popular Film and Television Comedy* set out to define the transgressive features of comic genres, examining variety acts, forms and performers such as Morecambe and Wise, *The Two Ronnies*, Ben Elton and Victoria Wood. They go on to argue that *Monty Python* contained as a central feature the impulse to undercut both established formats of variety and conventions of television. They conclude with a history of radio and television 'sit-com' structured commonly around familial relations with the comedy emerging from diverse threats to stability. The inverse of familial normality and respectability, they argue, can be seen in *Steptoe and Son* where normality remains an unattainable aspiration for Harold, consistently thwarted in his ambitions by his father.

Where Neale and Krutnik offer, essentially, formal and structural analysis of comic genres, a more historical perspective is preferred in John Corner's edited collection *Popular Television in Britain: Studies in Cultural History*. This is a useful survey of the period of the 1950s and 1960s, exploring the rise to dominance of the medium of television, early television drama and documentary, Hancock, *Z Cars*, *Grandstand*, *Quatermass*, the emergence of the TV 'personality', and the development of both television satire and pop music programmes (the major work of broadcasting history in its early phase is Scannell, Paddy, and David Cardiff. *A Social History of British Broadcasting: Serving the Nation. Volume One: 1922–1939*. Blackwell, 1991). This 'retrospective', historical perspective is also central to *Come on Down? Popular Media Culture in Post-War Britain* edited by Dominic Strinati and Stephen Wagg. This collection of essays seeks to cover:

> (a) the relationship between popular media culture and social difference – class, gender, ethnicity and race, and age (here embracing childhood and youth); (b) a diversity of popular cultural forms – the soap opera, the game show, the police drama, the women's magazine, the monarchy, the satirical comedy show, pop music, TV advertising; (c) popular cultural processes – consumption, Americanization, commercialization, cultural representations, audience interpretations, and ideological constructions; (d) the historical contexts provided by post-1945 British society.

The emphasis, then, is on diversity and an eclectic approach to theoretical perspectives which address the cultural politics of popular culture.

3. Europe

At the beginning of 1990 the editors of the *European Journal of Communication* (5:i) announced: 'we like to think that to an increasing extent unity in variation is a distinctive feature of European communication research – just as of Europe itself, perhaps'. In some ways this first issue of 1990 is typical of the journal generally in that contributors are drawn from Scandinavia and several regions of Europe and the articles concerned focus on three themes (political

communication, audience studies and media structure); articles tend
to tease out theoretical or methodological issues while there is a
recurrent preoccupation with comparative and localized empirical
studies. This was followed by a special double issue on 'Communications Research in Europe: The State of the Art' which the
editors saw as offering both a representative picture of current
research and an illustration of academic responses to the rapid
changes in the landscape of the European mass media. As we saw
earlier, James Curran's overview essay on the 'new revisionism' in
mass media research appeared in this issue alongside perspectives
from Scandinavia (Pietila, Malmberg and Nordenstreng, 'Theoretical
Consequences and Contrasts: A View from Finland', 5:ii–iii.165–85)
and from Southern Europe (Mancini and Wolf, 'Mass Media
Research in Italy: Culture and Politics', 5:ii–iii.187–205). Two
further essays focus on the dramatic developments in Eastern
Europe in 1989: Karol Jakubowicz's examination of Solidarity's
ideas for media reform in Poland and Kurt R. Hesse's analysis of
the influence of West German television on the collapse of Communist East Germany. Here we can see one of the paradoxes of
European media policy in that Western European public service
broadcasting systems are under threat from conservative and neo-
liberal governments wedded to market economics while Central and
Eastern Europe has responded to democracy by seeking to develop
some variant of a public service broadcasting system (see also
Nowell-Smith, Geoffrey, and Tana Wollen, eds. *After the Wall*. BFI,
1991). Denis McQuail seeks to develop a framework for the analysis
of media change in Western Europe while Blumler, Dayan and
Wolton examine 'West European Perspectives on Political Communication: Structure and Dynamics' (5:ii–iii.261–84). Hans Mathias
Kepplinger and Renate Kocher analyse the problematic of professionalism in journalism and the issue is completed by two useful
essays addressing audience research: Klaus Bruhn Jensen and Karl
Eric Rosengren provide a typology of existing traditions, arguing for
confluence in multi-method, cross-cultural research; Ien Ang's
'Culture and Communication: Towards an Ethnographic Critique of
Media Consumption in the Transnational Media System' (5:ii–
iii.239–60) takes apart the celebratory notion of 'the popular' as a
source of resistance to 'the hegemonic' and argues for a critical ethnography of reception as a useful way of exploring the complexities
of cultural identities and autonomy in relation to transnational, globalized media systems.

Clearly within the scope of this article I cannot do more than represent general tendencies within the journal over a three-year period. A special issue in 1992 focused on the 'Media and the Law: The Changing Landscape of Western Europe' (*European Journal of Communication* 7:ii) which addressed public service broadcasting and deregulation in the UK (Tony Prosser) and media law in Germany, Spain, Italy and the Netherlands. Perhaps unsurprisingly the period in question sees a range of articles on the German press, radio and television, while it is also worth noting that only two articles appeared which addressed explicitly feminist analyses: Elizabeth van Zoonen's 'The Women's Movement and the Media: Constructing a Public Identity' (*European Journal of Communication* 7:iv.453–76) and Joke Hermes and Veronique Schutgens's 'A Case of the Emperor's New Clothes? Reception and Text analysis of the Dutch Feminist Magazine *Opzij*' (*European Journal of Communication* 7:iii.307–34).

The concern with European media cultures, often seen in relation to Americanization, is central to *Media Cultures: Reappraising Transnational Media* edited by Michael Skovmand and Kim Christian Schroder. This is a collection of essays largely by Scandinavian academics with two excellent contributions from Graham Murdock on 'Citizens, Consumers and Public Culture' and David Morley on 'Electronic Communities and Domestic Rituals: Cultural Consumption and the Production of European Cultural Identities'. Morley suggests that the very concept of cultural identity has to be interrogated as a purely relational product of difference and 'oppositions to American culture, Asian culture, Islamic culture, and so on'. Soren Schou also investigates the postwar Americanization of European culture, while Jostein Gripsrud's textual analysis of Godard's *A Bout de Souffle* and Jim McBride's American remake *Breathless* traces mutual influence and cultural determinations on the framing of a common fabula. Michael Skovmand examines 'Barbarous TV International: Syndicated *Wheel of Fortune*' and Peter Larsen discusses 'News in the Multi-Channel Universe'. The final section focuses on 'Popular Audiences and Cultural Quality' with essays on Dennis Potter's drama (Ib Bondebjerg), on 'cult film' (Anne Jerslev) and on 'cultural quality' (Kim Christian Schroder). It has to be said that Schroder's conclusion that 'in a cultural democracy all tastes are legitimate and should be catered to, through a cultural policy of variety and diversity' begs more questions than it answers.

A more coherent, perhaps because more narrowly focused, exploration of transnational media systems can be found in Jeremy

Tunstall and Michael Palmer's *Media Moguls*. Their analysis considers not only the politics of entrepreneurial ownership through figures such as Berlusconi, Murdoch and Maxwell but also trends such as the emergence of a European media policy and a European–US–Japanese global media industry. The role of Reuters as a reconstituted global news-and-data agency and the influence of media lobbies and advertising are also seen as significant shaping forces on European media policy. Some of the issues surrounding national culture and 'television without frontiers' are also taken up in part 3 of Philip Schlesinger's collection of essays *Media, State and Nation*. Schlesinger provides a penetrating analysis of the paradoxes of European media policy statements and reflects widely on problems of national identity and collective identities in social theory.

Parts 1 and 2 of *Media, State and Nation* address the 'relations between news media and the use of political violence within the capitalist, liberal-democratic, national state'. Provoked originally by the perception of the impact of the conflict in Northern Ireland on British media politics, Schlesinger's subtle analysis ranges more widely over the issues involved in the interpretation of 'violence', 'terrorism' and such case-studies as the Iranian Embassy siege (see also Paletz, David L., and Alex P. Schmid, eds. *Terrorism and the Media*. Sage, 1992). Part 2 considers cold war media politics and the constructions of Communism as 'a cultural category' and of Eurocommunism as an ideological field of contention.

Finally, *The New Television in Europe,* edited by Alessandro Silj, concludes that 'television without frontiers' remains a chimera and that deregulation has not produced an integrated European market. Part 1 offers seven essays on general issues for a multi-channel European market while the rest of this comprehensive volume focuses on domestic markets in Italy, the UK, Spain, France, Germany, Eastern Europe and Scandinavia. The consistent themes in each context are the development of commercial television in relation to public service broadcasting and the impact upon programming, schedules and audiences.

4. Audience Studies

As can be seen, then, the last decade has witnessed an intensified concern with audiences, with text–'reader' activity, with the social discourses which interact with interpretive processes and with the everyday contexts within which audiences consume the media. To provide a detailed overview of this research here is impossible and also redundant in that both David Morley in *Television, Audiences and Cultural Studies* (1992) and Shaun Moores in *Interpreting Audiences* (1993, to be reviewed in a later volume) can be commended for offering clear and incisive accounts of the issues and debates surrounding audience analysis. Morley's book, in fact, collects articles previously published elsewhere during the previous decade and is useful, particularly for students, as an elaboration of theoretical and methodological frameworks and as a group of essays addressing the themes of 'Class, Ideology and Interpretation', 'Gender, Domestic Leisure and Viewing Practices', 'Television, Technology and Consumption' and 'Between the Public and the Private'. In my view, Morley's commitment to social scientific paradigms of analysis is positively to be welcomed and there is little doubt that he has been a centre of influence within the whole domain of media theory.

Ien Ang provides a rather different perspective on the audience in her *Desperately Seeking the Audience*. Ang argues that knowledge(s) of the audience is/are constructed by media institutions and by mainstream research in the effort to categorize and 'fix' the audience in a way which bears little relation to the everyday viewing practices of real audiences. She examines both PSB and commercial television in their attempts to define the audience as citizens and/or consumers and asserts that much mainstream academic research has been complicit in this institutional perspective on 'the' audience.

John Hartley also addresses these issues in *The Politics of Pictures* and *Tele-Ology: Studies in Television*. As he argues:

> Media audiences have often been subjected to strategies designed to turn them into something else, something more organized, more recognizable as a community, more responsible, responsive, biddable. Chief among these is the attempt to turn the audience into the public. The public, conversely, has been subjected to a campaign, initiated more than 300 years ago, to turn it into an audience.

Hartley offers wide-ranging excursions into journalism, popular culture, the everyday location of television in popular realities, and along the way challenging the new hegemony of ethnography:

> Ethnographies of reading must presuppose that they'll reveal something in the 'other' that can be observed – the act of reading, the real or 'natural' audience. So ethnographic research runs counter to textual theory, which holds that nothing outside meaning exists for

humans, that discourses organize practices, and that when you ask people what they think of texts, or how they read, even when you go into their very living rooms to do it, you don't end up with the real, but with more text, requiring just the same sort of critical reading as is given to television texts themselves.

Hartley advances a notion of what he terms 'power viewing' to eradicate the conceptualization of the audience as 'other' and to bring academic critical theory into an engagement with the interaction of 'textual power and social power'.

This interface is investigated also in Sonia Livingstone's *Making Sense of Television: The Psychology of Audience Interpretation*, in which she argues that viewers draw upon their social knowledge in relation to programme structures in order to 'make sense'. She provides a valuable overview of recent social psychological theory and its contribution to media theory and then offers an empirical case-study of viewers' 'readings' of soap opera. On occasion the data provokes the reaction of 'so what?' as many of the conclusions are rather obvious and the overall assessment that general conceptions of 'the audience' and 'viewing' need to be broken down into more complex categories is now generally accepted. A somewhat different approach to these matters is to be found in Justin Lewis's *The Ideological Octopus: An Exploration of Television and its Audience,* in which the statutory overview of news audience research is followed by case-studies of qualitative analyses of the *News* and *The Cosby Show* with Lewis's title registering the somewhat distinctive slant he develops. Finally, Liebes and Katz in *The Export of Meaning* analyse the ways in which respondents draw upon cultural values in order to decode *Dallas*. One problem with their cross-cultural examination is that they do not explicitly address the sources of cultural values, rather assuming their communal existence and then arguing that the audience points to a polysemic 'openness' of meaning in the interpretation of media texts.

Ann Gray's ethnographic survey of video technology and gender in *Video Playtime* also references *Dallas,* but here the focus of study is upon gendered subjectivities understood in their specific social contexts and on the ways in which differential cultural capital impacts upon gender and class. The study ranges across audience research in relation to textual analysis but also, importantly, looks at domestic leisure and technology – an interest which has been developed in more recent media theory (see, for instance, Silverstone, Roger, and Eric Hirsch, eds. *Consuming Technologies: Media and Information in Domestic Spaces.* Routledge, 1992. Also see Silverstone, Roger. *Television and Everyday Life.* Routledge, 1994).

5. Conclusion

From the foregoing account of media theory in the early 1990s it is evident that there has been a significant shift away from the analysis of television explicitly in relation to ideological and social structures and a heightened focus upon processes of reception and the contexts of consumption. Such work has sought also to redress the balance of the media–society nexus by seeing the media not as mono-causal but as one factor among many in shaping cultural experience. The best of this work, however, seems to me to be that which seeks to hold on to some exploration of the media in relation to political order and cultural power. Where these location-points dissolve there is a very great danger of a descent into banality and a simplistic celebration of reader/consumer power and polysemy. Fortunately, the evidence is that more recent work in media theory (especially that of John Corner and Douglas Kellner) will provide constructive approaches to the politics of media culture.

Books Reviewed

Ang, Ien. *Desperately Seeking the Audience.* Routledge (1991). pp. 203. pb £10.99. ISBN 0 415 05270 X.

Barrett, Oliver Boyd, and Daya Kishan Thussu. *Contra-Flow in Global News: International and Regional News-Exchange Mechanisms.* John Libbey. pp. 154. £20. ISBN 0 86196 344 X.

Corner, John, ed. *Popular Television in Britain: Studies in Cultural History.* BFI (1991). pp. 211. pb £12.95. ISBN 0 85170 270 8.

Curran, James, and Michael Gurevitch, eds. *Mass Media and Society.* Edward Arnold (1991). pp. 350. pb £14.99. ISBN 0 340 51759 X.

Dahlgren, Peter, and Colin Sparks, eds. *Communication and Citizenship: Journalism and the Public Sphere in the New Media Age.* Routledge (1991). pp. 266. $69.95. ISBN 0 415 05779 5.

Garnham, Nicholas. *Capitalism and Communication: Global Culture and the Economics of Information.* Sage (1990). pp. 216. pb £11.95. ISBN 0 8039 8258 5.

Gray, Ann. *Video Playtime.* Routledge. pp. 269. £37.50. ISBN 0 415 05865 1.

Hartley, John. *The Politics of Pictures: The Creation of the Public in the Age of Popular Media*. Routledge. pp. 240. pb £10.99. ISBN 0 415 01542 1.

——. *Tele-Ology: Studies in Television*. Routledge. pp. 245. £35. ISBN 0 415 06818 5.

Lewis, Justin. *The Ideological Octopus: An Exploration of Television and its Audience*. Routledge (1991). pp. 218. pb £9.99. ISBN 0 415 90288 6.

Liebes, Tamar, and Elihu Katz. *The Export of Meaning: Cross-Cultural Readings of Dallas*. Oxford University Press (1991). pp. 200. pb £11.95. ISBN 0 7456 1295 4.

Livingstone, Sonia M. *Making Sense of Television: The Psychology of Audience Interpretation*. Pergamon (1990). pp. 390. £34. ISBN 0 08 036776 0.

McQuail, Denis. *Media Performance: Mass Communication and the Public Interest*. Sage. pp. 350. pb £12.95. ISBN 0 8039 8295 X.

Morley, David. *Television, Audiences and Cultural Studies*. Routledge. pp. 325. pb £11.95. ISBN 0 415 05445 1.

Neale, Steve, and Frank Krutnik. *Popular Film and Television Comedy*. Routledge (1990). pp. 291. pb £10.99. ISBN 0 415 04692 0.

Nowell-Smith, Geoffrey, and Tana Wollen. *After the Wall: Broadcasting in Germany*. BFI (1991). pp. 87. pb $9.95. ISBN 0 85170 296 1.

Porter, Vincent, and Suzanne Hasselbach. *Pluralism, Politics and the Marketplace: The Regulation of German Broadcasting*. Routledge (1991). pp. 248. £37.50. ISBN 0 415 05394 3.

Scannell, Paddy, ed. *Broadcast Talk*. Sage (1991). pp. 231. pb £10.95. ISBN 0 8039 8375 1.

——, Philip Schlesinger and Colin Sparks, eds. *Culture and Power*. Sage. pp. 357. pb £11.95. ISBN 0 8039 8631 9.

Schlesinger, Philip. *Media, State and Nation: Political Violence and Collective Identities*. Sage (1991). pp. 202. pb £11.95. ISBN 0 8039 8504 5.

Silj, Alessandro, ed. *The New Television in Europe*. John Libbey. pp. 629. £66. ISBN 0 86196 361 X.

Skovmand, Michael, and Kim Christian Schroder, eds. *Media Cultures: Reappraising Transnational Media*. Routledge. pp. 222. pb £11.99. ISBN 0 415 06385 X.

Strinati, Dominic, and Stephen Wagg, eds. *Come on Down? Popular Media Culture in Post-War Britain*. Routledge. pp. 391. pb £12.99. ISBN 0 415 06327 2.

Thompson, John B. *Ideology and Modern Culture: Critical Social Theory in the Era of Mass Communication*. Polity (1990). pp. 362. pb £12.95. ISBN 0 7456 0082 4.

Tunstall, Jeremy, and Michael Palmer. *Media Moguls*. Routledge (1991). pp. 258. pb £10.99. ISBN 0 415 05468 0.

Part II

Critical Theory: An International Perspective

13

Critical and Cultural Theory in Germany Today

RAINER EMIG

1. (Pre-)History

Mention 'critical theory' to a German-speaker not familiar with Anglo-American academic jargon and you are likely to cause confusion. *Kritische Theorie* in Germany still refers primarily to the Frankfurt School, and although Cultural Studies seem to have made a hasty arrival in some of the more consciously trendy English departments around the country, your average academic would still place them firmly in an Anglo-American context. There is not even a common German term for theories in the humanities. In fact, theory holds a very different status in Germany from the one it has achieved, not without pains, in the English-speaking world. Check the lecture list at even the most progressive universities and polytechnics and you will be surprised at the small number of lectures and seminars on theory. Yet far from indicating the neglect, or worse the absence, of theory, it signals, on the contrary, how deeply the humanities and sociology in Germany have become theoretical in the last decades – to the extent that it is almost deemed unnecessary to point out that theory has a firm place in one's courses or to advertise and discuss the theoretical approaches dominant in one's department.

This is partly the effect of the long-standing treatment of the humanities on an equal footing with the natural sciences, as a *science* that is, a view already expressed in the umbrella term for the humanities: *Geisteswissenschaften*. This forces academics in these disciplines to base their research and teaching on a framework of thought and terminology that indicates clearly that a 'scientific' approach has been taken. It also produces the heavy jargon and sometimes unnecessarily complicated construction of arguments for which German academia has become notorious. Often this complexity merely indicates an awareness that it is indispensable to demonstrate one's knowledge of, and position in, ongoing theoretical debates.

Another historic reason for the strong foothold of theory in the humanities in Germany is the attempt of all sciences, but especially the humanities, history, sociology and political science, to bury their heads in the sand in Germany after the Second World War. Although most disciplines had been deeply compromised in the Third Reich, after its violent end it became the order of the day to pretend that one had only ever followed value-free and unideological science – and would continue to do so. The established scientificity of German academia seemed to provide a loophole of responsibility. This caused considerable unrest among students and intellectuals alike, a feeling of betrayal and the suspicion of a continued presence of fascist thinking, which culminated in the late 1960s in slogans such as *Unter den Talaren Muff von tausend Jahren* [Under the gowns stale air of the Third Reich].

As a consequence, the humanities and other disciplines were forced to scrutinize their ideological and theoretical premises, and this opened up German academic thinking to a variety of influences which have continued to influence the range of theories and vogues since then. It introduced French structuralism to Germany in the 1960s, but more noticeably Marxist criticism, first from exiled German thinkers and later from Anglo-American scholars. Some of the names deserving of mention in this connection are Herbert Marcuse, Margarete and Alexander Mitscherlich, Theodor W. Adorno, Max Horkheimer and Bruno Bettelheim. After an ebb of theoretical interest in the 1970s when 'hard' theory was threatened with becoming submerged in more subjectivist outlooks – which led to a resurgence of 'feeling' as opposed to theoretical thinking – theory was back in vogue in the 1980s and now has a firm presence in all areas of the humanities. Some names that have continued to be revered and influential in theoretical debates since the 1970s are Odo Marquard, Peter Sloterdijk, Oskar Negt and Alexander Kluge.

Even in the more conservative field of literary studies, there remains only a handful of traditionalist universities, such as Heidelberg and Mainz, which have managed to perpetuate philology in its established sense as the close reading of texts combined with an introduction to their historical and biographical backgrounds. Much more common are universities that mix this approach with the now firmly-established teachings of the Konstanz School of Wolfgang Iser and Hans Robert Jauss. Their theories of reader-response and aesthetics of reception are now common currency in the study of literature, in the same way as the hermeneutic approach of Hans-Georg Gadamer. Yet few universities manage to go beyond an amalgam of established interpretation studies and some newer ideas, and produce departments in which an actual forging of contemporary theory takes place.

In this niche the quite recent *Graduiertenkollegs* have found their *raison d'être*. First established in 1987, their number has mushroomed since then, and now there are about sixty such institutions in the humanities, uniting PhD students and postdoctoral scholars who pursue individual research under the common designation of the school. The most renowned of these institutions are perhaps the Konstanz Graduiertenkolleg whose theme is the theory of literature and the Siegen Graduiertenkolleg concerned with literary and communication studies. There the current trends in theory receive special attention, and theoretical debates can be fought with a ferocity that a standard university department could hardly provoke and much less endure.

2. State of the Art(s)

In some way it seems appropriate that some of the most vivid theoretical debates in the humanities in Germany in recent years should involve the so-called last remaining member of the Frankfurt School, the philosopher Jürgen Habermas. The Frankfurt School proper now rests in its historical grave, for better or worse, and even Adorno, though quoted at regular intervals, is hardly read by students or lecturers. The twenty-fifth anniversary of his death in 1994, quite tellingly, hardly caused a stir. One of the few theorists who have continued to perpetuate *Kritische Theorie* into the 1980s and 1990s is Axel Honneth. Walter Benjamin, never quite a proper member of the Frankfurt School, has experienced a renaissance in Germany in the last few years, but one hardly on the scale of the attention he has been receiving in the United States and Britain. Indeed the German interest in Benjamin's works seems to derive more from a reinterpretation of his aesthetic concepts than an enthusiasm over his ideas on politics and ideology. A sign of the different appropriations of Benjamin in Germany and elsewhere is his ranking among philosophers in Britain and the United States, whereas he is esteemed as a writer on aesthetics in Germany.

Calling Habermas a member of the Frankfurt School is a problematic move. Even when he was taught by Adorno in the 1960s, it was apparent that his teacher's negative utopias and dialectics did not agree very well with the pragmatism characteristic of Habermas's thought. His most influential contribution to debates in the humanities and politics in the last decade has been his *The Theory of Communicative Action*. In the two volumes of the study he develops a model of communicative exchange that seemingly transcends differences of education, social status or political power by assuming a utopian starting-point for the interchange in a power-free realm that can be achieved, he claims, by an agreement between the participants in the communicative action. Out of this starting position, Habermas has been busy creating a theory of discursive ethics in the last few years. It is evident that such a positive utopia can only be the result of Habermas's continual trust in reason, in the Enlightenment or modernity – which also finds its expression in his repeated attempts to defend this modernism against those who wish to announce its demise and the advent of postmodernity. It is this attachment to modernity that provoked his dispute with Jean-François Lyotard in the 1980s. Habermas retired in 1994, but he will certainly continue to be a decisive force in all areas involving theory.

The second major debate involving Habermas has been with Niklas Luhmann. Against Habermas's ontological dichotomy of system and lifeworld, the latter being the horizon of individual experience that can never be overcome, Luhmann sets a constitutive difference constituting system as well as lifeworld and a complex (and in the final analysis structuralist) model of mutual influence in his *Systemtheorie*. Reality is understood as a complex machinery of systems and subsystems inside which processes of regulation and legitimation take place. What is created inside these monadic bubbles are autopoeitic systems which reproduce in miniature the modernist creation *sui generis*. The rigour of Luhmann's model is as startling as is the difficulty of his writings. He, too, is guided by an extreme rationalism that often strikes the reader as reductive. One can easily see the problem when one takes into account that Luhmann has tried to apply his system not only to the social and political spheres, but also to the realms of art, religion, trust and love. His inability to explain how systems communicate creates the greatest problem when it comes to applying his ideas to literature, the media and culture. None the less, exactly this gap in his theory seems to provoke a large number of scholars in the humanities, who have tried either to take over Luhmann's model or merge it with others, for instance Foucault's discourse theory. 'Radical Constructivism' under its spokesman Siegfried J. Schmidt is such a variant of systems theory attempting to branch out into literary and media studies. What it has produced so far, however, hardly transcends a very detailed empirical (as in: subtly differentiated) form of context studies.

A more interesting contribution that manages to combine the seemingly antithetical positions of Luhmann and Habermas and unites them with a general study of communication and the media society is Richard Münch's *Dialektik der Kommunikationsgesellschaft* [Dialectic of the Communication Society]. It establishes links between the structural models of systems theory and discourse ethics and a broad look at economic theory, the changing relation of mass and elitist culture as well as the media-powered discourse of politics.

Foucault is perhaps the most pervasive force in the humanities in Germany today. While Derrida has been consigned to some specialists and Lacan's fame seems to be on the wane (not that a serious engagement with him has ever taken place), it is difficult to escape Foucault's influence, and even more traditional forces in the humanities have had to take over some of his concepts. Gilles Deleuze will perhaps assume a similarly crucial position in a couple of years' time. It is interesting to note that, unlike in the English-speaking world, some of the translations of his works, e.g. *Difference and Repetition*, *Logic of Sense* and especially *What is Philosophy?* are taken rather more seriously than, for instance, *A Thousand Plateaus*. Apparently they are regarded as more easily compatible with the German desire to categorize and differentiate, between science, philosophy, and art or reference, composition and terms. Yet so far, the German scene lacks established Deleuzians. The scholar who has most profitably adapted Foucault to his purpose is Jürgen Link. For the last couple of years he has been working on a concept of *Normalismus* that takes into account the paradigms of late capitalist societies and joins them with a highly structured model of cultural shifts. The most important aspect of his theory is the description of the current state of things as 'flexible normalism' which is capable of integrating, and indeed thrives on, its own contradictions, oppositions and crises. So far Link has not combined the many aspects of his research in one study, but has published them in a large number of articles, often in his own periodical which is provocatively named *KultuRRevolution* [Cultural Revolution].

It is quite startling that, although usually influenced by the same Marxist and sociological background as their Anglo-American counterparts, the German faction of ideological criticism (and that includes Luhmann as well as Link – and to a certain degree even Habermas) have abstained from reifying certain basic paradigms of their models. There are no attempts to locate authentic spots of oppression and/or opposition in the system, as in the cult of the working class, Irishness, etc., that sometimes oozes from British ideological criticism. On the contrary, it is quite evident that concepts such as Luhmann and Link's do not recognize secluded realms exempt from the mechanisms of their respective systems. This makes them theoretically much more thorough, albeit at the cost of a relative pessimism concerning change and resistance. Of course, class structure in Germany, although not completely absent, finds its expression in very different and usually more subtle shapes than in Britain. Especially during the Social Democrat reign in the 1970s, an opening of higher education took place that virtually did away with social barriers and has made the German universities and polytechnics relatively egalitarian realms. There is no dominance of the upper middle class in professorships or among lecturers either. Nor is there a handful of prestigious universities on the scale of Oxbridge versus a mass of places with a lesser reputation. Reputation indeed has to be fought for with results, and as a consequence some of the smaller and more modern universities have easily achieved top ranking in recent (unofficial) quality polls.

Unfortunately and despite itself, though, this theoretical rigour occasionally conspires with much more reactionary positions in keeping the so-called minority studies out of or on the fringes of German academia. Women's studies (hardly a minority subject) still leads a shadowy existence in many literature and sociology departments, and lesbian and gay studies exist mainly as the pastime of some interested lecturers and students, but hardly receive academic recognition. Silvia Bovenschen, Sigrid Weigel, Marianne Schuller and Barbara Vinken are some of the names which come to mind in connection with a theoretical evaluation of femininity. Even more difficult to find are acknowledged authorities on lesbian and gay studies, although Gert Mattenklott and Wolfgang Popp have continued to produce contributions to the field, the latter by establishing a society for the promotion of the study of homosexuality and literature.

The restriction of postcolonial studies to English, French and Hispanic departments in Germany can be explained by the short career of German colonialism. It is noticeable, though, that the rich culture and artistic production of migrants, especially Turks, have not yet been considered by most German departments. The University of Essen has established a Centre for Turkish Studies, but it concentrates primarily on economic and social issues. It is telling that even the increasing violence against foreigners in Germany has led not so much to an interest in their cultural situation in Germany, but rather typically to a renewed delving into the German psyche.

3. Impasses/Trends

One of the major problems that the currently fashionable structural models of Habermas, Luhmann and Link face is their inability to contribute to an aesthetic debate. From an aesthetic point of view they can all be interpreted as mere offspring of Formalist concepts of thinking whose focus is the mechanisms and systems of utterances. They tend to neglect the significant ruptures of meaning and communication which are also part of their own models. This is the locus of the gap of communication in Luhmann's model. It is the source of the problematic binarism of Link's concept which only recognizes switches – from protonormalism to flexible normalism, for instance – but not what happens during the switch. In Habermas, this grey area is the ontological blur out of which both his realm of power-free discourse and its utterances emerge miraculously. While Luhmann at least acknowledges the possibility that communication might not take place, non-communication is not even considered by Habermas. That these areas of suspended signification are the realm of culture, history, memory and aesthetics makes the blindness of these theories so irritating for people working on art and literature. It is, however, a blindness that they share with the concepts of most Anglo-American thinkers. This deficit might be the reason why French theory, often against its own intentions – as in the case of Deleuze – is much more influential in literary and aesthetic disciplines in Germany, where its publications are often reappropriated to suit very different purposes.

Often this purpose is indeed a recourse to *Kritische Theorie* in the shape of Adorno's writings. Some theorists have begun to detect the topicality of the old master for a debate that leads out of his dialectic of modernity – or perhaps continues the debate in a more productive way. Albrecht Wellmer is the first name to mention in this connection. His reappropriation of Adorno is undertaken with the professed intention of highlighting the hitherto obscured links between Adorno's aesthetics and Derrida. Wellmer's pupil Christoph Menke has also produced an interesting study entitled *Die Souveränität der Kunst* [The Sovereignty of Art], while his sister Bettine Menke has appeared on the scene with a deconstructive revaluation of Benjamin. Wolfgang Welsch is a German philosopher who has not only continued to promote Lyotard in Germany, but has also produced the most useful study of postmodernism to date. His *Unsere postmoderne Moderne* [Our Postmodern Modernity] easily puts any Anglo-American study to shame and even makes Lyotard occasionally look rather vacuous. The study is infinitely preferable to studies such as Peter Bürger's attempts to put postmodernism in a perspective starting from problematic notions of the avant-garde. It is part of Welsch's concern for a proper understanding of the potentials of postmodernism that he returns to quite traditional ideas, such as the Romantic concept of the sublime, via Adorno's rejection of positive reconciliation. In a little volume entitled *Ästhetisches Denken* [Aesthetic Thinking] he unites essays on the topicality of aesthetics with those on the problem of resistance and identity in postmodernism in a manner that makes offhand rejections, such as Jameson's, look simplistic indeed. It is annoying that Welsch still lacks an English translation.

In connection with the renewed interest in aesthetics in German theory today, it is telling that the second strong voice in the discussion should come from a camp very much opposed to postmodern ideas. Karl Heinz Bohrer's book *Nach der Natur: Über Politik und Ästhetik* [After Nature: On Politics and Aesthetics] touches on ground that Terry Eagleton's studies of aesthetics and ideology tend to cover, but approaches the issues from an aesthetic angle that is not afraid to include questions concerning, for instance, evil as an aesthetic category. It is clear that the answers provided by Bohrer's book differ greatly from Eagleton's. Bohrer's books *Die Ästhetik des Schreckens* [The Aesthetics of Terror] and *Suddenness: On the Moment of Aesthetic Appearance*, although more clearly focused on literature, also provide some fascinating angles for the study of phenomena of the media age that even their author seems unaware of.

Incidentally, Eagleton's contributions to ideological criticism, now partly translated, have met with a rather mixed reception in Germany – with the exception of his introduction to literary theory. The more critical reviews tend to concentrate on the lack of originality of Eagleton's ideas – compared to those of Adorno and Marcuse – his unbroken trust in dialectic and 'pure' Marxist theory as well as his lack of self-criticism (see, for instance, the review of the translation of *The Ideology of the Aesthetic* in *Frankfurter Rundschau* of 27 August 1994).

Bohrer is often placed in the traditionalist camp, as opposed to positions like Welsch's. Yet the really conservative positions in Germany are held by scholars such as Hans Blumenberg and Manfred Frank. Frank has continued to show hostility towards contemporary theory, especially poststructuralism, which he continues to defame in questionable articles and books, especially his *What is Neostructuralism?*. Another dubious recent trend seems to be a return to pre-Foucauldian positions via, paradoxically enough, theoretical routes sometimes leading through Foucault, in the attempt to generate a redefined version of anthropology out of the discoveries of literary and media studies. Yet a greater danger than theoretical misreadings and rejections of contemporary critical theory seems to lie in a renewed vogue for anti-theoretical thinking. After the demise of the short wave of hostility to theory in the 1970s and 1980s, this current trend seems to be fed mainly by disappointment over the failure of utopias, both political and personal. The main harbinger of this movement is George Steiner. The translation of his irritating *Real Presences* has become quite popular with those tired of seemingly ever more complex theories. Unfortunately, Emmanuel Levinas also seems to be drawn into this move to reject complexity and desire for unquestionable presence.

Yet the most decisive influences behind restorative thinking have not been theorists but writers like Botho Strauss who use the *Feuilletons*, the arts and culture pages of the influential German papers such as *Die Zeit, Frankfurter Allgemeine Zeitung* and *Der Spiegel*, to promote their own mixture of lamentation and revisionism, often fuelled by a justifiable concern over symptoms of stagnation and shallowness in culture and society. The seeming demise of utopian thinking in the obvious failure of socialism has been experienced very closely in Germany as the sell-out of the former GDR and the histories and values of its inhabitants. It is now used by a small group of right-wing ideologists to attack in retrospect the achievements of ideological awareness since the 1960s and to promote a return to 'old values'. An absurd example is the unfortunate debate among sociologists and pedagogues about the responsibility of anti-authoritarian education for neo-fascist skinheads. One is tempted to dismiss these debates as artificially fuelled by the highbrow media, but they set the agenda for more than just media coverage. They also block the view on more pressing and realistic debates – such as the one on cultural identity in a completely changed unified Germany, which has been turned into a paradoxical discussion of nationalism by these very media. The most intelligent contributions to these issues have come from the likes of Reinhard Koselleck and Wolf Lepenies. Hauke Brunkhorst has been adding useful insights to the continuing (and typically German) debate about the problematic role of intellectuals.

But so far the reluctance to engage with complex theory seems to be greater on the side of established academics than of younger ones or interested students (an annoyingly large number of students in the humanities, just as in other countries, try to slip through their courses without touching on too much theory). The cliquey nature of the German academic hierarchy makes it easy to keep unorthodox influences – or at least their perpetrators – outside the doors of universities. This explains perhaps the fact that the immensely popular Klaus Theweleit, whose *Male Fantasies* has brought him international recognition, is still without even a simple lectureship. The follow-up to his earlier work, *Orpheus (und) Eurydike* in the series *Das Buch der Könige* [Book of Kings], promises another highly original look at some of the psychoanalytic and social foundations of art in the Western world.

A faction that has worked its way into the system consists of theorists concerned with the material or media aspect of culture. This encompasses not merely the theatre and film scholars who are now established at most German universities. Erika Fischer-Lichte's *The Semiotics of Theatre* has already become a classic, and Brecht expert Hans-Thies Lehmann stands for a more poststructuralist approach to theatre. On the film side, women rule the field: Heide Schlüpmann and Gertrud Koch are names to reckon with. The theorists who have caused the greatest stir, however, are the likes of Friedrich Kittler, who apply the concept of materiality of signification to the very production processes underlying art in a way that even the most materialistic endeavours of Anglo-American scholars have not dared. Kittler's *Aufschreibesysteme* [literally 'Systems of Notation', but translated as *Discourse Networks*] indeed gives to the tools of writing a role in the production of texts that can only seem blasphemous to more traditional hermeneutical philologists. The almost religious devotion to technology, and especially the computer, as the hyper-medium to end all media, which unites him with some other contemporary German theorists, occasionally borders on mania.

In a similar vein, but taking the still-structuralist ideas of Kittler into a poststructuralist realm where they coincide with those of Jean Baudrillard and Paul Virilio, are the writings on media and simulation by authors such as Norbert Bolz. His *Eine kurze Geschichte des Scheins* [A Short History of Illusion], while perhaps attempting to cover more ground than it can manage, can be seen as a German foray into a hitherto French-dominated sphere, namely that of perception and reality and the way they are linked via various media. Florian Rötzer's collection of essays entitled *Digitaler Schein* [Digital Illusion] combines some of the best and worst, but certainly a representative sample of German writers on new and established media and their effect on the perception of reality. Another important collection of essays that takes up the concept of *aisthesis* [perception] and links it with the media, appeared in 1990 under the title *Aisthesis: Wahrnehmung heute oder Perspektiven einer anderen Ästhetik* [Aisthesis: Perception Today or Perspectives of a Different Aesthetics], edited by K. Barck et al. It unites a wide variety of French writers – from Barthes to Virilio and Baudrillard – with German authors like Kittler and practitioners such as Robert Wilson.

While many of the scholars mentioned above have made interesting inroads into basic yet highly complex modes of understanding reality, it is noticeable that – with the exception of Jürgen Link – they are not very much concerned with the shifts within society itself which form the bases of their models. Two very successful recent studies of changes in the cultural set-up of society and the ways in which this influences perceptions of individual identity are Ulrich Beck's *Risk Society* and Gerhard Schulze's *Die Erlebnisgesellschaft* [The Society of Experience]. While staying within the well-defined empirical paradigms of sociology, these studies develop some perspectives that transcend the usual sociological nit-picking, towards areas in which they merge with other critiques of late capitalism. Schulze's study, in particular, utilizes models developed by the French sociologist Pierre Bourdieu. Bourdieu's theories of social distinctions and symbolic power, although developed in the much more class-determined French society, might become influential tools in debates transcending sociology in the direction of literary and cultural studies. In more mainstream sociology Anthony Giddens has become a name to be reckoned with.

This transformation of the established disciplines, such as the diverse philologies, into a unified field of cultural studies can be seen to be under way in Germany when one analyses publications and research projects. Yet so far it has not become established in departmental structures or course plans. It seems obvious, however, that the main impetus has come from sociology and not so much from the literature departments, which are increasingly returning to their traditional roots in a decade of cuts and the continual pressure of rising student numbers.

While the dominance of French authors is indisputable in the realm of media studies, cultural studies are still very much regarded as Anglo-American or rather American territory. While names like Stuart Hall or Dick Hebdige will ring a bell with at least some members of English departments or people in media studies, the works of the likes of Greil Marcus have achieved a far greater popularity, not least by being published in accessible and affordable translations. (Hall's writings are only accessible in two small selections in a rather obscure series and Hebdige has not appeared in translation apart from a collection of writings edited by himself and others.) There is still a strong reluctance to accept that popular culture and youth culture are subjects worth studying, at least in their contemporary shapes.

It is indeed noticeable that the most interesting debates on *Zeitgeist* are not fought in the universities or even the major national papers, but in a small number of youth monthlies such as *Spex* that have cropped up since the 1980s, usually emerging from a vaguely Marxist scene and aiming to become a politically correct version of *The Face*. Although crippled by their own jargon and their tendency to take themselves too seriously, they contribute provocative statements to the debate on the state of contemporary culture. (Now that the fatal term has been mentioned, it is perhaps necessary to point out that 'political correctness' has not made its way into German intellectual debates, much less legislation. There is not even a German word for PC yet. Some media attempts to provoke a discussion have met with a mixture of amusement and disbelief. Although discrimination of all kinds is a sad fact, an institutionalized overreaction against it does not seem to suit the established lethargy of the German intellectual establishment, a lethargy which, however, also grants a great amount of personal freedom and security. Witch-hunts of any sort are also understandably watched with great suspicion in a country that has been confronted with its fascist past over the last fifty years.)

Some people from the *Spex* crowd, noticeably Diedrich Diederichsen, are currently attempting a crossover into academia proper. Diederichsen has published not only a German translation of American writings on black culture, but also a controversial assessment of youth culture in the 1980s and 1990s entitled *Freiheit macht arm* [Freedom Impoverishes] in which he deals very rigidly with the utopian promises of the 'revolutionary' generation of 1968. The very fulfilment of these promises (of personal freedom, unlimited spare time, the end of pressures), he claims, has turned into its own travesty in an age of mass unemployment and lack of perspectives.

Although undoubtedly biased and not always very thorough, this seems to be the drift which cultural theory in Germany takes these days – transcending the borderlines of academia once more, but in the opposite direction to that of its ancestors, namely towards youth and popular culture. It does not pull up its roots in Gramsci and Bakhtin, but relativizes them and – this seems even more important – disentangles them from their links with the middle-aged hang-ups and disappointed ideals still so much cherished by established academics in Germany and elsewhere, hang-ups and ideals which often block the view on important shifts happening under everyone's astonished eyes.

References

The following list of works by authors mentioned above is far from complete and should merely serve as an orientation for further reading. English translations are listed where available. The titles of German works are provided in translation in square brackets.

Barck, K. et al., eds (1990). *Aisthesis: Wahrnehmung heute oder Perspektiven einer anderen Ästhetik* [Aisthesis: Perception Today or Perspectives of a Different Aesthetics]. Leipzig, Reclam.

Beck, U. (1992). *Risk Society: Towards a New Modernism*, trans. M. Ritter (Theory, Culture & Society). London, Sage.

Blumenberg, H. (1985). *The Legitimacy of the Modern World*, trans. R. M. Wallace (Studies in Contemporary German Social Thought). Cambridge, Mass., MIT Press.

Bohrer, K. H. (1978). *Die Ästhetik des Schreckens: Die pessimistische Romantik Ernst Jüngers* [The Aesthetics of Terror]. Munich and Vienna, Hanser.

—— (1988). *Nach der Natur: Über Politik und Ästhetik* [After Nature: On Politics and Aesthetics] (Edition Akzente). Munich, Hanser.

—— (1994). *Suddenness: On the Moment of Aesthetic Appearance*, trans. R. Crowley (European Perspectives). New York, Columbia University Press.

Bolz, N. (1991). *Eine kurze Geschichte des Scheins* [A Short History of Illusion]. Munich, Fink.

—— (1992). *Chaos und Simulation* [Chaos and Simulation]. Munich, Fink.

Bovenschen, S. (1980). *Die imaginierte Weiblichkeit: Exemplarische Untersuchungen zu kulturgeschichtlichen und literarischen Präsentationsformen des Weiblichen* [The Imagined Femininity: Exemplary Analyses of Cultural and Literary Presentations of the Feminine]. 2nd edition. Frankfurt am Main, Suhrkamp.

Diederichsen, D. (1993). *Freiheit macht arm: Das Leben nach Rock'n'Roll 1990–93* [Freedom Impoverishes: Life after Rock'n'Roll 1990–93]. Cologne, Kiepenheuer & Witsch.

——, ed. (1993). *Yo! Hermeneutics! Schwarze Kulturkritik, Pop, Medien, Feminismus* [Yo! Hermeneutics! Black Cultural Criticism, Pop, Media, Feminism]. Berlin and Amsterdam, Edition ID-Archiv.

Fischer-Lichte, E. (1992). *The Semiotics of Theatre*, trans. J. Gaines and D. L. Jones (Advances in Semiotics). Bloomington, Indiana University Press.

Frank, M. (1981). *What is Neostructuralism?*, trans. S. Wilke and R. Gray (Theory and History of Literature 45). Minneapolis, University of Minnesota Press.

Gadamer, H. G. (1994). *Literature and Philosophy in Dialogue: Essays in German Literary Theory*, trans. R. H. Paslick (SUNY Series in Contemporary Continental Philosophy). Albany, State University of New York Press.

Habermas, J. (1984–9). *The Theory of Communicative Action*. 2 vols, trans. T. McCarthy. Boston, Beacon Press.

—— (1989). *The Structural Transformation of the Public Sphere: An Inquiry into a Category of Bourgeois Society*, trans. T. Burger (Studies in Contemporary German Social Thought). Cambridge, Mass., MIT Press.

Honneth, A. (1991). *Philosophical Interventions in the Unfinished Project of the Enlightenment* (Studies in Contemporary German Social Thought). Cambridge, Mass., MIT Press.

—— (1993). *The Critique of Power: Reflective Strategies in a Critical Social Theory* (Studies in Contemporary German Social Thought). Cambridge, Mass., MIT Press.

Iser, W. (1978). *The Act of Reading: A Theory of Aesthetic Response*. Baltimore, Johns Hopkins University Press.

——. (1989). *Prospecting: From Reader Response to Literary Anthropology*. Baltimore, Johns Hopkins University Press.

Jauss, H. R. (1982). *Towards an Aesthetic of Reception*, trans. T. Bahti (Theory and History of Literature 2). Minneapolis, University of Minnesota Press.

——. (1982). *Aesthetic Experience and Literary Hermeneutics*, trans. M. Shaw (Theory and History of Literature 3). Minneapolis, University of Minnesota Press.

Kittler, F. (1990). *Discourse Networks*, trans. M. Metteer. Stanford, Stanford University Press.

Kittler, F. and G. C. Tholen, eds (1989). *Arsenale der Seele: Literatur- und Medienanalyse seit 1870* [Arsenals of the Soul: Literary and Media Analysis since 1870] (Literatur- und Medienanalysen 1). Munich, Fink.

Koch, G. (1992). *Die Einstellung ist die Einstellung: Visuelle Konstruktionen des Judentums* [The Point of View is the Point of View: Visual Constructions of Jewishness]. Frankfurt am Main, Suhrkamp.

Lehmann, H.-T. and R. Voris (1992). *The Other Brecht I/Der andere Brecht I* (The Brecht Yearbook). Madison, University of Wisconsin Press.

Link, J. (1983). *Elementare Literatur und generative Diskursanalyse* [Elementary Literature and Generative Discourse Analysis]. Munich, Fink.

Luhmann, N. (1982). *The Differentiation of Society*, trans. S. Holmes and C. Larmore (European Perspectives). New York, Columbia University Press.

—— (1984). *Soziale Systeme: Grundriß einer allgemeinen Theorie* [Social Systems: Outline of a General Theory]. Frankfurt am Main, Suhrkamp.

—— (1986). *Love as Passion: The Codification of Intimacy*, trans. J. Gaines and D. L. Jones. Cambridge, Mass., Harvard University Press.

—— (1990). *Essays on Self-Reference*. New York, Columbia University Press.

—— (1993). *Risk: A Sociological Theory*, trans. R. Barrett (Communication and Social Order). New York, de Gruyter.

Marquard, O. (1989). *Farewell to Matters of Principle: Philosophical Studies*, trans. R. M. Wallace (Odéon). London and New York, Oxford University Press.

Menke, B. (1991). *Sprechfiguren: Name: Allegorie: Bild nach Benjamin* [Figures of Speech: Name: Allegory: Image after Benjamin] (Theorie und Geschichte der Literatur und der schönen Künste 81). Munich, Fink.

Menke, C. (1991). *Die Souveränität der Kunst: Ästhetische Erfahrung nach Adorno und Derrida* [The Sovereignty of Art: Aesthetic Experience after Adorno and Derrida]. Frankfurt am Main, Suhrkamp.

Münch, R. (1991). *Dialektik der Kommunikationsgesellschaft* [Dialectic of the Communication Society]. Frankfurt am Main, Suhrkamp.

Negt, O. and Kluge, A. (1983). *Geschichte und Eigensinn* [History and Stubbornness]. 3 vols. Frankfurt am Main, Zweitausendeins.

Rötzer, F., ed. (1991). *Digitaler Schein: Ästhetik der elektronischen Medien* [Digital Illusion: Aesthetics of Electronic Media]. Frankfurt am Main, Suhrkamp.

Schlüpmann, H. (1990). *Unheimlichkeit des Blicks: Das Drama des frühen deutschen Kinos* [The Uncanny Glance: The Drama of Early German Cinema]. Basel and Frankfurt am Main, Stroemfeld/Roter Stern.

Schmidt, S. J. and Hauptmeier, H. (1984). 'The Fiction is that Reality Exists: A Constructivist Model of Reality, Fiction, and Literature'. *Poetics Today* 5:ii.253–74.

Schulze, G. (1992). *Die Erlebnisgesellschaft: Kultursoziologie der Gegenwart* [The Society of Experience: Cultural Sociology of the Present Age]. Frankfurt am Main, Campus.

Sloterdijk, P. (1988). *Critique of Cynical Reason*, trans. M. Eldred (Theory and History of Literature 40). Minneapolis, University of Minnesota Press.

Theweleit, K. (1987–9). *Male Fantasies.* 2 vols, trans. S. Conway (Theory and History of Literature 22–3). Minneapolis, University of Minnesota Press.

—— (1988). *Orpheus (und) Eurydike. Das Buch der Könige 1* [Orpheus and Eurydice. The Book of Kings 1]. Basel and Frankfurt am Main, Stroemfeld/Roter Stern.

Wellmer, A. (1991). *Persistence of Modernity: Essays on Aesthetics, Ethics & Postmodernism*, trans. D. Midgley (Studies in Contemporary German Social Thought). Cambridge, Mass., MIT Press.

Welsch, W. (1988). *Unsere postmoderne Moderne* [Our Postmodern Modernity]. 2nd edition. Weinheim, VCH.

—— (1990). *Ästhetisches Denken* [Aesthetic Thinking]. Stuttgart, Reclam.

I would like to thank my friends and colleagues at the Siegen Graduiertenkolleg, especially Eva Erdmann and Armin Schäfer, and also Gerald Siegmund, for their advice concerning names and trends worthy of inclusion. They have helped a great deal to make my attempt at a review more objective.

14

Feminism and Theory in Italy

SHARON WOOD

In 1976 Lidia Ravera published *Porci con le ali* (*Pigs with Wings*), an ironic pastiche of the traditional boy-meets-girl theme set within the context of a revolutionary political movement clearly modelled on one of the many extra-parliamentary groups of the late 1960s and early 1970s. Ravera ruthlessly satirizes the pretentious ambition of the new cultural and political discourses, as her character Antonia listens to an earnest – and incomprehensible – analysis of pop music as 'metalanguage':

> Having fulfilled its associative function of collective – and collectiviz-ing – discharge of erotic energy repressed by civilization which 'kills Eros in the name of the reality principle' (Oh my!), 'pop music today is reduced to a mere consumer product, sucked right into the obscene market of the superfluous' ('Induced needs', he adds, with the air of someone who wants to make everything clear). 'Added to which this pop music finds itself playing the ambiguous role of metalanguage' (metalanguage?). There is general amazement, at least among the seven or eight who are listening (people who want to work in the arts when they grow up) (Ravera 1976: 64).

Confronted with the alienating and gender-blind discourse of Marxism and other leftist ideologies, many women on the radical Left in the late 1960s and 1970s sought to define their own cultural and critical spaces. The Centro Culturale Virginia Woolf was set up in Rome; women began to write their own syllabuses and set up their own small but successful publishing houses. Feminism in Italy was an eclectic movement, borrowing widely from American as well as other European feminisms and adapting a muliplicity of models to the specific, and dramatic, situation in which Italians found themselves in the late 1960s and 1970s. Feminism brought the dimension of gender not only to issues of divorce, abortion, sexual violence and rape, but to terrorism, institutional and parliamentary representation, the question of military service and ecology.

This new wave of feminism set out to uncover a new identity for women, no longer based on the political ethic of emancipation, a fallacious 'equality' with men, but rather on a rethinking of sexual difference which would embrace two quite distinct modes of being, which would no longer see femininity in terms of what it is not, as lack. Nor was women's liberation to be subordinate to socialist politics, for the programmes of political revolutionary groups clearly held their demands to be secondary to the goal of a global social revolution which took no account of women's own experience.

Given the strength of the Italian philosophical tradition, feminists in Italy did not share the Anglo-American distrust of theory, and drew on a number of diverse traditions to come up with a very particular mix of theory informed by political practice. As well as the practice of consciousness-raising, American feminism and writers such as Adrienne Rich contributed substantially to the debate on lesbianism. Italian feminists were much influenced by the work of French philosophical and psychoanalytical writing, Luce Irigaray in particular, and they have produced a large body of work on the vexed topic of sexual equality and sexual difference.

The most significant and original theoretical contributions of Italian feminism in the 1970s and early 1980s are its elaboration of theories of sexual difference and its continuing preoccupation with relationships between women. As is typical of most aspects of Italian feminism, these concerns have both a practical-political and a symbolic-theoretical value. Sexual difference, as it is understood in Italian theory, is to be equated neither with the determinism of biology nor with the social construction of gender. This is not the British and American concern with the sexism which inscribes women's social inferiority in language (equating humanity with maleness, for example, or referring to God the Father), nor is it the French preoccupation with elaborating the subversive potential of *écriture féminine* (not to be equated with writing by women). For the Italians, social recognition of equality is a poisoned chalice which would eliminate women's difference by assimilating them to the historically-dominant male modes of understanding and interpreting the world. Mistrust of the egalitarian principle was flatly stated by the influential Carla Lonzi in *Sputiamo su Hegel* (*Let's spit on Hegel*):

Subsuming the feminine problem to the classist conception of the master–slave struggle is an historical mistake. . . . . Subordination to the classist perspective means for woman the acceptance of terms borrowed from a slavery quite different from her own; terms which actually witness to her misrepresentation. Woman is oppressed as woman, at all social levels; not as a class, but as a sex (Bono and Kemp 1991: 42).

The philosopher Adriana Cavarero and the Diotima group continue to explore ways of thinking about sexual difference through a system of thought which itself expressly suppresses that difference. Cavarero calls for a dualistic philosophy, the recognition that 'being a man or being a woman is something originary which requires a dual conceptualization, an absolute duality, a kind of paradox for the logic of the one-many' (Bono and Kemp 1991: 191). (See also Diotima and P. Violi, *L'infinito singolare. Considerazioni sulle differenze sessuali nel linguaggio* [The Infinite Singular: Considerations on Sexual Differences in Language].) This dualism – similar in spirit perhaps to the 'due soli', the twin suns of Empire and Papacy, which Dante longed for as a just distribution of power and influence in the world – would require a fundamental shift not only in philosophical discourse but in the organization of the institutions.

The continuing strong regional basis of Italian cultural life was reflected in the establishment of influential local women's groups with their own specific identities and interests, brought together in a loose federal structure. Groups such as the Libreria delle donne di Milano (Milan's Women's Bookshop), Rivolta Femminile (Female Revolt, Milan), the Movimento Femminista Romano (Roman Feminist Movement), Diotima (Verona), published – and continue to publish – variously on questions of philosophy, ethics, history and politics. The creation of autonomous spaces outside the institutions in which women could meet, discuss strategy and evolve theory was also in accord with the separatism which marked Italian feminism, its increasing emphasis on locating and understanding female subjectivity in relation not to institutions or to men, but to other women.

Over the course of the 1970s Italian feminism, in its theoretical inflections, became less concerned with relations between women and men or institutions than with relations between and among women themselves. The practice of *affidamento* ('entrustment') clearly came out of the practice of *autocoscienza*, and was an attempt to acknowledge the social, intellectual and power differences, the tensions and inequalities between women in their public as well as their private lives. Through the notion of *affidamento* Italians reached for what they termed a 'dynamic separatism' (see the article 'Più donne che uomini', *Sottosopra* (January 1983) and translated by Rosalind Delmar as 'More Women than Men' in Bono and Kemp (1991): 111–23). 'Entrustment' implies supportive networking, the focusing on another woman as reference point in the effort to achieve one's ambitions and desires. While it is difficult to assess the success of this endeavour, it is interesting to speculate on the Italian emphasis on relations between women as a reaction to traditional cultural values. In their acknowledgement of the disparities between women, the Italians follow Irigaray in her belief in the need to prioritize the relationship with the mother as a model for other personal and social relationships, and the work of Luisa Muraro has been particularly influential in this sense. Caldwell speaks of 'the persistence in Italy of powerful common cultural accounts of mothers' (1991: 104), whose role – together with the pre-eminence of the male child – was underlined by the dominant ideology of Catholicism and reinforced in modern times through fascism. In this sense 'entrustment' sent a challenge to the dominant cultural and political representations of the relationship between women, for which the mother–daughter relationship served as a paradigm:

> They hoped that, by laying bare those psychic mechanisms which sought an idealized maternal figure either in the collectivity of women or in the leaders of groups, they would make it possible for women to work together and to develop relationships that would not depend on the abuse of power or the repetition of familial dynamics imported from earlier experiences (Caldwell 1991:105).

Italian feminism, abstract and abstruse as it can appear – and it has been accused by Italian women themselves of obscurantism – has always retained its links to political activism and a continuing commitment to social change and intervention in the public arena. The stormy social and political situation in Italy has always been crucial to the development of feminist thought in Italy, which offers a bridge between the preponderance of French theory and the pragmatism of the Anglo-American tradition. Teresa de Lauretis defines the specificity of Italian feminism, its parallel engagement with theory and practice:

> The essential difference of feminism lies in its historical specificity – the particular conditions of its emergence and development, which have shaped its object and field of analysis, its assumptions and forms

of address; the constraints that have attended its conceptual and methodological struggles; the erotic component of its political self-awareness, the absolute novelty of its radical challenge to social life itself. This is what is being addressed in the recent writings of some Italian feminist theorists, while their Anglo-American counterparts seem for the most part engaged in typologizing, defining, and branding various 'feminisms' along an ascending scale of theoretico-political sophistication where 'essentialism' weighs heavy at the lower end (De Lauretis 1989: 4).

With the increasing philosophical and critical dominance of deconstructionist theories and their Italian inflection, 'weak thought' (*il pensiero debole*) propounded in particular by Gianni Vattimo and Pier Aldo Rovatti, the strategic risks of essentialism were increasingly counterbalanced by the perception that it gave women not only a platform, but a position from which to speak and to assert their subjectivity.

'Weak thought' sets out not to impose truth but to proclaim the end of the metaphysical adventure, to safeguard thought but not as its 'master'. Vattimo and Rovatti launch an attack on theory 'understood as power, capacity to control, implication and totalization'. Proponents mark their distance from Marx, Nietzsche and Heidegger, who are still seen to be in search of the transcendental, engaged in uncovering what lies behind the world of appearances. 'Weak thought' on the contrary takes a more conciliatory look at the world of appearances, but without the perceived idealizing tendencies of Deleuze or Baudrillard; thought must 'articulate itself in the half-light', and Vattimo reaches for a new ontology which will not underpin but undermine notions of being. In his preference for aesthetic intuition over logical demonstration, 'truth' becomes not a dominant but an interpretive category. 'Weak thought' asserts the need to focus on the local rather than the global, to limit thought to ordinary experience and material context.

While 'weak thought' shares many discursive positions with feminist theory, it has been justly criticized for ignoring the fundamental site of difference, that of the body. It proclaims the superiority of difference to dialectics but simultaneously ignores feminism's revolutionary uncovering of sexual difference in the realms of the discursive and the symbolic as well as in material oppression. Other feminists are uneasy about the unseemly haste with which academics and theoreticians seek to dispel the subject: Braidotti comments that 'one can never deconstruct a subjectivity one has never been fully granted', pointing up the paradox of a discourse which liquidates the subject and the power of the word just at a point when disadvantaged and oppressed groups are asserting that subjectivity for the first time. Patrizia Magli puts the case for retaining a philosophical subject: 'There remains a strong desire to affirm subjectivity (which), even while it opts for a multiple and polymorphous vision of consciousness, rejects any suggestion of de-centred vision which dispenses with the "I".' The arguments about feminism and postmodernism rage on in Italy, as elsewhere. Cultural critics have been accused of naïveté, deconstructionist critics of creating an ahistorical impasse:

> Whereas cultural feminists have been accused of entertaining a too narrow idea of what woman is and wants as well as a naive concep-tion of woman as a free-willed subject capable of creating new experi-ences for herself, deconstructionist or postmodern critics have been under attack for painting too negative a picture of a socially and lin-guistically determined speaking subject who is helpless to discuss or effect any real political change (Lazzaro Weiss 1989: 384–5).

Despite the strong influence of French feminism in Italy, the Marxist underpinning of Italian feminism has led to a considerable scepticism as to the value of privileging discourse over the eradica-tion of oppression as the site of struggle. Although receptive to postmodern theories which undermine humanism and capitalism and which posit writing as a potentially revolutionary and subversive space, they are less convinced of the usefulness of uncovering a 'repressed feminine' in poetic discourse. Poet and critic Biancamaria Frabotta refutes the strategies of Elisabetta Rasy, Julia Kristeva's most significant follower in Italy, arguing that to privilege a pre-symbolic maternal state was to invite rather than forestall nostalgic regression. Other Italian thinkers demurred over Kristeva's view of the loss of identity and the self as potentially liberating, arguing that this position would keep women permanently locked into uncreative oppression. Like Kristeva, Frabotta is unconvinced that the solu-tions to women's problems are political, but she is wary that Kriste-va's semiotic politics would return women from collective action and struggle to individual, ethical isolation.

De Lauretis, in *Alice Doesn't*, argues for a redefinition of notions of the subject and experience in order to combat theoretical dis-courses which deprive the interpretant of subjectivity and simulta-neously objectify women, making of them 'a negative semantic space of the [male] imaginary fantasy of coherence' (1984: 161). She argues the need to theorize this exclusion, 'an experience to which sexuality must be seen as central in that it determines through gender identification, the social dimension of female subjectivity, one's personal experience of femaleness' (184). Otherwise we are left with the unresolvable paradox articulated by Rosi Braidotti that, since fragmentation of subjectivity and consciousness has been the historical condition of women, 'we are left with the option of theorizing a general becoming woman for both sexes, or else of flatly stating that women have been post-modern since the beginning of time'.

References

Birnbaum, Lucia (1986). *Liberazione della donna: Feminism in Italy*. Middletown, Wesleyan University Press.

Bono, Paola, and Sandra Kemp, eds (1991). *Italian Feminist Thought: A Reader*. Oxford, Blackwell.

—— (1993). *The Lonely Mirror: Italian Perspectives on Feminist Theory*. London, Routledge.

Braidotti, Rosi (1986). 'Io vedo nel tempo una bambina'. *Donna Woman Femme* 2: 45–50.

—— (1987). 'Envy'. In Jardine, Alice, and Paul Smith, eds. *Men in Feminism*. New York, Methuen.

—— (1991). *Patterns of Dissonance: A Study of Women in Contemporary Philosophy*, trans. Elizabeth Guild. Cambridge, Polity Press.

Caldwell, Lesley (1991). 'Italian Feminism: Some Considerations'. In *Women and Italy: Essays on Gender, Culture and History*. London, Macmillan.

De Lauretis, Teresa (1984). *Alice Doesn't: Feminism, Semiotics, Cinema*. Bloomington, Indiana University Press.

—— (1986). *Technologies of Gender*. Bloomington, Indiana University Press.

—— (1989). 'The Essence of the Triangle, or, Taking the Risk of Essentialism Seriously: Feminist Theory in Italy, the U.S., and Britain'. *Differences* 1.ii:4.

Diotima (1987). *Il pensiero della differenza sessuale*. Milan, La Tartaruga. Trans. as *Sexual Difference: A Theory of Social Symbolic Practice,* with introductory essay by Teresa de Lauretis (1991). Bloomington, Indiana University Press.

—— (1992). *Il cielo stellato dentro di noi: l'ordine simbolico della madre*. Milan, La Tartaruga.

Frabotta, Biancamaria (1981). *Letteratura al femminile*. Bari, De Donato.

Holub, Renate (1982). 'Towards a New Rationality? Notes on Feminism and Current Discursive Practices in Italy'. *Discourse* (1982), pp. 89–107.

Lazzaro Weiss, Carol (1989). 'The Experience of Don Juan in Italian Feminist Fictions'. *Annali d'Italianistica* 7: 382–92.

Libreria delle donne di Milano (1986). *Non credere di avere dei diritti.* Milan.

Lonzi, Carla (1971). *Sputiamo su Hegel.* Milan, Rivolta femminile. Trans. into English as *Let's Spit on Hegel* in Bono and Kemp (1991), pp. 40–59.

Magli, Patrizia, ed. (1985). *Le donne e i segni.* Ancona, Transeuropa.

Melandri, Lea (1988). *Come nasce il sogno d'amore.* Milan, Rizzoli.

Muraro, Luisa (1991). *L'ordine simbolico della madre.* Rome, Editori Riuniti.

Ravera, Lidia (1976). *Porci con le ali.* Rome, Savelli.

Vattimo, Gianni (1984). *Il pensiero debole* (ed. with Pier Aldo Rovatti). Milan, Feltrinelli.

Violi, P. (1987). *L'infinito singolare. Considerazioni sulle differenze sessuali nel linguaggio* [*The Infinite Singular: Considerations on Sexual Differences in Language*]. Verona, Essedue.

15

Althusser after Marxism

STEVE SMITH

One of the more remarkable events on the French intellectual scene of the past three years has been the revival of fortunes of the work of Louis Althusser. Deeply unfashionable for twenty years along with the Marxist philosophy with which his name was synonymous in the 1960s, his texts long out of print, the page – apparently – long turned on his project to establish the philosophical credentials of Marxism, Althusser's re-emergence has been prompted less by his death in October 1990 than by the decision of his nephew and heir, François Boddaert, in the absence of any will, to authorize the publication of the huge number of unpublished texts from every period of Althusser's life which he had discovered among his papers, as well as the establishment of an archive in Paris (The Institut Mémoires de l'Edition Contemporaine at 25, Rue de Lille, 75007 Paris) where researchers can consult numerous manuscripts and letters, as well as the (often annotated) contents of Althusser's personal library.

Of the writings so far published – which are already more voluminous than Althusser's relatively meagre output during his lifetime – and for reasons as obvious as they are dubious, it is the autobiography, *The Future Lasts a Long Time*, that has attracted most interest. Indeed, since its publication in 1992 it has been translated into (at least) eight languages, and has sold so well in France that it has now appeared as a *Livre de poche* paperback. The autobiography alone makes for a fascinating read, not least as a particularly 'knowing' example of the genre, indebted equally to Foucault's work on madness and criminality and to psychoanalysis, or as a portrait of French intellectual life in the 1960s, but what emerges clearly from the other posthumous texts that have appeared thus far is Althusser's continuing commitment to philosophy even in the period of solitude, increasing ill-health and legal anonymity that followed the 'drama' of 1980. (The drama is, of course, Althusser's infamous murder of his wife, Hélène, in November 1980. In what was perhaps an echo of De Gaulle's attitude to Sartre in the 1960s ('one does not arrest Voltaire') no prosecution followed, Althusser being granted a 'non-lieu', which effectively prevented him from publishing anything in his own name in France for what turned out to be the rest of his life.)

Surprisingly in the circumstances, Althusser viewed the autobiography, feverishly written in a period of only two months in 1985 and itself not devoid of philosophical interest, not as a valediction, but as a kind of self-exorcizing ground-clearing exercise that would facilitate his public reappearance on the philosophical scene (see Althusser 1993: 2), and most of his intellectual energies were given over to an ambitious radicalizing of (if not, in many respects, a break with) many of his earlier positions. Thus far, there have been sundry articles in journals. These comprise: 'Lettre à Merab' and 'Sur la pensée marxiste' in *Sur Althusser: Passages*, a special number of the journal *Futur Antérieur* (1993) which also includes a number of critical essays: 'L'Unique tradition matérialiste: Spinoza, Machiavel' in *Lignes* (vol. 18, 1993): 'Une conversation philosophique' in *Digraphe* (vol. 66, 1993). Also published thus far in book-form are Althusser's wartime writings, as *Journal de captivité, Stalag XA, 1940–5: Carnets, correspondance, textes* (Paris: Editions Stock/ IMEC, 1992) and a collection of writings on psychoanalysis, *Ecrits sur la psychanalyse* (Paris: Stock/IMEC, 1993). (All translations from French texts are my own.) Two collections of philosophical writings have also appeared: the first, *Sur la philosophie* (1994c), largely devoted to an interview with Althusser by a Mexican philosopher, Fernanda Navarro and first published in Mexico in 1988, was Althusser's only post-1980 work published in his lifetime. The 'interview' never took place as such, but was constructed by Navarro on the basis of texts, correspondence and interviews. The French edition comprises Althusser's own translation from the 'original' Spanish. Much of the correspondence on which the interview is based is also included in the volume. Here, in an accessible and even popularizing manner, Althusser reviews his own contributions to Marxist philosophy and outlines the later evolution of his thinking. The second volume of philosophical writings, *Ecrits philosophiques et politiques*, of more specialized interest, contains his unpublished 1947 thesis on Hegel, a book-length text written in 1978 called 'Marx dans ses limites', in which he develops his late 1970s position on Marxism's 'crisis', and a 1982 chapter from a projected book on materialism called *L'Authentique tradition matérialiste* in which he begins to set out the possibility of a new conception of Marxism. Also of theoretical interest are three texts appended to the new edition of the autobiography on Spinoza, Machiavelli and on the contemporary political situation.

In view of Althusser's abiding concern to position his own philosophical writings within a horizon determined in the last instance by the political, the latter text provides an appropriate starting-point for a discussion of Althusser's philosophical evolution in his final writings. Indeed, what is most immediately striking throughout his post-1980 writings is the extent of his political disenchantment with all existing forms of Communist politics. This disenchantment, which had been increasingly explicit in his work in the 1970s, is now expressed in unequivocal terms. He now acknowledges openly and with disarming frankness the spectacular historical failure of Marxist politics, not only in the Eastern bloc and China (where, he notes, Marxism had long ago been abandoned), but in the West too, where Communism has largely disappeared from the political agenda. Central to Althusser's schematic – not to say apocalyptic – analysis is the acknowledgement that Marxism's political failure is not simply a matter of contingent errors, which might have been avoided in different circumstances, but derives from fundamental theoretical errors which he will attribute to a serious misreading of Marx. Not the least of these is the concept of 'historical materialism', the touchstone of Marxism's claim to the status of science, which Althusser now terms a 'philosophical monstrosity' (Althusser 1994c: 31). The postulate of the absolute truth of Marxism had produced, at the level of politics, both a debilitating political and theoretical complacency grounded in a misplaced sense of the inevitability of social transformation under the pressure of capitalism's internal contradictions, and, equally seriously, had served to underpin the characteristically authoritarian and hierarchical structure of Communist parties East and West. In the case of the French Party (the PCF), of which Althusser had been a member since the late 1940s, despite numerous defections of fellow intellectuals in the 1960s, this had induced (notably in its response to the events of May 1968) a debilitating antipathy towards any oppositional movements that did not fit an aprioristic and hopelessly outdated model of class struggle. More importantly, it had produced an inability to analyse the contemporary mutations of capitalism, which had left it looking anachronistic and irrelevant in the face of such phenomena as neo-imperialism, the globalization of capital, consumerism and the leisure society, mass unemployment, the breakdown of the old model of factory-based production and increasing casualization of labour, and so on. This was not simply a theoretical error: it had contributed to a profound and widespread sense of depoliticization. As Althusser ruefully puts it:

> It is hardly surprising, then, that everyone and especially the young should turn completely away from theory and politics . . . . Unable to understand what is going on, having abandoned the old, now impotent explanation, that is, Marxism, they have finally, with nothing to take its place, passively given up trying to understand anything at all (1994a: 516, 520).

The pervasive disaffection with politics as irredeemably corrupt and irrelevant only serves all the more effectively to deliver those who had placed their hopes in the Marxist Left to the ever more imperious sway of capitalism. The electoral plight of the PCF in particular, coupled with the increasing grassroots quietism of the union movement, leads Althusser to the pessimistic prognosis that 'the traditional forces of the working class and its natural allies are undergoing such a prodigious decline that one wonders what political future they can really have' (Althusser 1994a: 513).

A comparable uncertainty also, of course, threatens the future of Marxism itself. Althusser's bold conviction is that the contemporary nadir in the fortunes of an intellectual movement to which he had devoted a lifetime's work cannot simply be put down to the ebb and flow of intellectual fashions, but indicates a deeper crisis, requiring a radical rethinking of Marxism. Implicitly, at least, he acknowledges that Marxist theory has in important respects been outmanoeuvred by other currents of contemporary thinking and made to look philosophically naïve. To cite briefly only two examples, Althusser takes on board Foucault's decentred conception of a micro-politics and his equation of knowledge and power – which is certainly at work in his critique of the PCF – while his thinking about philosophy and the nature of materialism is almost explicitly indebted to Derrida. Althusser, of course, had always practised a certain eclecticism, especially in his teaching at the Ecole Normale in Paris, but his thinking now is more than just eclectic. Whereas, in earlier texts, elements of structuralism, psychoanalysis, or Spinozist philosophy were invoked as a means of revitalizing and remodelling a Marxist philosophy that nevertheless remained the central focus of his thinking, it is now the case that non- or anti-Marxist currents of thought are welcomed as threatening the very existence and theoretical space of Marxist theory itself. Such a threat needs to be faced up to rigorously and dispassionately without the defensive theological or Hegelian assumption that, whatever its shortcomings at any particular moment, such shortcomings are merely the negative moment in a dialectical process that will assure their eventual and inevitable overcoming. Hence, the urgency of Althusser's stark limit-question posed at the beginning of 'Marx dans ses limites', a text that predates his own crisis and break with the PCF after 1980: 'what can we hold on to today from Marx?' (Althusser 1994b: 366).

In broad terms, Althusser's response to this question takes the form of an attempt to extricate Marx from (the history of) Marxism's errors, or at least to argue that Marx was not entirely responsible for what others (Engels, Stalin, Althusser . . .) had done with his writings and that other ways of reading them are possible. Scientific, theoreticist, humanist or historicist constructions of Marx's philosophy may have sustained Marxism for a century or more, but, Althusser now argues, their shared blind-spot was ever to have assumed that the construction of a coherent philosophical position was the most appropriate way to read Marx. Even his own project in *Reading Capital* to construct such a position, to write the 'Logic' that Marx 'did not have time to write' (Engels's words quoted in Althusser and Balibar 1970: 31) was, he now concedes, a 'fabricat[ion]', 'an "imaginary" philosophy for Marx, a philosophy which was not there in his work' (Althusser 1994c: 37). By the time of his final writings, Althusser is crucially less interested in making the case for his particular version of Marxist philosophy, than in questioning and undermining the claims of philosophical form as such, and, thereby, opening up a space for a new 'materialist' practice of philosophy – indebted to Marx, certainly, but irreducible to 'Marxist philosophy'.

To get a sense of what Althusser is driving at here it is worth quoting the following characterization of 'traditional' or 'idealist' philosophy, which is couched in terms that deliberately recall his own earlier version of 'scientific' Marxism, if not the whole of the Marxist philosophical inheritance:

> Traditional philosophy gave itself the historical and indispensable task of speaking the Truth of everything: of first causes, of first principles, and therefore of everything that is knowable, of the finality or the destiny of man and the world. Hence, its institution as a 'Science' of

the totality, able not only to produce incontestable knowledge, but also to possess Truth itself. This Truth is the *logos*, the origin, meaning . . . (Althusser 1994c: 50).

Althusser's new-found attentiveness to the difficulties of a simple overcoming of idealism stems from a new attitude of circumspection with regard to the philosophical heritage which he attributes explicitly to his reading, for the first time, of Heidegger after 1980. (That it was for the first time is Althusser's claim: see Althusser 1994: 112 and *passim*. It is probably untrue, as Yann Moulier Boutang informs us in a brief note (Althusser 1994a: 554). Volume 2 of the latter's 'authorized' biography of Althusser, covering the period after 1956 and due out in 1995, should be more enlightening on this point.) No longer can it be a question simply of commandeering a concept such as 'materialism', which, as Althusser now recognizes, is as old as philosophy itself, and of emptying it of its sedimented meanings so that it can be deployed within a new, revolutionary anti-idealist philosophy. This, in essence, was Althusser's strategy in his notorious conception of a clean 'epistemological break' between the early 'idealist' Marx of the *Theses on Feuerbach* and the later 'scientific', properly materialist Marx of *Capital*. Althusser now concedes that this was simplistic, and he argues now that the opposition of idealism and materialism is itself inscribed in the history of philosophy, opposition here, as in Derrida, functioning to mark a complicity:

> In the opposition of idealism to materialism, it is idealism – in so far as it is the dominant tendency of Western philosophy – which is the basis upon which the opposition itself is founded and developed . . . . Every time the word 'materialism' is used in our [i.e. Western] philosophy, we must understand that this appellation reproduces, as a negative, mirror image, the appellation 'idealism' . . . (1994c: 57).

At stake, fundamentally in idealism, even in its materialist form, is the assumption of the necessity and immanence of meaning as the ultimate ground of existence. As Althusser puts it:

> Heidegger would say that idealism, like materialism, obeys the 'principle of reason', that is, the principle that submits every existing object, ideal or material, to the question of the *reason for its existence* . . . and the fact of this question opens up a world of shadows (Nietzsche), a 'behind' of the thing, a reason hidden under the immediacy of appearance, of the empiricity of the thing given in the here-and-now (1994c: 96).

Althusser maintains that to locate the rational origin of the empirical in the intelligible necessarily entails a teleological account of history – regardless of what is invoked as the specific principle of its unfolding – for the question of origins is at once the question of ends:

> The question of the Origin is a question that arises from the question of the End. The End (the meaning of the world, the meaning of history, the finality (*finalité*: finitude) of the world and of history) projects itself, anticipating itself, in and on the question of origins. The question of origins is only ever raised as a function of the idea of ends (1994c: 97).

Or, more directly: 'Every materialism from the rationalist tradition is a materialism of necessity and teleology, which is to say, a modified and disguised form of idealism' (Althusser 1994c: 42). History, then, as a closed circle, anticipating its own ends, even before their empirical realization: herein lie the roots of the essential 'horror' (Althusser 1994b: 582) of Engels's dialectical 'science', which effectively authorized the Party's usurpation of the right to speak in the name of 'matter', of 'contradiction' or the Workers' Movement, and thereby to function as the vehicle of an always already anticipated 'end of history'.

It is in the complicity of idealism with a conception of history as the unfolding of a teleological process, governed by a principle which determines it from without but which can nevertheless be specified, where the principal theoretical stakes of what Althusser will call 'aleatory materialism' or 'materialism of the encounter' can be found. Of course, the critique of idealist conceptions of history had always exercised him; the earlier invocation of 'structural causality' and 'overdetermination' were precisely a means of loosening up the rigidity of economistic accounts of historical development and are generally regarded as among Althusser's most fruitful contributions to Marxist thinking about history. And yet, despite his evident attentiveness to the problem (see, for example, Althusser and Balibar 1970, especially Part 2, chapters 4 and 5), and, as he now recognizes (indeed, he now calls it 'absurd' [Althusser 1994c: 43]), the recourse to a determination 'in the final instance' by the mode of production (even when the final instance is said never to arrive as such) remained indebted to an idealist problematic. (See Derrida's interesting discussion of the concept of the 'last instance' in Derrida 1993a: 204–8.)

'Aleatory materialism', then, is conceived as a means of undermining any claim to understand the question of historical determination in terms of any governing principle. Although he does not explicitly acknowledge the work of Derrida specifically as an influence on his thinking on this, it is arguably here that Althusser's debt to Derrida is most marked. Such a borrowing is perhaps understandable. Etienne Balibar, Althusser's former collaborator, remarked in an interview published in 1982 that Foucault was Marxism's most thoroughgoing and scrupulous critic (Balibar and Macherey 1982: 48), but Althusser himself believes that it is the work of Derrida – who, unlike Foucault, had never explicitly been anti-Marxist – that poses the most acute philosophical questions for Marxism: Althusser's later writings are full of terms associated with Derrida ('logocentrism', 'outside', 'metaphysics', 'trace' are all used, if, as Derrida might say, a little quickly at times), while the autobiography refers to Derrida with unqualified admiration (see Althusser 1993: 178, 182, 220). In a text now appended to the new edition of *L'Avenir* he even cites Derrida as 'the most radical philosopher' of a list that includes Hegel, Nietzsche, Freud, Lenin and . . . Marx (Althusser 1994a: 491) and as 'the only great contemporary philosopher' (494). In connection with aleatory materialism, not only does Althusser's account of idealism and the difficulties posed in the project of its overcoming recall Derrida's remarks on Western metaphysics, but his wariness about the term 'materialism' – which must nevertheless still be applied now 'provisionally' (*par provision*) (Althusser 1994c: 96) to aleatory materialism – also suggests an awareness of Derrida's strategy of palaeonymics. (On this see 'Exergue' in Derrida (1982). Cf. Althusser (1994a: 476): 'Jacques Derrida has spoken much of strategy in philosophy and he is quite correct in this.')

Derrida's strategy of a deconstructive reading, it will be recalled, insists on the necessity of a double movement, whose first gesture is to propose the inversion of a 'metaphysical' opposition (in the name of a rational critique inherited and indissoluble from 'the history of metaphysics') so that the subordinate term becomes the primary one. This then gives way to the second movement wherein the structure that assigns primacy to one term within a hierarchy of opposites is itself questioned, which permits the formulation of an unstable third term (sometimes named as the 'non-word, non-concept' of 'différance', the fullest discussion of which is to be found in the essay 'Différance' in Derrida 1984. This undermines or, in the sometimes apocalyptic language of Derrida's *Of Grammatology*

(1976), 'destroys' the very logic of binary opposition, and discloses the unspeakable beyond, outside, before of metaphysical thought as such. In Althusser's case, the hierarchical opposition at stake is that between 'necessity' and 'contingency' (the precise terms mattering little as Althusser's analysis proceeds at quite an abstract level – rather more so than is the case with Derrida). In order to think history at all, idealism has always privileged the first term, which is also to privilege meaning, reason, teleology, as discussed above. What happens if we now overturn the opposition and propose that history is determined not by necessity but by contingency (which, of cause, would be no kind of determination at all)? Citing an obscure metaphor from Epicurus, Althusser writes:

> Let us recall the principal thesis [of aleatory materialism]: before the formation of the world, an infinity of atoms falls in the void, in a parallel formation. The implications of this assertion are striking: (1) before the world, absolutely nothing was *formed*, and, at the same time, (2) all the elements of the world existed already, isolated, from time immemorial, before the world ever was. This implies that before the formation of the world no meaning existed, no cause, no beginning, no end, no reason, no unreason. [. . .] Then, the *clinamen* occurs: an infinitesimal deviation, which takes place somewhere, somehow, at some point in time. The important point is that the *clinamen* provokes the deviation of an atom . . . and provokes an *encounter* with a neighbouring atom . . . and from atom to atom – whenever and wherever meetings endure and are not temporary – a world is born (1994c: 40).

Thought-provoking this may be, but it remains within the negative moment of a deconstructive reading, such that Althusser's insistence on the 'primacy of the void over form' (Althusser 1994c: 43) raises the spectre of a negative that posits emptiness as a substantive origin, always already inhabited by the potentiality of positive form. Further on, Althusser nuances the schema considerably. Not only is the deviation of the *clinamen* to be viewed as originary and not derived, but, pushing the metaphor further, Althusser contends that the very existence of the discrete atoms is an effect of the deviation:

> The encounter does not create the reality of the world, which is nothing but an agglomeration of atoms, but *gives reality to the atoms themselves* . . . . We may then say that the *very existence of the atoms only comes to them [ne leur vient que] through the deviation and the encounter* before which they led only a phantom existence (1994b: 542).

Emphasis Althusser's – is it by coincidence that Derrida in *Spectres de Marx* (Derrida 1993b) invokes the logic of spectrality as a deconstructive lever to undermine the logocentric opposition of presence/absence?)

This has the important effect of shifting the emphasis away from the deviation as the product of substantive causes which can be analysed and generalized as such, towards a conception of the deviation as a kind of pure effect, whose identity is not assured by or grounded in a specifiable cause that precedes it logically or temporally. To use a Derridean term which Althusser also employs, the clinamen produces an 'event' that marks a kind of absolute singularity. The only necessity exhibited by the encounter or the aleatory event, Althusser goes on, is that it took place at all: its necessity is constituted by the singularity of its particular configuration, its irreducibly material givenness. The concept of 'necessity' is thus transformed to become 'the becoming-necessary of the encounter of contingencies' (Althusser 1994b: 566). Patterns, tendencies, generalities may be inferred from the succession of events and conjunctures of events that constitute 'history' – and, indeed, must be if the 'event' is not to be conceived as purely self-generating and history, therefore, as an entirely random process – but such tendencies as can be discerned do not add up to generalizable concepts, and remain tied to a particular conjuncture. Tendencies may repeat themselves and endure, but, then again, if some new encounter takes place, they may not. No 'law' can be invoked that will adjudicate on this question. In other words, the motif of causality is essential but insufficient to the task of historical analysis, both of the past and the future.

If the foregoing sounds a little abstract, Althusser provides a brief analysis of historical causality focused on the classical Marxist conception of historical transition. Althusser's somewhat schematic analysis goes like this: in the first place, clearly something 'historical' took place which brought about the transition from feudalism to early capitalism, but it would be wrong to characterize feudalism as the 'cause' of capitalism, that is to analyse the feudal mode of production as harbouring capitalism within itself as a nascent possibility (or, rather, as its sole possible historical outcome) as the next stage of its historical development. On the contrary, capitalism came about by 'accident' as it were, as the ongoing process of an infinitely divisible conjuncture of elements, a complexity which cannot, in principle, be absolutely formalized into Engels's 'iron laws of the dialectic'. Citing Marx's chapter in *Capital* on primitive accumulation, a phenomenon whose consequences (to simplify somewhat) made available a dispossessed pool of labour that turned out to be crucial to the development of capitalism, Althusser writes:

> We see here the coming about of a historical phenomenon whose result we are familiar with: the dispossession of the means of production of a whole rural population in Great Britain, but *whose causes are unrelated to the result and its effects.* Was it for the establishment of great hunting lands or of huge estates for sheep-rearing? We don't really know (the sheep, no doubt) . . . and it matters little. The fact is that this process took place and ended up in a result that was immediately diverted from its presumed outcome by bourgeois entrepreneurs in need of cheap labour. *This diversion is the mark of the non-teleology of the process* and the inscription of its result in a process which made it possible but which was absolutely external (*étranger*) to it (Althusser 1994b: 572. Emphasis Althusser's).

In the light of this it comes as no surprise when we read in *The Future*: 'I am not sure that humanity will ever experience communism, Marx's eschatological view of things' (Althusser 1993: 224), or even that 'the inevitable transitional stage of socialism which Marx spoke about is "a lot of crap" ' (*ibid.*). But the dismissal of a facile optimism does not necessarily entail an equally facile pessimism. The 'aleatory' play within historical determination emphasizes history not so much as a *fait accompli* than as a *fait à accomplir*: history as a dynamic process, structurally open to a future 'uncertain, unforeseen, unfinished' (Althusser 1994c: 45). Notwithstanding the current paucity of indications of an effective encounter of elements which might bring about any effective transformation of capitalism, the lesson of the past – that things could easily have worked out differently – is concomitantly a source of hope. The motif of 'hope', however, should not be taken as a species of utopianism since it is grounded neither in subjectivist reverie nor in an eschatological conception of history as embodying some kind of progress towards human freedom or whatever. It is not just any hope but remains rooted in a profoundly negative impulse, a certain refusal of the existing state of things. It is in this connection that the figure of Marx emerges once more as a key one for Althusser, not now Marx as a Marxist, as the founder with Engels of the Communist movement, but Marx as the heretical, revolutionary thinker who refused to think within the conceptual tools he had inherited from Hegelianism and instead wrote *Capital* as an 'essentially subversive' work. (These are not Althusser's words – though they could be – but those of Maurice Blanchot approvingly cited by Derrida in his recent *Spectres de Marx* (Derrida 1993b: 64).) Althusser now views Marx's masterwork not so much in terms of a positive political or philosophical manifesto, but more narrowly as an exemplary critical and rigorous reading of the text of *Political Economy* that had previously furnished the terms of reference through which the capitalist mode of production had been understood. (In this connection at least Althusser's remarks on *Capital* in *Reading Capital* still hold (see Althusser and Balibar 1970, especially Part 2, chapters 1–4).) As such, Marx takes his place in a tradition of 'limit-thinkers' such as Spinoza and Machiavelli, who, in their respective fields of theology and political philosophy, similarly strove to think 'in extremes within a limited situation' (Althusser 1994a: 491). Whereas, for example, in Spinoza (or Althusser's reading of him), it was the old term 'God' that functioned to name an unnameable otherness that marks the possibility of a new thinking beyond the inherited problematic within which he was constrained to think, so, in the contemporary, particularly constricted conjuncture which is characterized by the apparent absence of the conditions of possibility of any social transformation, Althusser continues to invoke the old discredited term 'Communism'. The only definition of Communism he can come up with in all his post-1980 writings is appropriately profoundly negative, which is not to say it is not nothing:

> I think that the only possible definition of communism – if it is one day to exist in the world – is *the absence of relations based on the market*, that is, of exploitative class relations and the domination of the State. In saying this, I believe I am in line with Marx's thinking (Althusser 1993: 225, translation modified).

Communism is less now a matter of the realization of an idea or of substantial contents in the form of economic and social organization that can be anticipated as such, but more the simple injunction to think otherwise, to think heretically within – or, more properly, at the limits of – what is currently thinkable. As such, it is also an impossible injunction because Communism is not as yet thinkable at all. Such a conception is consistent with a certain reading of Marx. As Althusser puts it:

> Remember that when Marx thought of the form of a future State, he spoke of a State that would be a 'non-State': in short, an entirely new

form that brings about its own extinction. We can say the same thing about philosophy: what Marx was seeking was a 'non-philosophy', whose hegemonic function would perish to be replaced by new forms of existence of philosophy (Althusser 1994c: 39).

While I do not have space to pursue it here, it is interesting and perhaps not coincidental that Althusser's approach to the question of the future of Marxism in terms of a questioning of the concept of futurity itself should find an echo in Derrida's recent book, *Spectres de Marx*, in his remarks on 'democracy', 'emancipation', 'justice' – figures for what he calls the undeconstructable as such – as 'this absolutely undetermined messianic hope, this eschatological relation to the future-to-come (*à l'à-venir*) of an event and a singularity, of an unanticipated otherness' (Derrida 1993b: 111), or 'an event which we can neither anticipate as such nor recognize in advance' (*ibid.*).

What, finally, of the 'new forms of philosophical existence' of which Althusser speaks? In this connection, the key term for Althusser, as in some of his earliest texts, is that of 'practice'. Philosophy conceived as a practice, according to Althusser, 'is absolutely alien to the *logos*, is not Truth, and is irreducible to saying or seeing' (Althusser 1994c: 60), and 'there is no Truth of practice' (61). Unlike idealist forms of philosophy, whose purpose is given in the possibility of speaking the truth of everything, including the criteria by which truth itself is to be assessed, the materialist tendency in philosophy insists that philosophy has an 'outside', something which escapes its totalizing conceptual reach. The repressed 'outside' of idealist philosophy is constituted by its material insertion in a discursive history of philosophy, its indebtedness to the limits of what may be thought in any given epoch, which if it is to say anything new, philosophy must transform. The materialist practice of philosophy cannot embrace this 'outside' any more than idealist philosophies can, but it can take it into account in the strategic calculation of its effects. The necessity of a materialist philosophical practice, moreover, derives explicitly but not quite entirely from the positions it seeks to combat and undermine. It does so not in the name of Truth, but has only the force of its own (negative) critique to sustain it. Without a domain proper to itself, without an identity as such, it is impelled to take up the struggle with idealism wherever it finds it – that is, more or less everywhere – in every branch of philosophy from aesthetics to social theory. Why 'impelled'? Again, as with the definition of Communism, it is necessary to avoid a certain messianism, but the following formulation at least has the merit of bringing us back to Marx, and of suggesting ·that something more than immanent critique is at stake: 'If there exist philosophies which oppose each other antagonistically, it is because antagonistic class practices also exist . . . . Fortunately,' (Althusser 1994c: 68).

In his late writings (see, for example, 'Portrait du philosophe matérialiste' in Althusser 1994b) Althusser is fond of the curious metaphor of the materialist philosopher as a Wild-West cowboy-figure illicitly boarding an already moving train, knowing not where the train is heading, but only that he needs to be elsewhere. Whether he will end up where he wants to be is essentially unknowable. By the same token, philosophical interventions in the name of materialism may be oriented by the possibility of their transformative effects, within philosophy or beyond, and these effects may be constitutive of a history-to-come, but there can be no knowing in advance of particular undertakings what these effects will turn out to be. All that can be done is to pursue such an opening as rigorously and painstakingly as possible, with the awareness that philosophical struggles – as with more properly political ones – are hard-won, if they can ever be won at all. But if, as Althusser says, the future really does last a long time, then we can afford to be patient.

References

Althusser, Louis (1993). *The Future Lasts a Long Time*, trans. by Richard Veasey. London, Chatto and Windus.

—— (1994a). *L'Avenir dure longtemps* (Nouvelle édition augmentée, présentée par Olivier Corpet et Yann Moulier Boutang). Paris, Livre de poche/Editions Stock/IMEC.

—— (1994b). *Ecrits philosophiques et politiques: Tome I*. Paris, Editions Stock/IMEC.

—— (1994c). *Sur la philosophie*. Paris, Gallimard.

Althusser, Louis, and Etienne Balibar (1970). *Reading Capital*, trans. by Ben Brewster. London, New Left Books.

Balibar, Etienne, and Pierre Macherey (1982). 'An interview', trans. by J. H. Kavanagh, *Diacritics* 12:i.46–51.

Derrida, Jacques (1976). *Of Grammatology*, trans. by Gayatri Chakravorty Spivak. Baltimore and London, Johns Hopkins University Press.

—— (1982). *Dissemination*, trans. by B. Johnson. Chicago, Chicago University Press.

—— (1984). *Margins of Philosophy*, trans. by A. Bass. Chicago, Chicago University Press.

—— (1993a). 'Politics and Friendship: An Interview with Jacques Derrida', trans. by R. Harvey. In E. Ann Kaplan and Michael Sprinker, eds. *The Althusserian Legacy*. London and New York, Verso.
—— (1993b). *Spectres de Marx*. Paris, Gallilée.

16

Modern Western Literary Theories and Russian Cultural Policy

ANATOL V. LASHKEVITCH

Observing the recent history of Russian literary studies, we can mark at least three major historical events, each of which could be regarded as a turning-point of the cultural/political process. These are: (1) the First Congress of Soviet Writers (1934); (2) the Nineteenth Congress of the CPSU (1956); and (3) the Belovezh Summit of the leaders of three new independent states (1991). The first event opened the *totalitarian era* of Soviet culture; the second marked the so-called *Khrushchev's thaw* and the subsequent period of *zastoi* (stagnation); the third has started the period of *postperestroika* (i.e. the current liberalization) in all social fields. Each of the periods mentioned has its own special and particular attitudes to Western philosophical and cultural theories, and its own rules and modes of reception, analysis and evaluation.

The First Congress of Soviet Writers had two general interrelated effects: it *closed* the short post-revolutionary era of limited cultural pluralism and *opened* the time of strict Communist dogmatism in art, literature and philosophy. The conception of 'socialist realism' heralded in the report by Maxim Gorky and recognized personally by Stalin, pre-supposed the rejection of pre-revolutionary traditions of Russian philosophy and aesthetics. They were proclaimed 'reactionary, feudal-bourgeois, perspectiveless and simply unnecessary and useless for new Soviet proletarian culture'. New literature for the 'engineering of human souls' needed a special theory free from 'bourgeois prejudices' and traditional or 'abstract' humanism.

The 'natural' or 'organic' development of Russian theoretical thought was thus broken, but this didn't separate Russian from West European intellectuality; the relationship between the two had not, in any case, weakened Russian originality. But proletarian ideology regarded itself as a new tradition for a 'brave new world' and so it had no need for any previous values, whether national or international.

The period after the First Soviet Writers' Congress was one of intellectual and physical terror. It was a real war against 'inner and outer ideological enemies', who were condemned to total extermination for the sake of the final triumph of the new social order and culture. Lenin's advice 'to study all the best bourgeois achievements' was forgotten and all the ideas which originated from outside 'the first proletarian state' were considered useless to the Soviet people. Soviet culture was formed as a separate fortress of 'progressive' ideas and 'truly scientific conceptions'.

The systems of Soviet/Russian literary criticism and theoretical studies throughout the whole Soviet period were organized in terms of 'militarity' (Boris Paramonov). They were directed to take part in *party propagandist activity*, i.e. every critic, university professor or academic researcher of literature was obliged to pursue steadfastly the norms and prescriptions of Communist ideology (Marxist, Leninist and Stalinist conceptions of art).

All activities in the field of the humanities were put under the rigid control of the Communist Party and were subject to some special dogmatic demands: all teachers of literature were to organize their work in the subject according to strict laws of permanent 'ideological struggle and class war'. The 'tactic' of this war was to attack 'bourgeois' art, literature and theory, showing up their methodological weakness and political harmfulness, whereas 'the class war strategy' was to advocate Marxist and Leninist philosophy and Communist Party politics (later the 'achievements' of Russian national culture too) by means of professional (i.e. literary and theoretical) ideas.

Soviet literary critics and researchers were explicitly and implicitly mobilized for ideological battles against 'world bourgeoisie and imperialism'; any non-Marxist or non-Soviet ways of thinking, any attempt to quit the 'ideologically adapted' field of research, would lead to the truant's political condemnation or his/her professional penalization. Paradoxically, in this war of ideas the final victory had already been allocated by the Communists to themselves, and the battles were fought merely to justify their right to this victory.

In this intellectual-military climate there appeared a sort of special logic, formally originating in the texts of Marx, Engels, Lenin, Trotsky and Stalin, but essentially rooted in the old shamanistic model of 'the curse of the alien'. It was in some way a hysterical 'feminine' logic (in the old Victorian sense), where an emotionality ruled by subconscious 'class instincts' was considered more natural, important and accurate than considered rational arguments. This 'logic' was based on the general opposition of *own/alien* where the first member had a totally positive and the second a totally negative content.

This 'class' logic could generate nothing but special contradictory rhetorics for 'disputes with class enemies and ideological opponents'. These rhetorics seemed to be rooted in literal citations from a 'Marxist classic heritage' but had as a subtext a set of binary oppositions marked both ideologically and axiologically, as, for example, *materialist/idealist, dialectic/metaphysic, humanist/egoist, collective/individual*, etc. The second member of each was regarded as totally and always *alien*, i.e. politically suspect, ideologically wrong, or simply bad. The first one included, *vice versa* – the meaning of 'right, true, scientifically proved, realistic', or simply always good and even the best.

After the Second World War, of which 'the great Russian people' was proclaimed the only winner, there appeared some new negative intellectual objects and terms: '*Western* (i.e. not Russian or Chinese) = imperialistic = bourgeois = dangerous for weak young minds = corrupting'. The task for literary theoretical studies became twofold: to the old one – which was unmasking 'bourgeois idealism' plus defending 'the almighty as the only true' doctrine of Marxism-Leninism – a new task was added: protecting young Soviet citizens from the pernicious influence of Western cultural propaganda. Marxist dogmatism was complicated by 'Soviet patriotism' which was simply another name for Russian chauvinism. Ideology and cultural politics became more and more hypocritical: sophisticated 'humanistic' rhetorics covered over the primitive logic of bestial hatred and phobias.

Under such conditions the reception of any Western ideological and cultural phenomena was single-minded: 'to overcome the ideological enemy' meant just to show his 'idealistic roots' and 'formalist origins' and by doing so push him to his knees in front of triumphant, undebatable Marxism. Like the ancient rituals of bewitching, these terms were pronounced in a sacramental manner because the main aim in such 'disputes' was not to persuade the opponent of some realities but to repress him into '*gulag*'s dust'. All arguments by Western scholars (despite their possible intellectual validity) were regarded as ideological traps and provocations, their authors were under suspicion just because they were not born in 'the only country of victorious socialism'. Even those academicians who swore in the names of Marx and Lenin could not be sure of their full appreciation and personal security (remember Nikolay Bukharin, Georg Lukács, Louis Althusser or Roger Garodi). The idea of the *alien* was triumphant and all intellectual forces were concentrated upon the repulsion of Another and confirmation of Self.

This shamanistic military rhetoric formed the literary consciousness of several generations of Soviet critics and students of literature. Its final theoretical achievement was the creation of peculiar *simulacra* (names without essence, or copies without origin) like 'folkness' (*narodnost*), 'classity' (*classovost*), 'partyness' (*partiynost*), etc. It is quite impossible to translate these terms properly into any foreign language, and they can be used only for the theory of masterpieces of 'socialist realism'. But official Soviet theorists insisted that these simulacra had indisputable authority for all times and peoples and were applicable to any work of art.

The problem of 'socialist realism' (or SR) became the main subject of theoretical debate. Various groups of Soviet official theorists argued whether SR was a *method* of art, or a *movement* in literature, or a *system* of artistic means and aesthetic ideas. But despite these differences, all academicians were quite agreed in their opinion that 'socialist realism is the greatest achievement of world literature'. (See the works of Karkov, Dmitry. F., and A. C Bushmin, *The Science of Literature* (Moscow, 1984); Fridlender, G. M., *Methodological Problems of Literary Criticism* (Leningrad, 1984); Yegorov, A., *Problems of Aesthetics* (Moscow, 1977); Kikushina, N. J., *The October Revolution and Literature's New Ways* (Moscow, 1978), *On the Party-ness of Literature* (Moscow, 1987); Baranov, V. I., A. G. Botcharov and Y. I. Surovtsev, *Literary Fiction Criticism* (Moscow, 1982).) Literary theory, which had to serve the actual needs of party politics, was not allowed to touch on any philosophically complicated questions.

Special significance in this spiritual war was attached to the problem of *method*. It was proclaimed 'the central point' of the Marxist-Leninist philosophical system and thus one of the 'sacred cows' of Soviet ideology. All Marxists from Georgy Plekhanov to Georgy Fridlender considered method in art and aesthetics to be not just an instrument of investigation or a way of truth demonstration/ creation but also a 'weapon' for ideological struggle, the main reserve of Communist General Headquarters, used in the most crucial situations as a means to attack and destroy the enemies' intellectual castles.

Methodological studies were proclaimed the most important part of the intellectual syllabus but (one more paradox) all the results were obvious before the study had begun. The only correct and scientifically-proven method for research in the humanities and social sciences had already been revealed by the founding fathers of Marxism, and the task of their inheritors was to keep these principles intact. Their 'creative development' was permitted in very limited frames with the obligatory inclusion of crucial criticism of opponents. Any doubt as to the sanctity of Marxist–Leninist concepts was excluded; it was possible only to affirm and confirm this or that already-given axiom.

At the same time (and again paradoxically) those scholars who really read and analysed the original texts of Marx or tried to interpret rationally those of Lenin (for example Alexey Losev or Mikhail Livshits) were regarded as not being leading ideological authorities and their works were considered to be marginal and weak in comparison with the 'philosophical investigations' of Party chiefs and commanders (like Ivan Frolov or Mikhail Khraptchenko). Such leading philologists as Victor Vinogradov, Victor Shklovsky, and Victor Zhirmunsky were treated as 'narrow specialists' while such Party activists as Andrey Iezuitov or Vladimir Shcherbina were proclaimed 'grand Marxist scientists and literary experts'. Under these circumstances, the very thought of exploring any Western theory in modern literary studies was taken as political provocation against ideological unity and both thought and thinker were quickly got rid of. The best example of such confirmation of Marxism may be seen in the fates of two of the outstanding figures of Russian philosophy of art of the first half of the twentieth century.

At the very beginning of this century there existed a powerful intellectual movement in Russia which dealt with the problem of reception and understanding. The concept of Russian hermeneutics was developing in close contact with the Husserlian school but it proposed some theoretical ideas independently of German phenomenology. The leader of this movement, Professor Gustav G. Shpet (see Shpet, G. G., *Hermeneutics and its Problems.* Context 89; 90; 91; 92 (Moscow 1989–93)), was arrested after the Bolshevik revolution, his school was dispersed, manuscripts and publications were destroyed, and Shpet himself was executed in Stalin's prisons at the end of the 1930s (see *The Beginnings* 2 (Moscow, 1992)). So hermeneutics in Russia was over, and its doctrinal heritage removed from study.

Though the personal fate of Mikhail Bakhtin was not so grievous as that of Shpet, nevertheless his life was also a kind of permanent spiritual resistance to the official humanities. He was to carry on a sort of partisan activity in his works, propounding his own view of cultural phenomena, different from that of Marxists/Leninists. (See *Bakhtin Behind the Mask* 1–3 (Moscow 1993–4). The names of Bakhtin and Shpet are well known among Western literary scholars, but objective study of their works in Russia has commenced only since the final crash of the Communist ideological system.) In his theoretical works Bakhtin was to use a highly specific terminology, so that it was difficult for the party controllers to find in it any traces of anti-Marxist escapism. Bakhtin's works now look enigmatic even to his Russian followers, not to speak of his readers in the West. (The 'Bakhtinian' character of contemporary American literary theory deserves more attention than it has recently received in Russian studies of Western culture.)

For these reasons Soviet philosophy of art and theory of literature from the 1930s through to the 1950s stood apart almost completely from the broader world experience in the study and teaching of the humanities. Such trends as phenomenology, psychoanalysis, existentialism, linguistic philosophy, modernism and postmodernism were outside our understanding because the only thing we were permitted to know about them was their common feature – their 'bourgeois origin' – that excluded any possibility of their being acceptable. 'Bourgeois theory' – that phrase was enough to brand any concept as 'idealistic, improper, far from real-life problems, politically harmful and unnecessary for the Soviet reader'.

The same can be said about research methods in literary studies and critical analysis: the inventions of psychoanalysis, mythopoetics, New Criticism, later those of New Historicism, poststructuralism, hermeneutics, deconstruction and aesthetics of reception were simply neglected without having received any objective evaluation. They were treated as the 'product of bourgeois ideology' and that meant that their reviews did not go far beyond 'false', 'idealistic', 'politically innocent' (which was equal to 'harmful', 'useless' and 'unnecessary').

Political and ideological prescriptions blocked the free exchange of ideas and boxed Russian literary thought into its own set of analyses, methods and evaluations. But (paradox forever) the more the Communists tried to preserve Soviet intellectuals from 'hostile' ideas, the more interesting these ideas seemed to young philologists and theorists. Forbidden fruit seemed sweeter.

One more cultural phenomenon should be mentioned in this discussion of the 'Soviet' literary consciousness. This is the unique phenomenon of a *'Soviet' reader*. The texts produced under the supremacy of alienating logic, and according to the rules of hypocritical rhetoricity, demanded from their readers an unusual capacity – to read *through, between* or even *beneath* the lines. This special hyper-reading was applied not only to Communist propagandist newspapers or journals but also to the texts of philosophy and literary theory. When reading these texts we had to eliminate all party-political and ideological mannerisms and clichés if we wanted to uncover any relevant sense and meaning. Mental 'bracketing' of 'ideologically correct' sentences and passages in the special texts was the usual reading practice for those who started to deal with Western cultural and literary theories. Sometimes these brackets comprised ninety per cent of the whole book or article, but such hyper-reading was the only way to extract from the official texts some relevant content concerning Western intellectual life.

The Nineteenth Congress of the CPSU in 1956 ended this phase of bloody and repressive cultural politics and let some new theoretical ideas penetrate the dogmatist fortress of Bolshevik thought. It was not yet the end of the totalitarian era but it marked the first step out of the ideological prison-walls. At the end of the 1950s the contemporary system of literary criticism and theory began to be formed. We can mark three main trends in the attitude to Western cultural conceptions.

(1) Official Soviet literary studies.   This trend continued to some extent the previous tradition of ideological hostility to and neglect of Western intellectual achievements. Its representatives took the same position of defending Marxism-Leninism (but now without Stalinism) and rejecting 'bourgeois idealism', 'reactionary and conservative philosophy', 'non-realistic art' and 'ideologically immature theories'. Dogmatism and hypocrisy was now an obligatory element of any theoretical study. No article, book or dissertation could be presented without citations from Marx, Engels, Lenin or the latest decrees of the Central Committee of the CPSU (see for example, *The Resolution of the Central Committee of the CPSU* ('About Literary-Artistic Criticism'), 1972). By the beginning of the 1970s there was in the USSR a fully-formed dogmatic system of education and research in the humanities.

One of the main features of this system was its hyper-centralization. All information was concentrated in Moscow, and only in Moscow libraries could those who studied foreign culture get the necessary sources and files. This was very convenient for the Communist censors because it allowed control both of the information from abroad and of those who tried to gain access to it. In central Moscow libraries there were so-called *spetzkhrany* (special depositories) where 'politically reliable' scholars had the opportunity to read Western books and magazines unavailable to the wider public. Just as Communist chiefs received special food in the Kremlin buffets, so some Soviet official literary scholars received Western intellectual works in a clear (uncensored) form. Translations, reviews and original texts for these scholars were provided with the special stamp *Dlya sluzhebnogo pol'zovaniya* ('For official use only'). (See, for example, *New Studies in Hermeneutics* (Moscow: INION, 1983).) Other students, postgraduates, university tutors and simply those who were interested could receive only pre-prepared and specially (ideologically) interpreted texts (the best example is probably *Hermeneutics: The History and the Present Day* (Moscow: Thought, 1985)).

'Official' literary theory was completely subordinated to the political and propaganda tasks of the Communist Party; and for this reason modern Western theoretical concepts could expect from it nothing but abuse and ideological denunciation. This trend preserved the logics and rhetorics of the previous period; all its theoretical constructions stood inside Kantian-Hegelian dialectics and a 'class war' system of thought. It summarily rejected anybody who tried to reform it by the introduction of new ideas or independent thinking (for example, Evald Ilyenkov, Euphim Etkind or Andrey D. Sinyavsky). Some difference with the rhetorics of their Stalinist predecessors appeared in the use of radical revolutionary phrases: Brezhnev's ideologists were devoted rather to 'traditional' (not innovative) values though it was the tradition of Bolshevism.

(2) **'Non-formal' literary studies.** Another trend of post-Stalinist Soviet literary theory may be called 'unofficial' or rather 'non-formal'. It existed in a special milieu of young graduates, postgraduates and junior professors between the 1960s and the 1980s, and was a kind of a 'silent opposition' or 'inner emigration'. This generation was later called 'the generation of dvorniks [caretakers, janitors] and night watchmen' because many of them preferred not to serve in official structures but to be unskilled workers for the sake of integrity and personal liberty.

In this environment modern Western concepts like existentialism, psychoanalysis, structuralism, modernism and postmodernism met with extraordinary success and popularity. Information about them was obtained in different ways: from secret copying of the original

texts in *spetzkhrany* (special departments of libraries) to
half-underground meetings and conversations in the kitchens of
private houses with rare Western visitors. This interest in modern
theories was part of the general thirst for information on Western
culture and of the desire to escape the omnipresent Party control
and the hypocrisy of official scholars. Western theories of literature
and culture from Freud to Derrida were a kind of compensation for
the sterile ideas of social realism; they helped to restore the almost
forgotten Russian connections with a long European tradition of
liberal thought.

Not everything in these Western theories was clear and compre-
hensible, but the enthusiasm of neophytes made up for the deficit of
knowledge. The most brilliant example of this 'non-formal' trend
may be the so-called 'Tartu School' of semiotics under the leader-
ship of Professor Yuri M. Lotman. Western structuralism in this
School acquired a new and special (though provincial and naïve)
dimension. For the first time since the 'revolutionary' First Congress
of Soviet Writers there was an attempt to unite contemporary
Russian theoretical studies with the Western conception rooted
(paradox again!) also in a Russian (but not Soviet) tradition
(Roman Jakobson, Noam Chomsky, the Prague linguistic circle).

The activity of the Tartu School was a challenge to 'official'
literary studies because it tried to get round the traditional system of
primitive oppositional logic and hypocritical rhetoric. Tartu semi-
oticians were eager to replace the martial vocabulary of 'official'
theory with a kind of pure 'scientific' terminology free from political
propaganda. This structuralistic language ('discourse') was not easy
for a layman to comprehend and to the Soviet mind it looked like
secret code.

This group of Soviet theorists soon became an object of ideological persecution by official scholars. They were accused of a fiendish
ideological sin: neglecting the 'immortal Marxist dialectics and
Lenin's theory of reflection'. There was activated one more rheto-
rical/ideological term – 'formalism' – which meant not the specificity
of a particular research method but rather an alien and suspect theoretical position.

The Tartu group was not physically exterminated like that of
Shpet but it was forced to stop its activities. Some of the participants were assimilated by the 'official' trend (like Professor
Lotman), others preferred to emigrate, still others transferred to
alternative spheres of intellectual work. The main achievement of
the Tartu theorists seems to lie in the field of cultural philosophy.

Lotman and his disciples considered human cultural activity in terms of semiotics. For them all cultural phenomena are the results of total *semiosis* (cultural signification). There is nothing in the world except signs – this is the basic idea of Russian structuralists (Lotman, Y. M., *Culture and Explosion* (Moscow, 1993)). Though it was far from the theoretical depth of French *Tel Quel* scholars (Roland Barthes, Julia Kristeva, et al.), nevertheless Lotman's school played a significant role in the destruction of the mono-methodological Marxist 'official' system.

(3) The 'dissidents'. The third (and the smallest but the most authoritative) group of Soviet recipients of modern Western cultural theories may be defined as 'dissidents', or 'the underground'. This group included those intellectuals who dissociated themselves from the hypocritical official ideology, but led an active spiritual struggle against the regime. They were the most educated and open-minded part of the Soviet intelligentsia which acted to change society. They had direct contacts with some Western publishers and Russian émigrés, which is why they had access to original texts and authors. Some of them tried to disseminate Western ideas through underground magazines (the so-called *samizdat* and *tamizdat*), for example the almanac *The MetroPolis*, the magazines *Continent* and *Posev*. It was the most authoritative, albeit irregular, channel of information propounded within the Communist ideological fortress in the 1970s and 1980s.

After 1985 when Gorbachev began the politics of perestroika, all three trends started to come together on the ground of general dissatisfaction with the system of Party Diktat and control. Even the official scholars came to understand the stupidity and aimlessness of ideological prescriptions and taboos. Western work in the humanities ceased to be a propagandistic scarecrow and turned into a proper subject for study. Moreover, the pre-revolutionary traditions of Russian philosophy and aesthetics with their European orientation were restored. The time had come to re-establish an authentic national tradition of liberal intellectual work.

The last historical event (the agreement about the end of the USSR) finally destroyed the old Stalinist system of ideological control and opened new perspectives for contemporary Russian literary studies. The politics of Yeltsin's post-perestroika left almost nothing of the previous system of ideological opposition and opened up the way for Russian theorists to become acquainted with the world experience in the humanities.

But it is not so easy for new Russia to return to the family of civilized people. After the party propagandist pressure stopped, we immediately found ourselves in an ideological and methodological vacuum: the old principles and approaches (which were all we had been taught and had known) were now quite inadequate. Whole areas of Russian literature might as well have been foreign, while the newest phenomena of other cultures seemed like messages from another planet.

Russian literary and cultural theory still remains *homotextual* and monomethodological. 'Literature' is regarded as a sphere of pure poetic creation, imagination and fantasy, whereas the works of philosophers, theologians, historians, critics and aestheticians are not considered to be 'literary' texts. The main method of literary analysis is still the revealing of social-cultural context and the investigation of the class roots of literary activity.

Only now after the final crushing of the Soviet Communist ideological system have we begun to understand the essential need for the acceptance and critical evaluation of the actual ideas of our Western colleagues. We understand also that we should not simply imitate or copy them, but rather attempt to synthesize them with some original Russian concepts which have remained untainted by vulgar militaristic terminology and political simplification.

It has now become possible, and necessary, to open the way for independent theoretical thought. But there remain some old difficulties. The tradition of free philosophical thought was almost completely annihilated by dogmatic propaganda, but the new ideas of twentieth-century Western theories are still enigmatic. Russian theorists now face a host of new problems, without new means of finding solutions. I can mark only a few of the prevailing questions and issues.

At the end of the twentieth century we are witnessing a very interesting revolutionary (or at least unusual) process of cultural transformation: the dominance of literature as the written word is over. New kinds of aesthetic communication impose themselves in the field of the humanities. These innovations show themselves in three main aspects.

Firstly, the technology of information through its permanent penetration into the sphere of art will radically change the traditional culture of writing and reading. 'Gutenberg's galaxy' is collapsing; the written (printed) word as a particular form of modern knowledge will disappear. Simultaneously, another cultural universe is forming: 'the galaxy of Norbert Wiener'. A new cultural phenomenon is coming – the *electronic 'word'* – which will dislodge and replace the habitual contour of the book as a source of knowledge. (Even the 'Book of Books' – the Bible – will come to its contemporary recipients from TV and video screens.) Literature will be superseded by *hyper-literature* – computer software which imitates traditional genres but creates a totally new sort of aesthetic communication. Then will come 'virtual reality' – a unique synthesis of different kinds of creativity and reception.

Secondly, literature itself signals to us the exhaustion of its *usual* (i.e. creative) forms; the texts of postmodernist writers offer almost no new verbal artistic conceptions but consist of a free play of already-existing literary constructions, as sets of citation and recombination of older and more modern traditions. The favourite creative principle of postmodern prose and verse (and particularly of drama) is the ancient Latin genre *centon*: a composition organized as a complex of another's words, images and manners, through which an author plays with a reader.

Thirdly, the clearest dimension for the articulation of these shifting processes lies in the sphere of *literary criticism* and *literary theory*. Here we find not only indications of these *literary* transformations but the explication of their roots in general *cultural* development.

Modern Western cultural consciousness still remains totally *literary*; everything in it is *texte* in its literal and metaphorical sense, the process and the result of reading/interpretation. All modern Western intellectual history is centred round literature; a *European* (American as well as Russian) person derives the main part of his/her everyday, spiritual, and cultural experience from literary texts, breaking through books to the enigmas of Being and constructing his attitudes to God, nature, society, and himself on a foundation of written Word(s). Essentially, the whole history of the modern West has been the experience of reading, and the verbal substitution of all outer and inner phenomena.

A contemporary cultural person is formed in the universe of the already-elaborated (interpreted) word; his/her world is almost completely a world of readings, rereadings and (mis)interpretations where the *word* has become a measure of Being and a device for existence. And now, suddenly, the time has come to change the essence and form of this principal source of human cultural praxis; new modes of creating, keeping, transforming and representing knowledge have appeared, and these demand new ways of thinking about the basics of the verbal representation (or 'rationalities', as

Jonathan Culler presents it in 'Framing the Sign') of cultural experience.

From this point of view the modern world and its consciousness look overloaded with cultural signs and seem not to need any *new* signifiers. They appear to be satisfied with the process of recombination and reinterpretation of the *old*. Postmodern literature proves it brilliantly. *Homo structurus* is replaced by *homo interpretus*, writing is changed by interpretative reading, and the creation of new signs gives way to play with the old ones. Total signification is replaced by total interpretation. *Hermeneia versus Semiosis*.

This process of literary transformation puts modern theorists of culture up against a whole set of problems which had already appeared in the traditional systems of thought; but they are still waiting for investigation and solution in the framework of the new cultural *paradigm of (An)other*. Contemporary literature and those who study it now both yield to a kind of 'hermeneutic circle' where the first problem is to make a Word say more about itself; and the understanding of the word (i.e. the very existence of literary theory) itself becomes a second problem. The process of up-to-date verbal/ literary understanding/comprehension cannot be recollected and realized without attracting the experience of *another*.

One of these 'traditional/innovative' problems is that of aesthetic reception, critical interpretation and evaluation of literary work as a *cultural* (i.e. socially significant) phenomenon. What are the foundations of the aesthetic and communicative functions of literature? What is the basis of reading as an experience of (An)other? Where and how does a literary work realize itself as an aesthetic event with artistic value? These questions are still on the agenda and the new exploration of them seems vital, productive and provocative, especially in the present Russian cultural situation.

Contemporary literary theory is based on the notion of reading and interpretation as universal methods of dealing with life. However, the total textualization of being, started by structuralists, has now come to its logical conclusion: all the world around us appears as the process of our self-readings, and all signs become only the starting-points for nonstop interpretation.

This process seems to be worldwide, but it obviously takes place differently in different countries. Thus American culture is a leader not only because of its pre-eminence in information technology but also because it was American (or American-based) theorists of culture (though some of them have French names – Jacques Derrida, Paul de Man, Michel Foucault, Jacques Lacan, et al.) who succeeded in understanding and communicating the essence of this process. The experience of American thinkers seems really indispensable now, primarily in Russia where the new intellectual development has just started, and these thinkers constitute that necessary *voice of Another* which marks the border between old and new attitudes to the *word*.

According to modern philosophical and linguistic theory, 'World is Word given to mankind for reinterpretation'. A person receives this World/Word as already interpreted, and must then understand this universal text and translate it into the available intellectual forms. The chief precondition of this task is a scholarly dialogue between different cultural mentalities, grounded in a sophisticated *hermeneutic* theory of literature and its reception. (At the present time, some Russian theorists (including the author of this essay) are trying to reconstruct the tradition of hermeneutics broken in Russia in the 1930s. My Senior Doctoral Dissertation, 'Hermeneutic and Reader-Response Criticism in Modern British and American Literary Studies', was acknowledged by the Scientific Council as 'the first contemporary step in applying the hermeneutic approach to literature'.) The statement: 'Hermes has arrived here now, so we must let him speak' (Shapiro, Gary, and Alan Sica, eds. *Hermeneutics: Questions and Prospects*. Amherst: University of Massachusetts Press, 1984, p. 3) is more than topical in the process of Western–Russian intellectual convergence. But the new and real perspectives of Hermes' speech may be opened only through the process of dialogue between his different enthusiasts, who were previously divided by ideological barriers.

The broad-minded character of modern Western hermeneutics (seen in the works of Martin Heidegger, Hans-Georg Gadamer, Paul Ricoeur, Richard Palmer, William Spanos and Jonathan Culler), the latest concepts of reader-response criticism and multiculturalism give hope to Russian scholars who are studying the same methodological path and attempting a commitment to this mode of intellectual activity.

How can a literary investigation or any other sort of work in the humanities influence the political and cultural situation? What can a person of letters do professionally in the contemporary intellectual situation, one where we are not just losing *some* kinds of national tradition but destroying our essential cultural values and changing all kinds of identification: ethnic, social, racial, personal, linguistic and even sexual? Can our habits of text-analysis serve as an adequate means of cultural consolidation, or are they simply the toys of indifferent minds? These questions seem to have an existential interest for both Russian and Western theorists of culture.

The present period of Russian literary theory and cultural studies cannot avoid the experience of the Western humanities. In the new absence of ideological and political barriers let us bridge the artificial gaps between different cultures for our mutual development and understanding.

17

Specific Interliterary Communities and the Comparative Study of Literature

Yury Azarov

In the course of the last few years there has been born a tradition of co-operation between the Institute of World Literature of the Russian Academy of Sciences and the Institute of World Literature of the Slovak Academy of Sciences (Bratislava), and theorists of literature from other countries. All these scholars of literature were united by an international project, 'Specific Interliterary Communities', headed by Professor Dionýz Durišin of the Slovak Academy. The publication of ten books is planned. The present essay deals with some recently-printed books of the series.

Dionýz Durišin is a literary scholar, theorist and historian of literature well known not only in Slovakia and other European countries but throughout the world. His books on the methodology and theory of comparative literary studies have been translated into many languages. The centre-point of his works of the last few years lies in the theoretical problem of elaborating new criteria in comparative literary criticism.

The problem is to overcome all the imperfections of traditional comparatistics, which do not give adequate answers to the principal questions of historical-literary development. The most immediate question in that sense is that of transition from comparison to determination of the laws of literary evolution. The need to investigate problems of the kind is obvious, and the projected ten-volume series was founded as an attempt to draw general conclusions from the rich experience of investigating national literatures of various countries. This task has become an attempt to lift comparatistics above the level of the mere investigation of various influences and borrowings. National literary relationships and affinities on the one hand, and interliterary relationships and affinities on the other, are basically governed by the same laws. At the same time they are characterized by a whole series of differences that must not be forgotten in the methodics of research.

One of the direct stimuli for such a large-scale investigation has been the work on the 'History of World Literature' (or HWL) at the Institute of World Literature in Moscow, which has attempted to solve a whole series of theoretical questions of comparative literary studies. The most notable questions relate to the comparative characteristics of literature in various, geographical regions, and a working definition of the term 'world literature' or 'world-wide literature'. These questions have been touched upon in practical work by the founders of HWL, but they are still pressing problems for the theory of literary criticism.

It is necessary to stress that the theory of interliterary process is based on an understanding of world literature which repudiates the analytic methods that take only the best-known masterpieces of literature and the most distinguished writers. On the contrary, Dionýz Durišin is a follower of the so-called historical-literary conception, bringing out a complex rather than a selective analysis, and that very conception presupposes the use of the results of a general study of interliterary process.

Thus Durišin's theory, according to his intention, must give an exact meaning to the notion of 'world literature' and provide a concrete definition. Russian theorists of literature such as N. I. Conrad, V. M. Zhirmunsky, and I. G. Neupokoeva were his competent predecessors, whose ideas he used while formulating the problems of 'interliterariness'.

Thorough preliminary analysis of the interliterary process and an examination of its regularities presupposes the widest and most systematic study of various regional literatures. That is why specialists in literatures who have, as it seems, little in common are taking part in the project: beginning, for example, with national literatures of the Northern Caucasus and finishing with those of Latin-American and African countries. The essence of the aim and goal that have been put before the participants is to master in certain theoretical aspects the specific material of this or that national literature – the task that can be implemented by a numerous and highly professional collective of scholars.

The main feature, and the obvious advantage, of the proposed methodology is the formulation of the notion of literary centres. We would remind readers that in the discipline of 'History of World

Literature' the notions of national literature or history of national literature have been used as the main units of literary study. According to the theory of interliterary process, national literature is only one component of a complex analysis, which, contrary to common opinion, does not possess a universal character. It is also important that a literary process be analysed in synchronic and dia-chronic aspects. The goal of the analysis includes study of literature as a whole, from ancient times to the present day; that means making a general study of separate historical-literary units, and the final stage in that process is the community of world literature.

First it is necessary to single out initial and elementary categories and notions. None of these notions can exist in isolation, they have to be brought together in some initial system with its own inner hierarchy and with distinct terminology. Not claiming to be com-prehensive, Durišin introduces such notions as 'component of litera-ture', 'work of literature', 'author', 'literary school' and many others. He also introduces categories that have not been studied closely from the point of view of comparatistics: 'oral tradition of clan society', 'mediaeval ethnic literature', 'new age ethnic literature' and others. Most of these categories had already been widely used by literary critics and historians of literature, but had never been supplied with adequate theoretical explanation.

'National literature' is a category which predominates in con-temporary literary-critical study. Obviously it could quite possibly exist in its diachronic aspect, but it does not constitute an initial unit of 'interliterariness'. This can be explained by the fact that it is not nowadays easy to find a country with homogenous ethnic structure and culture. The articles of *Specific Interliterary Communities, 5* (we can take as examples E. K. Ryauzova's and V. D. Sedelnik's articles and some others) make quite clear the possibility of modifying the category depending on conditions of common existence of different peoples within a state boundary. Some other categories ('component of literature', 'groups', 'school') have been less studied and play a certain role as components in the complex analysis of literary phe-nomena. Also interesting is the inclusion within the context of 'interliterariness' of such categories as 'literature of nationalities'. Another important aim of the investigation is to single out various components and models of development on the basis of concrete literary material. Here lies one of the main advantages of Durišin's theory of comparison over other theories.

The fifth book of the projected series is a revised edition in Russian of the book *Osobitné medziliterárne spolocenstvá, 4* (Bratislava: Ústav svetovej literatúry SAV, 1992), which was prepared for publication at the Institute of World Literature of the Russian Academy of Sciences under the supervision of Professor I. D. Nikiforova and edited by Dionýz Durišin. His article, which is presented in the book, formulates a conception of the history of world literature which is compared with other widespread current conceptions: 'attended by conception', 'literary-critical', 'historical-literary'. Durišin understands world literature as a system of ideas, the result of extensive literary investigations and subjective notions of world literature. This is typical of human consciousness at a certain stage of its development. Hence, according to Durišin, the notion of 'history of world literature' is not invariable, because it continually modifies and reorganizes itself 'innerly' as literature itself develops.

The collective monograph under discussion demonstrates the logical continuation and development of the previous books of the series. Its authors, as do the authors of the fourth volume, use European literatures. At the same time, with respect to African literatures – this material has not been sufficiently studied from the point of view of 'interliterariness' – the investigation demonstrates clearly the complexity and historically developing forms of creative literary activity in former colonies and their very complicated but close relations in the metropolitan countries – England, Portugal, Spain and France. Comparative study of creative work in former colonies clearly demonstrates the possibility of thorough analysis of the literatures produced by the nationalities which, before colonization, were at a pre-national stage of development or in the process of nation formation.

A perfect example of this phenomenon is investigated in I. D. Nikiforova's article on literatures in tropical Africa. The author affirms that the material under discussion cannot be characterized objectively using old literary categories, which are based as a rule on the peculiarities of Western European literary studies. African countries, however, have a number of specific characteristics of their own: languages in former metropolitan states which have a unifying function; a community of national literatures using different languages within the boundaries of one state; a community of different national literatures using different languages in one country. It is notable that the theory of interliterary communities is applicable in all these cases, while other theories 'do not work'. Like Nikiforova's article, that of N. D. Lynkhovskaya examines the problem of place in the study of world literatures, focusing on the French language in

tropical Africa. The author has managed to demonstrate conclusively that on 'transitional stages' of historical-literary development there exist different types of artistic consciousness, the
literatures become 'open' that is, permeable to different types of
connections and influences – and these connections create starting-
points for the emergence of typological analogies.

A. F. Kofman's article 'Typological Peculiarities of the Spanish-
American Interliterary Community' presents another example of
theoretical generalization of concrete literary material. The author
investigates specific features of the Spanish-American community,
which differs greatly from the communities of the so-called
'European type', and demonstrates clearly that Spanish-American
literature presents a specific type of interliterary community which
has no equals in its scale (more than twenty countries), and the
strength of its influence.

One more article deserving of special interest is by K. K.
Sultanov. It touches upon an existing subject of interliterary process
in literatures of the northern Caucasus. An adequate analysis of
these literatures demands quite a new and different quality of interpretation and differentiation of the levels of analysis. According to
the author, existing conceptual contradiction can be explained by
the fact that an investigation limited within the bounds of national
literature misrepresents the real scale of national literary development. The potentialities inherent in national literary interpretation
have been completely exhausted, and without a new interpretation
of the communicative function of national literature, there arises a
kind of methodological crisis. At the same time, as Sultanov shows
in his article, the theory and systematics of interliterary process give
the scholar of literature a reliable frame of reference.

Literatures traditionally included in the so-called Russian literary
phenomenon are so original in their character that it is not an easy
task to compare them. N. S. Nadiarnykh, however, in her article on
interliterary community in the 'area of Russian literature' at the end
of the nineteenth and the beginning of the twentieth centuries,
rejecting the dogmatism of former times and making good use of the
theory of interliterary process, demonstrates a many-sided correlation between literary 'context' and 'text'. She shows that a national-
cultural 'code' constantly displays itself, because at every new stage
of development it enters into a new correlation with 'context'. In
Nadiarnykh's opinion, every literature develops according to the
logic and laws of historical and aesthetic choice. These laws are constantly modified in new historical conditions and determine the

character of interliterary communities and interliterary connections in many ways.

It is necessary to mention also E. K. Ryauzova's article on forms of development in Portuguese-language African literatures. The author worked in close co-operation with Dionýz Durišin for many years. In her doctoral thesis she analysed Portuguese-language African literatures according to the theory of interliterary communities. In the investigation presented in this book Ryauzova formulates the contemporary characteristics of the material under research: the community of Portuguese-language literatures is a living and constantly-developing phenomenon. In the course of its development it reflects different historical factors. The degree of their influence differs: at a certain stage some factors are dominant, while others are subsidiary. This 'unsteady balance' is connected with the specific character of cultural development and historical traditions.

A. G. Cheriomin's article 'Problems in Studying South African Literature as a Specific Type of Interliterary Community' also demonstrates the theory of 'interliterariness'. The analysis of this material, which is unique among the literary processes in Africa, reveals the peculiarities of English-language prose in local African languages. South Africa, in Cheriomin's opinion, is unique in respect of the formation and development of a multinational and multiracial cultural community, which integrates its own cultural traditions of local population and colonists (Afrikaners and Britons), as well as artistic experience of world culture.

Literatures of the Swiss confederation that could serve as a model for a study of the co-existence of different languages and literatures within state boundaries are analysed by V. D. Sedelnik, who also contributes to the collective book *Systematic of Interliterary Process*. His conclusions prove Dionýz Durišin's statements concerning historical conditionality and the temporal limits of specific interliterary communities. At the same time the author warns against a straightforward schematizing of state, national, and linguistic characteristics. It is obvious that a certain scheme exists, but it changes over time and is not invariable: according to Sedelnik, it is necessary to clarify the notions of 'standard' and 'specific' interliterary communities, because every single community has a unique character and shows resistance to any unification even if this resistance is on a theoretical level only. The subject of this article is even more significant, because Swiss literature is considered as a striking example of a tradition of peaceful co-existence of different languages and cultures.

If we turn our attention to the Slovak articles, written by the contributors from the Institute of World Literature of the Slovak Academy of Sciences (those articles are fewer in number than in the Slovak edition of the book), it is important to stress that they all demonstrate a highly professional approach. We would like to mention X. Colnarová's and M. Pokorný's articles analysing the connection of interliterary and extraliterary factors. This analysis, in the author's opinion, proves the necessity of taking into consideration social conditions in relation to literary evolution. E. Tkáciková's work also deserves interest. It deals with the Latin context of old Slovak literature, and it shows up some insufficiently studied problems in the literary works studied. The investigation demonstrates clearly the fruitfulness of this methodology in clarifying uninvestigated features in the separate literatures.

As can be seen, in all the examples just analysed, the theory of 'interliterariness' gives to the literary theorist a perfect set of laws governing the genesis and development of heterogeneous and constantly changing interliterary communities: these groupings can be analysed in terms of the connections between various literatures. The most significant examples of this are the literatures of former Portuguese colonies, literatures in Latin-American countries, and the very complicated material of English and American literature and literary criticism.

A significant indication of the universal character of the theory under discussion is that not only literatures, but also literary-critical trends, schools and theoretical conceptions can be analysed. The interdependence of these things has still not been sufficiently investigated, either as a worldwide or on a European scale, in spite of the fact that they are never confined in narrow national boundaries. In the present book the first attempts have been made at comparative analysis of literary theory and criticism, and this opens a new and broad area of literary investigation (Y. A. Azarov's article 'English and American Literary Criticism of the Twentieth Century as a Phenomenon of Interliterary Community'). From our point of view it would be interesting to analyse in terms of 'interliterariness' such trends as hermeneutics, structuralism, the mythological school and many others.

One of the most important tasks in the sphere of 'interliterariness' studies is a thorough working out of the terminology. This has been necessitated by the fact that participants in the project do not always use terms according to the rules of literary terminology.

The question of improving the system of 'notions' has been discussed at the most recent meetings of the collective of authors in Moscow and Bratislava. At these meetings, an outline of the future book (*Regularities of Interliterary Process*) has been worked out. This is being prepared for publication in 1995 and is planned to contain several special articles concerning the problem of the terminology of 'interliterariness' and its correlation with the traditional terminology of literary studies. The main attention will be focused on 'clear' theory and its connection with the basis of conclusions in previous books. In all the recent volumes of the project, a constant striving to master new concrete literary material is characteristic. In this connection it will be necessary to collect all the methodological discoveries and 'digress' from concrete material and clearly defined notions and categories. This could permit the formulation of well-composed theoretical conceptions of the unity and interdependency of world and national historically-literary process.

The search for an optimum methodological system – the initial goal of the project – has just been fulfilled. The chosen 'collective principle' of work is at present justified. Future investigations, undoubtedly, will not only broaden but deepen the investigation of the problems. A first significant step on this path is Dionýz Durišin's *What is World Literature?*, which considerably widens the range of literature studied by comparatistics.

The collective of authors hopes that the project 'Specific Interliterary Communities' makes a decisive contribution to the solution of current problems of the theory of literature and, in marking the ways for future development, raises contemporary comparatistics to a higher level. The future of this discipline depends not only on our willingness to leave the narrow circle of comparisons and search for further analogies, but also on our ability to understand what determines the broad regularities of interliterary process. To do this we must next turn to the sphere of our concluding category of literary investigation – that of world literature.

18

Home of Memory: Hospitality, Closure and Eastern Europe

TADEUSZ SŁAWEK

Thus – between the breath of Asia and the west . . .

C. K. Norwid, Memento

1. The Boat and the Plough

When the West, driven by economic and epistemological curiosity, begins to expand, Poland – despite its imperial power within Central Europe – chooses another course. Sebastian Klonowic, in his 1595 chorographical poem, *The Raftsman* (*Flis*), advises Poles to exercise restraint and resoluteness when faced with the prospect of the sea-bound exploratory economy in which the Other, seen as a distant and uncanny alien, figures so prominently. In the prefatory Latin poem 'Ad Zoilum' Klonowic qualifies as 'unhappy' (*infelix*) one who prefers 'boats, oars and sails' (*naves et remos, et lina tumentia ventis*) to the pleasures of the 'solid ground' (*solidissima tellus*) (Klonowic 1951: 3). The warning is serious and not to be easily dismissed as it comes also as a diagnosis of melancholy or madness. The Other-oriented self, the exploratory ego of the merchant/discoverer/politician is, in its choice of sea voyage, firstly guilty of madness and insane motivation, and, secondly, even when it reaches a safe harbour it is not so much to enjoy safety and shelter but to recognize and cure the mental malady. The name of the ancient port Antikyra appears in the poem to signify the safety and mental balance which we have ourselves disturbed by wrong (cultural) choices (the culture of *naves* rather than the culture of *solidissima tellus*): in the hills surrounding the harbour local inhabitants gathered veratrum, a herb used as a popular medication against insanity. It is in Antikyra that the troubled sailor will, by 'swallowing veratrum' learn whether the 'sea winds are safer than the solid ground'.

Thus, at the beginning of the era which, by a series of geographical discoveries was, in a not too distant future, to open both political and economic markets of free enterprise, a Polish poet and statesman (Klonowic was a mayor of Lublin, a major city of Eastern Poland) diagnoses this course of development as 'mad' and qualifies the culture of sea-journey as transgressive and therefore subject to therapy. The pathogenic character of this cultural turn is based on the interweaving of ethical and economic arguments. It is the pecuniary economy of mercantilism and debt which is largely responsible for the distortion of cultural models: Klonowic clearly indicates that 'we are happy' as long as we 'have our bread at home, and do not owe anything to anyone' (*Niechaj nie igra szczęściem, kto ma w domu / Swój chleb, a długu nie winien nikomu*) (Klonowic 1951: 47).

The debt/credit oriented husbandry is not only suspect in terms of monetary but, equally importantly, also of ontological imbalance: it is the desire to own more (and therefore the dire necessity to *owe* more) that violates the principle of *well-placedness of things* which organizes the world in terms of the familiar and domestic. *Home is where things are well placed*, i.e. where space is arranged by the laws of territorialization of things and the rigorous connections holding between them. Thus, Klonowic can write: 'Let not him play with luck who has at home / His bread, and does not owe anything to anyone' (Klonowic 1951: 47). The ethics of the Polish landed-gentry culture was founded upon the moderation and restraint ('restrain yourself, oh virtuous Pole') which allowed for both wealth and at-homeness ('You can have money without a vessel', Klonowic 1951: 47) and, at the same time, was perceived as a clear alternative to Western expansionism: 'Let us give priority to Spaniards and Germans / Frenchmen, Italians and other foreigners, / Let them discover new worlds and be paid with gold' (Klonowic 1951: 46). It is worth noting that, despite the dominating tendency towards self-confinement demonstrated by the landed gentry, mercantile developments in Europe did not remain unnoticed. Piotr Grabowski writing in 1596 notices with some anxiety and regret that 'other nations promulgate, spread and fix themselves all over the wide world, that the German spreads in all countries with his commerce, crafts, and soldiery and even agriculture . . . Englishmen spread over islands ‟and ocean shores unfathomable, over the wide and opulent India . . .' (Topolski 1986: 185).

The figure of the ship carries a moral signification; the late mediaeval ship of fools (the *Narrenschiff* of Sebastian Brandt) is as early as the late sixteenth century transformed into a metaphor of economic excess (the boat of greed) and ontological de-naturalization, i.e deregulation of being. The excesses of the economy lead to the ontological alienation of people from their own element: 'The ship was first conceived by greed' (Klonowic 1951: 39) and, ultimately, unnaturally change man's element. In this process the story of Icarus is paradigmatic: 'Icarus let you know in his testament / That you should not play with an alien element' (Klonowic 1951: 32).

It is the philosophy of 'home' (to which we shall be returning in this essay) which differentiates Poland from the West, which has evolved towards a dispersion resulting from curiosity. The 'solid ground' Klonowic espouses speaks not only of the stability of the soil but also of the familiar and the known as the essential human element. The ideas of 'measure' and of the 'Other' are central to this thought. The agricultural economy founded upon natural rhythms of production was particularly suited to support domestic exchange: production was based upon a natural contract between God's gift of productivity (God being the chief guarantor and, thus, a part of the domestic household) and man's reciprocal gesture of tenderness and grateful care extended towards the given. Hence, to tend fields was considered to be both productive (therefore *re*-creating a new life) and, what is particularly worth emphasizing, immune to the *hubris*, the excessive pride and greed, of 'original' novelty, of the creative genius which, in an offensive and blasphemous gesture, replaces God's *fiat* with its own initiative. To farm land was to be a recreative, therefore un-original creator, to humbly receive God's gift and reciprocate by sheltering and developing it in a manner which recognized the 'measure' (or as Shakespeare puts it in *Troilus and Cressida*, 'degree'). To be a farmer is to know the limit, also to know where to turn one's horses at the end of the field, and it is the violation of this limit that Klonowic notices in the Western economy: 'The sea knows no bottom / Neither does luxury, / It always wants more, and thus what labour gains / Luxury will lose' (Klonowic 1951: 39).

Re-productive production: a baroque rhetorical figure for a baroque husbandry in which man and God indulge in an economic bond based on the operation of gift-giving and sheltering. The repetitive character of this process seems the essence of the landed gentry culture; memory was, at the same time, trained by the agricultural actions undertaken each year at a specific season and relaxed by the absence of outrageous novelty, of the Other who/ which would be so alien and threatening (or, at least, exceedingly strange) that it would strain the memory in forcing (or even shattering) it to remember. *Home is where things are well placed and therefore memory is not* (and cannot be) *a source of pain.* In such a world memory can, in pleasurable mode, perform its main function which is 'to establish connections' (Terdiman 1993: 295), a task particularly difficult and even painful when one encounters absolute novelty, i.e. something which we cannot relate or be connected to. When Klonowic attacks Western European culture it is precisely with the help of the adjective 'new' (*nowy*) which speaks of the devastating role played by curiosity and of the negligent attitude towards the culture's memory which is interrupted by the excessive ordeals of the (absolutely) Other. Thus, a Pole is admonished not to look for anything in 'a distant county, in the new world' (Klonowic 1951: 32), and the cultural turn towards the new is interpreted as the exhaustion of the old, a restless movement of the mind and technology which, generating new desires, tries to destroy memory by exposing it to the radical and extreme challenge of the new: 'But the human thought [Klonowic uses the word *przemysł* which later acquired the meaning of 'industry'] is so bold, / That this old world seemed to man too small, / And therefore having crossed the ocean, he found a new world' (Klonowic 1951: 45–6). *Home* (the space of well-placed things) *is the paradise of memory: it leisurely remembers without effort, becomes unconscious memory of endless repetitive cycles of re-production, undisturbed by the dream (or nightmare) of the Other.*

The agricultural economy reinforced the sense of 'home' by the impression of opulence and luxury. Even if for some time in the sixteenth and seventeenth centuries this impression was true, nevertheless one has to notice with economic historians that such an economy, even if based on massive export of crops, does not construct a healthy general economy precisely because it is an extension of 'home', rather than a confrontation with the (economically) Other. Jerzy Topolski comments: 'If we were to look at the economy of 16th century Poland from the point of view of the export of corn which reached its apogee in the first half of the 17th century we could arrive at very optimistic conclusions. But, in fact, the export of corn was a mere function of the development of the manorial economy and cannot be considered as evidence of economic growth . . .' (Topolski 1986: 191).

The Other does not disappear from the picture, but it is allotted the place of a parasite, i.e. of someone who comes to share with us our feast in a position of one who is not so much invited as one whose needs are recognized in a taciturn ethical decision: 'It is good, everyone knows it, to lend bread to your neighbours, / But do not try to bring bread to him, / If he wants it, let him come himself' (Klonowic 1951: 49). Expansionism *à rebours*; the sense of well-placedness, of *habitus*, of a homogeneity of a specific style, is so strong that it does not allow for openness, but only for a further closure. I offer you a piece of my bread (we shall come back to the motif of eating later on in our essay) but only on condition that, firstly, you truly need it, and secondly, that you will come to me to fetch it, that I will not have to leave my premises, my home. A specific transformation of the Other which apparently looks like its neglect but which is, in fact, a definite ethical relationship (which we will describe later) with one who is received on our terms and only if he or she accepts the categories of the familiar. In the same way as the ocean is translated into the Vistula ('Give up the sea, and / Sail only on the Vistula', Klonowic 1951: 51), the Other is translated into a 'domestic', into one who eats my bread next to me with my permission. The Other as parasite: 'To parasite means to eat next to' (Serres 1982: 7). Both these elements (of proximity and nourishing) will come back later in our essay as instrumental in establishing the Slavonic model of the Other as subject to the relationship of hospitality, which I consider significantly different from the Anglo-Saxon.

Such a domestication of the Other who is 'remembered' as a part of one's household, accounts for the only type of excess allowed in the otherwise strictly regulated culture of measure and well-placed objects – the excess of hospitality. In this model of social intercourse the Other is neutralized by the complete translation into the cultural *habitus* of the host and, by the same process, it is incorporated by the host, becomes a part of his body. A religious undercurrent of the cultural enclosure: 'Gifted [the one to whom things are given] always eats the same thing, the host, and this eternal host gives over and over, till he breaks . . . The host is not a prey, but the host. The other one is not a predator but a parasite' (Serres 1982: 7).

What *Flis* documents is the moment of a certain cultural decision: whereas the West was moving outwards, Poland was more and more

involved in cultural self-enclosure. The momentum of memory aims
at conserving the known with the minimum amount of novelty, i.e.
memory does not have to struggle with the new material but merely,
in a less and less conscious manner, perpetuate old patterns, beha-
viours and structures. The attitude towards the Other is that of a
host who admits the Other within his own territory only to demonstrate the ethics of measure (giving out the surplus of bread, 'It is an
honourable thing / To give out bread you have the surplus of . . .',
Klonowic 1951: 48) which was soon transformed into the ethics of
excessive hospitality. Three partitions of Poland at the end of the
eighteenth century demonstrated the limits of this culture by
showing the limits of the philosophy according to which the Other
was always to be incorporated within one's own culture and turned
into a neighbour. Such a neutralization of the Other as a parasitic
guest, interesting and productive as it was as an ethical relation,
could not be held for long on the political plane. Politics changes
the Other into a predator, and the host becomes a prey.

2. Home and Well-placed Things

It is Romanticism which re-enacts the drama of memory: not only is
the nation bereft of the state and the official mnemonic machine of
archives, bureaucracy and education, but the memory function has
been replaced by the countermemory of other political powers
(Russia, Prussia and Austria) which exercise all their powers to erase
the traces of the original memory, to de-memorialize nation.

This task is approached through the slow, but permanent, en-
croachment of the alien official administrative structure upon the
familiar, unofficial mode of community life which was subsumed
under the name of 'home'. The 'state'–'home' dichotomy also
involves memory: if, as we have said, 'home' is a place of well
ordered things and pleasurable, effortless memories of the domestic
and the known, then the 'state' challenges memory with the new and
alien (one may wonder to what extent corruption, infamous malady
of Central European bureaucracy, was the effect of a popular attempt
to come to terms with the 'home'–'state' controversy splitting
people's lives. To corrupt and bribe was to turn a member of the
alien structure into one's domestic, to familiarize a foreign force by
puncturing its smooth and seemingly adamant face). In Tönnies's
terms, *Gemeinschaft* tries to salvage its territory against the incursions
of *Gesellschaft*: 'In *Gemeinschaft* with one's family, one lives from

birth on, bound to it in weal and woe. One goes into *Gesellschaft* as one goes into a foreign country' (Tönnies 1963: 33–4).

It is not difficult to see the work of the 'foreign country' in this passage: the West in the late nineteenth century evokes the nostalgia of the self-enclosed and self-contained community which for Poland was already a hegemonic cultural model in the seventeenth century. The only, but dramatic, difference was that *whereas western Europe thinks of the community as of a small, pre-state unit, the Polish landed gentry tries to visualize it on a gigantic scale as the model of an imperial political power*. For Polish culture it spells the extension of 'home' on a massive scale; Poland thrives on the utopian projection of political structure as a 'home'. Similarly, Western nostalgia for the *Gemeinschaft* (evident as late as the commune of the 1960s) is precisely a result of the wearing out of the sense of 'home'. Richard Terdiman is right in claiming in his work on memory that this nostalgia 'has little to do with our wistful contemporary regret for the past, but rather with what physicians of the eighteenth and nineteenth centuries described and treated as a full-blown illness precipitated by separating the sufferer from the familiarity and security of home' (Terdiman 1993: 42–3).

This implies: (1) a move from the world of well-placed things to a world where the placement of things is hypothetical and provisional, (2) a separation from the world where memory did not have to embrace the new but merely rehearse and reconfirm the past, and (3) a defence of the unconscious, lived memory against the proliferation of the alien (both in terms of character and political implications) official memory. This shift definitely tries to depoliticize memory and bring it in to the realm of the everyday, and in a silent, unspoken manner sees this move as cryptopolitical.

Nowhere is it more striking than in the 1834 Polish national epic *Pan Tadeusz* written by Adam Mickiewicz. Set amidst the cataclysms of the Napoleonic wars which reshuffled Europe and its social and political order, the poem deliberately focuses on the representation of the traditional community and its local pleasures and 'strifes'. Having described the life of the population of the country manor and its dependants, Mickiewicz says: 'Such were the pleasures and the petty strife / Of peaceful Lithuanian country life' (Mickiewicz 1966: 26). This domestic peacefulness is grounded in the transference of lived memory which is determined by (1) the perpetuation of the traditional mores which, (2) being directly related to the wisdom revealed by Transcendence, (3) have the power to repel the eroding forces of the Other threatening from the outside and extol the Other as a 'domestic' (see the whole series of domestics, of household servants and lease-holders in *Pan Tadeusz*). Thus, in a characteristic passage from Book I describing people returning from the fields at the end of the day's work we read:

> And now the company are turning home,
> Gay but in order: first the children come
> Accompanied by their tutor: in their train
> The Judge himself with Mistress Chamberlain,
> And at their side the Chamberlain is found,
> The rest of all their family around;
> Behind the old folk the young ladies stepped,
> The young men walked beside them, though they kept
> A half-pace back; decorum so demanded.
> This marching order no one has commanded,
> Each kept his proper place of his own will.
> The Judge observed the ancient customs still,
> Nor suffered disrespect or negligence
> For age or birth, rank or intelligence.
> 'Such order', he would say, 'makes nations great
> And families, and without it they abate.'
> The household grew accustomed to that style,
> And, kin or stranger, he that stayed awhile
> Within the Judge's house quickly acquired
> The customs that the very place inspired.
> (Mickiewicz 1966: 8)

There are, at least, two crucial moments in this passage. The first relates to the somehow 'objective', 'impersonal' character of the order which has not been 'commanded' by anyone. The philosophy of 'well-placed objects' results from the internalization of rules considered to be one's own integral decisions ('Each kept his proper place of his own will'). The second demonstrates that this internalization is the effect of a hegemonic structure of the group: we learn that it is the Judge who considers himself the warden of the 'style' and who can enforce its execution upon both 'kin and stranger'. *The secret of the community's lived memory seems to reside in its transference from one particular hegemonic individual (or group) on to the structure of reality itself*: despite the fact that the Judge is nominated as one whose work secures the customs, the final line speaks of the modes of social behaviour as belonging to the whole space rather than to one individual ('The customs that the very place inspired'). (For a more detailed discussion of this problem see Sławek and Wesling 1991).

From other passages in the same book of the poem we learn that the 'structure of feeling' (to use Raymond Williams's celebrated phrase) of the community is analogous to the cosmic structure determined by Transcendence ('The Lord of Earth knows when our toil should end, / And when the sun, his workman, doth descend / 'Tis time the husbandman should quit the land', Mickiewicz 1966: 7) and mistrust of importations from other cultures. The latter point is particularly interesting because not only does it spell a mistrustful attitude towards the Other, but it also conceives of a whole cultural theory according to which the society is not governed by a system of laws but by one specific Law. In other words, culture is not a question of laws (or a law) but of The Law. Hence the French Revolution is viewed as a product of 'French cafés' and 'novel laws' (Mickiewicz 1966: 15) which originate from a specific and blasphemous cultural forgetfulness or 'blindness'.

> Some clever Frenchmen had proclaimed as true
> 'All men are equal' – as if that were new,
> Though it had been declared in Holy Writ
> Of old, and every parson preaches it.
>   (Mickiewicz 1966: 14)

The world is revealed as the field of a struggle between the forces of memory which cement and centre the community around the Law, and forgetfulness which is based on the multiplicity of changeable and operational laws and de-centres the group by problematizing its very foundations. In the world governed by memory the new (and Other) is shown merely as a form of a certain 'as if', i.e. a kind of pretence and usurpation, an alienated part of the old which has been (temporarily) knocked off its 'proper place'; forgetfulness necessarily questions the system of 'well-placed objects' and thus tries to theorize it, to find the very foundations of the mnemonic system to demonstrate that it is not merely 'given' but constructed. It is interesting to note that the eponymous hero of the poem embodies the two traits of the mnemonic: a linkage with the past, and mistrust of the new and theoretical. We are told that his name was given him 'in memory of Kościuszko's fame' (Mickiewicz 1966: 6), and that although 'no dullard', he was loyal to the call of the group memory of the family and was more 'apt to the art of war, for learning less' (Mickiewicz 1966: 18).

The question which we are asking refers then to the problem of the relationship between memory and forgetting which, in Polish culture, received a particularly painful bias. On the one hand, the state with its machinery of memory (archives, administration, museums, education) was obliterated from the map of Europe in an unprecedented act of imposed forgetfulness, which European societies tolerated, very quickly incorporating it in their own cultural memories; on the other hand, the persistent memory of traditional mores preserved the nation and culture which, paradoxically, under normal circumstances would have needed forgetting (i.e. openness to the Other and unknown) in order to survive. The difficulty with the kind of memory which conserved (under extreme historical circumstance) Poland and other nations of Central Europe is that it tends to petrify and stabilize certain aspects of the past, thus monumentalizing them and therefore precluding people's attention from coming to terms with their everyday life. If the problem with cultural analysis is that it should not only identify a culture (with this, Polish tradition does not seem to have any difficulty) but try to 'grasp what it feels like to live within particular cultural and social circumstances, and how that feeling or "structure of feeling" . . . is embedded within and acts upon wider social practices' (Blundell et al. 1993: 3), then the preoccupation with the memory/memories of the past necessarily restrains (if not makes impossible) one's ability to understand the present. This has two crucial repercussions. One is the privileging of disciplinarity which is, as we have said, internalized and imagined as authentic personal choice. This attitude cast its shadow upon a divisionism of social life which is viewed as compartmentalized and segmented, and also in the embedded mistrust towards anything that refuses to be classified in its 'proper place' (this remark also refers to the academic tradition which with utmost suspicion looks at interdisciplinarity as a hybrid, and therefore dangerous, form of the Other). The Other is a clear juxtaposition of marked preference for a practice over a theory. *Practice secures the preservation of social mores by the unreflective use of lived memory; theory problematizes practices and could therefore potentially activate the sources of forgetting.*

It is also striking that both these effects were widely practised by the Communist authorities which, advocating amnesia of the bourgeois and aristocratic past, tried to focus maximum social attention precisely upon the past to dissuade the force of analysis from the present and theoretical. Already in 1907 Stanisław Brzozowski, the outstanding Polish philosopher of Marxist inclinations, saw the cultural predicament of an individual who is unable to perform acts of 'intricate and penetrating analysis' of one's 'state of spirit'. This inability was, according to Brzozowski, a result of the absence of one's awareness of the 'mechanisms of contemporary life' leading to ignorance of 'what evokes our spiritual states and into what kind of acts they are transformed' (Brzozowski 1984: 247). A contemporary Polish writer Kazimierz Brandys highlights the same inability forced upon the population by the Communist regime which discouraged the understanding of life as it is lived ('[t]he women are fighting with each other in long lines outside the butcher shops in the morning . . .') by the reinvigoration of the past: '[t]hey make sure that society continues to believe it has not lost its ancient traits. The Traditions of Uhlans, the slogans of positivism, romanticism, nationalism, and revolution, the world of Hussars – it is as if all this continued to be' (Brandys 1981: 122).

The ideal of absolutely interiorized memory is to restrain the (political, racial, economic) Other and regulate its appearance at our will so that the present can not be available for any theoretical analysis; this is necessarily so because of the absence of any breach, any crack in the monument of (imaginary) reality through which it could open some space for theory. We see here the trap of ideology as determined by Althusser: 'Ideology is indeed a system of representations, but in the majority of cases these representations have nothing to do with "consciousness": they are usually images and occasionally concepts, but it is above all as structures that they impose on the vast majority of men, not via their "consciousness". They are perceived-accepted-suffered cultural objects and they act functionally on men via a process that escapes them' (Althusser 1971: 155).

If nineteenth-century Poland, particularly after a series of tragic failures of national uprisings in 1830 and 1863, was a culture of mourning (with regard to both the nostalgic cultivation of the past and the style of sartorial behaviour which emphasized black colour and simple cut in ladies' dresses), the grounds of this bereavement are not merely political; due to the developments of history the Polish state with its history and legal and economic apparatus, annihilated by three partitions at the end of the eighteenth century, was transformed into the most essential Other around which circulated the processes of memory. The drama of repression following the 1863 January Uprising ('there was no home where someone would not be mourned', Brzozowski 1984: 409) marks also a change in the attitude towards the past, a modification of memory resulting from a turn towards *'theory', which we understand here as memory inspecting its own mechanisms and operations*. The past is not merely monumentalized but also critically reviewed. Brzozowski, writing in 1907, would even speak of a 'negation' of the past: 'A new life was rising as a negation of this past which has previously fought such an awesome battle. . . . Something nobler than stoicism, a renunciation of one's own pain and, simultaneously, dedication to the creative daily efforts aiming at the common future, is the most characteristic trait of the noblest representatives of the generation' (1984: 409).

A remarkable intervention: a turn towards the future refashions memory, which ceases to focus on the past exclusions of the Other and discovers the necessary participation of the Other in the construction of the familiar. The Other, who according to Derrida, 'resists the closure of our interiorizing memory' (Derrida 1986a: 34) thus problematizes dominating ideologies. The Other no longer supports (as a 'domestic') our home economy but is shown as a challenge and a source of possible agon. If Poland and Eastern Europe, viewed from the Western perspective, do not seem to be particularly inviting towards capitalism it is largely due to the cultural politics of a non-agonistic, mnemonic mode of life which stems from a different conceptualization of the Other.

3. A Domestic

The process which we refer to as the 'domestication' of the Other finds its roots in a more general cultural attitude which was developing in Poland from the end of the sixteenth century. This *weltanschauung* can be characterized in broadest terms as *countersublime*. In the passages quoted from Klonowic's symptomatic work one could easily find a decisive reluctance towards expansion, the obverse of which is also interpretable as a fascination with the border and the edge. The concept of Poland as *scutum* or *antemurale* of Christianity, which Poland took pride in, adds a military and religious dimension to the geographical and cultural focus on the border as a line which separates what is 'ours' from the land of *ubi leones*.

Claudio Magris, in his masterful exploration of the Danube cultures marks the border as a characteristically European phenomenon. Meditating on the remnants of the Roman ramparts Magris offers a general formula of European culture as being profoundly *liminal*: 'Our history, our culture, our Europe, are the daughters of that *Limes*. Those stones tell of the urge to frontiers, of the need and ability to give oneself limits and form. The *imperium* is a barrier, a defence, a rampart against the uncouthness of the indistinct and individualistic' (Magris 1990: 98). If the West confronts the unknown motivated by the desire to establish new frontiers, it also operates on the principle of the endless series: the border is established here and now only to be moved beyond or negotiated in the near future. *The call of the frontier: a wish to accommodate what is 'indistinct' within the clear pattern of a 'higher' culture where the categories are neatly divided and distinguished from one another.* The aesthetic aspect of this cultural politics is the Western European philosophy of the sublime which flourished at the moment of great geographical, economic, and political expansion and which was activated by two general tendencies: fascination with terror and astonishment which suspend the power of reason ('The passion caused by the great and sublime in nature . . . is Astonishment . . . In this case the mind is so entirely filled with its object, that it cannot entertain any other, nor by consequence reason on that object . . .', Burke 1958: 57), and a triumphant return of the rational in the critical discourse which subjected the previously untamed terror to the 'terror' of rational categories of description and analysis.

The countersublimity of the Polish cultural tradition would then signify a tendency towards stabilization of borders (a mode perfectly understandable in the light of the developments of history which were eventually to lead to a complete erasure of the Polish frontiers) and thus towards a clear mistrust for the movement beyond them. Already in our reading of Klonowic we emphasized the question of 'measure' and of a 'properly' demarcated place of one's own. The countersublimity has also its economic aspect. The corn trade which Klonowic refers to in his poem ought to be set against the weakening of the international activity of Polish merchants which was due, as a historian claims, to the political-economic doctrine of 'locking up the borders' (*zawarcie granic*). This policy was grounded upon the tradition of the 'right of storage' which obliged all merchants passing through a town to display and sell objects and upon a belief that the absence of native mercantile activities would force foreign traders to bring their goods to Poland and thus lower the prices (Topolski 1986: 194). With time this tendency augments and, as a historian of the book-binding industry notices, in the eighteenth century the Kraków merchants reluctantly travel not only to Frankfurt, Prague or Leipzig but even to Wrocław, which is the evidence of the downgrading and general collapse of local production unable to keep up competition with foreigners (Pachoński 1956: 228).

The two major consequences of this attitude, which we describe as the domination of the *politically and culturally beautiful* over its sublime counterparts, were a reluctance towards theory and an aversion from change or metamorphosis. The former is a result of the stability and measuredness of culture and the decorum of social and convivial life; if 'theory' connotes a confrontation with the Other who/which has already penetrated into our territory disturbing its established forms and institutions, then the stress on 'practice' aims at preservation, memorization of the well-grounded modes of thought and life. If Peter de Bolla is right, as I believe he is, in claiming that 'theory is excess' which 'is no longer grounded' (Bolla 1989: 93) then both the seriousness of the philosophy of the 'solid ground' (which we saw in Klonowic) and the loyalty to the historically preserved forms of political and cultural life defy and ostracize theory outside the *limes* of the state, as the 'easiest way to deal with the excess is to place it outside' (Bolla 1989: 98).

The aversion from metamorphosis works on a similar principle: Coleridge's dictum, according to which 'nothing not shapely . . . can be called beautiful: nothing that has a shape can be sublime' (Bolla 1989: 46), describes well the attitude of culture which tries to locate form exclusively within its own realm, looking at the sublime as belonging to the domain where we have no interest, or where even having this interest is morally suspect (see Klonowic's criticism of 'luxury' and 'excessive' profit which, when read next to de Bolla's comments on the politics of the National Debt in mid-eighteenth century England, must evidently point at the difference of attitudes of two cultures towards 'excess', 'theory', 'profit', and consequently towards capitalism as a system of sublime excessive overproduction and consumption). To metamorphose means to go beyond the limitations of one form, to theorize meaning by means of its translation into another system of signs, and this was precisely what the culture of the landed gentry in Poland was trying to avoid.

And then the question of the Other who is, as we have said, domesticated, i.e. not simply tamed, colonized, and deprived of his/her identity but just the opposite – turned into a 'domestic', a household servant who shares the life of his master and whose own position is determined by both dependence and familiarity. He/she is not a hired hand; a domestic is one who lives near or about the household of his/her master and participates in its development. The thesis we want to advance is outrageously general and would need much more detailed elaboration. At the moment we can afford no more than a very schematic presentation. What is at stake is the concept of the Other which, I want to argue, is in Poland (and Eastern Europe) fundamentally different from its Western European equivalent. In most general terms, what in the Western culture marks the Other is the notion of distance and separation: the Other (etymologically going back to Old High German *andar* and the Sanskrit *antara*) is a being distinct from the one already mentioned, one who is clearly not the same, i.e. different, may be even additional, excluded by and opposite to something or somebody else.

Unlike its English counterpart, the Polish term *bliźni* etymologically emphasizes in all Slavonic languages (Czech *blizni*, Russian *blizhniy*, Bulgarian *blizen*) the element of proximity. Thus, the domestication of the Other signifies its transformation into the 'one who is close', reducing at the outset the aspect of strangeness and curiosity. *Bliźni* is similar, if not identical (see *bliźniak*, a Polish word for *twin*); somebody who doubles and mirrors my own structure, contact with whom revives the memory of myself. *Bliźni* does not make me problematic; just the opposite – he reaffirms my own independence and the completeness of my being. If, for Levinas, ethical relationship is based on the experience of 'the putting into question of my spontaneity by the presence of the Other' (Levinas 1969: 43), the liaison I enter *vis à vis bliźni* is a confirmation of each other's spontaneity where the element of 'putting into question' plays a very limited role.

This widens the ethical relationship of 'neighbourhood' and extends it into the whole society (the traditional landed-gentry ethos is founded upon the principle of being a good neighbour) but, on the other hand, liberates one from 'theorizing' one's own self. If *bliźni* says 'yes' to my existence, if he/she is a good neighbour to whom I say 'drink and eat', and I ought to be able to say it to anyone, then I do not know and need not know the experience of being torn away from the security of my consciousness, I am able to retain the unity and harmony of the closed form (the term *bliźni* stands very close to the noun *blizna* which, signifying a 'scar left by a healed wound', brings up the notions of totality and absence of fissure and gap).

Once again we have collapsed into the discourse of the beautiful (closed form, harmony, etc.) abandoning the language of the sublime which seems more suited to the experience of the Other. Levinas himself uses such a discourse of sublimity when talking about the 'pure existence' of *il y a*: 'Horror is somehow a movement which will strip consciousness of its very subjectivity. Not in lulling it into unconsciousness, but in throwing it into an impersonal vigilance, a participation' (Levinas 1989: 32).

The concept of the Other as *bliźni*, i.e. the Other represented in the categories of the beautiful rather than sublime, stays away from 'impersonal vigilance' and focuses on the act of 'eating next to', on the philosophy of the domestic, or the parasite (Levinas seems close to this point when he claims that 'Only a being that eats can be for the Other', Levinas 1981: 74).

Therefore, the domestication of the Other which we consider to be a characteristic trait of Eastern Europe is not what it seems to be: it is not a mere translation of the Other into the language of my own culture responding to the postulate of my hegemonic control over the Other, but a recognition of the Other as a mirror in which I can find confirmation (rather than problematization) of my own self and reassertion of *limes*, of the protected ground which with its frontier secures me from the intervention of the Other. The Western world of 'we are challenges to each other' is replaced by the reality of 'we are each other's domestics (or parasites)' and, in consequence, the borders are seen less in terms of the external obstacles to be overcome and more in terms of the internal, domestic spatialization of the public sphere which we learn to obey and respect.

Some sixty years before Bourdieu's use of the term *habitus* Brzozowski had recourse to this concept to describe his stance *vis à vis* both crucial problems – that of the *limes* (and the interiorizing movement of a culture which sees the value as inherent to its own territory) and of the Other (understood as a cluster of ideological assumptions). 'Each class has its own mode of life and the satisfied or unsatisfied needs resulting from it. This is its necessary limitation, but beyond these borders there can exist and, *in potentia*, does exist the ability and will towards social construction . . . . Most of the time, however, we consider the habitus other than our own class habitus as a source of all possible disasters and faults of our own social system . . .' (Brzozowski 1913: 168). To rethink the concept of the border and its relationship to culture is a most responsible part of Eastern European intellectual life.

4. Memories and (of) Home

The predicament of memory concerns the status of novelty; the Enlightenment project advances the view according to which originality, i.e. what is not so much a mere rehearsal of memory but an arduous task for it, ought to be trimmed and restrained by a desire for perfection for which memory is an indispensable tool. Tillotson's phrase 'correctness was a likely preservative' (Wesling 1985: 42) summarizes the rational model grounded in two principles: firstly, that perfection, elimination of errors, is a most welcome task for thought, and, secondly that memory 'conserves' well, performs its duty, only when mistakes have been eliminated. To remember, to preserve, is tantamount to establishing *errata*, to work separating errors from truths; and therefore memory, which is activated only at the moment of the determining of truth by means of corrections, is the best measure of truth. Forgetfulness is an action which results from un-truth: I do not 'preserve' what is in the state of error, I doom mistakes to the oblivion of forgetting.

One can risk a thesis that this model of memory inhabited already by a crucial operation of censorship is, for two reasons, instrumental for any authoritarian power. Firstly, it implies a clear distinction between truth and illusion and makes the state a depository of the discriminatory force. Wielding this force the state can always segregate more from less desirable ideas, 'remembering' the former and 'forgetting' the latter. Secondly, it assumes a wider project of purposes which somehow has been pre-formed and now needs only implementation. Thus, we encounter a double denial of 'theory': (1) validation of one's judgements is to be done on the basis provided by some external mechanism, (2) a society needs only to concentrate on the 'practice' the task of which is to actualize the prerogatives of the systematic solutions worked out in advance either by the knowledgeable elite(s) or promoted to the status of the model by the flow of time (as in the case of the reverential attitude taken towards ancient aesthetic principles). Memory originating in this eighteenth-century project is thus antitheoretical (in terms of its ambition to neutralize the practices of the everyday as something given) and disciplinarian (since it calls for a strict regimentation of epistemological processes centring them round the idea of rationality).

It is interesting to note that the 'forgetfulness' implied in the Enlightenment model refers, in fact, to a specific form of memory: what has been censored as 'un-true', i.e. barred from the domain of memory, does not sink into oblivion but is 'remembered differently'. The memory of these facts or forms carries a 'negative' sign which serves as a warning: 'this is not to be remembered, this ought to be forgotten, and the mark which you see here is nothing else but a memorable indicator which tells you that you must remember to forget'. This specific phenomenon of forgetfulness/memory is indispensable as it enables society to segregate the desirable from the undesirable, and was crucial for the Communist authorities (which, in their rhetoric, considered themselves to be the heir to the Enlightenment tradition of rationality and perfectibility, and which with its help could relegate threatening political, social and aesthetic phenomena to the realm of temporary oblivion from which they could always be awakened in case of political necessity). By 'remembering' undesirable occurrences (be it an underground publication of a suppressed book, or commemoration of a 'forbidden' historical event) man participates both in the subversive force of 'suppressed memory' and, not being oblivious of the state dictate which compels one to 'forget', he or she sees this ambiguity of memorizing and forgetting as a force which alienates him or her from the well-established procedures of the everyday. The practices of life in Eastern Europe, for many decades formed under the command of a hostile presence, were always punctuated by the dual manoeuvres of remembering and forgetting which, from within, both strengthened the sense of 'home' (in the sense of belonging to a vast majority which remembered against the dictate) and considerably weakened it (through a reflection on forgetting, recognized as an alien strategy which successfully channelled incomparably great social energies in the strenuous effort to overcome 'forgetting'). In other words, the practices of the everyday focused on survival (in the political and economic senses of the term) skills rather than on 'living' (by which term was meant the pleasurable aspects of life). *To problematize, or to use our terminology, to 'theorize' 'home' was then to oscillate between the movements of remembering and forgetting, remaining within the confines of 'home' and simultaneously reflecting on its dubious status* (whose 'home'?).

The situation of memory in Poland (and probably in other countries of this part of Europe) evolves round the question and meaning(s) of 'home'. So far we have emphasized the 'home'-supporting aspect of the culture of this area which constructed the world along the lines of familiarity and proximity. Historical development in the nineteenth and twentieth centuries showed another reading of 'home' in which the familiar is used not to facilitate but thwart cultural actions due to the antiquarian passion for conservation and thus petrification of certain facts and events. Writing at the beginning of our century Stanisław Brzozowski launched an attack on the 'musk-smelling Enlightenment pattern' according to which man was to feel 'at home' in the world. The philosophical crisis of Enlightenment in Eastern Europe seems to be caused by the recognition of the limitations of the 'home' philosophy and by the critique of the eighteenth-century thought which, in most general terms, strove towards the domestication of the Other (through the processes of rational explanation, de-theologization of the everyday, and economic conquest of the exotic). 'I do not know why we always speak only about September 1793 as the moment of the bankruptcy of the philosophical dreams of nature. The partition of Poland, rivers of blood with which this sacrifice was sanctified . . . the defeat of the intelligentsia at the hands of black-shirt squadrons, all this belongs to the same musk-smelling Enlightenment pattern. The history of modern culture needs a radical revisioning; one must be liberated from the rational superstitions which do not respect the true life of our psyche' (Brzozowski 1910: 483).

The radical revisioning of which Brzozowski conceives must imply theorization of the notion of 'home' and 'homely memories'. It is not co-incidental that Brzozowski was one of the first enthusiastic and understanding Polish commentators and critics of Nietzsche; the Nietzschean necessity of 'forgetting' as a way of getting over the illness of history which the German philosopher discusses in *The Untimely Meditations* is parallel to Brzozowski's critical comments concerning the debilitating power exercised by the uncritically repeatable history which was a screen preventing culture from facing contemporaneity. In this sense, the debate over the 'uses and abuses of history' carried out by Brzozowski early in the twentieth century (particularly striking in the philosopher's devastating criticism of Henryk Sienkiewicz who was not only the main representative of the uncritically antiquarian memory of the past but also, as his 1905 Nobel Prize for *Quo Vadis* demonstrates, was considered by the West to be the 'ambassador' of Eastern European mentality) introduced Poland into the project of modernity, the main point of which was to question man's 'at-homeness' in the world.

If, as Jürgen Habermas claims, Nietzsche's thought 'demonstrates that the embodied, speaking and acting subject is not master in its own house' (Habermas 1980: 310), then Eastern European historical developments focusing on political imposition of foreign rule and violence show this statement to be doubly true. First, the subject is alienated from its own house for political reasons (a long tradition of living under a foreign dictate). Second, the subject must realize that in order to regain the feeling of 'at-homeness' it should retain a critical distance from the idealized and monumentalized memory which can threaten the subject with a mere repetition of past gestures, thus screening it from contemporaneity. It is the possibility of facing 'now' that is a difficult moment in Eastern European history which for many centuries was dominated by a tendency to domesticate the Other and live the present according to the scenario of the past.

5. Living on the Edge

A complex interweaving of literature and politics seems to mark Eastern Europe, where the sense of political life for many decades was concealed in the *écriture* and where the bardic remained alive longer than anywhere else. One has to take the concept of *écriture* with full responsibility: it was the very fact of recording which carried a subversive message, whereas the substance could be free of any overt political importance. To record and write was to engrave letters of the politically forbidden alphabet, to indulge in the act of scribbling a transgressive graffiti. The misery of this part of the world where *écriture* was a political luxury which, belying the superficial. Marxist dichotomy of base and superstructure, turned unobserved into a most potent political device. Literature was a psychoanalysis of Central Europe. Again let us turn to Brzozowski's *Diary*: 'Literature in general is a luxury if one believes in politics, but literature if one knows it subtly and amorously constitutes one of the most dependable ways towards liberation from brutally stupid and depraving political superstitions' (Brzozowski 1913: 42).

To practise politics is to know literature, but this knowledge is not a mere exercise in epistemological memory which rehearses facts and dates; it is the 'amorous and subtle knowledge' which bursts in the moment of personal, private, intimate *anamnesis* but, in consequence, has a powerful impact upon the public sphere; the amorous, fragmentary knowledge 'which recovers only insignificant features in no way dramatic, as if I remembered time itself and only time' (Barthes 1979: 216). It is difficult to avoid a reflection that it was precisely this 'amorous' knowledge of literature (Mallarmé, Poe, Shelley) which turned Derrida towards philosophy which he reads and thinks as a kind of literary discourse, a task in which he was preceded by Martin Heidegger's readings of Hölderlin and Trakl. Deconstruction 'amorously' shelters the last and crumbled ramparts of the bardic.

It is this turn towards the fragmentary and amorous which, coupled with the traditionally strong position of literature in a society which considered *écriture* to be a form of subversive

countermemory, somehow ironically prepared the ground for deconstruction in Eastern Europe; for a questioning of the discourse of
the beautiful by the rhetoric of the sublime, i.e. for the meditation
on borders (edges, frontiers) and the repositioning of the Other. 'I
wish to raise the question of the *bord*, the edge, the border, and the
bord de mer, the shore . . .' (Derrida 1979: 83).

In this passage of an early work by Derrida we can locate at least
two important calls which could potentially unsettle the Eastern
European scene. The first voice speaks of the border, i.e. of the line
which demarcated 'ours' from 'theirs' and which helped to carry out
the stratification of the society within the fenced-in territory where
the Other obtained the status of a domestic. The other one brings
what has always been dangerous for Central European culture: the
sound of the sea and the breakers which filled Klonowic with terror,
made him cringe and, quitting the fluid area of the sublime, turn
towards the 'solid ground' of the beautiful.

With these two voices another crucial problematics slips in: they
bring back to our attention proximity and its values. The Nietzschean metaphors of boats, seas and sailing have paved the way for
the Derridean *bord de mer* and the question of distance (Nietzschean
'pathos of distance') inherent in it and stretching before one who
stands on the shore. Thus, to the dominating thought of proximity
and familiarity deconstruction has brought the concepts of necessary
distance and therefore otherness and the non-identifiability of what
has been considered familiar. To think deconstruction is to meditate
upon the scene of hospitality. In the continuation of the same
passage Derrida speaks about 'all those boundaries that form the
running border of what used to be called a text, of what we once
thought this word could identify . . .'.

The chance of deconstruction in the Eastern European context
depended much less on its subversive potential threatening the metaphysics of *presence* and the foundations of Western linguistics and
semiotics, than on the political ethics which, capitalizing on the traditionally high position of literature in society, could transform the
philosophy of *différance* into the politics of non-identifiability, i.e. it
knocked the familiar and memorable off its trajectory of the Same,
pulling it more and more strongly towards difference and forgetfulness. Whereas structuralism, by far the most popular scholarly
approach of the academic mainstream in Poland, tried to oppose the
dangers of totalitarianism by identifying phenomena as belonging to
competitive units and dichotomies, deconstruction pointed at the
interruptions in the series of social substitutions which constituted

the very mechanism of the system. 'Totalitarianism . . . is that political form of society governed by a logic of identification whereby
all areas of social life represent incarnate power: the proletariat is
identified with the people, the party with the proletariat, the politburo with the party, the leader with the politburo. It is the representation – or rather, fantasy – of a homogeneous and transparent
society, a unified people among whom social division or difference is
denied . . .' (Critchley 1990: 208).

The practices (always in the plural) of deconstruction were aimed
then at the dis-incarnation of power (demonstration of the fact that
power is deprived of *one* specific body in which authority would be
completely sedimented, a discovery of the fact that politics is a
question of *bodies* rather than of one body) and at introducing the
necessity of thinking in terms of distance, which always works in the
apparently homogeneous identification procedures. Thus, deconstructive strategies could modify a traditional Eastern European
attitude which we can refer to as 'value memory' and which focused
on preserving and sheltering certain values threatened by the system,
rather than mapping out specific political decisions and purposes to
be achieved (Szacki 1992: 330). The undecidability of deconstructive
interpretation problematized the memory of values not in order to
destabilize the values themselves, but to make one aware of values
as certain constructs which remained in specific relationships with
the political reality of the day.

If I refer to deconstruction (a very imperfect term for a whole
cluster of textual strategies: one tends to agree with Derrida that 'I
do not think . . . it is a good word . . .', Wood and Bernasconi
1988: 5) as an important and impactful element of Polish intellectual
life in the early 1980s, it is with the purpose of highlighting its
(perhaps somewhat against Derrida's own intention) sceptical and
heterogeneous turn.

As scepticism, deconstruction enabled one to liquidate the privileged position of the signified, i.e. to question the clear structure of
'host' and 'guests' which, as we have been trying to argue, shaped
the Polish understanding of the Other as a 'domestic'. If a standard
'definition' of *différance* proclaims it to be 'a relay to mark that
there is never anything but relays' (Derrida 1987: 298), then evidently the division of roles implied by and in the notion of 'home'
turns out to be volatile and insecure. The architecture of home is
now modified by the architecture of the void, a move already
foreseen by Brzozowski who in the first years of the twentieth
century was arguing on behalf of two cultural revisionisms which

Poland must undertake. To begin with there is a need to open Poland to the 'new' (and this necessarily implies a rethinking of the frontier and 'home'); then there comes the time for the unconcealment of the Other not as a 'domestic', living on and off my mercy and always on my – albeit noble – conditions, but as a challenging force. Both revisions meet in the metaphor of the abyss (a well-known trope from both Nietzsche's and Derrida's works) and – more importantly – in the postulate of the supplanting of the traditional protocols of 'hospitality' and hegemony of the 'host' over the 'guest' which determine and map the sense of place ('home') by a more radical move towards a 'less naive metaphorics of place' (Derrida 1987: 212).

This must also imply a decisive intervention in the forms of memory which cannot function merely on the basis of automatic and mechanical recall but is now modified by the aura of the abyss. 'One has to break with all the hitherto existing forms of thinking of that which is. . . , one has to, as it were, hang suspended in the void of nonexistence and not to lose courage, walk forward and work . . . One needs the heroism of thought and constant dignity of act' (Brzozowski 1910: 178).

A 'home' is modified by the sense of *chora* (of which Derrida writes in *Psyche*), a place of creativity of the individual which is (un)based on any *Grund*. What deconstructive practices reveal, then, is another type of 'hospitality', a non-foundational hospitality which is not based on the hegemonic relationship between the 'host' and the 'guest' but which, rather, springs from the fact that it is no longer possible to claim two different territories for the two roles: the 'host' does not belong to the world of 'home' (and its dogmatic, remembered truths imposed upon the 'guest'), the 'guest' does not come to the host's manor from the outside (and as we have learned from *Pan Tadeusz* quickly learns to obey the general truth). Now both, the host and the guest, are turned into 'domestics', i.e. beings entertained by some larger power which rejects our efforts to lock it in the formula of 'hospitality', 'truth', 'welcoming care', etc. Thus, what deconstructions were found to teach was the placing of notions like 'truth' and 'falsehood' in a wider context which enabled resistance against the simplified interpretative schemes upon which any totalitarian system is founded. Christopher Norris comments: 'Deconstruction can invoke standards of truth and falsehood because . . . it locates those moments of resistance in a text where the sense holds out against simplified or premature forms of interpretive grasp' (Norris 1991: 130). 'Home' is thus a place of resistance (against the pretences of the solidity of a political system) not because it is a system of well-placed objects (as we have shown in our analysis of the foundations of the traditional hospitality model) but because it is a place where various objects entertain various roles and whose enigmatic nature does not allow us to 'consider it as the homogeneous and serene milieu of dynamic and economic processes' (Derrida 1978: 215).

In other words, the 'guest' and 'host' coalesce to form one category of the 'ghost' which, first, shows provisionality of the socially accepted roles preserved by social and cultural memory, and second, narrates a different story of the Other (or, rather, *an* other) which now has a different status: no longer merely entertained by me, he/she/it is also able to show me his/her/its grace and solicitude. Hence a radical theorizing of otherness as proximity (so crucial for the concept of *bliźni*): the proximity which was previously taking place somehow at my decision and will ('I will give you food if you come and ask') is now changed into a different mode – it speaks of a generosity which belongs essentially to an other and the roots of which are never to be ultimately traced and named ('I have some bread to give you only because I have previously received a generous gift from you who have arrived within my confines, invading my territory'). As Derrida puts it: '. . . the ghost effect, more radically heterogeneous insofar as it implies the topography of an other, of "a corpse buried in the other"' (Derrida 1986b).

What we observe, then, is a different hospitality which belongs to another economic sphere and which can save the virtue of generosity in the epoch of the post-Ford massification of production and consumption, in the time of what Naomi Goldbenberg, noticing 'the progressive and systematic disappearance of people from each other in the routine practices of daily life', calls the 'Apocalypse in Everyday Life' (Blundell et al. 1993: 140). Early in the twentieth century Ludwik Krzywicki, an eminent Polish philosopher and sociologist, analysing the phenomenon of traditional hospitality, which consisted in the total overwhelming of the Other by the 'host' who turned himself into a dictatorial figure, claims that its sources were to be looked for in the dominating economy of Renaissance and Enlightenment Poland. Characteristic of the landed-gentry culture, a reluctant attitude towards both commerce and cities resulted in the accumulation of harvested crops in granaries and sheds rather than in their circulation on the market. Hence, it was more economic (and economical) to 'force' various foodstuffs on your guests than to allow products to be eaten by animals or insects (Gloger 1972: vol. 2, 208). We can see how this model of hospitality is based on excess open spaces for the deconstructive mode of thought (see the Derridean focus on Bataille and his notion of *dépense*), and simultaneously how it differs from it due to the centrality of the concept of 'me' and clearly dichotomous roles of the 'host' and 'guest'. The deconstructive hospitality arises also out of the economy of excess and overabundance, but in its deregulated and unstructured movements of signifiants it opposes and undoes the stability of a 'home', of a solidified, sedimented and determined meaning, replacing it with the semiotics of the nomadic, deterritorialized wandering. An Other in this situation does not belong to a 'me' who is its entertaining and hegemonic 'host', but the very 'me' finds out that it cannot think itself otherwise than through an Other which has offered its hospitality before the 'host' could make its appearance. The deconstructive thought which, according to the logic of *différance* sketched by Derrida himself, 'marks the separation and the relation to the entirely other (an entirely other which it is necessary to think "at the same time" as the same . . .)' (Wood and Bernasconi 1988: 85) can find its moorings in the Eastern European scene of hospitality and, as a thought essentially 'homeless', try to accommodate itself to the traditionally 'home'-oriented culture.

References

Althusser, L. (1971). 'Ideology and the state'. In *Lenin and Philosophy, and Other Essays*. London, Verso.

Barthes, R. (1979). *A Lover's Discourse: Fragments*, trans. R. Howard. London, Jonathan Cape.

Blundell, V., et al. (1993). *Relocating Cultural Studies: Developments in Theory and Research*. London and New York, Routledge.

Bolla, P. de (1989). *The Discourse of the Sublime: History, Aesthetics and the Subject*. Oxford, Blackwell.

Brandys, K. (1981). *A Question of Reality: Answers from Poland*, trans. I. Barzun. London, Blond & Briggs.

Brzozowski, S. (1910). *Legenda Młodej Polski: Studia o strukturze duszy kulturalnej*. Lwów, Księgarnia Polska Bernarda Połonieckiego (my translation).

—— (1913). *Pamiętnik* ['Diary']. Lwów, Księgarnia Polska Bernarda Połonieckiego (my translation).

—— (1984). *Współczesna powieść i krytka*. Kraków, Wydawnictwo Literackie (my translation).

Burke, E. (1958). *A Philosophical Enquiry into the Origin of Our Ideas of the Sublime and the Beautiful*, ed. J. T. Boulton. London, Routledge and Kegan Paul.

Critchley, S. (1990). *The Ethics of Deconstruction: Derrida and Levinas*. Oxford, Blackwell.

Derrida, J. (1978). *Writing and Difference*, trans. A. Bass. London, Routledge and Kegan Paul.

—— (1979). 'Living on Border Lines'. In *Deconstruction and Criticism*, ed. G. Hartman. London, Routledge and Kegan Paul.

—— (1986a). *Memoires for Paul de Man*, trans. C. Lindsay, J. Culler, E. Cadava. New York, Columbia University Press.

—— (1986b). 'Fors: The Anglish Words of Nicolas Abraham and Maria Torok', trans. B. Johnson, N. Abraham, M. Torok. In *The Wolf Man's Magic Word: A Cryptonymy*. Minneapolis, University of Minnesota Press.

—— (1987). *The Post Card: From Socrates to Freud and Beyond*, trans. A. Bass. Chicago and London, University of Chicago Press.

Gloger, Z. (1972). *Encyklopedia staropolska*. Warszawa, Wiedza Powszechna.

Habermas, J. (1980). *The Philosophical Discourse of Modernity: Twelve Lectures*, trans. F. Lawrence. Cambridge, Massachusetts, MIT Press.

Klonowic, S. (1951). *Flis*. Wrocław, Ossolineum (my translation).

Levinas, E. (1969). *Totality and Infinity*, trans. A. Lingis. Pittsburgh, Duquesne University Press.

—— (1981). *Otherwise than Being or Beyond Essence*. The Hague, Martinus Nijhoff.

—— (1989). 'There Is: Existence without Existents'. In *The Levinas Reader*, ed. S. Hand. Oxford, Blackwell.

Magris, C. (1990). *Danube: A Sentimental Journey from the Source to the Black Sea*, trans. P. Creagh. London, Collins Harvill.

Mickiewicz, A. (1966). *Pan Tadeusz*, trans. K. MacKenzie. London and New York, Dent & Dutton.

Norris, Christopher (1991). *Spinoza and the Origins of Modern Critical Theory*. Oxford, Blackwell.

Pachoński, J. (1956). *Zmierzch sławetnych, Z życia mieszczan w Krakowie XVII i XVIII wieku*. Kraków, Wydawnictwo Literackie (my translation).

Serres, M. (1982). *The Parasite*, trans. L. Schehr. Baltimore, Johns Hopkins University Press.

Sławek, T., and D. Wesling (1989). 'The Exiled Voice in Adam Mickiewicz's *Pan Tadeusz*'. Budapest, *Acta Litteraria Acad. Sci. Hung.* 31:iii/iv. 311–40.

Szacki, J. (1992). 'Odrodzenie liberalizmu?'. In *Historia i wyobraźnia*, ed. S. Amsterdamski et al. Warszawa, PWN (my translation).

Terdiman, R. (1993). *Past Present: Modernity and the Memory Crisis*. Ithaca, Cornell University Press.

Tönnies, F. (1963). *Community and Society* (first edition 1887), trans. C. Loomis. New York, Harper & Row.

Topolski, J. (1986). 'Zagadnienia goapodarki w Polsce'. In *Polska w spoce Odrodzenia: Państwo, społeczeństwo, kultura.* Ed. A. Wyczański. Warszawa, Wiedza Powszechna (my translation).

Wesling, D. (1985). *The New Poetries: Poetic Form Since Coleridge and Wordsworth.* Lewisburg, Bucknell University Press.

Wood D., and R. Bernasconi, eds (1988). *Derrida and Différance.* Evanston, Illinois, Northwestern University Press.

19

Post-1989 Bulgarian Literary Theory and Criticism

TATYANA STOICHEVA

The thought of writing on recent Bulgarian literary theory and criticism came as a challenge, but one mixed with anxiety. Literary transformations have been profound over the last five years or so. What I think we all agreed about some time before November 1989 was that we wanted a different identity. Of course this is not to say that we were prepared to go to any lengths to get it. By the 1980s the health of socialist realism was hardly likely to alarm literary theory and criticism, as long as important anniversaries were dutifully supplied with celebratory volumes and the writers' union conferences could mobilize a bit of international attention. Now the five years' perspective makes it easier to suggest that the Party grasp was already relaxing somewhat and Bulgarian theory and criticism were taking advantage of a trickle of Western theory in translation. The criteria of selection were resolutely shifting from 'classics' to more recent texts. A few random examples: Tzvetan Todorov's *Poetics of Prose* (1985), Gombrich's *Art and Illusion* (1988), Frye's *Anatomy of Criticism* (1987), Freud's *Introductory Lectures on Psychoanalysis* and Nietzsche's *Birth of Tragedy* (both 1989), or the assignment for translation in early 1989, by the largest publishing house for academic texts, of *A Semiotic Anthology* (2 volumes), Eco's *Semiotics and the Philosophy of Language* and Roger Fowler's *Dictionary of Modern Critical Terms*.

Of course the trickle has now become a flood which reaches even to street corner stalls and underpasses. The newly-found freedom of the spirit blew away the tight cultural constrictions of the past, so familiar and so uniform. The laws of the market turned literature out of its cosy place into the open as former bookshops became more profitable, elegant stores. This new form of existence has erased the dividing line between low-brow and high-brow culture, and the two are equal: this means literature being subject to the whims of the weather and the vendor's taste and sense of profit. It is quite normal to get your Freud, Foucault or Ricoeur round the corner, prominently arranged next to Harlequin novels, horoscopes, or guidebooks on magic.

As for publishing, censorship has gone, but financial constraints spell new rules, and the good or bad opinion of sponsors may decide the life or death of a journal. Developments in early 1990 did not point to such an anticlimax. At the time high-minded enthusiasm was the rule since literary journals and newspapers saw their task as carrying out a corresponding 'revolution'. Well-established journals, while recognizing their successful existence, offered new platforms (*Literaturna missul* celebrated its thirty-fifth birthday in 1991 and so did *Plamuk*). Others, of equal longevity, changed their names to shake off the burden of the ideological referent: *Literaturen front* became *Literaturen forum* newspaper, and *Septemvri* was substituted by *Letopissi*. The greatest optimism was displayed towards the emergence of new periodicals. These included the dissident *Glas* and *Most* followed by, among others, *Prilep, Znak, Kambana* or *Nov Zlatorog*. The list of literary newspapers, magazines and journals in the National Library catalogue is truly impressive; the same, however, cannot be said about their record. Publishing is extremely late, appearance is irregular, the survival of most is problematic at best. Financial difficulties have also influenced the policies of even the most solid ones. Production costs now dictate larger issues but at irregular intervals, and this increases delay and uncertainty. Yet the reasons are not only financial, as the desperate cry of Professor Toncho Zhechev, editor-in-chief of *Letopissi* shows: 'Literary periodicals are expiring. If no miracle takes place, we shall be closing *Letopissi* and *Plamuk* down by the end of the year.' This, he thinks, is due to the fact that literary periodicals lack vivid characteristics; they are not the expression of a well-established literary group with its own literary and public ideas and aesthetic programmes. There is a possible analogy with the difficulties for periodicals between 1944 and 1948 (Zhechev 1994b).

When one looks at the issues for the years 1990 and 1991, literary magazines and journals seem to be bursting; there is an overflow of materials. A couple of years later they have shrunk greatly. Yet there is a welcome eagerness to offset the loss: enthusiasts must be die-hards. Despite difficulties, 1994 saw the beginning of yet another academic journal, *Literaturata* (for studies in Bulgarian literature in the Slav Faculty at Sofia University).

In the kaleidoscopic picture of transformations, newspapers were the first to respond and to start debates. Looking at them, one notices that they tend to boil with strong emotions: there is much froth. Blackening one's enemies or enhancing the importance of one's distress easily get mixed up with more substantial topics. The anxiety of journalists to meet the demands of the day and attract attention may border on fabrication, as did the announcement in *Standart* newspaper of 7 March 1993, according to which Malcolm Bradbury's *Rates of Exchange* had been denounced in Bulgaria. Part of the effect must have been to advertise more effectively the forthcoming British Council conference and Malcolm Bradbury's visit, and this probably struck home.

Newspapers were the first to outline new literary tasks, well ahead of magazines and academic journals: the need for a change in the literary canon, the listing of forgotten/ignored authors and texts, the recharting of literary space to accommodate names and works previously denied access or suppressed for political reasons, the re-examination of facts about major authors and books which might have caused embarrassment and were hushed up (the activity and murder of Georgi Markov, the pressure upon Dimiter Dimov concerning the rewriting of *Tyutyun*).

The survey of periodicals demonstrates a clash of literary opinion which stands out as a major gain against the uniformity of the past. The most varied spectrum of opinions exists in *Literaturen forum*. It ranges from cautious optimism to extreme nihilism, not surprising when one keeps in mind the established audience (the writers' union) which brings together different generations, political views and aesthetic conceptions. Here are current writers like Dimiter Korudjiev, Encho Mutafov, Ivo Indjev, whose political affiliations are strongly connected with the newspaper *Demokratsiya*, or Alexander Spiridonov and Vassil Kolevski, former adherents of socialist realism. The tolerance of co-existence is striking when one thinks that Bulgarian society of the last five years has been extremely politicized and sharply divided into antagonistic political affiliations. Critical practice is part of the reason. But the interconnection is far from simple. Bulgarian literature and politics have ever been in a tight symbiotic embrace, with propagandist discourse usually dominating the hierarchy of literary discourses. The literature–politics relationship of the past fifty years was one of frank subordination to

Party criteria, with open instructions for both writers and critics. This trend has now been renounced through the publishing of various documents which remind us of the distortions and the response (Georgiev 1990b; Todorov 1991; Slavov 1990). Censuring the past has not managed to halt this trend, because it has proved all too easy to insert substitutes with the opposite ideological sign into the slots which literature and criticism were used to keeping available for political propaganda. There is an example in *Literaturen vestnik* which was started, and continued until 1994, as the literary supplement to a party organ. In it literature adopted yet again a political programme to the extent of acting as 'homologous politics'. The resemblance to the experience of literature-cum-politics of the past was less obvious because authors felt free to make a choice and to engage without hindrance in the current political debate. Insightful comments about the present state of Bulgarian society went with poststructuralist theory and with the ostensible rejection of the years of totalitarianism, and the literature and culture they produced.

In a theoretical perspective literary scholarship has shown great interest in Stefan Stambolov, one of the most famous politicians in modern Bulgarian history (Terziev 1991; Nedelchev 1991; Mateev 1991).

Probably the most characteristically Bulgarian illustration of literature doing the job for politics could be the incorporation of literary scholars into politics in the past few years. They went to the National Assembly, became ministers, and a woman poet was elected vice-president. The situation did attract the attention of a literary scholar and it may well merit future analyses (Kamenov 1994).

Direct involvement aside, literary scholarship also interprets the immersion of literature into politics with its subsequent effects (Georgiev 1990a). This debate shows the abundance of information shared by its participants, professional critics and literary scholars, on the crucial role Party ideology enjoyed, and their ignorance about theory on the subject. Scholarly myopia might be due to the very straightforwardness of the political link for Bulgarian literature with a concomitant blunting of the critical sense. External reasons should superimpose Party vigilance against the profanation of Marxism even if attempts came from well-intentioned Marxists. Whatever the interpretations, the fact remains that Bulgarian literary theory, regardless of its eagerness to appropriate modern Western theory, is still reluctant to employ the tools that will enable it to study critically and transcend the past. To my mind, critical ineptitude in this respect goes to extremes in the opening platform of *Kritika i humanizm* journal (1991:5–10). Although it carefully acknowledges that critical theory should take account of existing social structures, the editorial board decides against it because 'that would be impossible unless one hypostasized uncritical appearances and automatized conceptual patterns which "think for" the critics themselves'. The concentration upon the uncritical appearances and conceptual commonplaces tends to screen the role of literature as praxis and to have appearances and commonplaces embedded in the past. To show concern for man in research after the Foucauldian 'death of man in theory' is fine but again it skirts what is existing here and now.

The need to approach socialist realism was formulated in the *Literaturna missul* platform (Nichev 1991) but has not been debated yet. As for the study of literature in terms of its service to political assignments, there have been studies on the use of detective fiction (Saparev 1991) and the failure of socialism to create mass art (Stefanov 1991). Clearly interest in this field is still lacking and its absence signifies that our society ˉstill seems to be in the early emotive stage of transition when strong reactions suffice for both personal and social fulfilment. The foregrounding of socialist realism as a reading practice, for example, the analysis of its discursive features as constituting a particular view of the world, or the fact that it invariably authorized writing and reading from the centre of political power only, ruling out the margin, could add something to our awareness of Bulgarian literature. Also, I imagine, it might be worthwhile to judge from the text how deep and how far authors were cowed into subordination.

One of the fascinating things about the radical transformation in social and political life was the change in language. What we could watch was language emerging out of a prison house to turn into a house of Being. The emergence of a free press and the discussion of the relationships between language and power also became part and parcel of the process (Popovski 1990; Dimitrov 1990; Mladenov 1990; Purvev 1993; 'Ezik i obshtestvo' 1994).

The language of literary theory and criticism changed no less radically. The appropriation of poststructuralist theories legitimated the professionalism of young authors in *Literaturen vestnik*. From the very first, the language they employed and that of *Kambana* (a socialist literary newspaper) posited different worlds. The language of the former was supposed, according to the opening platform, 'to name things unnamed'; it evokes centrality, disallows argument and lends its value judgements the naturalness and universality that go with the defence of power. The group round it tend to appropriate to themselves epistemological secrets and wave the wolfskin to the uninitiated. They reject any difference of opinion on what is identified by them as the (post-)totalitarian cultural vacuum.

Yet if we trust the opinions of critics, the changes that have surfaced in Bulgarian literature in the past five years are the effect of undercurrents in the 1980s. Poetry then constructed a new identity as experimentalism, started some twenty years earlier, came to a climax. It appropriated bold philosophical, cultural, and historical allusions, freely incorporating spiritual and physical concepts. It displayed ideas of time and space as strongly distorted, reversed and taken to absurdity. Poets of the 1980s are said to be fond of the absurd and to be in conscious search for it in a journey moving backwards in time and space. What they conceptualize is the loss of a sense of identity, the destruction of the ego and its disorientation (Malinov 1993).

In fiction Belyaeva sees the interposing of temporality by means of displacement where the mind busies itself with the construction of mental networks out of different components such as temporal perspectives, mythological symbolism and images of the concrete (Belyaeva 1986). Rozaliya Likova argues that parody and the grotesque either dislocated the fiction of the 1980s as they intersected with power and the absurdity of totalitarianism, or constructed a curious interplay between a fantastic reality and the world of everyday existence. Under such conditions the grotesque demonstrates vitality and polyvalence and she sees them in action juxtaposing eternity, space, fantasy, the subconscious, as well as public and political life. The result is the projection of a multiple complex vision (Likova 1991).

With the tearing down of the political barriers and the appropriation of a new identity, literary theory and criticism have drawn attention to the need for discussing the specifics of Bulgarian language and literature. For Pierre Rouve (Peter Uvaliev) the fact that Bulgarian was for centuries *lingua peregrina* gave it epistemological and ontological functions: 'Bulgarian philology became Bulgarian ontology'. The effect of this was that Bulgarian acquired great prestige and instead of being doubted or mistrusted it was invested with tremendous authority (Rouve 1991). For Bogdanov, the surveys of the present and future of Bulgarian literature are important in respect of the broad European boundaries, and thus he foregrounds features that constitute 'otherness'. Bulgarian literature and culture are characterized by intolerance of variety and by a primitive impulse to attain clarity and unity. Their hierarchy privileges representation in black-and-white and the validation of the here-and-now, whereas universal and transcendental impulses are mistrusted (Bogdanov 1991). Exciting as it may appear, Bogdanov's representation manages to marginalize Bulgarian literature by measuring it with criteria imposed from the outside. He offers two examples of Bulgarian translations for one and the same excerpt from ancient Greek, and as far as I can judge (Greek is Greek to me) the second translation does anything but prove the devoidness of baroque ornamentality and the occlusion of extra-denotative meanings in Bulgarian. What it does prove is that the different strategies of the translators result in entirely different effects and that skilled translators make wonderful use of the target language even to the extent of transcending alleged boundaries. As for the drive towards clarity and unity, Radichkov's fiction over the past thirty years disproves it. It is also a good example of the successful appropriation of universal and transcendental impulses to the here-and-now. And finally, outlining the specificity of Bulgarian literature against the centre is not the best way of validating it. The peripheral position is identified with peripheral status rather than with a centre from which Bulgarian writing can mediate between European and other literatures. By insisting on the privileges such a position gives, the Bulgarian language and its literature would legitimate their truly original potential, for example the constitution of subjectivity and the characteristic view of the world in the re-narrated (non-witness) mood, the articulation of self and other in the sphere of the speaker, and so on.

Bulgarian literary and critical practice is evidently searching for postulates of self-representation and this is also confirmed by the continual foregrounding of the concept of self–other. A re-formulation of self is more than desirable since the new political orientation dislocated our original notion of self. Our image abroad has been affected as well. Previously we would have been known as 'the most faithful ally', now we have reverted to our geographical location and its troubled affairs (Kyosev 1991). But regardless of political motives, self–other enjoys a vitality which Bulgarian literature has tested time and again, at least since its early modern period. Its present revival has expanded our idea of Bulgarian literary space through the incorporation of émigré texts (Tikhanov 1992; Zlatarska 1994). Another aspect is evoked in the specific constructions of the

Bulgarian national character (Kirova 1991; Slavov 1991), of representations of professional groupings (Dichev 1990; Kirov 1991; Nachev 1990), or in the charting of national destiny (Zhechev 1994a).

Critical practice in relation to 'self–other' also intersects with a parodic version of Bulgarian history (Genchev 1990) or with the savage representation of Bulgarianness as a blending of the individual, the type and the sample (Pozharliev 1993; for the contribution of the media, see Dimitrov 1990; Andreev 1994). In its early stage 'self–other' was also validated in political discourse (one political platform was named 'The Journey to Europe') as different parties had different ideas of the routes. 'Other' invariably meant Europe and the issue of Europeanization brought together émigré writers and insiders, all working hard for its appropriation (Ognyanov 1991; Uvaliev 1991; Zhechev 1994a, 1994b; Todorov 1991; Kristeva 1992, 1993).

The critical model is very diversified. It ranges from the detailed study of Bulgarian authors and the way they explored the subject (Georgiev 1991) to studies of encouragement which guard against misgivings and disillusionment with recipes for the successful Europeanization of Bulgarian intellectuals in the early twentieth century (Zhechev 1994c; Djokova 1991). Special mention ought to be made of the rehabilitating sketch of Bay Ganyo with its recognition of the good aspects in his character, a guarantee of successful resistance to and final acceptance of others (Dimitrov-Robanov 1993).

Critical practice intersects with an abundance of literary interpretations. To quote just a few: Dimiter Tomov's story *A Journey to Europe* (1992), Pissarski's *Homo Bulgaris* (1992), a prognostico-fantastic novel, and then the most famous ones: Stanislav Stratiev's *Bulgarskiyat model* (1991) and *Uprazhneniya po drugost* (1993). These qualify as the most successful sketches of the Bulgarian condition after 1989, with pungent insights into our mentality. Stratiev succeeds in telling the bitter truth without giving offence. Otherness, for example, is seen as an act of mimicry we perform in order to stay as we are: its appropriation is a formula for survival. The ridicule provokes and soothes anxiety at one and the same time as it explores and dramatizes the most unpalatable aspects of everyday life and its less obvious effects.

The popularity of Stratiev's sketches is worth thinking about and so is the current use of the 'self–other' idea. As Roman Jakobson stated, the literary table of a period describes a certain image of the past, 'not only the literary production of any period but also that part of the literary tradition which for the stage in question has remained vital or has been revived . . .' The Bulgarian experience of Europe has often been mobilized, by Paissy, Drumev, and Voinikov among others; its evocation lay behind Aleko Konstantinov's success in *Bay Ganyo* and in Chudomir's humorous stories. 'Self–other' ostensibly marks for Bulgarian literature a change in perspective where the familiar image of self is exceeded to be substituted by a new one. The reference to other (Europe) with self allows a bracketing and a critical distancing from self. It is in fact the threshold phenomenon of generalization. 'Self–other' constitutes a new epistemic focus; it acts like a mirror to show what self is and what else it might be (Eco 1984: 203, 218). Or to take it further to Lacan's mirror stage with its primary narcissism and semantic latencies, it might be said that Bulgarian literature experiences this stage when it has to disrupt former images and templates which have been accumulated, only to be subsequently distorted in self-complacency. The constituting of a new *I* falls back upon 'self–other' as it acknowledges insufficiency in its own world. The dialectic of identification with the other will help establish for self a new relation between *Innenwelt* and *Umwelt*. The European perspective formulates the required exteriority and the process is to lead from insufficiency through anticipation to an alienating identity. The symbolic matrix of the new *I*, as Lacan asserts, will evolve to a social function while telling itself *Thou art that* ('Europeans we are, yet still not quite', Aleko Konstantinov 1895; 'To become an-other, one should first understand what one really is like', Stratiev 1993). Exteriorization through self-parody and injection of negativity in strong doses start a maturation in the subject's new mental development (Lacan 1980: 1–7). So why not imagine that it might extend an invitation for another journey to self and the nonfulfilled trends of Bulgarian literature?

References

Andreev, A. (1994). 'Ot totalitarna durzhava kum totalitarna natsiya.' *Kultura* 32.4 (3 November).

Belyaeva, S. (1986). *Vreme, literatura, chovek*. Sofia, Narodna kultura.

Bogdanov, B. (1991). 'Za bulgarskata literatura i predelite na ezika.' *Literaturna missul* 35.11–30.

Dichev, I. (1990). 'Inteligentsiyata. Opit za mitologiya'. *Plamuk* 34:iv.95–109.

Dimitrov, R. (1990). 'Zhurnalistika ili "suobrazistika"?'. *Plamuk* 34:iv.119–26.

Dimitrov-Robanov, I. (1993). 'Bay Ganyo i gravitatsiyata'. *Literatura i izkustvo* 1.28–31.

Djokova, T. (1991). 'Ivan Andreichin – cherti ot portreta na bulgarskata inteligentsiya'. *Plamuk* 35:vii.43–6.

Eco, U. (1984). *Semiotics and the Philosophy of Language*. London, Macmillan.

'Ezik i obshtestvo' debate (1994). *Ezik i literatura* 69:i.52–65.

Genchev, N. (1990). 'Smeshna istoriya'. *Septemvri* 43:v.138–92; vi.139–201.

Georgiev, N. (1990a). 'Ideologiya i literatura' debate. *Plamuk* 34:x.109–26; xi.95–106.

—— (1990b). 'Ilyuziyata Aprilsko obnovlenie 1963'. *Plamuk* 34:xi.3–33.

—— (1991). 'Putuvane kum Evropa'. *Literaturna missul* 35:iv.3–40.

Kamenov, Y. (1994). 'V zashtita na literatorite-polititsi'. *Letopissi* 3:vii–viii.109–12.

Kirov, K. (1991). 'Shto e inteligentsiya?'. *Nov Zlatorog* 2:i.49–55.

Kirova, M. (1991). 'Nashiyat totalitaren kharakter'. *Letopissi* 1:vii.139–57.

Konstantinov, A. (1895). *Bay Ganyo*. Sofia, Daskalov & Co.

Kristeva, J. (1992). 'Tozi chuzhdenets'. *Literaturen vestnik* (30 March–5 April). 13.

—— (1993). 'Kak se prisazhda kultura'. *Kultura* 31 (30 July). 3.

'Kum chitatelite' (1991). *Kritika i humanism* 1. 5–10.

Kyosev, A. (1991). 'Sredna Evropa i Balkanite na pazara na geopoliticheskite obrazi'. *Kritika i humanizm* 3.243–57; 4.101–12.

Lacan, J. (1980). *Écrits*. London, Routledge.

Likova, R. (1991). 'Groteskno-parodiyni elementi v nai-novata ni beletristika'. *Vek 21* (11–17 December). 1,3.

Malinov, A. (1993). 'Prostranstvo i vreme v bulgarskata poeziya ot osemdesette godini'. *Literaturen vestnik* 2 (10–24 January). 4,5.

Mateev, E. (1991).'Durzhavnikut Stambolov v bulgarskata istoriya'. *Letopissi* 1:x.67–88.

Mladenov, I. (1990). 'Metaforata pri totalitarizma'. *Vek 21*:xxxiv (21 November). 6.

Nachev, V. (1990). 'Zanayatchiyata'. *Literaturen vestnik-Veliko Tirnovo* 9 (14–27 September). 1–2.

Nedelchev, M. (1991). Biografskiyat obraz na Stambolov – tipove mitologizatsii i demitologizatsii'. *Letopissi* 1:iii.140–56.

Nichev, B. (1991). 'Kum nov prochit na suvremennata bulgarska literatura'. *Literaturna missul* 35:i.5–10.

Ognyanov, M. (1991). 'Evropeizmut kum koito se stremim'. *Literaturen forum* (17 January). 1,7.

Popovski, V. (1990). 'Metaforite na vlastta'. *Literaturen forum* (13 December).1,4.

Pozharliev, R. (1993). 'Bulgarinut – individ, ekzemplyar ili eksponat'. *Literaturen vestnik* 32 (16–22 August).1,3.

Purvev, H. (1993). 'Razmisli vurhu kharakternite osobenosti na nashata literaturno-ezikova suvremennost'. *Ezik i literatura* 68:ii.3–19.

Rouve, P. (Peter Uvaliev) (1991). 'Ezik i poeziya. V chest na Hristo Ognyanov'. *Literaturna missul* 35:x.3–22.

Saparev, O. (1991). 'Ideologizirane na trivialnoto'. *Literaturna missul* 35:iii.3–33.

Slavov, A. (1990). 'Novata kritika'. *Plamuk* 34:xii.103–17.

—— (1991). 'The Shoppi Mind'. *Literatura* 1.91–104.

Stefanov, S. (1991). 'Edin neuspeshen opit za massovo izkustvo'. *Literaturna missul* 35:iii.133–41.

Stratiev, S. (1991). *Bulgarskiyat model*. Sofia, Ivan Vazov.

—— (1993). *Uprazhneniya po drugost*. Sofia, Ercul.

Terziev, K. (1991). 'Stambolov i Ferdinand'. *Letopissi* 1:i.16–39.

Tikhanov, G. (1992). 'Emigrantskata literatura i natsionalniyat literaturen prozes'. *Plamuk* 36:i.84–90.

Todorov, P. (1991). 'Paradoksi na literaturnata nomenklatura'. *Vek* 21:ii(9–15 January).6.

Todorov, T. (1991). 'Ideyata za obshtochoveshkoto: Evropa i drugite'. *Kritika i humanizm* 1:ii.115–17.

Uvaliev, P. (1991). 'Za suzdavaneto na evropeetsa'. *Literaturen vestnik* 31(9 September).1.

Zhechev, T. (1994a). 'Natsionalizmut i noviyat istoricheski opit'. *Letopissi* 3:iii–iv.3–10.

—— (1994b). 'Interview'. *Letopissi* 3:v–vi.5–14.

—— (1994c). 'Simeon Radev i Aleksandur Balabanov'. *Letopissi* 3:vii–viii.3–6.

Zlatarska, S. (1994). 'Slavyanskata emigrantska literatura kato sotsiokulturen problem'. *Letopissi* 3:iii–iv.144–56.

Books Received

Critical Theory: General

Bannet, Eve Tabor. *Postcultural Theory: Critical Theory after the Marxist Paradigm.* Macmillan (1993). pp. 226. ISBN 0 333 58456 2.

Bennett, Andrew, ed. *Reading Reading: Essays on the Theory and Practice of Reading.* University of Tampere (1993). pp. 237. ISBN 9 5144 3429 3.

Burnett, David. *The Olive of Odysseus: Function and Form in Poetry.* New Century Press (1993). pp. 79. ISBN 0 9485 4504 6.

Clifford, John, and John Schilb, eds. *Writing Theory and Critical Theory.* MLA (1994). pp. 374. ISBN 0 87352 576 0.

Cunningham, Valentine. *In the Reading Gaol: Postmodernity, Texts, and History.* Blackwell (1994). pp. 418. ISBN 0 631 15198 2.

Fairlamb, Horace L. *Critical Conditions: Postmodernity and the Question of Foundations.* Cambridge University Press (1994). pp. 271. ISBN 0 521 45665 7.

Gans, Eric. *Originary Thinking: Elements of Generative Anthropology.* Stanford University Press (1993). pp. 225. ISBN 0 8047 2114 9.

Gubar, Susan, and Jonathan Kamholtz. *English Inside and Out: The Places of Literary Criticism.* Routledge (1993). pp. 138. ISBN 0 415 90668 7.

Harrison, Charles, and Paul Wood, eds. *Art in Theory 1900–1990: An Anthology of Changing Ideas.* Blackwell (1992). pp. 1189. ISBN 0 631 16575 4.

Jackson, Leonard. *The Dematerialisation of Karl Marx: Literature and Marxist Theory.* Longman (1994). pp. 312. ISBN 0 582 06655 7.

Lechte, John. *Fifty Key Contemporary Thinkers: From Structuralism to Postmodernity.* Routledge (1994). pp. 251. ISBN 0 415 07408 8.

McNay, Lois. *Foucault: A Critical Introduction.* Continuum (1994). pp. 196. ISBN 0 8264 0778 1.

Marshall, Donald G. *Contemporary Critical Theory: A Selective Bibliography.* MLA (1993). pp. 201. ISBN 0 87352 964 2.

Menocal, Maria Rosa. *Shards of Love: Exile and the Origins of the Lyric.* Duke University Press (1994). pp. 295. ISBN 0 8223 1419 3.

Patterson, Annabel. *Reading Between the Lines.* Routledge (1993). pp. 339. ISBN 0 415 09241 8.

Peck, John, and Martin Coyle. *Literary Terms and Criticism.* Macmillan (1993). pp. 222. ISBN 0 333 58887 8.

Purdie, Susan. *Comedy: The Mastery of Discourse.* Harvester Wheatsheaf (1993). pp. 186. ISBN 0 7450 0724 4.

Radcliffe, David Hill. *Forms of Reflection: Genre and Culture in Meditational Writing.* Johns Hopkins University Press (1993). pp. 232. ISBN 0 8018 4500 9.

Ronell, Avital. *Crack Wars: Literature Addiction Mania.* University of Nebraska Press (1993). pp. 175. ISBN 0 8032 8944 8.

Ronell, Avital. *Finitude's Score: Essays for the End of the Millennium.* University of Nebraska Press (1994). pp. 368. ISBN 0 8032 3911 4.

Selfe, Cynthia L., and Susan Hilligoss, eds. *Literacy and Computers: The Complications of Teaching and Learning with Technology.* MLA (1994). pp. 387. ISBN 0 87352 580 9.

Wales, Katie, ed. *Feminist Linguistics in Literary Criticism.* D. S. Brewer (1994). pp. 157. ISBN 0 85991 411 9.

Woodmansee, Martha, and Peter Jaszi, eds. *The Construction of Authorship: Textual Appropriation in Law and Literature.* Duke University Press (1994). pp. 462. ISBN 0 8223 1412 6.

Wilding, Michael. *Social Visions.* Sydney Studies (1993). pp. 196. ISBN 0 9494 0506 X.

Williams, Eric B. *The Mirror and the Word: Modernism, Literary Theory, & Georg Trakl.* University of Nebraska Press (1993). pp. 350. ISBN 0 8032 4756 7.

Rhetoric and Deconstruction

Allen, Graham. *Harold Bloom: A Poetics of Conflict.* Harvester Wheatsheaf (1994). pp. 200. ISBN 0 7450 0944 1.

Bennington, Geoffrey, and Jacques Derrida. *Jacques Derrida.* University of Chicago Press (1993). pp. 417. ISBN 0 226 04261 8.

Blanchot, Maurice. *The Work of Fire.* Stanford University Press (1995). pp. 344. ISBN 0 8047 2493 8.

Caputo, John D. *Against Ethics: Contributions to a Poetics of Obligation with Constant Reference to Deconstruction.* Indiana University Press (1993). pp. 292. ISBN 0 253 20816 5.

Cavell, Stanley. *Philosophical Passages: Wittgenstein, Emerson, Austin, Derrida.* Blackwell (1995). pp. 200. ISBN 0 631 192271 9.

de Graef, Ortwin. *Serenity in Crisis: A Preface to Paul de Man 1939–1960.* University of Nebraska Press (1993). pp. 240. ISBN 0 8032 1694 7.

de Graef, Ortwin. *Titanic Light. Paul de Man's Post-Romanticism 1960–1969.* University of Nebraska Press (1995). pp. 289. ISBN 0 8032 1695 5.

de Man, Paul. *Romanticism and Contemporary Criticism.* Johns Hopkins University Press (1993). pp. 212. ISBN 0 8018 4460 6.

Derrida, Jacques. *Memoirs of the Blind. The Self-Portrait and Other Ruins.* University of Chicago Press (1993). pp. 141. ISBN 0 226 14307 4.

Derrida, Jacques. *Points . . . Interviews 1974–1994.* Stanford University Press (1995). pp. 499. ISBN 0 8047 2488 1.

Derrida, Jacques. *Spectres of Marx: The State of the Debt, the Work of Mourning, and the New International.* Routledge (1994). pp. 198. ISBN 0 415 91045 5.

Elam, Diane. *Feminism and Deconstruction: Ms en Abyme.* Routledge (1994). pp. 154. ISBN 0 415 09166 7.

Harland, Richard. *Beyond Superstructuralism.* Routledge (1993). pp. 259. ISBN 0 415 06359 0.

Johnson, Barbara. *The Wake of Deconstruction.* Blackwell (1994). pp. 112. ISBN 0 631 18963 7.

Johnson, Christopher. *System and Writing in the Philosophy of Jacques Derrida.* Cambridge University Press (1993). pp. 234. ISBN 0 521 41492 X.

Madison, Gary, ed. *Working through Derrida.* Northwestern University Press (1993). pp. 284. ISBN 0 8101 1079 2.

Mailloux, Steven. *Rhetoric, Sophistry, Pragmatism.* Cambridge University Press (1995). pp. 251. ISBN 0 521 46780 2.

Miller, J. Hillis. *Topographies.* Stanford University Press (1995). pp. 376. ISBN 0 8047 2379 6.

Nealon, Jeffrey T. *Double Reading: Postmodernism after Deconstruction.* Cornell University Press (1993). pp. 200. ISBN 0 801 422853 X.

Payne, Michael. *Reading Theory. An Introduction to Lacan, Derrida, and Kristeva.* Blackwell (1993). pp. 250. ISBN 0 631 18289 6.

Rockmore, Tom. *Heidegger and French Philosophy: Humanism, Antihumanism and Being.* Routledge (1995). pp. 250. ISBN 0 415 11181 1.

Silverman, Hugh J. *Textualities: Between Hermeneutics and Deconstruction.* Routledge (1994). pp. 269. ISBN 0 415 90819 1.

Smith, Robert. *Derrida and Autobiography*. Cambridge University Press (1995). pp. 194. ISBN 0 521 46581 8.

Spivak, Gayatri Chakravorty. *Outside in the Teaching Machine*. Routledge (1993). pp. 335. ISBN 0 415 90489 7.

Vattimo, Gianni. *The Adventure of Difference: Philosophy after Nietzsche and Heidegger*. Polity (1993). pp. 192. ISBN 0 7456 0497 8.

Wheeler, Kathleen M. *Romanticism, Pragmatism and Deconstruction*. Blackwell (1993). pp. 302. ISBN 0 631 18964 5.

Wigley, Mark. *The Architecture of Deconstruction: Derrida's Haunt*. MIT Press (1993). pp. 278. ISBN 0 262 23170 0.

Wihl, Gary. *The Contingency of Theory: Pragmatism, Expressivism, and Deconstruction*. Yale University Press (1994). pp. 215. ISBN 0 300 05798 9.

Wood, David, ed. *Of Derrida, Heidegger, and Spirit*. Northwestern University Press (1993). pp. 149. ISBN 0 8101 1093 8.

Psychoanalysis

Balint, Enid. *Before I was I: Psychoanalysis and the Imagination*. Free Association Books (1993). pp. 248. ISBN pb 1 8534 3187 7.

Bléandonu, Gérard. *Wilfred Bion: His Life and Works, 1897–1979*. Trans. Clare Pajaczkowska. Free Association Books (1994). pp. 303. ISBN pb 0 898 62185 2.

Bowie, Malcolm. *Psychoanalysis and the Future of Theory*. Blackwell (1993). pp. 162. ISBN 0 631 18925 4.

Bowlby, Rachel. *Shopping with Freud*. Routledge (1993). pp. 134. ISBN 0 415 06006 0.

Breen, Dana, ed. *The Gender Conundrum: Psychoanalytic Perspectives on Femininity and Masculinity*. Routledge (1993). pp. 304. ISBN 0 415 09163 2.

Brenkman, John. *Straight Male Modern: A Cultural Critique of Psychoanalysis*. Routledge (1993). pp. 269. ISBN 0 415 90217 7.

Brennan, Teresa. *History after Lacan*. Routledge (1993). pp. 239. ISBN 0 415 01116 7.

Brooks, Peter. *Psychoanalysis and Storytelling*. Blackwell (1993). pp. 144. ISBN 0 631 19007 4.

Brunner, José. *Freud and the Politics of Psychoanalysis*. Blackwell (1995). pp. 238. ISBN 0 631 16404 9.

Butler, Judith. *Bodies that Matter*. Routledge (1993). pp. 288. ISBN 0 415 90365 3.

Chodorow, Nancy J. *Femininities, Masculinities, Sexualities: Freud and Beyond.* Free Association Books (1994). pp. 132. ISBN pb 1 8534 3380 2.

Cohan, Steven, and Ina Rae Hark, eds. *Screening the Male.* Routledge (1993). pp. 272. ISBN 0 415 07758 3.

Copjec, Joan. *Read my Desire: Lacan against the Historicists.* MIT Press (1994). pp. 272. ISBN 0 262 03219 8.

Creed, Barbara. *The Monstrous Feminine.* Routledge (1993). pp. 182. ISBN 0 415 05258 0.

Edelman, Lee. *Homographesis: Essays in Gay Literary and Cultural Theory.* Routledge (1994). pp. 284. ISBN 0 415 90258 4.

Elliott, Anthony. *Psychoanalytic Theory: An Introduction.* Blackwell (1994). pp. 183. ISBN 0 631 18846 0.

Elliott, Anthony, and Stephen Frosh, eds. *Psychoanalysis in Contexts.* Routledge (1995). pp. 254. ISBN 0 415 09703 7.

Flax, Jane. *Disputed Subjects: Essays on Psychoanalysis, Politics, and Philosophy.* Routledge (1993). pp. 188. ISBN 0 415 90789 6.

Fordham, Michael. *Freud, Jung, Klein – the Fenceless Field.* Routledge (1995). pp. 284. ISBN 0 415 11080 7.

Frosh, Stephen. *Sexual Difference: Masculinity and Psychoanalysis.* Routledge (1994). pp. 153. ISBN 0 415 06843 6.

Gilman, Sander L. *Freud, Race, and Gender.* Princeton University Press (1993). pp. 277. ISBN 0 691 03245 9.

Hart, Lynda. *Fatal Women: Lesbian Sexuality and the Mark of Aggression.* Routledge (1994). pp. 201. ISBN 0 415 10081 X.

Heald, Suzette, and Ariane Deluz, eds. *Anthropology and Psychoanalysis: An Encounter through Culture.* Routledge (1994). pp. 244. ISBN 0 415 09742 8.

Holland, Eugene W. *Baudelaire and Schizoanalysis.* Cambridge University Press (1993). pp. 306. ISBN 0 521 41980 8.

Kavaler-Adler, Susan. *The Compulsion to Create: A Psychoanalytic Study of Women Artists.* Routledge (1993). pp. 356. ISBN 0 415 90710 1.

Kochhar-Lindgren, Gray. *Narcissus Transformed.* Pennsylvania State University Press (1993). pp. 138. ISBN 0 2710 0907 1.

Lacan, Jacques. *The Psychoses (1955–56).* Routledge (1993). pp. 341. ISBN pb 0 415 10183 2.

Maclean, Mary. *The Name of the Mother: Writing Illegitimacy.* Routledge (1994). pp. 269. ISBN 0 415 10686 9.

Myers, Diana T. *Subjection and Subjectivity: Psychoanalytic Feminism and Moral Philosophy.* Routledge (1994). pp. 199. ISBN 0 415 90471 4.

Newman, Robert D. *Transgressions of Reading*. Duke University Press (1993). pp. 179. ISBN 0 8223 1280 8.

Otis, Laura. *Organic Memory*. University of Nebraska Press (1994). pp. 297. ISBN 0 8032 3561 5.

Payne, Michael. *Reading Theory: An Introduction to Lacan, Derrida, and Kristeva*. Blackwell (1993). pp. 250. ISBN 0 631 18288 8.

Phillips, Adam. *On Flirtation*. Faber & Faber (1994). pp. 226. ISBN 0 571 14496 9.

Pontalis, J.-B. *Love of Beginnings*. Free Association Books (1993). pp. 171. ISBN pb 1 8534 3129 X.

Ragland, Ellie. *Essays on the Pleasures of Death: From Freud to Lacan*. Routledge (1995). pp. 240. ISBN 0 415 90721 7.

Rose, Jacqueline. *Why War?* Blackwell (1993). pp. 274. ISBN 0 631 18923 8.

Salecl, Renata. *The Spoils of Freedom: Psychoanalysis and Feminism after the Fall of Socialism*. Routledge (1994). pp. 167. ISBN 0 415 07357 X.

Shamdasani, Sonu, and Michael Münchow, eds. *Speculations after Freud*. Routledge (1994). pp. 227. ISBN 0 415 07655 2.

Spensley, Sheila. *Frances Tustin*. Routledge (1995). pp. 154. ISBN 0 415 09262 0.

Feminism

Afshar, H., and M. Maynard, eds. *The Dynamics of 'Race' and Gender: Some Feminist Interventions*. Taylor and Francis (1993). pp. 263. ISBN 0 7484 0212 8.

Anthias, E, and N. Yuval-Davis. *Racialised Boundaries: Race, Nation, Colour and Class and the Anti-Racist Struggle*. Routledge (1993). pp. 240. ISBN 0 415 10388 6.

Brown, L., H. Collins, P. Green, M. Humm and M. Landells, eds. *International Handbook of Women's Studies*. Harvester Wheatsheaf (1993). pp. 449. ISBN 0 7450 1413 5.

Butler, J. and J. Scott. *Feminists Theorise the Political*. Routledge (1992). pp. 485. ISBN 0 415 90274 6.

Cornell, D. *Transformation: Recollective Imagination and Sexual Difference*. Routledge (1993). pp. 239. ISBN hb 0 415 90746 2, pb 0 415 90747 0.

Dodd, K., ed. *A Sylvia Pankhurst Reader*. Manchester University Press (1993). pp. 304. ISBN hb 0 7190 2888 4, pb 0 7190 2889 2.

Ellman, M. *The Hunger Artists: Starving, Writing and Imprisonment.* Virago (1993). pp. 136. ISBN 1 85381 675 2.

Flint, K. *The Woman Reader: 1837–1914.* Oxford University Press (1993). pp. 366. ISBN 0 19 811719 1.

Frazer, E., J. Hornsby, and S. Lovibond, eds. *Ethics: A Feminist Reader.* Blackwell (1992). pp. 500. ISBN hb 0 631 17829 5, pb 0 631 17831 7.

Gever, M., J. Greyson and P. Parmar, eds. *Queer Looks: Perspectives on Lesbian and Gay Film and Video.* Routledge (1993). pp. 413. ISBN 0 415 90742 X.

Grant. J. *Fundamental Feminism: Contesting the Core Concepts of Feminist Theory.* Routledge (1993). pp. 240. ISBN hb 0 415 90825 6, pb 0 415 90826 4.

Greene, G., and C. Kahn, eds. *Changing Subjects: The Making of Feminist Literary Criticism.* Routledge (1993). pp. 283. ISBN 0 415 08685 X and 0 415 08686 8.

Griffin, G. *Heavenly Love? Lesbian Images in Twentieth Century Women's Writing.* Manchester University Press (1993). pp. 202. ISBN 0 7190 2880 9 and 0 7190 2881 7.

Griffin, G., ed. *Outwrite: Lesbianism and Popular Culture.* Pluto (1993). pp. 204. ISBN 0 7453 0688 8.

Hennessy, R. *Materialist Feminism and the Politics of Discourse.* Routledge (1993). pp. 176. ISBN 0 415 90480 3.

hooks, b. *Sisters of the Yam: Black Women and Self-Recovery.* South End Press (1993). pp. 200. ISBN 1 8732 6203 5.

Jackson, S., with K. Atkinson, D. Beddoe, T. Brewer, S. Faulkner, A. Hucklesby, R. Pearson, H. Power, J. Prince, M. Ryan, P. Young, eds. *Women's Studies: A Reader.* Harvester Wheatsheaf (1993). pp. 525. ISBN hb 0 7450 1187 X, pb 0 7450 1188 8.

Kaplan, E. A. *Motherhood and Representation: The Mother in Popular Culture and Melodrama.* Routledge (1992). pp. 256. ISBN hb 0 415 01126 X, pb 0 415 01127 2.

Kennedy, M., C. Lubelksa, and V. Walsh, eds. *Making Connections: Women's Studies, Women's Movements, Women's Lives.* Taylor and Francis (1993). pp. 210. ISBN 0 74840 098 2.

Kramarae, C., and D. Spender, eds. *The Knowledge Explosion: Generations of Feminist Scholarship.* Harvester Wheatsheaf (1993). pp. 533. ISBN 0 7450 1549 4.

Landry, D., and G. Maclean. *Materialist Feminisms.* Blackwell (1993). pp. 270. ISBN 1 55786 185 4.

Luftig, V. *Seeing Together: Friendship between the Sexes in English*

Writing from Mills to Woolf. Stanford University Press (1993). pp 320. ISBN 0 8047 2168 8.

Meaney, G. *(Un)Like Subjects: Women, Theory, Fiction.* Routledge (1993). pp. 255. ISBN hb 0 415 07098 8, pb 0 415 07099 6.

Mernissi, F. *The Forgotten Queens of Islam.* Polity Press (1993). pp. 240. ISBN 0 745 61419 1.

Morris, P. *Literature and Feminism.* Blackwell (1993). pp. 220. ISBN hb 0 631 18419 8, pb 0 631 18421 X.

Oliver, K. *Reading Kristeva: Unravelling the Double-Bind.* Indiana University Press (1993). pp. 218. ISBN 0 253 34173 6 and 0 253 20761 4.

Ostriker, A. S. *Feminist Revision and the Bible.* Blackwell (1993). pp. 148. ISBN 0 631 18798 7.

Palmer, P. *Contemporary Lesbian Writing: Dreams, Desires, Difference.* Open University Press (1993). pp. 141. ISBN 0 3350 9039 7 and 0 3350 9038 9.

Probyn, E. *Sexing the Self: Gendered Positions in Cultural Studies.* Routledge (1993). pp. 189. ISBN 0 415 07356 1.

Scheman, N. *Engenderings: Constructions of Knowledge, Authority and Privilege.* Routledge (1993). pp. 254. ISBN 0 415 90740 3.

Singer, L. *Erotic Warfare: Sexual Theory and Politics in the Age of Epidemic*, ed. and introduced by J. Butler and M. McGrogan. Routledge (1993). pp. 210. ISBN 0 415 90202 9.

Stacey, J. *Star Gazing: Hollywood Cinema and Female Spectatorship.* Routledge (1993). pp. 282. ISBN 0 415 09179 9.

Still, J. and M. Worton, eds. *Textuality and Sexuality: Reading Theories and Practices.* Manchester University Press (1993). pp. 242. ISBN hb 0 7190 3604 6, pb 0 7190 3605 4.

Wolfe, S., and J. Penelope, eds. *Sexual Practice, Textual Theory: Lesbian Cultural Criticism.* Blackwell (1993). pp. 388. ISBN 1 5578 6100 5 and 1 5578 6101 3.

Historicism

Adorno, Theodor. *Hegel: Three Studies.* MIT Press (1993). pp. 160. ISBN 0 262 01131 X.

Adorno, Theodor. *Notes to Literature*, vol. 2. Columbia University Press (1994). pp. 350. ISBN 0 231 06913 8.

Bahti, Timothy. *Allegories of History: Literary Historiography after Hegel.* Johns Hopkins University Press (1992). pp. 336. ISBN 0 8018 4342 1.

Bird, Jon, et al., eds. *Mapping the Futures: Local Cultures, Global Change.* Routledge (1993). pp. 288. ISBN 0 415 07018 X.

Bourdieu, Pierre. *The Field of Cultural Production.* Polity Press (1993). pp. 322. ISBN 0 7456 0987 2.

Bygrave, Stephen. *Kenneth Burke: Rhetoric and Ideology.* Routledge (1993). pp. 124. ISBN 0 415 02211 8.

Cox, Jeffrey, and Larry J. Reynolds, eds. *New Historical Literary Study: Essays on Reproducing Texts, Representing History.* Princeton University Press (1993). pp. 337. ISBN 0 691 01546 5.

Dworkin, Dennis L., and Leslie G. Roman, eds. *Views Beyond the Border Country: Raymond Williams and Cultural Politics.* Routledge (1993). pp. 364. ISBN 0 415 90276 2.

Glenny, Michael, and Richard Taylor, eds. *S. M. Eisenstein: Selected Works. Volume II: Towards A Theory of Montage.* BFI Publishing (1991). pp. 428. ISBN 0 85170 211 2.

Grossberg, Lawrence, Cary Nelson and Paula Treichler, eds. *Cultural Studies.* Routledge (1992). pp. 788. ISBN 0 415 90345 9.

Haverkamp, Anselm. *Gewalt und Gerechtigkeit: Derrida-Benjamin.* Suhrkamp (1994). pp. 444. ISBN 3 51811 706 8.

Hays, Michael, ed. *Critical Conditions: Regarding the Historical Moment.* University of Minnesota Press (1992). pp. 152. ISBN 0 8166 2022 9.

Hestetun, Oyunn. *A Prison-House of Myth?* Uppsala (1993). pp. 261. ISBN 9 1554 3064 3.

Hewitt, Andrew. *Fascist Modernism: Aesthetics, Politics, and the Avant-Garde.* Stanford University Press (1993). pp. 222. ISBN 0 8047 2117 3.

Hitchcock, Peter. *Dialogics of the Oppressed.* University of Minnesota Press (1993). pp. 244. ISBN 0 8166 2107 1.

Inglis, Fred. *Cultural Studies.* Blackwell (1993). pp. 262. ISBN 0 631 18454 6.

Jackson, Leonard. *The Dematerialisation of Karl Marx: Literature and Marxist Theory.* Longman (1994). pp. 312. ISBN 0 582 06655 7.

Jenkins, Richard. *Pierre Bourdieu.* Routledge (1992). pp. 190. ISBN 0 415 05798 1.

Kaplan, E. Ann, and Michael Sprinker, eds. *The Althusserian Legacy.* Verso (1993). pp. 245. ISBN 0 86091 594 8.

Leitch, Vincent B. *Cultural Criticism, Literary Theory, Poststructuralism.* Columbia University Press (1992). pp. 186. ISBN 0 231 07970 2.

Lukács, Georg. *German Realists in the Nineteenth Century*. Libris (1993). pp. 360. ISBN 1 8703 5260 2.

McGuigan, Jim. *Cultural Populism*. Routledge (1992). pp. 290. ISBN 0 415 06295 0.

McIlroy, John, and Sallie Westwood, eds. *Border Country: Raymond Williams in Adult Education*. National Institute of Adult Continuing Education (1993). pp. 343. ISBN 1 8729 4128 1.

Morgan, W. John, and Peter Preston, eds. *Raymond Williams: Politics, Education, Letters*. Macmillan (1993). pp. 215. ISBN 0 312 08357 2.

Reed, Walter L. *Dialogues of the Word; The Bible as Literature According to Bakhtin*. Oxford University Press (1993). pp. 223. ISBN 0 19 507997 3.

Rella, Franco. *The Myth of the Other: Lacan, Foucault, Deleuze, Bataille*. Maisonneuve Press (1994). pp. 127. ISBN 0 94462 421 9.

Resch, Robert Paul. *Althusser and the Renewal of Marxist Social Theory*. University of California Press (1992). pp. 436. ISBN 0 520 06082 2.

Wollen, Peter. *Raiding the Icebox: Reflections on Twentieth-Century Culture*. Verso (1993). pp. 222. ISBN 0 86091 578 6.

Wright, Crispin. *Realism, Meaning and Truth*, Second edition. Blackwell (1993). pp. 509. ISBN 0 631 17118 5.

Colonial Discourse/Post-Colonial Theory

Azim, Firdous. *The Colonial Rise of the Novel*. Routledge (1993). pp. 253. ISBN hb 0 415 07024 4, pb 0 415 09569 7.

Behdad, Ali. *Belated Travellers: Orientalism in the Age of Colonial Dissolution*. Duke University Press (1994). pp. 165. ISBN 0 8223 1471 1.

Bharucha, Rustum. *Theatre and the World: Performance and the Politics of Culture*. Routledge (1993). pp. 253. ISBN hb 0 415 09215 9, pb 0 415 09216 7.

Chatterjee, Partha. *The Nation and Its Fragments: Colonial and Postcolonial Histories*. Princeton University Press (1993). pp. 282. ISBN hb 0 691 03305 6, pb 0 691 01493 6.

Dirks, Nicholas, Geoff Eley and Sherry Ortner, eds. *Culture/Power/History: A Reader in Contemporary Social Theory*. Princeton University Press (1993). pp. 621. ISBN 0 691 02102 3.

Donaldson, Laura. *Decolonising Feminisms: Race, Gender and*

Empire-Building. Routledge (1993). pp. 175. ISBN hb 0 415 09217 5, pb 0 415 09218 3.

Gilroy, Paul. *The Black Atlantic: Modernity and Double Consciousness.* Verso (1993). pp. 261. ISBN hb 0 86091 401 1, pb 0 86091 675 8.

Gilroy, Paul. *Small Acts: Thoughts on the Politics of Black Cultures.* Serpent's Tail (1993). pp. 257. (ISBN not given).

James, Stanlie, and Abena Busia, eds. *Theorising Black Feminisms: The Visionary Pragmatism of Black Women.* Routledge (1993). pp. 300. ISBN hb 0 415 07336 7, pb 0 415 07337 5.

Jordan, Glen, and Chris Weedon. *Cultural Politics: Class, Gender, Race in the Postmodern World.* Blackwell (1995). pp. 624. ISBN 0 631 16228 3.

King, Bruce, ed. *The Later Fiction of Nadine Gordimer.* Macmillan (1993). pp. 249. ISBN hb 0 333 53416 6.

Kramer, Fritz. *The Red Fez.* Verso (1993). pp. 292. ISBN hb 0 86091 465 8.

Larrain, Jorge. *Ideology and Cultural Identity: Modernity and the Third World Presence.* Polity (1994). pp. 190. ISBN pb 0 7456 1316 0.

Rajan, Rajeswari Sunder. *Real and Imagined Women: Gender, Culture and Postcolonialism.* Routledge (1993). pp. 153. ISBN hb 0 415 08503 9, pb 0 415 08504 7.

Richards, Thomas. *The Imperial Archive: Knowledge and the Fantasy of Empire.* Verso (1993). pp. 179. ISBN hb 0 86091 400 3, pb 0 86091 605 7.

Said, Edward. *Culture and Imperialism.* Chatto & Windus (1993). pp. 444. ISBN hb 0 7011 3808 4.

Sprinker, Michael, ed. *Edward Said: A Critical Reader.* Blackwell (1993). pp. 272. ISBN hb 1 55786 228 1, pb 1 55786 229 X.

Spurr, David. *The Rhetoric of Empire: Colonial Discourse in Journalism, Travel Writing and Imperial Administration.* Duke University Press (1993). pp. 212. ISBN hb 0 8223 1303 0, pb 0 8223 1317 0.

Ukadike, N. Frank. *Black African Cinema.* University of California Press (1994). pp. 371. ISBN 0 520 07748 2.

White, Jonathan, ed. *Recasting the World: Writing After Colonialism.* Johns Hopkins University Press (1993). pp. 255. ISBN 0 8018 4606 4.

Williams, Patrick, and Chrisman, Laura, eds. *Colonial Discourse and Post-Colonial Theory: A Reader.* Harvester Wheatsheaf (1993). pp. 570. ISBN hb 0 7450 1490 9, pb 0 7450 1491 7.

Art History

Antliff, Mark. *Inventing Bergson: Cultural Politics and the Parisian Avant-Garde*. Princeton University Press (1993). pp. 237. ISBN 0 691 03202 5.

Baker, Steve. *Picturing the Beast: Animals, Identity and Representation*. Manchester University Press (1993). pp. 242. ISBN hb 0 7190 3377 2, pb 0 7190 3378 0.

Benjamin, Andrew, ed. *The Problems of Modernity: Adorno and Benjamin*. Routledge (1992). pp. 220. ISBN pb 0 415 06029 X.

Bernstein J. M. *The Fate of Art: Aesthetic Alienation from Kant to Derrida and Adorno*. Polity Press (1993). pp. 292. ISBN hb 0 7456 0406 4, pb 0 7456 1241 5.

Bianchini, Franco, and Michael Parkinson, eds. *Cultural Policy and Urban Regeneration: The West European Experience*. Manchester University Press (1993). pp. 220. ISBN 0 7190 3556 2.

Bown, Mathew Cullerne, and Brandon Taylor, eds. *Art of the Soviets: Painting, Sculpture and Architecture in a One-party State, 1917–1992*. Manchester University Press (1993). pp. 231. ISBN hb 0 7190 3734 4, pb 0 7190 3735 2.

Brooker, Peter. *Modernism/Postmodernism*. Longman (1992). pp. 268. ISBN hb 0 582 06358 2, pb 0 582 06357 4.

Cheetham, Mark A. *The Rhetoric of Purity: Essentialist Theory and the Advent of Abstract Painting*. Cambridge University Press (1993). pp. 194. ISBN hb 0 521 38546 6, pb 0 521 47759 X.

Cherry, Deborah. *Painting Women: Victorian Women Artists*. Routledge (1993). pp. 275. ISBN hb 0 415 06052 4, pb 0 415 06053 2.

Cottle, Simon. *TV News, Urban Conflict and the Inner City*. Leicester University Press (1993). pp. 252. ISBN hb 0 7185 1447 5, pb 0 71851 4629.

Daniels, Stephen. *Fields of Vision: Landscape Imagery and National Identity in England and the United States*. Princeton University Press (1993). pp. 257. ISBN 0 691 03273 4.

Diawara, Manthia. *African Cinema: Politics and Culture*. Indiana University Press (1992). pp. 192. ISBN hb 0 253 31704 5, pb 0 253 20707 X.

Distelberger, Rudolf, et al. *Western Decorative Arts*, Part I. National Gallery of Art, Washington, and Cambridge University Press (1993). pp. 333. ISBN 0 894 68162 1.

Easthope, Anthony, ed. *Contemporary Film Theory*. Longman (1993). pp. 218. ISBN hb 0 582 09031 8, pb 0 582 09032 6.

Docker, John. *Postmodernism and Popular Culture: A Cultural*

History. Cambridge University Press (1994). pp. 313. ISBN hb 0 5214 6045 X, pb 0 5214 6598 2.

Fer, Briony, David Batchelor and Paul Wood, *Realism, Rationalism, Surrealism: Art Between the Wars.* Open University in association with Yale University Press (1993). pp. 243. ISBN hb 0 300 05518 8, pb 0 300 05519 6.

Fine, Ben, and Ellen Leopold. *The World of Consumption.* Routledge (1993). pp. 361. ISBN hb 0 415 09588 3, pb 0 415 09589 1.

Frascina, Francis, Nigel Blake, Briony Fer, Tamar Garb and Charles Harrison. *Modernity and Modernism: French Painting in the Nineteenth Century.* Open University in Association with Yale University Press (1993). pp. 297. ISBN hb 0 300 05513 7, pb 0 300 05514 5.

Gee, Malcolm, ed. *Art Criticism since 1900.* Manchester University Press (1993). pp. 240. ISBN 0 7190 3784 0.

Gidley, Mick. *Modern American Culture: An Introduction.* Longman (1993). pp. 407. ISBN hb 0 582 05111 8, pb 0 582 05110 X.

Glassie, Henry. *Turkish Traditional Art Today.* Ministry of Culture of the Turkish Republic and Indiana University Press (1993). pp. 947. ISBN 0 253 32555 2.

Greenhalgh, Paul. *Quotations and Sources on Design and the Decorative Arts.* Manchester University Press (1993). pp. 246. ISBN hb 0 7190 3964 9, pb 0 7190 3965 7.

Hall, Marcia. *Color and Meaning: Practice and Theory in Renaissance Painting.* Cambridge University Press (1992). pp. 274. ISBN 0 521 39222 5.

Harrison, Charles, Francis Frascina and Gill Perry. *Primitivism, Cubism, Abstraction: The Early Twentieth Century.* Open University in association with Yale University Press (1993). pp. 270. ISBN hb 0 300 05515 3, pb 0 300 05516 3.

Harvey, Charles, and Jon Press. *William Morris: Design and Enterprise in Victorian Britain.* Manchester University Press (1991). pp. 257. ISBN hb 0 7190 2418 8, pb 0 7190 2419 6.

Haskell, Thomas L., and Richard F. Teichgraeber III, eds. *The Culture of the Market: Historical Essays.* Cambridge University Press (1993). pp. 524. ISBN 0 521 44468 3.

Hopkins, Jim, and Anthony Savile, eds. *Psychoanalysis, Mind and Art: Perspectives on Richard Wollheim.* Blackwell (1992). pp. 383. ISBN 0 631 17571 7.

Jencks, Chris. *Culture.* Routledge (1993). pp. 182. ISBN pb 0 415 07278 6.

Jencks, Chris, ed. *Cultural Reproduction.* Routledge (1993). pp. 257. ISBN hb 0 415 07182 9, pb 0 415 07183 6.

Johnson, Dorothy. *Jacques-Louis David: Art in Metamorphosis*. Princeton University Press (1993). pp. 316. ISBN 0 691 03218 1.

Johnson, Lewis. *Prospects, Thresholds, Interiors: Watercolours from the National Collection at the Victoria and Albert Museum*. Cambridge University Press (1994). pp. 250. ISBN hb 0 521 44488 8, pb 0 521 44927 8.

Julier, Guy. *Encyclopaedia of Twentieth Century Design and Designers*. Thames and Hudson (1993). pp. 216. ISBN pb 0 500 20269 9.

Kuspit, Donald. *The Cult of the Avant-Garde Artist*. Cambridge University Press (1993). pp. 175. ISBN hb 0 521 41345 1, pb 0 521 46922 8.

Kuspit, Donald. *Signs of Psyche in Modern and Post-Modern Art*. Cambridge University Press (1993). pp. 387. ISBN hb 0 521 44056 4, pb 0 521 44611 2.

Lewis, Justin. *Art, Culture and Enterprise*. Routledge (1990). pp. 164. ISBN hb 0 415 04449 9, pb 0 415 04450 2.

McEvilley, Thomas. *The Exile's Return: Toward a Redefinition of Painting for the Post-Modern Era*. Cambridge University Press (1993). pp. 231. ISBN pb 0 521 41672 8.

McGuigan, Jim. *Cultural Populism*. Routledge (1992). pp. 290. ISBN hb 0 415 06294 2, pb 0 415 06295 0.

McWilliam, Neil. *Dreams of Happiness: Social Art and the French Left 1830–1850*. Princeton University Press (1993), pp. 385. ISBN hb 0 691 03155 X.

Mainardi, Patricia. *The End of the Salon: Art and the State in the early Third Republic*. Cambridge University Press (1993). pp. 210. ISBN hb 0 521 43251 0, pb 0 521 46921 X.

Mattick, Paul, Jr., ed. *Eighteenth-Century Aesthetics and the Reconstruction of Art*. Cambridge University Press (1993). pp. 256. ISBN 0 521 43106 9.

Nash, David. *Secularism, Art and Freedom*. Leicester University Press (1992). pp. 211. ISBN 0 7185 1417 3.

Nigro, Salvatore. *Pontormo: Paintings and Frescoes*. Harry N. Abrams (1993). pp. 160. ISBN 0 8109 3727 1.

Parton, Anthony. *Mikhail Larionov and the Russian Avant-Garde*. Princeton University Press (1993). pp. 254. ISBN 0 691 03603 9.

Petric, Vlada. *Constructivism in Film*. Cambridge University Press (1993). pp. 325. ISBN hb 0 521 32174 3, pb 0 521 44387 3.

Plant, Sadie. *The Most Radical Gesture: The Situationist International in a Postmodern Age*. Routledge (1992). pp. 226. ISBN hb 0 415 06221 7, pb 0 415 06222 5.

Rifkin, Adrian. *Street Noises: Parisian Pleasure 1900–40*. Manchester University Press (1993). pp. 221. ISBN hb 0 7190 3835 9.

Satkowski, Leon. *Giorgio Vasari: Architect and Courtier*. Princeton University Press (1993). pp. 176, 239 ills. ISBN hb 0 691 03286 6.

Smith, Terry. *Making the Modern: Industry, Art, and Design in America*. University of Chicago Press (1993). pp. 512. ISBN hb 0 226 76346 3, pb 0 226 76346 3.

Smyth, Craig Hugh, and Peter M. Lukehart. *The Early Years of Art History in the United States*. Princeton University Press (1993). pp. 205, 122 ills. ISBN pb 0 691 03645 4.

Takeuchi, Melinda. *Taiga's True Views: The Language of Landscape Painting in Eighteenth-Century Japan*. Stanford University Press (1992). pp. 211. ISBN pb 0 8047 1915 2.

Tester, Keith. *The Life and Times of Post-Modernity*. Routledge (1993). pp. 168. ISBN hb 0 415 07545 9, pb 0 415 0983 2.

Tomlinson, John. *Cultural Imperialism*. Pinter (1991). pp. 187. ISBN hb 0 8618 7746 2, pb 0 8618 7751 9.

Walker, John. *Art and Artists on Screen*. Manchester University Press (1993). pp. 226. ISBN hb 0 7190 3780 8, pb 0 7190 3781 2.

Waugh, Patricia. *Practising Postmodernism, Reading Modernism*. Edward Arnold (1992). pp. 176. ISBN pb 0 340 55050 3.

Wood, Paul, Francis Frascina, Jonathan Harris and Charles Harrisson. *Modernism in Dispute: Art since the Forties*. Open University in association with Yale University Press (1993). pp. 267. ISBN hb 0 300 05521 8, pb 0 300 05522.

Young, Julian. *Nietzsche's Philosophy of Art*. Cambridge University Press (1993). pp. 170. ISBN hb 0 521 41124 6, pb 0 521 45575 8.

Zurbrugg, Nicholas. *The Parameters of Postmodernism*. Routledge (1993). pp. 183. ISBN hb 0 415 10561 7, pb 0 415 10562 5.

Popular Music

Beadle, Jeremy J. *Will Pop Eat Itself? Pop Music in the Soundbite Era*. Faber (1993). pp. 269. ISBN 0 571 16241 X.

Bennett, Tony, Simon Frith, Lawrence Grossberg, John Shepherd and Graeme Turner. *Rock and Popular Music: Politics, Policies, Institutions*. Routledge (1993). pp. 306. ISBN 0 415 06369 8.

Blundell, Alda, John Shepherd and Ian Taylor, eds. *Relocating Cultural Studies: Developments in Theory and Research*. Routledge (1993). pp. 236. ISBN 0 415 07549 1.

Bowie, Angela, and Patrick Carr. *Backstage Passes: Life on the Wild Side with David Bowie.* Orion (1993). pp. 262. ISBN 1 85797 021 7.

Boyes, Georgina. *The Imagined Village: Culture, Ideology and the English Folk Revival.* Manchester University Press (1994). pp. 285. ISBN 0 7190 4571 1.

Brett, Philip, Elizabeth Wood and Gary C. Thomas. *Queering The Pitch: The New Gay and Lesbian Musicology.* Routledge (1994). pp. 355. ISBN 0 415 90752 7.

Bussy, Pascal. *Kraftwerk: Man, Machine and Music.* SAF (1993). pp. 192. ISBN 0 9467 1909 8.

Clarke, Donald. *The Rise and Fall of Popular Music,* Viking (1995). pp. 620. ISBN 0 670 83244 8.

Clayson, Alan, and Spencer Leigh. *Aspects of Elvis: Tryin' To Get To You.* Sidgwick & Jackson (1994). pp. 346. ISBN 0 283 06217 7.

Cole, Richard, with Richard Trubo. *Stairway To Heaven: Led Zeppelin Uncensored.* Simon & Schuster (1993). pp. 391. ISBN 0 671 71232 2.

Coleman, Ray. *Clapton: The Authorised Biography.* Sidgwick & Jackson (1994). pp. 332. ISBN 0 283 06211 8.

Cope, Julian. *Head-On: Memories of the Liverpool Punk-Scene and the Story of the Teardrop Explodes; 1976–82.* Magog (1994). ISBN (none given).

Corbett, John. *Extended Play: Sounding Off from John Cage to Dr Funkenstein.* Duke University Press (1994). pp. 342. ISBN 0 8223 1473 8.

Coyne, Kevin. *Show Business.* Serpent's Tail (1993). pp. 162. ISBN 1 85242 251 3.

Crafts, Susan D., Daniel Cavicchi and Charles Keil. *My Music.* Wesleyan University Press (1993). pp. 218. ISBN 0 8195 6264 5.

Docherty, Thomas, ed. *Postmodernism: A Reader.* Harvester Wheatsheaf (1993). pp. 528. ISBN 0 7450 1242 4.

Doty, Alexander. *Making Things Perfectly Queer.* University of Minnesota Press (1993). pp. 146. ISBN 0 8166 2245 0.

During, Simon, ed. *The Cultural Studies Reader.* Routledge (1993). pp. 478. ISBN 0 415 07709 5.

Ennis, H. Philip. *The Seventh Stream: The Emergence of RocknRoll in American Popular Music.* Wesleyan University Press (1993). pp. 445. ISBN 0 8195 6257 2.

Flanagan, Bill. *U2 at the End of the World.* Bantam (1995). pp. 480. ISBN 0 593 03626 3.

Frith, Simon, Andrew Goodwin and Lawrence Grossberg, eds. *Sound and Vision: The Music Video Reader.* Routledge (1993). pp. 215. ISBN 0 415 09431 3.

Gaar, Gillian G. *She's a Rebel: The History of Women in Rock & Roll*. Blandford (1993). pp. 467. ISBN 0 7137 2379 3.

Gambaccini, Paul, Tim Rice and Jonathan Rice. *British Hit Singles*. Guinness (1993). pp. 432. ISBN 0 85112 526 3.

Gammond, Peter. *The Oxford Companion to Popular Music*. Oxford University Press (1993). pp. 739. ISBN 0 19 280004 3.

Gill, John. *Queer Noises: Male and Female Homosexuality in Twentieth-Century Music*. Cassell (1995). pp. 184. ISBN 0 304 34302 1.

Goldman, Albert. *Sound Bites*. Abacus (1993). pp. 299. ISBN 0 349 10464 6.

Goodwin, Andrew. *Dancing in the Distraction Factory: Music Television and Popular Culture*. Routledge (1993). pp. 237. ISBN 0 415 09170 5.

Gray, Ann, and Jim McGuigan. *Studying Culture: An Introductory Reader*. Edward Arnold (1993). pp. 242. ISBN 0 340 55628 5.

Haralambos, Michael. *Right On: From Blues to Soul in Black America*. Causeway Press (1994). pp. 187. ISBN 1 873 92923 4.

Hayward, Philip, Tony Mitchell and Roy Shuker, eds. *North Meets South: Popular Music in Rotearoa/New Zealand*. Perfect Beat Publications (1994). pp. 125. ISBN 0 646 16901 7.

Heath, Chris. *Pet Shop Boys Versus America*. Viking (1993). pp. 250. ISBN 0 670 85274 0.

Herman, Gary. *Rock'n'Roll Babylon*. Plexus (1994). pp. 224. ISBN 0 85965 199 1.

Heylin, Clinton. *From The Velvets To The Voidoids: A Pre-Punk History for a Post-Punk World*. Penguin (1993). pp. 384. ISBN 0 14 017305 6.

Hutcheon, Linda. *Irony's Edge: The Theory and Politics of Irony*. Routledge (1994). pp. 248. ISBN 0 415 05453 2.

Johnson, Holly. *A Bone in My Flute*. Century (1994). pp. 310. ISBN 0 7126 6145 X.

Jordan, Stephanie, and Dave Allen. *Parallel Lines: Media Representations of Dance*. John Libbey (1993). pp. 234. ISBN 0 86196 371 7.

Kent, Nick. *The Dark Stuff: Selected Writings on Rock Music 1972–1993*. Penguin (1994). pp. 338. ISBN 0 140 23046 7.

Kureishi, Hanif, and Jon Savage. *The Faber Book of Pop*. Faber & Faber (1995). pp. 862. ISBN 0 571 16992 9.

Lomax, Alan. *The Land Where the Blues Began*. Minerva (1994). ISBN 0 749 39733 0.

Lydon, John, with Keith and Kent Zimmerman. *Rotten: No Irish,*

No Blacks, No Dogs. Hodder & Stoughton (1994). pp. 342. ISBN 0 450 60182 X.

Mackinnon, Niall. *The British Folk Scene: Musical Performance and Social Identity.* Open University Press (1993). pp. 151. ISBN 0 335 09773 1.

Marcus, Greil. *In The Fascist Bathroom: Writings on Punk 1977–1992.* Viking (1993). pp. 438. ISBN 0 670 83845 4.

Marsh, Dave, ed. *Mid-Life Confidential.* Hodder & Stoughton (1994). pp. 222. ISBN 0 340 61754 3.

Meyer, Moe. *The Politics and Poetics of Camp.* Routledge (1994). pp. 203. ISBN 0 415 08248 X.

Miller, Simon, ed. *The Last Post: Music After Postmodernism.* Manchester University Press (1993). pp. 192. ISBN 0 7190 3609 7.

Moore, Alan F. *Rock: The Primary Text.* Open University Press (1993). pp. 227. ISBN 0 335 09786 3.

Moore-Gilbert, Bart. *Cultural Closure? The Arts in the 1970s.* Routledge (1994). pp. 312. ISBN 0 415 09906 4.

Murray, Charles Shaar. *Blues on CD: The Essential Guide.* Kyle Cathie (1993). pp. 452. ISBN 1 85626 084 4.

Nehring, Neil. *Flowers in the Dustbin: Culture, Anarchy and Postwar England.* University of Michigan Press (1993). pp. 404. ISBN 0 472 06526 2.

Otis, Johnny. *Upside Your Head! Rhythm and Blues on Central Avenue.* Wesleyan University Press (1993). pp. 171. ISBN 0 8195 5263 1.

Picardie, Justine, and Dorothy Wade. *Atlantic and the Godfathers of Rock and Roll.* Fourth Estate (1993). pp. 310. ISBN 1 85702 085 5.

Redhead, Steve. *Rave Off: Politics and Deviance in Contemporary Youth Culture.* Avebury (1993). pp. 192. ISBN 1 85628 465 4.

Redhead, Steve. *Unpopular Cultures.* Manchester University Press (1995). pp. 136. ISBN 0 7190 3652 6.

Roberts, Chris, ed. *Idle Worship: How Pop Empowers the Weak, Rewards the Faithful and Succours the Needy.* HarperCollins (1994). pp. 158. ISBN 0 00 638266 5.

Rosenberg, Neil V. *Transforming Tradition: Folk Music Revivals Examined.* University of Illinois Press (1993). pp. 340. ISBN 0 252 01982 2.

Ross, Andrew. *Microphone Fiends: Youth Music and Youth Culture.* Routledge (1994). pp. 276. ISBN 0 415 90908 2.

Sandford, Christopher. *Clapton: Edge of Darkness.* Victor Gollancz (1994). pp. 320. ISBN 0 575 05623 1.

Shuker, Roy. *Understanding Popular Music.* Routledge (1994). pp. 331. ISBN 0 415 10723 7.

Simpson, Mark. *Male Impersonators: Men Performing Masculinity.* Cassell (1994). pp. 290. ISBN 0 304 32808 1.

Slobin, Mark. *Subcultural Sounds: Micromusics of the West.* Wesleyan University Press (1993). pp. 127. ISBN 0 8195 6261 0.

Starr, Victoria. *K.D. Lang: All You Get Is Me.* HarperCollins (1994). pp. 316. ISBN 0 00 638240 1.

Thomson, Elizabeth, and David Gutman, eds. *The Bowie Companion.* Macmillan (1993). pp. 252. ISBN 0 333 57226 2.

Thorne, Tony. *Fads, Fashions and Cults.* Bloomsbury (1993). pp. 310. ISBN 0 7475 1384 8.

Trynka, Paul, ed. *The Electric Guitar.* Virgin (1993). pp. 159. ISBN 0 8522 7437 9.

Turner, Steve. *Van Morrison: Too Late To Stop Now.* Bloomsbury (1993). pp. 191. ISBN 0 7475 1565 4.

Walser, Robert. *Running With the Devil: Power, Gender and Madness in Heavy Metal Music.* Wesleyan University Press (1993). pp. 222. ISBN 0 8195 6260 2.

Watson, Ben. *Frank Zappa: The Negative Dialectics of Poodle Play.* Quartet (1994). pp. 597. ISBN 0 7043 7066 2.

Williams, Paul. *Bob Dylan: Performing Artist 1960–1973: The Early Years.* Omnibus (1994). pp. 310. ISBN 0 7119 3554 8.

Williams, Paul. *Bob Dylan: Performing Artist 1974–1986: The Middle Years.* Omnibus (1994). pp. 334. ISBN 0 7119 3555 6.

Wilson, Brian, and Todd Gold. *Wouldn't It Be Nice: My Own Story.* Bloomsbury (1993). pp. 398. ISBN 0 7475 1504 2.

Index

Baudrillard, Jean 3, 5, 6, 10, 63, 125, 127, 220, 251, 261
Bauer, Dale M. 129
Baxandall, Michael 183, 184
Bay Ganyo 337
Beal, Tim 59
Beard, Mary 192
Beatles, the 200, 205, 210–11, 212, 213, 215
Beck, Ulrich 251
Beckett, Samuel 17, 61
Beech, Christopher 60–1
Beezer, Anne 215
Behn, Aphra 104
Belfrage, Sally 113
Bell, Clive 3, 182
Bellour, Raymond 11
Belovezh Summit 280
Belsey, Catherine 13, 33
Belyaeva, S. 335
Benjamin, Andrew 37
Benjamin, Jessica 87
Benjamin, Walter 4, 10, 32, 121, 123, 124, 125, 126, 127, 130, 133, 134, 135, 141, 142, 161, 243–4, 248
Benn, Gottfried 46, 128
Bennett, Benjamin 50
Bennett, Tony 130
Benson, Ross 199–200
Benstock, Shari 89–90, 114
Benzel, Kathryn N. 109
Bercovitch, Sacvan 14
Berg, Alban 122
Berger, Peter 208
Berman, Marshall 155
Bernasconi, R. 324, 327
Bernstein, Jay 121
Berthoff, Ann 36
Bettelheim, Bruno 242
Beuys, Joseph 134
Bhabha, Homi 69, 139, 142, 146, 171
Bhartrhari 28, 29
Bingham, George Caleb 166, 192
Birmingham Centre for Contemporary Cultural Studies 229
Black Power 50
Blackmore, Ritchie 209
Blackmur, R.P. 14
Blake, Andrew 207, 208
Blanchot, Maurice 10, 30, 276
Bloch, Ernst 122, 127, 133
Block magazine 189
Bloom, Alan 14

Bloom, Harold 37, 59, 60
Blumenberg, Hans 249
Blumler, Jay 223–4, 225, 232
Blundell, V. 312, 326
Boatmans Bancshares Inc. 166
Bock, Gisela 80
Boddaert, François 265
Bogdanov, B. 336
Bohlam, Philip V. 210
Böhrer, Karl Heinz 248, 249
Bois, Yve-Alain 177
Bolan, Marc 202–3
Boldy, Steve 55
Bolla, Peter de 316
Bolz, Norbert 251
Bon Jovi 209
Bonaparte, Marie 73
Bonner, Frances 108–9
Booth, Wayne 43
Borch-Jacobsen, Mikkel 67
Bordo, Susan 79, 81
Bosnia 4
Botcharov, A. G. 283
Botticelli 192
Bourdieu, Pierre 134, 251, 318
Boutang, Yann Moulier 270
Bove, Paul 14–15
Bovenschen, Silvia 246
Bowers, Susan 107
Bowie, David 200, 203
Bowlby, Rachel 75–6
Boyd, David Lorenzo 63
Boyd-Barrett, Oliver 223
Brackett, David 210
Bradbury, Malcolm 332
Bradley, Dick 198, 213
Brady, Kristin 83
Bragg, Wayne 175
Braidotti, Rosi 80, 263
Brandt, Sebastian 305
Brandys, Kazimierz 313
Braque, Georges 172
Brasillach, Robert 17
Brean, Marcus 207
Brecht, Berthold 124
Brenkman, John 67–8
Brennan, Teresa 86–7
Brennan, Tim 144, 145
Brisman, Leslie 60
Bristow, Joseph 91
Bronfen, Elisabeth 74–5, 84
Brontë, Anne 106
Brontë, Charlotte 144

and hermeneutics 46–7
literature in 21–2
Eiener, Norbert 290
Eisenman, Stephen 172, 177
Elam, Keir 44–5
Eliot, George 83
Eliot, T. S. 21
Ellington, Duke 214
Elliot, John 33
Elshtain, Jean Bethke 80
Emerson, Ralph Waldo 135
empire
   colonial discourse/postcolonial theory
      138–59
   race and feminism 92–104
Engels, F. 34, 269, 274, 275, 281, 286
Engler, Balz 61
Epps, Brad 54, 55
Epstein, Brian 211
Erickson, Peter 21–2
Ernstrom, Adele M. 192
Eskelinn, Markku 31
Esman, Milton J. 151
Etkind, Euphim 287
European Journal of Communication 219,
   227, 231–2, 233
European Romanticism 10
Evans, J. Claude 33–4
'Ezik i obshtestvo' debate 334

Face, The 252
Fairclough, Norman 135
Fanon, Frantz 69, 148, 149
Farah, Nuruddin 142–3
Farley-Hills, David 33
Farocki, Harum 195
Featherstone, Mike 121
Felman, Shoshana 70, 71, 72
feminism 78–116
   and autobiography 113–16
   and death 84
   in Italy 257–63
   and lesbianism 90–2
   and literature of the past 104–7
   and mythology 111–13
   and psychoanalysis 73–6, 85–90
   race and empire 92–104
   and representation 107–13
Fenves, Peter 124
Ferris, David 126
Fewell, Danna Nolan 59
Fichte, J.G. 125
Fielding, Sarah 108

film
   and art history 186–91
   and historicism 132–3
   and intertextuality 52–3
First Congress of Soviet Writers 280–1
Fischer-Lichte, Erika 250
Fish, Stanley 37, 49
Fiske, John 206, 219, 220–1, 230
Flaherty, Robert 190
Flaubert, Gustave 62, 84
Flax, Jane 80, 87
Fleischer Museum of California 167
Fleming, Marie 83
Fletcher, Pauline 14
Fontana, Ernest 59–60
Fontane, Theodor 121
Forrester, John 73, 74
Forster, E. M. 141, 144
Forsyth, Lucy 174
Fortunati, Vita 61
Foshay, Toby 28
Foster, Elaine 97
Foster, Hal 177
Foucault, Michel 6, 10, 11, 13, 15, 32,
   47, 80, 81, 134, 162–3, 245, 249, 268,
   272, 292, 331
Fowler, Roger 330
Fox, Aaron A. 209
Frabotta, Biancamaria 262
Franchise Federated Financial
   Corporation 167
Frank, Manfred 11, 48, 249
Frankenberg, Ruth 139
Frankfurt School 120, 121–2, 185, 225,
   241, 243, 244
Frankfurter Allgemeine Zeitung 249
Franklin, Sarah 228
Frascina, Francis 175
Frazer, Elizabeth 229
Freadman, Richard 12–13, 16
Freud, Anna 73
Freud, Sigmund 66, 67, 69, 71, 73, 74,
   75, 76, 84, 86, 87, 121, 272, 288, 330,
   331
Freud-Halberstadt, Sophie 75
Fridlender, G. M. 283
Fried, Michael 176
Frisby, David 121
Frith, Simon 207, 212–13
Frolov, Ivan 284
Fry, Roger 173, 182
Frye, H. N. 133, 330
Fuchs, Cynthia J. 107